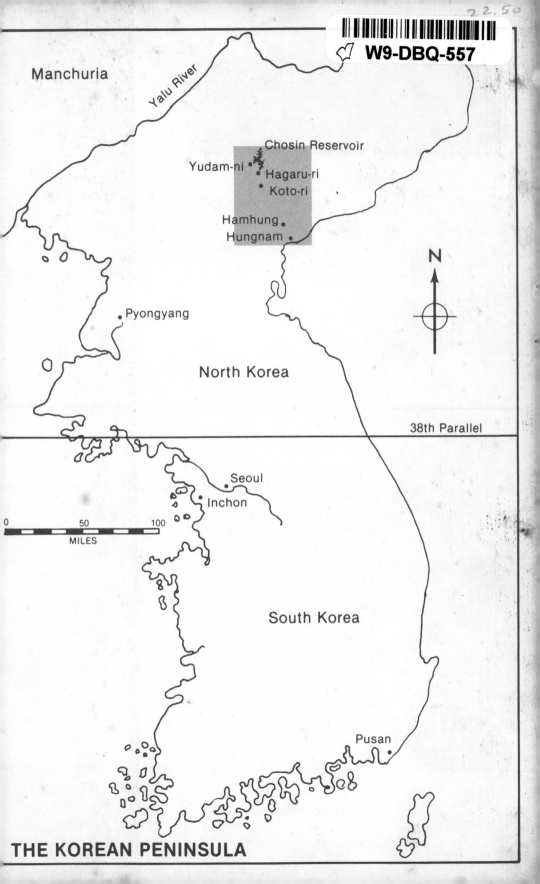

22.50

W9-DBQ-557

Manchuria

Yalu River

Chosin Reservoir

Yudam-ni Hagaru-ri
Koto-ri

Hamhung
Hungnam

N

Pyongyang

North Korea

38th Parallel

Seoul
Inchon

0   50   100
MILES

South Korea

Pusan

THE KOREAN PENINSULA

C H O S I N

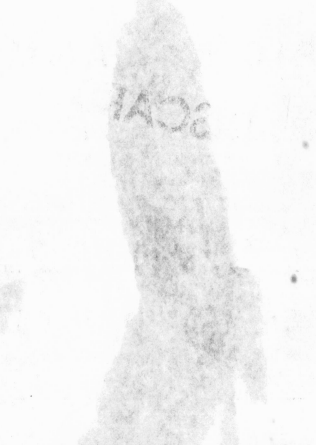

CHOSIN

Heroic Ordeal of the Korean War

BY

ERIC M. HAMMEL

WITH AN INTRODUCTION BY

GENERAL LEMUEL C. SHEPHERD, JR.

UNITED STATES MARINE CORPS

(RETIRED)

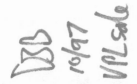

THE VANGUARD PRESS
New York

Library of Congress Cataloging in Publication Data

Hammel, Eric M.
Chosin: heroic ordeal of the Korean War.

Bibliography: p.
Includes index.
1. Korean War, 1950–1953—Campaigns—Korea
(North)—Changjin Reservoir.   I. Title.
DS918.2.C35H35   1981   951.9′042   81-16089
ISBN 0-8149-0856-X   AACR2

This book is for my children,

REMY and DANIEL,

in the fervent hope that their lives

will be untouched

by the evil that is war.

MAPS

Contents

Introduction

CHOSIN is a stirring account of the combat operations of the United States X Corps of General Douglas MacArthur's Far East Command during the Chosin Reservoir campaign in North Korea in the fall months of 1950.

The intense fighting that took place between Marine and Army units of the X Corps, and North Korean and Chinese Communist forces on the snow-covered plateau of the Chosin Reservoir is accurately described in detail by the author.

Eric Hammel has made an exhaustive research of U.S. Army and Marine Corps records of the Chosin Reservoir Campaign, as well as interviewing many participants and obtaining written accounts from others who were present during the conflict.

Hammel's manuscript briefly reviews the outbreak of hostilities in Korea in June 1950, when the North Korean Communist army invaded South Korea and advanced to within a hundred miles of the Southern tip of the peninsula.

General MacArthur's brilliantly conceived amphibious landing at Inchon by Marine and Army troops of the X Corps, supported by the First Marine Air Wing, resulted in complete victory, and the liberation of Seoul, the capital of South Korea.

As a result of this successful operation, General MacArthur ordered the U.S. Eighth Army and South Korean forces to press forward in pursuit of the retreating Korean Communists, and directed the X Corps to make an amphibious landing at Wonsan in Northeastern Korea, in an effort to prevent further withdrawal of the North Korean Army.

In spite of relentless pressure by the Eighth Army and X Corps, the bulk of the North Korean army was able to continue its withdrawal to the Chosin Reservoir plateau.

It was on this high plateau that the Chosin Reservoir and hydroelectric plants that provided electricity for North Korea were located. On the Northern side of the plateau, the Yalu River forms the boundary between Communist China and North Korea.

Although conflicting intelligence reports had been received by the Far East Command concerning the massing of Chinese Communist forces just North of the Yalu, General MacArthur chose to discount the likelihood of Chinese intervention and directed the X Corps to continue pursuit of the North Korean army to the Yalu River.

It was in November that the X Corps began its advance up the steep unimproved 78-mile road from Hamhung to the Reservoir plateau. Although sporadic fighting took place during the advance of the X Corps, including contacts with elements of three Chinese divisions, it was not until the troops approached the Yalu River that they came under attack by overwhelming numbers of Chinese Communist army forces, which had been concealed in wooded areas surrounding the frozen reservoir.

Upon organizing defensive positions on the snow-covered plateau, the soldiers and Marines of the X Corps found it impossible to dig emplacements in the solidly frozen ground with temperatures of minus-twenty degrees.

The combat that took place, frequently hand to hand, between the troops of the X Corps and the superior numbers of North Korean and Chinese Communist soldiers is recorded in detail in this stirring narrative of individual bravery and suffering in the bitterly cold winter of North Korea.

Courageously defending their positions against continued enemy assaults, the Marines and soldiers of the X Corps fought with valor until ordered by General MacArthur to withdraw to the seaport of Hungnam.

During the conflict on the plateau, the dive-bombing and strafing attacks on the Communist troops by the First Marine Air Wing contributed materially to the defense of the infantry positions.

As the withdrawal of the First Marine Division began, an observer inquired of General O. P. Smith if his Marines were retreating, to which General Smith replied, "Certainly not, we are just fighting in a different direction." Furthermore, General Smith insisted on bringing out with his troops the Division artillery, tanks, and heavy equipment that the Far East Command had given him permission to abandon.

During the withdrawal, the troops of the X Corps were under constant attack by Chinese Communist forces. It was only by a courageous delaying action supported by constant sorties of the Marine Air Wing that the survivors of the Chosin Reservoir battles were able to fight their way down from the plateau to Hungnam, where they embarked on ships of the U.S. Seventh Fleet for transportation to South Korea.

The detailed account of the heartbreaking Chosin Reservoir campaign forms an epic of individual heroism and physical hardship by the Marines and soldiers of the X Corps during the Korean War.

To the readers of military history and those who take pride in the achievements of the Armed Forces of the United States, I commend their reading CHOSIN.

> Lemuel C. Shepherd, Jr.
> General, U.S.M.C. (Ret.)
> Commanding General,
> Fleet Marine Force, Pacific 1950–1952
> 20th Commandant of the Marine Corps

Author's Foreword

America's best-remembered battles have always been defeats. The American military credo is a dedication to overcome initial defeat, to rise from the ashes, to master adversity, to conquer an evil foe, to make things right again. The American military psalm is a litany of despair and defeat: Bunker Hill, the siege of Washington, the Alamo, Fredericksburg, the Little Big Horn, the Maine, Pearl Harbor, Guam, Wake, the Philippines, Pusan, the Chosin Reservoir. . . .

I have wondered why this is so, and I perceive an answer in the position our military holds in our society. We see ourselves as a nation of citizen soldiers, of minutemen — peaceable souls in peaceable times, tigers when we are treated poorly or stabbed in the back. It is our duty and our fate to rise from the ashes to fashion our near-run victories. And for the greater part of our history we have done so. It is as though we subconsciously crave an early defeat so that we can better gird ourselves for the struggle and the victory we know will follow.

We did it in our Revolution, in the War of 1812, with the Mexicans, amongst ourselves and within our own borders during the Civil War, to our native Indians, to the Spaniards, to the Germans, to the Germans again, and to the Japanese. And to the North Koreans.

We did it time and again for precisely one hundred seventy-five years, every time we were called upon to do so: we turned initial defeat into ultimate, though not always lasting, victory. We did it right up through the end of September, 1950, when we defeated the North Korean armies that had defeated us in South Korea the previous June and July.

And then we stopped turning initial defeat to ultimate victory.

There is nothing in the chain of events forming the retreat from the Chosin Reservoir that would uncover this profound change in the national military tradition. But there it is. We were defeated, and we never quite rose from the ashes. Our luck, or our will, had been played out.

We survived the defeat. Indeed, the people who literally survived the defeat fought on and achieved *military* victories well into the spring and summer of 1951. But our soldiers have never again won a political victory, which is the ultimate aim of the ultimate political sanction, the ability and the will to wage war.

If anything, the defeat that was meted out at the Chosin Reservoir was the defeat of possibly the most professional force of American men-at-arms ever assembled to that time. Most of the officers and a great many of the enlisted men had been bloodied in World War II. They knew precisely how to wage the war they waged, and they waged it well. They were defeated by overwhelming numbers, which is forgivable. They were defeated by incredibly bad weather, which is understandable if not entirely forgivable. And they were defeated by the political game that their highest commanders chose to play against one another and, ultimately, against them. That last was not without precedent, but it is utterly unpardonable.

This is decidedly not a book about the machinations of generals and the so-called statesmen of the world. It is a book about ordinary American men, caught up in an extraordinary situation. It is a book about common American men who were defeated in every measurable way save one: they survived, and most of them fought on future battlefields. It is their story, above all, which interests me. And it is their story that this book was written to tell.

Lest we end upon too profound a note, let me caution the reader that this is a book about individuals and small units. There is much action described. The aim is to get across to the reader through the poor medium of words the agony of battle, the ultimate milieu of terror. That requires detail heaped upon detail, the stuff of which the mind's eye is aware.

There is much in this book of the tactical permutations of small-unit battle, and that is as it should be. Battles are won by men who do their duty, and they are lost by generals who do not. In that light the defeat at the Chosin Reservoir was the defeat of generals by generals, of an army by another army, of masses of men by nature. But there is victory in the carnage, and that is the victory that each living participant found in his personal survival.

Look to the common, ordinary, suffering, groaning, bitching, wisecracking, duty-bound, fearful, terrorized men who fought this battle. They are the ones who froze and starved and suffered and died. And survived.

Eric M. Hammel
Pacifica, California
1981

Background

INVASION/

COUNTERINVASION/

COUNTER-COUNTERINVASION

They spread like clumsy green ants over the brown-white roadway, clumping forward in quick spurts, dropping behind what meager cover the barren landscape yielded. The antlike ducking and weaving advance slowly brought the first of them to the first of the roadside houses and huts.

Tension was mounting, and so was the exhaustion which the parka-clad running men shared. They had done it all before, were good at it, feared it.

There was *something* out there . . . in the town, or beyond it. No one could quite say what it was, but it made the hair stand tall on the necks of those veterans, and that alone was an ill omen. Those riflemen were so attuned to visceral tensions as to give the lie to educated fools who would say that humans have lost all but the vestiges of their primal animal cunning.

For the moment, though, there was just one more town to secure. More doors to kick down. More miserable, fearful civilians to rout out into the wind-whipped street. In the end, perhaps, more of their dwindling number to be stacked upon the charnel wagons.

Puffs of blue breath preceded them, then were whipped away by the brutal Manchurian wind that moaned down from the great mountain plateaus surrounding the narrow five-fingered valley of Yudam-ni. The scraggly-bearded, parka-clad riflemen gasped the thin, frigid mountain air into aching lungs,and set their teeth against the shocking chill.

On the heights to the rear friendly machine gunners peered over the sights of their incredibly cold steel weapons, eyes slowly traversing the barren vista in practiced sweeps, senses keenly modulated to detect the alien movement of the elusive enemy.

There were several young men entering that valley who *knew*, but could not decisively prove, that they and their fellows were in mortal danger from an unseen but not unperceived enemy. Lacking masses of hard evidence, those young men, and others, had no hope of convincing superiors far from the field that danger lurked beyond the next line of hills, or the next after.

If most of the young riflemen entering that chill, windswept valley town did not actually know there was a new enemy nearby, it was a rare man indeed who could not *feel* the enemy's presence.

★

In a refreshingly blatant act of aggression the North Korean People's Army crossed the 38th Parallel on June 25, 1950, and invaded South Korea.

The 38th Parallel had become the de facto international boundary in August, 1945. At that time the brave Russian despot, Stalin, committed his eastern armies to a final (and, at the same time, maiden) offensive against the battered vestiges of the Empire of Japan. The Russians were awarded a military zone in Korea north of the 38th Parallel — a zone that was to become North Korea — while the American victors of the Pacific War installed an ostensibly democratic regime south of that Parallel, in what is now South Korea.

It had been the avowed intention of the World War II Allies to see to the eventual reunification of Korea in much the same manner as it had been the avowed intention of these same allies to reunite, say, Germany.

The years following World War II had been a period of sparring, testing, posturing, and rearranging global balances. In that period the West had been found by its Communist rivals to be lacking in resolve. Though some backbone had been exhibited during the Berlin Crisis of 1949–50, the Russians were bolstered in their determination to test the resolve of their rivals by the West's inability to prop up the weak Chiang Kai-shek regime in China.

The North Korean invasion of South Korea in late June, 1950, was the ultimate test of the West by the Russians (using, as was — and is — their custom, non-Russian surrogates). The West, to the profound amazement of the entire world, reacted quickly and forth-rightly.

While mainly American combat units sought to stem the swift North Korean tide, still larger United Nations contingents were readied, mainly under United States command, to launch a massive counterblow against a manifestly hard-driving but ultimately insuf-ficient North Korea People's Army (NKPA).

Basing their tactical preparations upon a master plan outlined by General Douglas MacArthur, American combat divisions mounted a classic amphibious assault against the NKPA flank in September, 1950, at Inchon, South Korea's major west coast port, just below the 38th Parallel and only miles from Seoul, South Korea's overrun cap-ital. Trapped between the Inchon invaders and a drive by several American and South Korea corps operating at the foot of the Korean Peninsula, the NKPA was routed in a few short weeks of exception-ally bitter warfare.

The Korea War — or "police action" — should have ended there. But Douglas MacArthur, the American proconsul in East Asia, stilled the dissenting voices of both military and civilian superiors, and a just "punishment" was meted out to the North Korean aggres-sors: their own country was invaded by the victorious UN-backed Republic of Korea (ROK) forces then in the field. It was the express desire of General MacArthur, the man who had shaped modern Japan from the ashes he himself had sown, to reunify all of Korea under the South Korean president, Dr. Syngman Rhee, a despot who was at least no Communist.

The disintegrating NKPA was hounded northward along the west coast of Korea by the bulk of the UN/ROK force. Other, smaller, units were to be chased and run down in northeastern Korea by several ROK Army corps and the same two-division American corps, the X, that had undertaken the brilliant Inchon landings and the lightning drive to recapture Seoul.

The objective of the armies invading North Korea was the military occupation of the country, which was to be followed by a UN with-drawal just as soon as the last vestiges of Communist domination could be rooted out and run up against a wall. It was to be a quick, clean, surgical operation.

The linchpin of this new phase of the war was Douglas Mac-Arthur's vision of a pro-West or neutral East Asian cordon surround-ing the new and as yet unassessed Communist government in mainland China. Strangely, it does not appear to have fazed Mac-

Arthur that his relatively small multi-national army was bound to cause some concern in China as it was drawn ever northward by the fleeing NKPA.

There were, at the time, 600,000,000 Chinese, and millions upon millions of them had become inured to the wars that had been ravaging their nation continuously since the first decade of the twentieth century, and for millennia before. The new Red Chinese regime had bested the West-backed Nationalists less than a year before the outbreak of war in Korea, and its reasons for casting a jaundiced eye upon the UN advance into neighboring North Korea were manifold.

It was then understood in the West that the Communist world was "monolithic." North Korea, China, and Russia were seen by Western policymakers as having governments chiseled from the same stone, as it were. Thus, the invasion of North Korea — a Russian surrogate — was seen as a demonstration to the *Russians* that the West would stand firm in the event of Communist adventures into Western Europe, where the interests of nearly all the Western governments readily lay. At the same time throttling North Korea would put the Chinese on notice that any effort by them to bring down a pro-West or neutral government in East Asia would be met on the field of battle.

For all the smiling pretensions of the Chinese and Russians in maintaining a comradely façade, the two major Communist powers were squabbling in earnest behind doors closed to a West that chose not to eavesdrop. North Korea was a Russian surrogate, and the Chinese appear to have held few qualms about accepting a neutral or even pro-West regime ruling all of Korea if such could be done at the expense of the Russians and *without direct Western intervention*. This position, in fact, was communicated to the West through neutral third parties, but it was either misconstrued or lost in flights of anti-Communist paranoia.

At all events, the Chinese could not tolerate a Western military presence north of the 38th Parallel, no matter how much North Korea's defeat might cost the Russian rivals.

Chinese fears had been roused, and rightly, by the anti-Communist purges that were then gutting the U.S. State Department and other government agencies. The Red Baiters were clearly in the ascendant in the United States, and China feared an all-out invasion of Manchuria, the province bordering North Korea, as a manifestation of ultimate resolve by the West.

At stake for China was her most-developed industrial base.

Blessed with ample hydroelectric potential, which had been exploited by the Japanese after their 1910 accession of Korea and their 1931 invasion of Manchuria, the region was of critical importance to the new Communist Chinese regime.

The value of a secure hydroelectric grid to the Red Chinese cannot be overemphasized, for it held in its promise the vast dreams of that regime. That cheap energy source was to be fully exploited for powering the new China to a positon of prestige and economic strength in an increasingly industrialized world.

Given the respective mental sets of the potential antagonists, a clash was inevitable.

When she saw her warning go unheeded, China began infiltrating her armies into the barren wastes of North Korea's central mountain plateaus in mid-October, 1950. Moving by night, or obscured in the daytime by intentionally set forest fires, Chinese divisions — *whole divisions at a time* — padded silently, virtually without a trace, into North Korea.

The Chinese commander, General Lin Piao, recognized the limitations imposed by material poverty upon his ability to wage a protracted land campaign over long lines of supply, so contented himself with accumulating his strength while waiting for the fast-moving United Nations armies to advance within striking range.

PART ONE

Before

CHAPTER

1

It is a cardinal rule of military intelligence that contingencies be recommended on the basis of an enemy's capabilities, and not upon his intentions, or what his intentions are perceived or hoped to be.

It was a common failing at virtually every level of the United States-dominated United Nations command in Korea that wishful thinking brought on the abeyance of this rule with respect to the Chinese People's Liberation Army (PLA).

For a time, following the the liberation of Seoul and the cautious advance by ROK Army units across the 38th Parallel, American General Headquarters in Tokyo (GHQ-Tokyo) and its chief operating arm, 8th Army, considered the possibility of Chinese intervention in North Korea. Indeed, this possibility grew more pronounced at successive points along the way: at the beginning of the UN drive into North Korea in support of the ROK Army; at the fall of Pyongyang, the North Korean capital; and with the seizure of Wonsan, the major port in northeastern Korea.

Strangely, as UN forces closed on the Yalu River, the boundary between North Korea and Manchuria in China, both GHQ-Tokyo and 8th Army relaxed their vigils. It had been thought, wishfully, that China would intervene early. It was later thought, yet more wishfully, that she had missed her best chance and would never intervene. No thought was given as to her *ability* to intervene, early or late.

★

Intelligence gathering and assessment is a quirky art at best. As with writing history or touting the horses, good intelligence springs from good information. Unlike writing history, where the results are known, or touting the horses, where choices are finite and measurable, intelligence assessment requires the moral strength to write scenarios that stand a very good chance of never taking place, or of conflicting with the fondest notions of a superior whose imagination has settled upon dreams of glory best left unencumbered by bothersome probability or fact. Good intelligence assessment requires that the assessor be wrong far more than he be right, just so long as he is right when he needs to be right.

When a campaign is going badly, no commander really enjoys having a man around who will say that the effort will go yet less well. And when victory is in the offing, few generals want to be reminded that the effort might fail. So, for all the lip service paid Intelligence by its counterparts in Command and Operations, there can come a time when even the finest general might choose to ignore the best, most honest assessment presented by his intelligence advisors.

But all this presumes that intelligence matter of the highest quality has been gathered. If it has not been, the best, most honest intelligence assessor has no more chance of successfully fulfilling his mandate than has a reader of tea leaves.

After the creation of the mightiest military machine ever forged on this planet the United States dismantled her military might with incredible vigor, utterly emasculating her armed forces after 1945. Intelligence hardware went the way of the rest, to the scrap heap.

Missing the Chinese buildup in Manchuria and the subsequent move by the PLA into North Korea was less a matter of chance than of total inability. A scarcity of vital aerial photo-reconnaissance lay at the root of the intelligence failure. The United States lacked not only the hardware, but the experience as well — the years of human expertise gained in truly remarkable intelligence-gathering and assessment feats during the war years. The finely honed minds that had, by 1945, mastered the art were gone, or gone soft from inactivity.

★

From the night of October 15, 1950, onward hundreds of thousands of highly disciplined Chinese combat infantrymen walked across the Yalu bridges and hid themselves in the mountainous North Korean hinterland. The UN Command did not detect the move until the PLA picked a few fights late in the month. The results of these fights were so at odds with prevailing wisdom and desires as to confuse rather than enlighten. Given only a hint of the news and the preconceptions of the men to be convinced, the intelligence assessors were likely to come to erroneous conclusions. And they did, in perfect harmony with the fondest hopes of the Chinese.

By the end of October, 1950, the smattering of reports alleging a Chinese intervention in North Korea began adding up. But intelligence summaries from the field were rejected by senior intelligence officers and the commanders they served. Those generals, it is clear, had not the will to comprehend the gravity of those reports. Eyes were fixed firmly upon the goal, on the Yalu River, and upon the rewards that would be bestowed for "getting the boys home" in keeping with promises made in the heat of a congressional campaign. Having passed safely beyond all the preconceived crisis points — crossing the 38th Parallel, capturing Pyongyang, seizing Wonsan — the American generals ignored the implications so abundant even in the anemic intelligence summaries that did exist.

The Chinese proffered one last, best chance for the American generals to see the light.

Crippled by a paucity of intelligence matter regarding the intentions and capabilities of *their* enemies, Chinese generals authorized an intelligence-gathering program of their own. Its form was of a particularly brutal variety. Because they lacked material means for gathering information, the Chinese mounted a series of limited offensive operations in the hope of learning how well their enemies would stand up in a hard fight, what weapons those enemies might bring to bear, what determination those enemies might show in the face of adversity.

In the very last days of October and the first week of November, very large Chinese infantry formations struck at a half-dozen points throughout North Korea. It seemed to the victims that whole Chinese divisions emerged from the ether. There was no warning and no time to think. There was barely time to man the defenses.

A number of ROK units were utterly defeated in exceptionally savage fighting, and a United States Army battalion was nearly obliterated in northwestern Korea.

The Chinese were elated with the results of their so-called First Phase Offensive. They had found nearly every weak spot in the enemy organization, and they had learned that their tactics of surprise and mass assault worked against a modern Western army.

There was one negative point recorded. In the narrow Sudong · Gorge, about thirty miles above the northeastern port city of Hungnam, on the road to the Chosin Reservoir, several Chinese divisions had been soundly defeated by the 7th Regiment of United States Marines. It was not an important defeat, for the Chinese were seeking information, not territory. But that single American victory was so at odds with everything else they learned from the bloodletting of the First Phase Offensive that the Chinese generals decided to take special steps to insure a victory over those same Marines later in November, when the Second Phase Offensive was slated to scour North Korea of the Western armies.

★

While the First Phase Offensive was hot, the American generals were appropriately attentive. But the sudden, total disappearance of a full Chinese field army of several hundred thousand men gave the illusion of a UN victory. Senior intelligence staffers were quick to take the lead from their generals, announcing that the Chinese "volunteers" had been resoundingly defeated and sent into headlong retreat across the Yalu River.

Curiously, no one asked where so many Chinese had hidden themselves through the latter half of October — nor how.

Because they lacked the will to know, the UN commanders could not know of the threat poised across their fronts and athwart their flanks.

C H A P T E R

2

The decision for X Corps to attack through the Chosin Reservoir westward to hook up with 8th Army was made at GHQ-Tokyo. It was an insane plan. You couldn't take a picnic lunch in peacetime and go over that terrain in November and December.

Major General Clark L. Ruffner, USA
Chief of Staff, X U.S. Army Corps

The United States Marine Corps is bound by tradition. Its lore is its soul.

First Marine Division is an old division, as old as any in the Corps. In late 1950 it was also a new division, as new as any in the American military establishment.

Formed in early 1941 as the then-largest formation of Marines ever assembled under one command, the division had been hurled unexpectedly into combat for the first time in August, 1942, at Guadalcanal. It thus became the first American division to be used offensively in World War II. Later, in the Pacific War, 1st Marine Division fought at New Britain, Peleliu, and Okinawa. And following the demise of Japanese military power in East Asia, the division had been sent to mainland China to keep several important coastal cities, with their important commercial interests, from the hands of those dubious allies, the Russians and Communist Chinese.

Weakened by postwar demobilizations and years of budget cutbacks, 1st Marine Division had been reduced to a mere remnant by the time Mao Tse-tung's People's Liberation Army won control of mainland China in 1949. By 1950, following the American withdrawal from the new People's Republic, the division and several of its key components had all but ceased to exist.

The 5th Marine Regiment, one of the proudest in the Corps, had survived in some shadow form as the core of the depleted division. Reduced to one-half its wartime establishment, the 5th Marines was the only major Marine unit in the western United States on June 25, 1950, the day the NKPA crossed the 38th Parallel to unify the Korean nation under the red banner.

The 5th was hurriedly filled out with Regular Marines from nearby duty stations and a sprinkling of early-arriving Marine Reservists. As the core of the 1st Provisional Marine Brigade, it was shipped directly to the South Korean port city of Pusan and committed to the defense of that isolated bastion, used by the American-manned UN Command as a "fire brigade" in some of the closest fighting of any recent war.

While the brigade bought time at Pusan, the commander of the parent 1st Marine Division rushed to re-form his other two infantry regiments, the balance of his four-battalion artillery regiment, and the dozen special and support battalions that comprised, on paper, a Marine division of the period.*

Trained on the ocean voyage, picking up units and parts of units shipped from stations the world around, the bulk of the reconstituted division landed in Japan, then hurriedly re-embarked — reabsorbing the reluctantly released brigade which was only then brought to full strength — and hurled into the west coast area of Korea in Douglas MacArthur's brilliantly conceived end run at Inchon. It was the last time (to the present) in its history that 1st Marine Division carried out its best maneuver, an amphibious assault against a defended beach, its mission by tradition, temperament, and training.

The invasion at Inchon, followed by the swift, bitter drive up the Inchon-Seoul Highway to liberate the South Korean capital in Sep-

* See "A Word About Organization," p. 421.

tember, brought the division to a tough, well-honed level of cooperation and expertise.

First Marine Division was withdrawn from west-central Korea in early October, 1950, and landed at Wonsan, North Korea's main east coast port, later in the month.

The seizure of Wonsan had been designed by MacArthur's GHQ-Tokyo as an end-run affair to rid geographically isolated northeastern Korea of the last vestiges of the fading NKPA. Operating as it had at Inchon, as part of United States X Corps (which also comprised the veteran 7th Infantry Division, and the newly arrived and untested 3rd Infantry Division), 1st Marine Division initially worked at clearing the coastal corridor around Wonsan. Later the Marines embarked upon a northerly drive toward the twin cities of Hamhung and Hungnam, a major commercial-industrial complex farther up the east coast.

Most of the narrow coastal strip had been secured by the end of October. While several ROK divisions led the advance to the Yalu, 1st Marine Division's vanguard advanced north and west from Hungnam on the narrow mountain road ascending toward the Chosin Reservoir, an intermediate objective beyond which the Marines had no firm goal.

★

Trained and equipped to operate as a cohesive, balanced fighting force, undertaking primarily amphibious missions, 1st Marine Division was, first, a bit out of its element on the Asian mainland and, second, thrown into some organizational confusion by the nature of simultaneous and divergent missions handed it by X Corps. Moreover, the division had been roughly used in the Inchon-Seoul drive, and it had not been brought back to strength following its withdrawal from west-central Korea.

First Marine Division was neither equipped nor trained for a protracted land campaign so far from its sources of supply, nor was it adequately outfitted for a mountain campaign in sub-zero weather. That the war was thought to be nearing a conclusion did not mitigate the fact that the Marines were being misused.

There is a natural disdain shared by military professionals for the doctrines of other branches of service, but the disdain is casual, usually friendly. There is, however, an enduring abrasive quality to the relationship between the United States Army and the United States Marine Corps. It arises from differing perceptions of the mission of the Marine Corps. Contrary to the views of Marines, many Army officers tend to see the capabilities of the two services as being essentially interchangeable. Thus, in part, the use of an amphibious force in the North Korean mountains, and the feeling on the part of senior Marine officers that 1st Marine Division was being mishandled, possibly sacrificed.

Far from having a merely impossible mission, X Corps had no firm mission at all. It was to hold itself in a "state of readiness" even as it advanced piecemeal north and west from Hamhung into the truly great unknown of the northeast Korean hinterland.

Tiny elements of 7th Infantry Division, another component of X Corps, reached the Yalu, as did larger ROK Army forces which were working independently in the same zone of operations as X Corps. To the rear, the main bodies of 7th Infantry Division and 1st Marine Division were advancing northward, filling space but serving no vital strategic purpose.

X Corps lacked sufficient strength to amply secure all of northeastern Korea, so was forced to rely upon an inadequate plan. Trusting to the superiority of Western arms and mechanized mobility, and hampered by having too much ground to cover, X Corps had a tendency to impose manifold tasks requiring its components to commit elements too small to perform adequately and too far apart to support one another.

During the second week of November, for example, the 5th and 7th Marines had been assigned parallel tracks along either shore of the Chosin Reservoir. Unable to support each other across the wide stretch of intervening water, the two regiments were on roads leading essentially nowhere, though both were bound vaguely for the Yalu. The third infantry regiment of 1st Marine Division, the 1st Marines, was just then being ordered up from duties nearer the coast to act as a reserve force and to guard the seventy-eight-mile-long Main Supply Route (MSR), the vulnerable one-lane road linking the Marines to their base at Hamhung.

★

The first of the war-weary, bone-chilled riflemen of the 7th Marines entered Yudam-ni, about halfway up the rugged western shore of the Chosin Reservoir, on November 25, 1950. There were 120,000 Chinese infantrymen concealed in the mountain country around the valley town, nearly 500,000 total in North Korea or immediately across the Yalu River, as the green-clad, hypersensitive American riflemen cautiously combed through the outlying buildings on the southern edge of town.

The Chinese generals' efforts at concealment were in no way hindered by the curious deployment of the UN forces.

Eighty miles to the east of Yudam-ni, the American 8th Army and several ROK corps — several hundred thousand men — held the United Nations left flank along the west coast of North Korea. The main body of the ROK Army was already situated at or near the Yalu River, though it was, like the American forces, divided into two widely dispersed components. The four forces — 8th Army, X Corps, and the divided ROK Army — were not under unified tactical command, and the eastern and western wings were not attached by even the most tenuous physical contact on the ground.

An eighty-mile-wide corridor separated X Corps from 8th Army, and the inland flanks of both were totally exposed.

The thirty-five-hundred-man 7th Marine Regiment was staging into Yudam-ni specifically to secure the town's road junction, which was vital to the plans of X Corps, 8th Army, and GHQ-Tokyo. The latter, MacArthur's headquarters, had belatedly seen the light, and had ordered X Corps to link itself physically with 8th Army across the eighty-mile gap within a week.

As the first Marine riflemen were kicking down doors throughout Yudam-ni during the afternoon of November 25, the Chinese were opening their Second Phase Offensive against 8th Army. By mid-morning, as the first Marine battalion command groups were moving into the valley of Yudam-ni, an entire American division of 8th Army, twenty-five thousand combat infantrymen, was cracking, plunging into headlong retreat. By lunchtime the Chinese in the west had unseated 8th Army's front and were infiltrating entire ten-thousand-man divisions into the rears of successive 8th Army units.

No word of 8th Army's rout reached any tactical unit or headquarters in northeastern Korea. X Corps did not know that the Second Phase Offensive had begun. And the 7th Marines did not know that the road junction at Yudam-ni was not in the least bit vital any longer. In the absence of up-to-date information, however, the main body of 1st Marine Division was on the move toward Yudam-ni and the mountain tracks to the west.

The plan calling for the Marines to turn west to link up with 8th Army envisaged a brief concentration followed by an even wider dispersement. The 7th Marines, which had been leading the way into the mountains for over a month, was to hold at Yudam-ni and expand its domination far enough in all directions to ensure the security of the road net. The 5th Marines was to quit its intermediate positions east of the Chosin Reservoir, stage into Yudam-ni as soon as it could be relieved by elements of 7th Infantry Division, and take to the road leading westward from Yudam-ni into the vastness of the Taebek Mountain range. Elements of 8th Army, it was thought, were moving eastward on a reciprocal track. When joined with 8th Army, the 5th Marines was to turn northward and race for the Yalu River, the sooner to end the war.

As a consequence of preliminary moves in accordance with the corps plan, the entire fighting strength of 1st Marine Division was to be briefly concentrated within an area serviced by thirty-five miles of mountain road. All fighting elements of the division would be within supporting distance of all other fighting units for roughly forty-eight hours, from November 26 through November 28.

★

Though 8th Army was the greatest threat poised against the Yalu hydroelectric plants, the eighty-thousand-man X Corps had not been left out of the Chinese commander's plans. It would be hit, hard, when it entered the monstrous trap the Chinese field armies in northeastern Korea had prepared.

As for the Marines, the fate the Chinese had planned for the only troops to best them during the First Phase Offensive was something special, something awesome. The entry of the 7th Marines into Yudam-ni was like the passing of a condemned man's head through a noose.

C H A P T E R

3

The PLA's Second Phase Offensive in northeastern Korea began with a fistfight.

A squad of riflemen from How Company, 3rd Battalion, 5th Marines, bolstered by a section each of heavy machine guns and anti-tank guns, was manning an outpost on the approaches to a dam on the east side of the Chosin Reservoir on the night of November 25, 1950. There had been no contacts with any hostile forces that day, so the outpost was on a standard fifty-percent alert. Half the men were asleep while the other half, wrapped in their down sleeping bags to ward off the minus-30-degree cold, were scanning the front in anticipation of trouble.

Suddenly there was a scuffle of feet on the frozen ground, and the passage of dark forms through the line. Unable to pick targets, and fearful of hitting friends, the sentries held their fire and screamed alarms.

Thirty-odd Chinese had swooped down in the tiny, isolated perimeter and, in a trice, had formed a tight knot around a sleeping bag containing a recumbent Marine. The Chinese fought off rescuers with their fists and dragged the wailing American from the perimeter, bumping him down a rocky slope.

Unable to unzip the bag, the captive screamed for machine-gun fire, but the gunner froze, fearful of killing friend as well as foe. The kidnapped man unleashed a bloody oath, shaking the gunner free of his concern. A short burst brought down several of the raiders, and the captive was released while the surviving Chinese fled from range.

The midnight fistfight was the most overt contact Marines in North Korea had had with the Chinese since the first week of November. It was a chimera, a touching of armies so brief as to give the impression of never having taken place. That had been the basic characteristic of all contacts made since the 7th Marines beat back a large Chinese force in the Sudong Gorge at the start of the month.

★

November 26 was the day the 5th Marines turned the east side of the Chosin Reservoir over to a battalion of 7th Infantry Division.

Sergeant Jim Matthews, a rocket section leader with Fox Company, 2nd Battalion, 5th, was tired and cold, and sick of the ripe odor rising from the clothing he had not been able to change in over a month. As he stood by a roadside bonfire, such as Marines had learned to build in an instant for any break over five minutes long, Matthews wiggled his toes and felt the dampness in his heavy woolen socks. His feet where shod in rubberized shoepacs, an innovation that was not quite filling the need for reliable arctic footgear. It would soon be time to change his sweaty socks. Meantime the Michigan-bred Marine reservist stomped his feet on the hard ground to keep the blood circulating a minimal warmth. He glanced down the road just in time to see the first trucks bringing up the Army relief force.

The 2nd Battalion, 5th, was to be the first Marine unit to turn its position over to the Army and board trucks for a lift partway to Yudam-ni. Jim Matthews did not know the plan, but he had been ordered to keep his section together to facilitate the loading that would presage the latest of innumerable rides and marches into the unknown.

★

The 1st Battalion, 32nd Infantry Regiment, the first United States Army unit to reach the east side of the Chosin Reservoir, was a typical sort of outfit, given the declining standard of the day.

It was a Regular Army battalion that had been permanently based in Japan until mounted out with 7th Infantry Division to support the X Corps drive up the Inchon-Seoul Highway in September. Many of its members had been drawn from other units as the battalion left Japan, or had arrived as replacements in recent weeks, and many of these had not yet been fully integrated into the outfit. About two hundred of the battalion's nine hundred soldiers were ill-trained South Korean conscripts. The Regulars in the battalion were openly contemptuous of the Koreans. In fact, they were openly contemptuous of many of their fellow Americans. But everyone had a high opinion of the thirty-two-year-old paratrooper who commanded the battalion, Lieutenant Colonel Don Faith.

Despite its composition, the 1st Battalion, 32nd, was no worse off than just about any other Army infantry battalion then in northeastern Korea. Its morale was running high, and had been since General MacArthur's unequivocal Thanksgiving Day announcement that he would have the troops "home by Christmas." Don Faith's battalion was expecting to undertake a fast sweep to the Yalu, and gain a fast ride out of Korea.

After a day on the road from Hungnam, Faith met the commander of the 5th Marines, thirty-seven-year-old Lieutenant Colonel Ray Murray, a broad-shouldered, wasp-waisted six-foot-five-inch Navy Cross recipient who had three Pacific battles and two Korean campaigns under his belt. In crisp, professional language, Murray and his staff briefed Faith on the terrain and the tactical situation on the east side of the Reservoir. Among the incidents discussed was the fistfight of the night before; no one knew quite what to make of it, nor of any of the meager intelligence matter that had been dribbling in over the past few days.

Whatever misgivings Don Faith might have felt about replacing a thirty-five-hundred-man regiment with a nine-hundred-man battalion, he was secure in the knowledge that he would be joined over the next thirty-six hours by the balance of the 32nd Infantry and all of its sister regiment, the 31st. And most of the Marines would not have transportation out at least until the next afternoon.

Once the formality of the relief had been completed, Ray Murray bounded into his waiting jeep for a drive to Yudam-ni so that he could be properly briefed on his new mission by day's end.

Murray's ride was longish, but uneventful, taking him south through the bustle of the new divisional base at Hagaru-ri, then north over Toktong Pass and on down into Yudam-ni. It would not register for days, but the one noteworthy event came at the top of the pass, which was the only way in or out of Yudam-ni from the south. There Ray Murray glanced up to see a motionless Asian man sitting on an outcropping, doing nothing but watching the traffic.

While Faith's battalion moved in, the 2nd Battalion, 5th, was trucked to the top of Toktong Pass, where the bitching Marines were ordered to march the rest of the way into Yudam-ni. The battalion commander, Lieutenant Colonel Harold Roise, drove ahead with key staffers to attend a briefing and examine the ground with Ray Murray. Roise's battalion would be leading the 5th Marines through the lines of the 7th on the road west, beginning the next morning, November 27.

As Ray Murray and Hal Roise met with the 7th Regiment's staff to plan the passage of lines, the divisions that had once comprised 8th Army were plunging southward in headlong retreat. Thus far, however, no one had troubled to alert X Corps or any of its widely scattered components.

★

There were few Marines in the know who were at all happy about being stuck out at the end of a tenuous seventy-eight-mile-long line of supply. And they were less happy about the prospect of having to lengthen the route in the course of a winter campaign of dubious value in some of the world's most rugged mountains.

For his part, Colonel Alpha Bowser, the 1st Marine Division's skeptical operations officer, steadfastly and doggedly used every de-laying tactic he could without courting the spectre of relief. For example, with the tacit approval of 1st Marine Division's com-mander, Major General Oliver Prince Smith, Al Bowser had slowed the advance of the 7th Marines to a crawl on the approaches to Yudam-ni, taking five days to accomplish the work of two.

Bowser, the brilliant forty-year-old tactician who had faced in-credible adversity to perfect the flawless plans for the Inchon land-ing, was buying time, hoping against hope to concentrate the bulk of his division around the vital road junction at Hagaru-ri, sixty-four miles from the sea and fourteen miles south and east of Yudam-ni.

Bowser's game was to wait for the newly committed 3rd Infantry

Division, a fresh unit of unknown ability, to achieve control over the MSR as far north as the railhead at Chinhung-ni, about twenty-one miles south of Hagaru-ri. One battalion of the 1st Marines was to hold at Chinhung-ni, at the southern extremity of the division zone; another battalion of the 1st was to hold at Koto-ri, a tiny mountain hamlet only ten miles south of Hagaru-ri; the last of the 1st's rifle battalions was to stage into Hagaru-ri through November 26 and 27 to relieve the 2nd Battalion, 7th, which was to move forward to Yudam-ni.

First Marine Division headquarters was itself in a state of flux. General Smith would be moving to Hagaru-ri from Hamhung on November 28 to open a new division forward command post (CP). Al Bowser would follow later in the day with his lightly manned forward operations center. The remainder of the division senior staff would move from Hamhung at some future date, when the division's mission had been more fully revealed by X Corps.

Smith and Bowser needed forty-eight hours to consolidate the main strength of their division between Chinhung-ni and Yudam-ni. In the interim, their battalions would be strung out over thirty-five miles of roadway and, in some cases, dispersed and off balance.

O. P. Smith and Al Bowser were racing an hourglass they did not even know had been turned.

★

The sand had started running on November 2, when the PLA First Phase Offensive had collided with the 7th Marines in the Sudong Gorge, nearly thirty-five miles south of Hagaru-ri. The 7th had slaughtered several thousand Chinese in that dogged three-day battle. And then the PLA divisions had vanished.

Impressed, the Chinese had set about preparing a special fate for the Marines. Massed infantry formations, far superior in relative strength to any committed against comparable 8th Army units, were slated to isolate, segment, and destroy 1st Marine Division.

When the 5th and 7th Marines took diverging routes to seize the two shores of the Chosin Reservoir, the Chinese commanders had split their force, establishing independent wings whose simultaneous assaults would catch the two Marine regiments in motion and unable to support each other.

The blow was set to fall the night of November 27.

Lacking telephonic and radio field communications, PLA senior commanders and their intelligence staffs were deprived of a quick, certain means for discovering, reporting, and assessing a changing tactical situation.

It is probable that the PLA field force commander east of the Reservoir — the man charged with destroying the 5th Marines and penetrating the MSR in order to isolate Hagaru-ri from the sea — had relatively up-to-date intelligence regarding the slow advance by the Marines in his sector through November 25. It is unlikely, however, that he received the news until a day later, November 26, by which time the 5th was turning its sector over to Don Faith's 1st Battalion, 32nd Infantry.

At the same time, the field force commander west of the Reservoir must have heard that the vanguard of the 7th Marines had invested Yudam-ni on November 25. But he probably did not receive the news until the 26th, just as the 2nd Battalion, 5th, was staging into town to pass through the 7th.

It is highly unlikely that any PLA commander heard that 1st Marine Division's center of operations was being moved into Hagaru-ri on November 26. Thus, the force assigned the task of taking Hagaru-ri could not be bolstered in time. It was of a size to overwhelm a single one-thousand-man rifle battalion, but not a battalion that could be thickened by hundreds of Marines who were holding service billets but who had all been trained as basic infantrymen.

PLA blocking forces strung out along the MSR might have realized that the axis of the Marine division was shifting northward, but they had no means for quickly effecting a warning, nor were they as yet strong enough to limit so massive a flow in any decisive manner.

The situation on the night of November 26 was this: As the independent PLA main forces completed their deployments against two Marine regiments thought to be isolated on either side of the Reservoir, those same regiments were consolidating temporarily in a small area preparatory to mounting a long-range sweep into the mountains. And, as a detached and unsupportable PLA force was maneuvering against the base at Hagaru-ri, that base was being manned by thousands of combat-trained Marines rather than the hundreds envisaged by the plan.

Had the Chinese plan and order of battle been known to the American commanders, none of them would have offered much hope for the survival of any of the Marine forces spotted around the Chosin Reservoir. But the Chinese scheme was not known. Even the Chinese presence was being seriously debated at the highest levels of authority.

★

About midday on November 26, and far to the north, Captain Harry Henneberger, a twenty-seven-year-old professional Marine airman, was leading his division of four gull-winged F4U Corsair fighter-bombers back from a reconnaissance sweep to the Yalu River. A member of Marine Fighting Squadron 312 (VMF-312), Henneberger had been in Korea since Inchon, and was then based with several other Marine Corsair squadrons at Yonpo, an excellent all-weather air facility outside of Hungnam.

Henneberger was looking forward to a warm meal and warm quarters after what should have been a routine and unproductive flight, when he glanced down at the ground ten thousand feet below, and was startled to see a solid mass of Chinese infantry come to a complete halt in full marching order on the snow-covered wastes beneath his wing tips.

Marine Corsair pilots were hot; they considered themselves the best in the business. Harry Henneberger did not even think about what he did next, and the three airmen following him instantly took his lead.

Descending to five hundred feet to begin his run from the front of the mile-long column of solidly massed infantry, Henneberger cooly went through the routine of charging his guns and lining up his sights while his mind sought some reason for so many men lying so perfectly motionless in the face of so much airborne firepower.

Then the moment arrived. Henneberger lined up his illuminated ring sight and squeezed the gun-button knob on his joy stick. The six .50-caliber machine guns mounted in the fighter's wings shuddered and roared, jarring the airplane as Captain Henneberger corrected and recorrected his aim with detached, practiced nonchalance.

Henneberger banked right to make room for his wingman, then started clawing for altitude, hauling a pair of 500-lb bombs against the pull of gravity. Turning to look down at the Chinese column over his left shoulder, he saw the mass of men lie still under the hammering guns of his division, then break in unison, a mass of green-clad humanity roiling in confusion upon the white and gray-brown landscape below.

The Corsair division's second run planted eight 500-lb bombs among the roiling survivors. Subsequent runs spread twenty-four 5-inch rockets over the charnel scene below. The Marine pilots doggedly made pass after pass until every bullet had been loosed upon the writhing, spreading carpet of miserable death. Another Corsair division joined as Henneberger's flew off.

Harry Henneberger was too hyped on adrenalin as he highballed to Yonpo to give any thought to the destruction he had wrought that clear, cold November afternoon. He landed, made his report, warmed up as best he could, and discussed the fine points of the day's slaughter with a detached, professional air.

★

At Yudam-ni, Captain Donald France, the 7th Marines' intelligence officer, was mulling over the gleanings of the day's haul. Three Chinese prisoners had been taken by a patrol of the 3rd Battalion, 7th. The Chinese privates had revealed, in the cathartic manner of Asian captives Westerners find both pathetic and helpful, that the PLA 29th Army (a corps-size unit of three ten-thousand-man divisions) was poised north and northwest of Yudam-ni, set to mount an attack against the 7th Marines within the next thirty-six hours. The prisoners did not say so, but it seemed evident from other bits and scraps of data that a whole lot more than 30,000 Chinese were out there in the uncharted wilderness of the Taebek Plateau. But neither Don France nor any of his intelligence associates could uncover anything of real substance. There was no concrete resolution to the jumble of rumors and fears and partial truths that had been percolating out of the silent hills since the Chinese had vanished after three days of fierce combat at Sudong.

Fact: An intelligence sergeant from the 2nd Battalion, 7th, had crawled into one of the abandoned gold mines that dotted the plateau, more as a way to mollify some hysterical civilians than in the hope of finding anything. He had found a mine shaft crammed full of factory-fresh Russian-pattern infantry weapons and ammunition.

Fact: The discovery of abandoned bunkers and fighting holes in the hills on either side of the MSR was so commonplace as to have become largely unreportable.

Fact: A command bunker, complete with Chinese-language terrain maps and carefully stored equipment, had been uncovered when the vanguard of the 7th Marines had moved into Hagaru-ri more than a week earlier.

★

As Don France grappled with these fragments and a dozen more like them, he was awaiting word from a combat patrol sent out that morning by the 1st Battalion, 7th. While most of the regiment's patrols were fanning out across the ridges overlooking Yudam-ni, 1st Lieutenant Frank Mitchell's reinforced platoon of Able Company, 7th, was legging its way down a little side valley to the southwest in response to civilian reports that "many, many Chinese" were holed up in the huts of the village of Hansang-ni. The rest of Able/7 was following Mitchell at the slower pace necessitated by greater numbers.

The terrain was brutal, but within norms these Marines had mastered in a solid month on the trail. Mitchell cannily led his platoon along the snow-covered ridgeline overlooking the side valley. The platoon was above Hansang-ni at 1600 hours, and the platoon leader ordered the point, a four-man fire team, to continue on to screen the approaches.

Asian soldiers wearing green quilted uniforms were spotted in heavy woods overlooking the valley. When the point fire team passed word back that the strangers showed no inclination to fight, First Lieutenant Gene Hovatter, the Able/7 commander, who happened to be with Frank Mitchell at that moment, trudged forward with his Korean interpreter. As soon as he got to the point, Lieutenant Hovatter had the interpreter engage the strangers in conversation. The Korean said he thought they were Chinese, and that they appeared to want to surrender. Hovatter asked the interpreter to tell them to hold fire while he went down the slope to talk.

As Gene Hovatter and his interpreter moved forward about ten yards, the point fire team was ambushed by unseen soldiers in the brush and weeds that abounded throughout the area. Hovatter hit the deck as machine-gun fire sheared off small trees and bushes all around. The interpreter was hit, the fire-team leader was killed, and the team Browning Automatic rifleman was severely injured.

Frank Mitchell sprang forward, seized the BAR from the wounded Marine, and fired cover while directing the remainder of the platoon to safer ground a bit to the rear. Gene Hovatter managed to drag the wounded Korean into a large hole. Then, as Mitchell directed a greater volume of fire at the Chinese, Hovatter left the interpreter and raced back fifty yards to Mitchell's position to direct the deployment of the remainder of Able/7 by voice radio.

Second Lieutenant Jim Stemple quickly maneuvered his thirty-five-man back-up platoon to a spur north of Mitchell's position. And, while Gene Hovatter moved to join Stemple, the company's three 60mm mortars were deployed to support both rifle platoons.

The action was hot, and getting hotter, as additional Chinese were fed into the firing line facing Mitchell's platoon.

As the fight raged into the gathering darkness, Gene Hovatter realized that his one-hundred-seventy-man company could not possibly hold through the night against an enemy force whose size he could not begin to determine; he ordered Frank Mitchell to withdraw toward Stemple's position.

Easier said than done. Mitchell's platoon was pinned, but feisty. The BAR-man who had been wounded earlier, and the injured Korean interpreter, were beyond the Marine line. Mitchell, who had been lightly wounded twice, was not about to pull back without them, so he organized an attack to retrieve them. Firing off the last magazine of BAR ammunition, he grabbed a pair of hand grenades and moved to lead the rescue. The shock of the attack knocked the Chinese from their forward positions just long enough for the wounded Marine to be retrieved. But, as Mitchell closed with the enemy to fight it out hand to hand, the twice-wounded platoon leader was shot to death. Another Marine became separated from his companions in the darkness, and neither he nor Gene Hovatter's Korean interpreter were seen again.

The bulk of the company, holding a ridgeline to the northeast, fired heavy concentrations at the Chinese below while Mitchell's platoon sergeant reorganized the platoon and led it out of the fight.

Though Gene Hovatter's platoon leaders wanted to stay the night and recover several bodies in the morning, he feared that the wounded would not survive the night. The company moved out to undertake an exhausting forced march back to Yudam-ni. The wounded BAR-man was evacuated by helicopter, but he died of his wounds.

When Gene Hovatter reported in well before dawn on November 27, Don France, the regimental intelligence officer, had the first hard news that a large Chinese force was operating in the vicinity of Yudam-ni. Active, aggressive patrolling would commence at sunup.

PART TWO

November 27

CHAPTER

4

Monday, November 27, 1950, began with a clatter and confusion at Yudam-ni that must have been unprecedented in the indeterminate history of that obscure mountain valley town.

The 7th Marines began the day with such a fury of activity as to seem in total confusion. Colonel Homer Litzenberg, a tall, ruddy-faced man, built all of rectangles and squares, was determined to scour and secure the Valley of Yudam-ni within a day or two, and he had ordered out a profusion of company- and platoon-sized patrols to search or seize the confusing jumble of towering hills and twisting, climbing side valleys that comprised the terrain in and around his objectives. The regiment, like the man leading it, was a vigorous veteran of long marches and intense combat, fully competent to bring another Korean town and its environs under firm control.

Yudam-ni sits in a long, narrow north-south valley bisected by the MSR. There is a road junction north of town: one fork continues north to skirt the western shore of the Chosin Reservoir, while the other fork bends abruptly west to snake through the formidable Tae-bek Mountains. The valley of Yudam-ni gives off into five smaller valleys, each separated from the next by a high, hilly ridge complex. North and northeast of town is the Reservoir, and to the south is Toktong Pass, a potential bottleneck reached from Yudam-ni by way of a steep, narrow section of the one-lane MSR.

On the morning of November 27 there were nearly four rifle battalions and the bulk of three artillery battalions in and about the town. Two of the rifle battalions, and part of another, were Litz's. The last was the 2nd Battalion of Ray Murray's 5th Marines, which had arrived the previous afternoon from the east shore of the Reservoir. Lieutenant Colonel Murray was overseeing the establishment of a temporary regimental command post in a stubbly, frozen field just to the left of the roadway and just south of the vital road fork.

The rifle battalions had largely unrelated missions. Lieutenant Colonel Hal Roise's 2nd Battalion, 5th, was to step off that morning to link up with 8th Army. Lieutenant Colonel Ray Davis's 1st Battalion, 7th, was to mount a series of company and platoon sweeps to the south and southeast, probing the side valleys and the jumble of hills and ridges in those quadrants. The 3rd Battalion, 7th, commanded by Lieutenant Colonel William Harris, was to sweep the heights on either side of the road that the 5th Marines would be using that day and the next. Two companies of the 2nd Battalion, 7th, were in the hills east of town, awaiting the arrival of the remainder of their battalion from Hagaru-ri.

While the rifle battalions expanded outward, the three artillery battalions continued to move into battery sites along an arc north of town, from northwest to east. Lieutenant Colonel Harvey Feehan's 1st Battalion, 11th Marines, an eighteen-gun 105mm light battalion, was to support the drive of the 5th Marines, so its weight was to the northwest. Feehan's howitzers would displace forward with the 5th Marines. Major Francis Fox Parry's 3rd Battalion, 11th, had only twelve of its eighteen 105s at Yudam-ni; the missing six-gun battery was at Hagaru-ri and was expected to arrive the morning of the 28th. Once fully assembled, Parry's battalion was to be concentrated north and northeast of town to support the seizure of the high ground by the 7th Marines. The last of the artillery battalions at Yudam-ni was Major William McReynolds's 4th Battalion, 11th, an eighteen-gun 155mm medium battalion. Normally parceled out as the general support battalion for the entire division, McReynolds's unit was fully assembled for the first time in weeks, a reflection of Division's concern about sending the 5th Marines into the mountains. The long-range 155s, strung out in battery sites east of town but aimed to the west, were to support the 5th for as long as it remained in range.

★

As was typical in a Litzenberg order, the 1st and 3rd Battalions, 7th, had to contend with precisely drawn missions assigned by Regiment to specific companies and platoons. Lieutenant Colonel Bill Harris's 3rd Battalion was given the task of securing the defile through which Ray Murray's regiment would have to pass to get out of the valley. George and Item Companies were to secure several hills on Southwest Ridge while How Company was to seize Hill 1403, the first hill on adjacent Northwest Ridge.

Though Harris knew of contacts with Chinese troops in the vicinity, no special alert was issued by Regiment, and no special precautions were taken. Harris's troops were quite adept at securing hills, had been doing so for weeks on end all the way up the MSR. The battalion, however, had never had a day quite like November 27 was going to be.

★

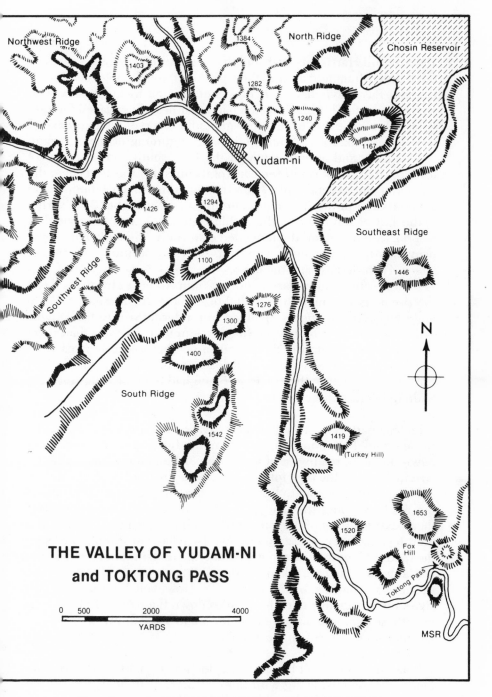

Northwest Ridge

1403

1384

North Ridge

Chosin Reservoir

1282

1240

1167

Yudam-ni

1426

1294

Southeast Ridge

1100

1446

1276

1300

1400

South Ridge

1542

1419

(Turkey Hill)

N

1653

1520

Fox
Hill

THE VALLEY OF YUDAM-NI
and TOKTONG PASS

Toktong Pass

MSR

| 0 | 500 | 2000 | 4000 |
YARDS

(See endpapers for GUIDE TO MAP SYMBOLS AND ABBREVIATIONS.)

While Bill Harris, his staff, and the company commanders sweated
the familiar fragmentation of their battalion, tough, bold Lieutenant
Colonel Ray Davis had an even wider-ranging fragmentation with
which to contend. Able/7, which had been heavily engaged the previous afternoon, was to be the regimental reserve, resting. Baker/7
was given a patrol assignment which, beginning at dawn, would
send it over and around many of the hills south and southeast of
town to see what it could see. One of its missions was to recover the
bodies of the several Able/7 Marines who had been killed or had
gone missing in the Hansang-ni fire fight on November 26. Charlie/
7, the last of Ray Davis's three rifle companies, was to be held in
reserve through noon; if not needed elsewhere, the bulk of the company was to march south, uphill, to secure a position midway between Toktong Pass and the town.

With no apparent unease resulting from Able/7's stiff fire fight of
the previous afternoon, two battalions of the 7th Marines were to
undertake routine chores involved in rendering secure the heights
—though not the dominating heights—around the vital road junction. Rumors concerning the presence of Chinese in the area were
rife among the troops. Some unit leaders voiced weak, ambivalent
warnings of a nature they and their men had been hearing since the
Sudong fighting three weeks earlier.

★

For his part, Ray Murray had an advance to plan and control. Hal
Roise's 2nd Battalion, 5th, was to move by column of companies
down the main road west of town. The 3rd Battalion, 5th, would be
arriving later in the day, followed still later by the 1st Battalion.

It was Murray's plan to leapfrog his three veteran battalions down
the road, stopping the lead unit when it encountered opposition,
then passing either of the following battalions around the fight while
the blocking force was ground down by whatever it took to reopen
the road. At length, if all went well and the remainder of the division
was able to close on Yudam-ni, Murray hoped to be relieved by the
fresher 1st Marines, or the rested 7th. However, he was really resigned to advancing alone forty miles down the road to link up with
the 8th Army troops arriving from the west. The 5th was then to turn
northward and "race" to the Yalu.

★

If all was going well by day's end, the greater parts of two veteran
Marine regiments, along with three artillery battalions, were to be
concentrated in and around the valley of Yudam-ni.

At the same time, three divisions of the People's Liberation Army — about thirty thousand troops — were already in the hills overlooking Yudam-ni, ready to swoop down that night upon the Marines holding the town. Three fresh divisions were behind them, and three more were on the way from Manchuria, prepared to render a killing blow if necessary.

C H A P T E R

5

Hal Roise, at thirty-four, was at the peak of his professional military career. An exceptionally capable combat commander, the chain-smoking Idahoan had spent most of the Pacific War stationed aboard battleships. He had commanded his 2nd Battalion, 5th, since a year before the outbreak of the Korean War, then through Pusan and Inchon-Seoul, where he had impressed his superiors as a singularly pugnacious combat officer who would allow nothing to stand between his command and success. Roise was known by his contemporaries to be particularly blunt of speech, a trait much admired by the men who served him.

There was no particular reason for placing Roise's battalion in the vanguard of the 5th Regiment's advance that morning. The battalion had been the first to be relieved east of the Reservoir, the first to arrive at Yudam-ni, and the most conveniently placed to start the advance to link X Corps with 8th Army. It was the luck of the draw.

★

Hal Roise's day began with a toast. As the battalion commander was preparing to move out, the battalion executive officer, Major John Hopkins, placed a canteen cup in Roise's hands and measured out half of a rare two-ounce bottle of medical brandy. "It's my birthday, Hal," Hopkins explained. "I bummed this from the doc."

The battalion commander raised his cup: "To your health!"

"To the longest fifty-five miles we'll ever travel," Hopkins replied, "if we get there."

The major was feeling an indefinable "something," and so were

many of the regimental and battalion officers assembled in Yudam-
ni that Monday morning.

★

Roise's battalion assembled in the fields north of town and arranged itself for the day's advance. Captain Uel Peters's Fox Company would be leading the move, followed by Dog/5. Easy/5 was the
battalion reserve and was not expected to get into a fight that day.
Backing the battalion were elements of the regimental 4.2-inch
Heavy Mortar Company, Harvey Feehan's 1st Battalion, 11th, and a
platoon of combat engineers.

Uel Peters, a slight, blond young man with sharp, aquiline fea-
tures, received over the command radio network the order to advance, uttered orders of his own, passed a few stock hand signals,
and moved out along with his veteran riflemen. The pace was slow,
cautious; there had been word from the 7th Marines that Chinese
troop formations were in the area.

At 0935, just after Fox/5 stepped off down the west branch of the
MSR, the battalion point was fired on at long range from the commanding height to the immediate right, Hill 1403. Neither Captain
Peters, Lieutenant Colonel Roise nor any of the troops was overly
concerned by the desultory fire. It seemed to be part of a long-standing Chinese delaying tactic, much discussed by briefers from the
7th Marines. It seemed meant to caution the Marines and slow the
advance; weak as the fire was, it could do little actual harm at so
great a range.

Fox/5 sideslipped a bit to the right, moving up the slope of Hill
1403 in order to use the intervening ground to screen its movement
from the Chinese riflemen on the heights.

To Peters's rear, elements of How Company, 3rd Battalion, 7th,
were already advancing cautiously up another slope of Hill 1403.
The danger would be eliminated by the time the remainder of
Roise's battalion passed the hill.

As the point slowed and swerved toward Hill 1403, a Marine light
observation plane tilted in over Fox/5 and the pilot dropped a message, which was brought to Captain Peters: A number of unmanned
roadblocks had been spotted ahead on the roadway, just beyond Fox
Company's view.

Peters had been briefed about such an eventuality, and he resorted
to a preplanned response. The riflemen stood aside as a platoon of
Able Company, 1st Engineer Battalion, rushed forward. In addition
to its complement of flamethrower teams and demolitions special-

ists, the engineer platoon was equipped with several diesel bulldozers, which aggressive drivers would use to clear the rubble
constituting the first of nine unmanned road obstructions to be uncovered by the advance that day.

As the engineers clanked forward, Fox Company continued to
advance on the right side of the roadway. At 1015, as the regimental
4.2-inch mortars and Feehan's 105s softened the ground to the front,
the point crossed a deep draw at the foot of Hill 1403 and began a
cautious advance against a steep, flat-topped ridge running several
hundred yards on a bearing parallel to the roadway. The point drew
fire from the ridge, and Fox/5 recoiled while Uel Peters coolly established a base of fire and prepared to mount platoon assaults against
the reachable opposition.

While Fox/5 maneuvered to subdue the ridge defenses, Dog/5 was
ordered to bypass the block by moving southward from the roadway,
using the intervening ground to screen its move. Easy/5 remained
well to the rear, prepared to move to the aid of either of its sister
companies or take on any other mission necessitated by the course
of the action.

Fox/5 got into an unexpectedly heavy fight against what turned
out to be prepared bunkers. At least a company of Chinese was dug
in along the east-west axis of the flat-topped ridge overlooking the
roadway. Probes soon determined that the Chinese flank was weak,
and that a flank assault might roll up the entire defensive line from
end to end.

While Dog/5 continued to file past the strongpoint, Captain Peters
ordered his three-gun 60mm mortar section to set up in a frozen
plowed field across the road. At the same time, Peters's 1st Platoon,
about thirty-five Marines, was moved into the draw while the bulk
of the company established positions partway up the eastern slope
of Hill 1403 overlooking the Chinese bunkers. A platoon of Dog/5
was placed south of the roadway to block a Chinese retreat.

Fox Company's 1st Platoon braced to do the job it had learned to
do best — take another hill. The 4.2-inch and 105mm barrage
ceased, and a pair of heavily laden Marine Corsair fighter-bombers
roared in, smoking the Chinese emplacements with bombs, rockets,
and .50-caliber machine-gun fire.

As the Corsairs pulled up from the final pass, Fox/5's 1st Platoon
surged forward, hitting the strongpoint where it was weakest, rolling
it up a bunker and a foxhole at a time while the balance of the
company peppered the ground ahead from the slope of Hill 1403.

Most of the defenders pulled out, heading west. Three were taken alive. They were cowed little men in raggedy quilted fighting togs and canvas tennis shoes topped by cloth puttees.

First Platoon scoured the killing ground with practiced caution while another Fox/5 platoon passed through to assume positions overlooking the road. Long-range heavy machine-gun fire from Chinese positions to the north slowed the consolidation, forcing the Marines to take time-consuming precautions.

In the meantime, Dog Company moved westward down the road, covering the engineers, who busily swept aside one unmanned road-block after another.

Several hundred yards west of the flat-topped ridge the main defile branches to the south of the roadway. It was at this point that Dog Company's vanguard was driven to ground by pre-sited fire from Sakkat-san, the dominant height in the vicinity of Yudam-ni. As the firing intensified, it became clear that the Chinese had installed an extensive network of tiered bunkers and gun emplacements all along the eastern slope of the mountain. So extensive was this network, in fact, that Dog Company's point found itself in a cross fire placed upon it by machine guns at either end of the Chinese position.

That was a bit more than even the sanguine Hal Roise cared to contend with that day. He called off the attack at 1430 and ordered his companies to dig in: Fox Company on the flat-topped ridge north of the roadway, Dog Company in a blocking position astride the MSR, and Easy Company covering the draw between Hill 1403 and the flat-topped ridge.

★

What transpired as the companies dug in revealed the ambivalent attitude Marines at all levels still held regarding possible Chinese intentions.

It was a cardinal rule in the 5th Marines — indeed, throughout 1st Marine Division — that each night in the field be viewed as a night of potential combat. Regular or Reservist, every Marine in Roise's trim battalion was a veteran of a dozen or more fire fights. The organism that was the 2nd Battalion, 5th Marines, undertook a hundred standard precautionary measures, from the establishment of a viable communications grid to the siting of every machine gun to form an endless network of cross fires over every reachable square foot of ground in front of the defensive lines.

The heavy fighting of the day should have prompted troop leaders to increase the normal level of vigilance. If that was not sufficienct, the experience of the troops along Fox/5's line that afternoon should have been ample evidence of Chinese intentions.

Sergeant Jim Matthews had done a lot of profitless running around during most of the day's fighting. Now, as Fox/5 settled in for the night, Matthews collapsed behind a large, flat-topped boulder, facing northward toward a much higher hill about one thousand yards out.

Looking up after stowing his bazooka and rockets, the veteran noncom was amazed to see that a blue-uniformed Chinese political officer was carefully surveying the Marine dispositions from atop the distant hill, and that a covey of green-clad Chinese infantrymen was quietly kindling cooking fires in plain sight of Matthews and the rest of Fox/5.

The arrogance of the Chinese was too, too galling, so a number of Marines opened fire on the clumps of men on the far hill, particularly at the unflappable political officer. But the fire was appallingly inaccurate, for the Chinese continued about their business without so much as looking at the Americans.

At length, a Marine sharpshooter, armed with a bolt-action Russian-made 7.7mm sniper rifle, moved to the line, took careful aim, and squeezed off several rounds. None of the soldiers on the higher hill seemed to have been hurt, but the sharpshooter stirred them up a bit, for the Fox/5 line was soon peppered in earnest by gunfire from the heights.

The bloodless exchange continued until nightfall, by which time Jim Matthews and many others drifted off to sleep, so tiring had been their day.

★

As Easy/5 moved into position between Fox/5 and Hill 1403, Sergeant Jim Friedl, the 81mm-mortar forward observer seconded from the battalion weapons company, approached Captain Sam Jaskilka, the Easy/5 commander. In accordance with established procedure, Friedl requested permission to register the two-gun medium-mortar section normally assigned to the company. Jaskilka, however, told Sergeant Friedl that he thought there would be no need of the guns that night, and that he preferred not running the risk of taking casualties in the event a registration round fell short, a rare but terrifying possibility.

At twenty-five, Jim Friedl was a thoroughly indoctrinated veteran of three Pacific campaigns and the fighting between Seoul and the Reservoir. He had strong feelings about not registering the guns, and informed the company commander that failure to do so meant that the company could be refused supporting fires in the event it was attacked that night. More importantly, it was possible that the mortars, if reassigned to the company, would be delayed in providing support because the gunners would have no trustworthy figures when the time came to compute ranges and deflections. Friedl truly expected to change the mind of the usually detail-conscious captain, but Jaskilka placed a hand on the forward observer's shoulder and assured him that registering the guns would be a superfluous exercise.

Upset, but powerless, Friedl trudged over to the spot where he had left his radio operator and placed a call to inform the mortar-section leader that he would not be registering the guns. Then Jim Friedl climbed wearily into his down sleeping bag, pulled off his leather boondockers, massaged his cold feet, and lay back to get some needed sleep.

★

Minutes after dismissing Jim Friedl, Sam Jaskilka was joined by his company officers. It was common knowledge that the company commander had just received orders to return to the States for advanced schooling. He was a man marked by his superiors for rapid advancement, and the school assignment was a big bonus. More important, Jaskilka hoped to be home in time for the birth of his next child.

The officers kidded the veteran captain, accusing him of performing unseemly acts to curry the favor of his superiors — the usual banter of men in the field. With luck, the next day would be Jaskilka's last with the battalion; his replacement had already arrived and had joined the company as a supernumerary, just to get the feel of things.

Minutes before sunset, following a good-natured, bantering briefing, the group of officers split up to return to their platoons. One, 2nd Lieutenant Ed Deptula, walked several paces, let out a surprised yelp, grabbed a leg, and fell heavily to the frozen earth. Following the ribbing he had just taken, a beaming Sam Jaskilka readily assumed that Deptula was feigning injury. "Knock off the grab-ass," he admonished. "Don't pull a phony like that!"

"I'm really hit," Deptula protested. "Take a look."

Jaskilka bounded forward and took the look. Sure enough, Ed Deptula had taken a round through his right calf. Corpsmen were called out, and Deptula was carried away for treatment. A last, kidding exchange took place: "See you Stateside, Skipper." Jaskilka chided the lieutenant that he would be lucky to be evacuated as far as Japan.

It was a sobering moment.

★

Roise's battalion was at that moment under seige, but neither the battalion commander nor any of his subordinates knew that for sure.

CHAPTER
6

At 0815 on November 27, just as Roise's battalion launched its drive down the road west of Yudam-ni, Captain Leroy Cooke's How Company, 7th, opened its precautionary sweep up the southwestern slope of Hill 1403, the terminal height of Northwest Ridge. Cooke was to secure the height as proof against attacks on Yudam-ni from that quarter, and to support Roise's initial thrust.

Although Fox/5 drew fire from the summit of Hill 1403 early in its advance, How/7's drive up the steep slope went off without a hitch in the face of zero opposition. Whatever PLA infantry there had been on the hill early in the day had fled, for none was found as the first files of How/7 Marines probed the crest.

Not so the efforts of the remainder of Lieutenant Colonel Bill Harris's 3rd Battalion, 7th.

★

George and Item Companies, 7th, had first set foot on Southwest Ridge the previous afternoon, barely gaining a toehold on the terminal height before the waning sun forced them to establish defensive perimeters for the night.

Later that evening, November 26, the battalion commanders and senior staff of the 7th Marines attended a briefing at Regiment. Harris's two companies on Southwest Ridge were to launch an attack parallel to Roise's to secure the skyline above the road junction so that Roise could concentrate on moving his battalion rapidly forward.

Although regimental and battalion intelligence officers noted the increasing Chinese presence in the area, no great concern was expressed over the division of Harris's battalion into two mutually unsupportable segments. Given the regiment's experiences throughout the long advance from the sea, there was no reason to be overly apprehensive about the fairly routine division of a veteran unit, even in the face of possible action.

★

The day's initial objective on Southwest Ridge was Hill 1426, which was occupied by Captain Thomas Cooney's George/7 without opposition at 0845, barely thirty minutes after the battalion assault began.

Roise's battalion, downhill to the right rear of George/7, did not seem to be moving forward as rapidly as expected.

Captain Cooney called in his company officers for a fast powwow, leaving the troops to gulp down half-thawed mouthfuls of C-rations and slushy fruit cocktail. The decision was made to press rapidly on. Cooney coordinated air and artillery support with Battalion while the platoon leaders readied the troops for the next move.

The battalion's supporting-arms center, overseen by the battalion weapons-company commander and comprising a forward air-control team and artillery and mortar observer teams, was initially located on Hill 1282, just over two miles to the rear and across the main valley of Yudam-ni. From there, the observers had a clear view of all the objectives of the 3rd Battalion, 7th, and the initial objectives of the 2nd Battalion, 5th. The forward air controller's work began with calling an air strike against the numberless hill that would be facing attack by George/7. A four-plane division of Royal Australian Air Force F-51 fighter-bombers was unleashed, and a thorough artillery preparation followed. The precision softening-up process was marred when a short 105mm round fell on the back slope of Hill 1426, cutting down a knot of Item/7 Marines waiting to support the attack.

For Sergeant Bob Oldani, a veteran Reservist from Seattle, the losses incurred by friendly fire in no way mitigated the effects of the strongest support he had seen since the Sudong fighting three weeks earlier. Oldani was surprised and elated to see that a platoon of heavy water-cooled .30-caliber machine guns had been emplaced on the brow of Hill 1426, the better to rake the nearby objective with concentrated bursts designed to discourage a stand by the defenders, if there were any defenders.

Sergeant Ray Aguirre, a squad leader in Oldani's platoon, was keenly aware of the yelling of the Marines around him as the first assault elements raced down Hill 1426. Aguirre and his buddies had been told to raise as much hell as possible in the hope of making the Chinese defenders think that a good deal more than one rifle company was mounting the attack.

Bob Oldani got only ten yards down the hill before he saw clearly that the Chinese were not about to be rattled. The return fire, mainly automatic, was fearsome, arriving in sheets rather than bursts. All Oldani could think of was avoiding the trees and scrub that impeded his progress. When he had arrived safely in the draw between the hills, the sergeant looked up in the hope of catching sight of the defenders. He saw nothing, so began puffing up the steep slope, dodging the undergrowth at a far slower pace than he had mustered on the downhill leg.

For Ray Aguirre, the objective was a numberless hump in an endless series of Korean hills he had taken and abandoned since coming ashore at Inchon in September. He began each new assault with a dread that had become commonplace. And he continued on his way, building up a rage that would have frightened him in civilian life. Inwardly, he demanded that the unseen enemy step into the open to fight it out, man to man. Ray Aguirre raged and ran, ran and raged, mounting the hill in front of him, steeling himself against the moment when his luck failed.

Two-thirds of the way to the crest, Sergeant Bob Oldani realized with a start that the withering cross fire had ceased, that all was quiet but for the clanking of his gear and the wheeze of his own labored breathing.

Captain Cooney was in the draw overseeing the deployment of his left platoon when the unit was held up by a Chinese machine gun that could not be silenced. The fire from the Chinese-held hill was particularly heavy on this flank, and Cooney, a career officer who had just ordered Marines to attack into that fire, commented to the platoon leader that it was the strongest he had seen in a long time. That said, Cooney was pitched over on his back, dead with a bullet through the chest.

Without orders, the platoon right guide, Sergeant John Hamby, a big bear of a man, yelled for volunteers and took off after the nearest Chinese machine gun in the lead of a determined group of six self-motivated riflemen. Using the terrain to screen its movements, Hamby's group came nearly within range when it was pinned securely, unable to advance or withdraw. Hamby checked his own movement momentarily, then stood up. The big sergeant fired his rifle, lobbed one hand grenade after another, made it to the edge of the emplacement. He killed three gunners before he was shot through the shoulder. Despite the painful, bloody wound, Hamby made the two surviving Chinese gunners comprehend that their war was over, then guided them to the rear while hurling orders to fellow Marines to secure that sector of the objective. John Hamby refused medical treatment until loss of blood forced him out of the fight.

While Sergeant Hamby was opening the way on the left, Sergeant Bob Oldani, on the right, was about to say something about how quiet things had gotten when an explosion threw him and the only other Marine nearby to the ground. Momentarily stunned, Oldani checked himself over, finding that the backs of his gloves had been shredded and that he was bleeding from superficial wounds in both hands. The nearby rifleman was complaining of a severe leg injury, so Oldani moved crablike across the slope and checked for a wound. Despite the absence of blood, the other Marine continued to complain of a stunning pain in one leg. In a moment the sergeant found that a can of jam the man had in the cargo pocket of his trousers had taken the impact of a sizable grenade shard. The pain emanated from a large bruise caused by the secondary impact of the jam can on the leg. The two Marines collapsed in mirth until it occurred to Sergeant Oldani that whoever had thrown the first grenade might still be stalking them.

Oldani looked up the slope and spotted the earth spoils marking a fighting hole. Quickly he threw a hand grenade, which fell short onto the lip of the hole. A second hand grenade landed dead on and exploded. As he sprinted uphill, Oldani found a pair of broken bodies flopping around on the frozen earth and fired into them to make certain they were dead.

Bob Oldani looked upslope again and spotted a second fighting hole. He snapped his Garand rifle to the ready and charged up the steep slope, killing the men he could see, unaware of the toll he was taking, risking his all to get out of the line of fire from the men he was dueling to the death. Marines coming up behind counted thirteen Chinese corpses in Bob Oldani's wake, a number that would not be revealed to him until some weeks later.

It was midafternoon by the time George/7 Marines surged to the crest and watched PLA infantrymen tumbling down the reverse slope, tearing for safety under the protection of guns guarding the next knob down Southwest Ridge.

★

By about 1500 hours, while George Company officers and noncoms strove mightily to sort the company out, other Americans

scoured the scrub-covered ground to the rear to find dead and
wounded comrades. Corpsmen from Battalion moved forward from
Hill 1426 to bear a hand, and litter teams were told off from the rifle
platoons, a measure that would temporarily weaken the company's
ability to fight, but not so much as leaving the injured to their fates
would have ruined the resolve of those weary Marines.

George/7 found itself dangerously low on ammunition. The company executive officer sent an urgent message to the rear, requesting
that Item Company be sent forward to help hold the hill in the event
the Chinese, who could be seen massing in the distance, decided to
mount a counterattack.

Lieutenant Colonel Bill Harris, who had not directly observed any
of the fighting on Southwest Ridge, was not convinced that
he should send Item Company as far forward as the newly won
hill. Even as he was contemplating the options, George/7 reported
that it was under massed machine-gun fire from the tiered bunkers
on Sakkat-San. In the end, Harris decided to allow Item/7 to establish a secure position atop Hill 1426, where it could support
George/7 from afar. The battalion supporting-arms center was already in motion from Hill 1282, two miles to the rear, to establish
a new post on Southwest Ridge. At the same time Harris alerted
Regiment that the situation seemed to be turning against George
Company, and that he needed whatever assistance was available.
Troops from Item Company were sent forward with parcels of ammunition to make good some of the supplies the assault company
had expended.

While the officers sought a solution to the rapidly changing situation, Sergeant Bob Oldani settled in to await The Word. He was
surprised to see two massed columns of PLA infantry form up at the
base of Sakkat-San and begin trudging toward his position. No order
had come through, so Oldani continued to watch with growing incredulity until, after thirty minutes, the columns were obscured by
the intervening ground. More time passed. Then a lone Chinese
soldier appeared on the crest of the next hill forward, seemingly
oblivious to the company of Marines just across the way. Bob Oldani
watched for a moment longer, then steadied his Garand rifle and
squeezed off a single round, knocking the Chinese soldier from his
feet. Ever conscientious, Oldani fired twice more into the inert
body.

Bob Oldani's killing shots seem to have galvanized George Company into taking action to save itself.

★

Waiting for orders a moment before the new fighting erupted, Sergeant Ray Aguirre watched as his platoon leader stood on the skyline with two riflemen, oblivious to the approaching danger. Aguirre yelled a warning just as both enlisted Marines were bowled over, one shot through the head and killed, the other severely injured. The lucky officer dove for cover, untouched.

From his vantage point on a razorback ridge to the right rear of George Company, Captain Bill Earney, the battalion operations officer, watched as the first artillery and heavy mortar rounds fell into the advancing Chinese columns. Then Earney, who had escaped the ennui of the battalion command center to spend the day with the supporting-arms group, was sent racing for cover as friendly 105mm rounds exploded around him. Major Jeff Smith, the battalion supporting-arms coordinator (and commander of the parceled-out battalion weapons company) got on the line with Captain John McLaurin, whose six-gun Item Battery, 11th Marines, was supporting the 3rd Battalion, 7th. McLaurin, a fine artilleryman, was contrite, and immediately checked fire and confirmed the alignment and elevation of all of his guns. The 105mm fire resumed, but continued shorts and overs sent the supporting-arms group scampering back and forth over the summit of the razorback ridge. It became clear that the problem was not in the laying of the guns, but in a deterioration of the ammunition propellants in the extremely cold climate. The result was a drastic abatement of the needed artillery support, which was reduced to single "sniping" rounds. In time, Jeff Smith was happy to inform John McLaurin that more rounds were hitting the Chinese than the friendly observation post.

But there was not enough friendly artillery and mortar fire, and *no* air support. The George Company officers decided among themselves to pull back to Hill 1426 while the Chinese on the next hill took the time to mass for its expected counterattack. The withdrawal could not be precipitous, for the company was in real danger of being caught from behind and in the open as it scrabbled up the steep slope of Hill 1426. It was decided to establish a base of fire with knots of infantry supporting several machine guns. The bulk of George Company then moved out.

The move was made at agonizingly slow speed. The troops of both sides were slowed by their heavy winter clothing, the incredible steepness of the terrain, and the debilitating effects of the freezing weather. In the end, however, the more numerous Chinese can be said to have won the race, for the first of them were firing from the summit of the contested hill before the last of the George/7 Marines disappeared over the summit of Hill 1426.

Sergeant Ray Aguirre was only halfway up Hill 1426 when streams of tracer bullets began passing overhead, thudding into the scrub-covered frozen earth around him. Looking to see how other Marines were faring, the San Antonio Reservist was stunned to find himself alone and off course. The rest of George Company was far to the left.

The Chinese gunners made a game of it, squeezing off long bursts as Aguirre dodged and weaved and grabbed and scrabbled uphill. A hundred feet shy of the crest, Sergeant Aguirre dove behind a huge boulder as a line of bullets stitched the face of the rock. Sweating from the physical ordeal, the veteran squad leader felt that he would freeze to death if he tried to stay put until dark. He steeled his nerves, recovered his breath and moved out, clambering uphill like a madman between converging lines of tracer. Ten feet from the summit, he saw that a pair of Marine machine guns were firing overhead too. Aguirre screamed for the gunners to cease firing, but they did not hear him. There was a three-foot gap between the friendly guns, and Ray Aguirre dove through with the last of his strength and resolve — safe, breathless, thankful.

George Company, 7th, somewhat chastened after the daylong fighting with the Chinese, dug in with Item Company for the night.

CHAPTER

7

Private First Class Raul Rendon, a light-machine-gun squad leader with Baker Company, 1st Battalion, 7th Marines, was fiddling with the remnants of his cold lunch when the main body of the company was ordered to its feet and pointed in the direction of another of the high, steep hills with which it had been contending through the morning of November 27.

Born and bred in the dry heat of southwest Texas, Rendon felt that he would never become used to the traps the cold was forever springing upon the uninitiated. The water in his canteen had frozen, and he had had the devil's own time coaxing out a drop or two at a time in order to relieve an unquenchable thirst. Sweat was beginning to freeze on the gunner's skin, attesting to the heavy loss of body fluids brought on by the day's exertions. The clincher in his hate relationship with the sub-zero weather came when young Rendon innocently pried some frozen jam from a tin and placed it on the tip of his tongue to melt. This project left his bayonet frozen to his tongue, and the resulting struggle caused an ugly wound where the sensitive pink flesh was torn away.

It was in moments like this that Rendon recalled how eagerly he had gone to war, how in first combat on the road to Seoul the gunners had raced the riflemen up enemy-held hills, winning despite the heavier loads they had had to pack. But no more. When The Word to saddle up interrupted his lunch break, Raul Rendon rose sluggishly to his feet, still willing to fight, but not so eager now to go out of his way to meet the risk.

Baker/7 was patrolling the hills and side valleys southwest of Yudam-ni, moving in the direction of Hansang-ni, the tiny village where Able/7 had fought a day earlier, and where 1st Lieutenant Frank Mitchell's body awaited recovery.

Higher up, on a spur overlooking the route of Baker/7's main body, 1st Lieutenant Woody Taylor, commander of the 1st Platoon, received over the company command net the order to move out. Taylor had been in Korea for only three weeks and had yet to work off the extra bulk accumulated as a civilian between wars. Besides, the 32-year-old Alabamian was more than ten years older than many of the eager young Marines in his care. But Woody Taylor was a dependable sort, a man whose intense personal pride made him a distant but outstanding troop leader. First Platoon was simultaneously to lead and screen Baker/7's advance over the ridgeline. If there were Chinese up there, Woody Taylor would be among the first to know.

Another member of Baker/7 usually took time during breaks to reflect upon the beauty of the snowy hills and mountains of the Taebek Plateau. Navy Corpsman Bill Davis was a native of a small western Maryland town whose setting was very much like the valley of Yudam-ni. Like many of the corpsmen serving with 1st Marine Division, Davis was a professional who had volunteered for duty with the Marines following a cushy stint at a Stateside hospital before the new war. When the call came to mount out, Bill Davis grabbed his medical bag and took his place in the shambling column.

Second Lieutenant Joe Owen, a profane twenty-six-year-old six-foot-five-inch mustang, was resigned to the prospect of a fight. A smiling, talkative giant, Owen had made the Marine Corps his life. He had had to work hard to wangle a billet in Baker/7 when the unit was forming in California, and he had remained the unit's junior lieutenant despite the comings and goings of several of his slightly more senior colleagues. As such, he had been denied command of a rifle platoon, though he had turned in a sterling performance as permanent commander of the company's three-gun 60mm mortar section. When he received his orders, Joe Owen unfolded his long bones and ordered his gunners to begin moving up the long draw toward the distant ridgeline.

Raul Rendon pulled out the hobo remnants of the socks he used in place of gloves and grabbed his load — two chests of .30-caliber ammunition for his squad's light machine gun.

At about 1300 hours, elements of Baker/7 observed a dozen Chinese soldiers far ahead along the route of advance. The artillery forward observer with the company quickly called a brief artillery fire mission. That dispersed the small knot of hostile soldiers, and Baker/7 continued struggling up the steep grade. Well over an hour later, however, the company was ordered onto a new heading to counter a force of about sixty Chinese which was maneuvering to threaten the heavy traffic on the MSR.

At about 1500 hours — by which time George/7 had secured part of the unnumbered hill west of Hill 1426 — Baker/7 was ascending a slope that could be reached by fingers of fire from the prepared positions on Sakkat-San. Baker/7 was mousetrapped as it climbed into the killing zone.

The fire hit Woody Taylor's 1st Platoon from north, south, and west without preamble, then sought the balance of the company. It was a well-conceived trap sprung by patient gunners.

Raul Rendon, initially crouched over to facilitate the steep climb, stood up so fast at the first shots that he lost his helmet, which rolled down the hill, taking with it treasured letters from home that he had stowed in the liner. He grabbed another helmet as it rolled down from above, and called his diminished squad together, bird-dogging the tired gunners to the crest of the ridge, bellowing instructions as they broke out the tripod and gun and cracked open a new chest of ammunition. Aimed generally at the source of the hostile fire, Rendon's air-cooled light machine gun cranked out several rounds and fell silent, a temporary victim of the brutal cold. Incoming fire increased as the gunners sought to warm the parts, clear nonexistent jams, and get the gun firing smoothly.

Farthest up the slope, Woody Taylor's 1st Platoon went to ground momentarily, then charged forward in fits and starts in an effort to grapple with a line of Chinese infantry that was firing down on the rest of the company. The attack stalled.

Chinese gunfire drove Raul Rendon's gun squad from its initial position. As he instinctively searched for leadership, Rendon saw the machine-gun platoon leader scramble behind a rock outcropping. He approached the officer from behind, tapped the man on his back and asked if his gun could be placed on the right, where another light machine gun had just been put out of action. The green lieutenant nodded his assent without turning, so Rendon led the way and set up the gun, firing at distant figures. To the right, out of the corner of his eye, Rendon saw Marines engage in a hand-to-hand melee with white-clad Chinese soldiers. Baker/7 was surrounded.

Too busy to panic, Rendon cranked off several more bursts, then gave vent to a bloodcurdling scream as his legs and lower abdomen were stitched by a string of bullets. His only sensation was the unlikely feeling that a huge watermelon had been crammed between his thighs.

Oaths dripping from his open mouth, Raul Rendon flipped onto his back, feeling in his heart of hearts that death was near. The crippled gunner spit several times to see if he could bring up any blood; he had seen men die with blood on their lips, and when he saw his frothy spittle freeze white upon the ground he calmed down despite the unremitting pain. Lacking control over the lower part of his body, he used his arms to force his legs together, then managed to roll a dozen feet downslope, out of the line of fire. Unable to become totally immersed in his own suffering, the proud Marine noted that his gun crew was firing despite his absence.

The bleeding gunner rolled some more and landed on top of a rifleman, who nearly jumped out of his skin when what he thought was a corpse collided with him. Rendon assured the man that he was alive, if not exactly kicking.

While the rest of Baker Company formed a 360-degree perimeter to beat off repeated attacks, Woody Taylor prodded 1st Platoon closer to the line of Chinese arrayed at the top of the slope. It took some hard fighting, but the Marines closed to within twenty-five yards of the bushwackers before being driven firmly to ground. The opposing sides traded bullets and blood.

Mortar crews love a good fight because it gives them a perfect pretense for unloading a lot of heavy rounds they would otherwise have to hump across often impossible terrain. In that respect, Second Lieutenant Joe Owen's colorful assemblage of gunners was no different from other mortarmen, though they rated themselves among the best shots in the business. Spotting several squads of PLA infantry maneuvering across his left front about four hundred yards out, Owen challenged his gun crews to score on a made-to-order shot. A gun was quickly turned, and the first round sent on its way. Owen watched the shell rise, certain it was to be a direct hit. And it was, landing right in the midst of a Chinese squad. But it was also a dud, one of the many such that made life hell for men who prided themselves on the accuracy of their fire. The Chinese dispersed before the gunners could get off a second round.

★

Corpsman Bill Davis found Raul Rendon at length and probed the wounded machine gunner to assess the extent of his injuries. Rendon did not know it, but he was being triaged; if he was too damaged, Davis would be forced to move on to a man who stood a better chance of being salvaged. Concentrating on the examination, Rendon could feel sticky blood all over his backside and lap. He asked Davis to check his genitals, and was assured that they seemed intact, a relief of the first magnitude.

After Davis moved on, an exchange right out of the movies took place. Though bullets were hitting near his head. Rendon focused on the cigarette-smoking man next to him. Noting the gunner's interest, the other Marine proffered the butt. Rendon replied that he was a nonsmoker, that he had been warned of the harm smoking could cause. The other Marine insisted, however, so Rendon took a few deep drags, which seemed to help him relax.

Corpsman Davis returned after some minutes and began patching holes. Morphine was controlling Raul Rendon's pain. While watching Marine Corsairs flash by to deliver napalm and bombs to Sakkat-San, Rendon dozed mercifully, sensing that Baker/7 was holding its own in a fight for its life.

Later, with four wounded Marines to care for, Bill Davis was called out to treat another injured man. As he grabbed his medical kit, he saw two of his patients rise to help bring in the newly injured man. Davis turned to motion the volunteers back and came face to face with the full force of a mortar shell as it exploded between him and the casualties. He went down with numerous shrapnel wounds in his face, chest, arms, and legs. A nearby Marine sergeant pulled the injured, bloody medic to safety and treated him beside his patients.

★

A platoon-size PLA maneuvering element Joe Owen had been keeping an eye on made its move from behind a rock outcropping forty yards from the Marine line, heading right for the company mortars. Owen took an instant, irrational, personal dislike to the Chinese officer leading the assault, and stood to challenge the man.

No one could help noticing the six-foot-five-inch lieutenant, dressed as he was in a filthy, ragged calf-length parka and decorated about the face with a wild, scruffy, snot-festooned beard. The Chinese officer had no trouble picking Joe Owen out of the crowd, and the two men stared at each other as the Chinese drew nearer. After considering the probability that he would be dead meat if the towering Marine ever laid hands on him, the Chinese platoon leader turned on his heel twenty feet from the American line. Joe Owen took off after him, wielding a bayonet at the end of his tiny carbine. Luckily for Owen, a Marine rifleman tumbled the Chinese officer into the snow before the mortarman could pass beyond the friendly line.

★

By that time, George/7, about two miles to the west and north, beyond the next ridgeline, had made its withdrawal to Hill 1426, and that left Baker/7 the only American unit still in mortal danger.

One of the people following the action, on the battalion tactical radio net, was the battalion commander, Lieutenant Colonel Ray Davis, a decorated veteran of three Pacific campaigns, the only rifle-battalion commander in the division to have held a similar command in combat before the Korean War, and one of the most respected field officers in the Marine Corps. Once Baker Company was firmly pinned, Ray Davis rang up Regiment and spoke with Colonel Homer Litzenberg, who agreed to release elements of Charlie/7, which was guarding the regimental command post. Davis decided to lead the relief himself.

★

Baker/7 was by then under the orders of 1st Lieutenant Joe Kurcaba, who had assumed control when the company commander was shot through the mouth. Kurcaba was a quiet, tough, cool combat officer, and he saw no reason to hang around waiting for help to come. The platoon leaders were ordered to effect a fighting withdrawal in the direction of the MSR.

With Woody Taylor's platoon fighting rearguard actions, the Baker/7 perimeter moved downslope, virtually intact. Small groups of Chinese mounted snapping, snarling wolflike attacks, but they appeared reticent about really pressing home their many advantages.

Ray Davis arrived on the MSR with Charlie/7 and had the company mortars fire white phosphorous rounds to mark the most secure route for Baker Company, which was slowed considerably by the many wounded who had to be humped down the treacherous slopes.

As the first files of Baker/7 Marines struggled off the ridge, Charlie/7 moved into defensive positions in a draw on the east side of the road. Ambulances and trucks were dispatched from the town to pick up the wounded and tired troops. The juncture was made just after sunset.

Among the wounded was Private First Class Raul Rendon, punctured in four palces by Chinese machine-gun bullets, exhausted and dozing fitfully in a poncho borne by rotating four-man teams. Bill Davis — still in shock, still bleeding, still worrying about the other wounded men — came down from the ridge on the arm of a Marine platoon sergeant. Joe Owen arrived intact, wondering if the loss of the company commander might result in his finally being shifted to command a rifle platoon. And Woody Taylor boarded his truck mulling over the important lessons he had learned in the day's disaster.

Raul Rendon's next moments of awareness came in a hospital tent at Yudam-ni, where Navy corpsmen cut off his shoepacs, shirt, and pants, and changed his bloody, frozen battle dressings. A bottle of plasma was dripping away into each of his arms. Later in that long night, Rendon's bladder would be pierced to relieve pressure backed up by a bullet-severed urethra. In a perverse way, Raul Rendon was one of the luckiest Marines wounded around Yudam-ni that day and night, for he was one of the very few to be evacuated by helicopter. Within twenty-four hours, the Texas Regular would be in an Army hospital in Hamhung, receiving the best medical treatment available for his critical, crippling wounds.

Leaving Charlie/7 to guard the MSR from positions in a draw on the roadside slope of Hill 1419, Ray Davis rode back into Yudam-ni with exhausted, bleeding Baker/7.

The 7th Marines had seen better days, and would have worse.

C H A P T E R
8

First Lieutenant Ralph Abell felt completley out of his depth. Until a month earlier the St. Louis Reserve officer had been doing what he felt he did best, leading a rifle platoon through enemy territory, his chance for helping win the war and getting everyone home again. Then he had been assigned to the staff of the 2nd Battalion, 7th Marines, to act as a liaison officer with the regimental headquarters, an envoy of his battalion to the regimental staff. But at the beginning of the third week in November Abell's education (he was a graduate of the University of Missouri School of Journalism) had caused him to be dragooned to fill the vacant post of the 7th Regiment's Public Information Officer. His job was to assure Colonel Litzenberg's regiment at least as much Stateside publicity as the rival 5th Regiment PIO was getting for his regiment.

But the new job was not why Ralph Abell felt out of his depth. He had been sent that Monday afternoon to pick up a visitor from the new division base at Hagaru-ri, fourteen miles to the south along the MSR. The visitor was the X Corps commander, Lieutenant General Edward Almond. Ralph Abell had never spoken to a man ranked higher than colonel, and he had a silly fear that he might pull a gaffe that would dishonor his regiment.

He need not have worried. Some of the senior sergeants at Regiment had told him to act naturally, and General Almond had shown himself to be a good enough sort, honoring his hosts by choosing to ride in a rickety, battle-worn Marine jeep when he could have chosen from among several brand-new Army jeeps that were pulled up beside the tiny helicopter pad at Hagaru-ri. He had even invited 1st Lieutenant Abell to ride along, relegating several of his staffers to lesser vehicles. But the fourteen-mile road journey had been a real nightmare for the rank-conscious lieutenant whose job it was to build images.

A short way out of Hagaru-ri, while ascending the approaches to Toktong Pass, the general's party became entangled with a small convoy of large Marine trucks. The road was narrow and the trucks were wide and heavily laden. Almond had shown commendable restraint for a while, but he finally became impatient over the delay. A traffic jam in the mountains was no place for a busy man with a corps to run.

The general ordered his senior aide, a full colonel, to walk ahead of the jeep, find the convoy master and direct him to clear a path for the general's vehicles. Ralph Abell, realizing himself that there was a perfectly good lieutenant at hand to do the job, pulled deeper into the parka in which he was swaddled, hoping that his keen embarrassment would not be noticed.

At length, a bulky, parka-clad figure appeared beside the jeep and motioned for the door to be opened. The man was the convoy master, a young Marine sergeant, sent back by the Army colonel who thought his rank might be of definitive use in unsnarling the clogged roadway. The sergeant had no way of knowing that he was climbing into a jeep occupied by the corps commander, and the late afternoon shadows and insignia-obscuring clothing worn by all did nothing to relieve him of his burden of ignorance.

To Ralph Abell's red-faced consternation, the sergeant, typically, read the riot act against the Army colonel. His monologue was obscenely accurate. Ralph Abell dared momentary peeks at the corps commander for the next quarter hour, but Ned Almond did not so much as turn a hair in response to the Marine sergeant's diatribe.

Those fifteen minutes were the most exhausting of Ralph Abell's career. He would vastly have preferred storming an enemy bastion single-handed to the tongue-lashing he expected to receive back at Regiment.

In time the Army colonel managed to clear a path for the general's vehicles, and the yattering sergeant was sent back out into the cold. The general's party passed the Marine trucks, topped Toktong Pass, and descended into the valley of Yudam-ni to make directly for the 7th Regiment's command compound. There 1st Lieutenant Abell turned Lieutenant General Almond over to Colonel Homer Litzenberg before rushing back to his own tent to await punishment that would never come.

There was some banter at Regiment for a while, then General Almond turned to the task of pinning medals on the parkas of several Marines who had stepped in out of the cold for the brief ceremony. When the formalities had ended, Ned Almond turned to Captain Don France, Litz's intelligence officer, and asked for the latest news. France had been collecting data for weeks on end and, though he was known as a rather sober type, the studious captain blurted out in the presence of the medal winners and the regiment's senior staff, "General, there are a fucking lot of Chinese in those hills."

Almond did not blink, though many of the thirty-odd bystanders had to duck out of the cozy tent to keep from choking on their laughter.

The general stood through what little remained of his briefing and stalked out in the the evening chill to board his helicopter, which had been flown up from Hagaru-ri earlier.

★

The Army general who set the tone of the northeastern Korea campaign was a contradictory figure even in Army circles, where he was known. He was the object of a special brand of scorn on the part of Marine officers, who failed utterly to understand his style or appreciate his worth.

Lieutenant General Edward Almond was a Virginia Military Institute alumnus in an Army dominated by West Pointers. He had commanded an all-Negro infantry division in the mountains of Italy, and even in the newly integrated Army that might have been seen as a stigma; he was, at all events, a superlative division commander, exceptionally adept at the sort of mountain warfare X Corps was waging in North Korea.

Almond was an extremely intelligent man, and an exceptionally hard worker, who drove his staff to match his own output, an achievement requiring fifteen-to-twenty-hour workdays. He always knew to within a hairsbreadth the location of each battalion under his command, and the contact points of every unit in X Corps. He had been a tireless leader at Inchon-Seoul, getting to the front, often under fire, every day he had troops in combat.

But he had shown a serious lack of technical expertise to Marine officers with whom he came in contact. At Inchon, on seeing lines of amphibious tractors making for the beaches with their loads of Marine riflemen, he had asked a very senior Marine general if he thought they would remain afloat, a possibly understandable lapse by a man who had never before witnessed an amphibious assault. On another occasion he had spotted a battery of Marine 105mm howitzers set for high-angle fire, their barrels pointing almost straight up. The corps commander marveled aloud at the speed with which Marines could set up 90mm antiaircraft guns. That was unpardonable; Almond had certainly seen his share of 105mm howitzers in battery since 1940.

Those were just the sort of gaffes that could turn combat troops away from even as robust a field commander as Ned Almond.

The general's worst problems arose from the ambiguity of his position in the chain of command. In addition to his duties as the commander of an independent corps operating directly under GHQ-Tokyo, Almond served as Douglas MacArthur's chief of staff. But he was a virtual outsider on the staff of which he was, nominally at least, chief. The MacArthur clique was manned largely by highly politicized generals, all personally loyal to Douglas MacArthur; they were men who had served their general throughout the Pacific War, talented sycophants who appear to have shunned Almond both as their superior and as a subordinate corps commander.

While in the field — and he never left it when his corps was in action — Almond was totally at the mercy of GHQ-Tokyo for the support he required if he was to operate an independent command.

There is no way to be certain, but it is just possible that Tokyo intentionally withheld from Almond news of the rout of 8th Army. At the moment the general was being berated by the Marine convoy master, 8th Army was a rabble in headlong retreat. Neither Almond nor any man in northeastern Korea knew that. It is possible, of course, that GHQ-Tokyo merely misdiagnosed the fighting on the western wing, never considering the impact it might have upon X Corps. But that is doubtful, for 8th Army had received crippling hammer blows over all of the previous forty-eight hours, and Tokyo never murmured the merest warning.

Don France's singularly inept presentation did not move Ned Almond at the eleventh hour mainly because Ned Almond had been programmed by GHQ-Tokyo to accept no such warning.

★

The final movements in setting the stage for the ordeal of the Chosin Reservoir took place through the afternoon and early evening of November 27, as tens of thousands of PLA infantrymen moved to within striking distance of 1st Marine Division and those elements of 7th Infantry Division east of the Reservoir.

Lieutenant Colonel Bob Taplett's 3rd Battalion, 5th, hiked down from Toktong Pass in the late afternoon and was placed in a "staging area" north of town, a flat field dominated by several nearby hills and approachable through several wide draws. Taplett was assured upon querying Regiment that his bivouac was guarded by a company of the 2nd Battalion, 7th, which was holding the dominating heights to the northeast. Taplett could not see any activity on the designated hills and he accepted Regiment's word only with the greatest reluctance.

★

First Lieutenant Richard Primrose arrived at Yudam-ni late in the afternoon of November 27 as part of an experiment he was not certain had succeeded.

A day earlier the crews of four World-War-II-vintage Sherman M4 medium tanks had attempted to traverse the unimproved packed-earth track from Hagaru-ri, but icy conditions had forced the crews to abandon one of the tanks and turn back. Primrose had arrived at Hagaru-ri early on November 27 leading his platoon of five modern Pershing M26 heavy tanks. He had agreed to try to get one of these more stable vehicles over Toktong Pass.

As he stood in the turret of the wide Pershing, muttering minutely detailed orders to his volunteer driver, Dick Primrose had sweated out the arduous ascent to the pass, teetering on the brinks of bottomless chasms, scraping against rock outcroppings, squeezing by the abandoned Sherman tank. Impeded by ice, which caused his tank's steel tread shoes to slip and skew, Primrose did not crawl over the top of the pass until well into the afternoon.

The descent was at least as arduous as the ascent. The driver had to stand on his right brake almost the whole way down in order to use the verge of the narrow roadway to help slow the skidding hulk. It took three hours to get into town from the top of the pass. Primrose and the driver were worn to a frazzle, not certain that they should recommend that any other Pershings be brought forward before the engineers had an opportunity to widen the roadway.

★

The last large unit to arrive at Yudam-ni was Lieutenant Colonel Jack Stevens's 1st Battalion, 5th, which hiked into town as Ray Davis was completing the relief of Baker/7 on the MSR south of town. Stevens's battalion was literally dumped into an open field after dark, but the battalion commander was assured by Ray Murray that everything would be sorted out correctly in the morning.

★

If Jack Stevens's troops were the last to arrive at Yudam-ni that night, 1st Lieutenant Robert Messman appears to have been the last to leave. The commander of King Battery, 4th Battalion, 11th, Messman had been detailed to pick up needed 155mm ammunition from Hagaru-ri, where several truckloads had been cached.

Messman had little to fear, though a drive at night through unpacified mountains is never without an element of risk. However, shortly before the artillery officer left Yudam-ni, a vast column of empty trucks had set out for Hagaru-ri. The trucks, in fact, did not clear Toktong Pass until well after dark, and the drivers had had to turn on their headlights in order to safely traverse the treacherous route. If there was to be any trouble along the MSR, Bob Messman was betting that the larger column would draw it.

The column made the fourteen-mile journey without incident, stopping at the base's casualty clearing station to drop off more than a dozen men who had been wounded around Yudam-ni that day. But as Bob Messman's jeep breasted Toktong Pass, PLA infantry cut the road, establishing a succession of manned and unmanned road-blocks. Lieutenant Messman was taken prisoner when at one of these barriers he was forced to brake the jeep he was driving.

As Bob Messman was marched into the hills to begin three years in captivity, the world was falling in on the Marines strewn about the valley of Yudam-ni.

PART THREE

Assault

CHAPTER
9

The first files of Chinese skirmishers crept down from the heights opposite the slumbering Marine lines along the northwest, north, and northeast arcs of the Yudam-ni perimeter. The 79th and 89th Divisions of General Sung Shin-lin's 9th PLA Army Group had come to destroy an isolated regiment of American Marines.

Farther south the 59th PLA Division was swinging into position on either side of Toktong Pass, cutting the tenuous route to Hagaru-ri and the sea. To the east two additional PLA divisions were preparing to descend upon what their scouts had told them was another isolated Marine regiment.

Though their commanders did not know of the changes that had taken place in American dispositions over the preceding twenty-four hours, the PLA soldiers surrounding Yudam-ni certainly had detected the increased strength their quarry had been able to muster in that time.

But even the deployment of two reinforced Marine regiments, rather than one, would not have deterred the unknowing Chinese commanders from their plan, for they had deployed overwhelming superiority in numbers for just about any contingency.

The first light probes made contact three hours before midnight on November 27, 1950.

★

The 2nd Battalion, 5th, had had a grueling day of winter combat on the road west of town. All that the nine-hundred-odd men of the battalion wanted that night was rest and warmth. When the sun set at 1830 hours, the temperature had plunged to −20 degrees. The troops were on fifty-percent alert; half were asleep while their foxhole buddies stood watches ranging from one to four hours, depending upon whatever arrangements they had made amongst themselves in the long months of campaigning since Pusan and Inchon.

Those who were awake fretted about the cold and its effect upon their weapons, which often proved balky at extreme temperatures. Those who slept, or tried to, were concerned lest parts of their bodies freeze. Most had removed their imperfect shoepacs to dry so that trapped perspiration would not freeze toes and feet. The sleeping men could be awake in a moment, but they could lose whole minutes banging the ice from their footgear and handling slippery laces. The battle, when it came, would be in the hands of the men who happened to be awake and ready at the first onslaught.

★

The Marines on the northwest perimeter were deployed along a fairly straight line, their backs to the roadway leading west from the town.

The westernmost unit was Dog/5. Next in line was Fox/5, which had borne the brunt of the day's fight; but for supporting arms, every Fox/5 Marine was on the line, facing northward. Next was Easy/5, holding the wide draw between Fox/5's flat-topped ridge and Hill 1403, the terminal knob of Northwest Ridge. Easy/5 and How/7, which was holding the height, were not in direct physical contact, and there was no Marine unit within supporting range of How/7. Backing Lieutenant Colonel Roise's line was a single platoon of Easy/5 and a fifty-man combat-engineer platoon.

The first serious flare-up, a diversion, occurred when a group of Chinese mounted a grenade assault against a roadblock manned by a platoon of Dog/5 on the roadway of the western extremity of Roise's line. The Chinese did not seriously press the attack, and the Marines killed two grenadiers.

While attention was drawn to the roadblock fight, masses of PLA infantry maneuvered to within yards of the main line held by Fox and Easy Companies. As mortar fire near the roadblock died away, very light probes were launched by very small Chinese groups along the Fox/5 line. The Chinese recoiled wherever they met resistance, but by drawing fire they exposed the positions of most Marine automatic weapons.

While attention was drawn to the light probes, infiltrators intent upon breaching the Marine line crawled to within a few feet of the junction of Fox and Easy Companies, the weakest point along that part of Roise's line.

This was a skillful series of ruses and deployments by an enemy whose battlefield tactics are yet denegrated by their adversaries. In every case, Marines reacting to minor harassments helped sketch in the defensive layout of their own lines. Satisfied in time that he had found all that could be revealed, the PLA commander ordered his assault columns to work.

Bugle calls cut the frigid night air and grenadiers hurled bunches

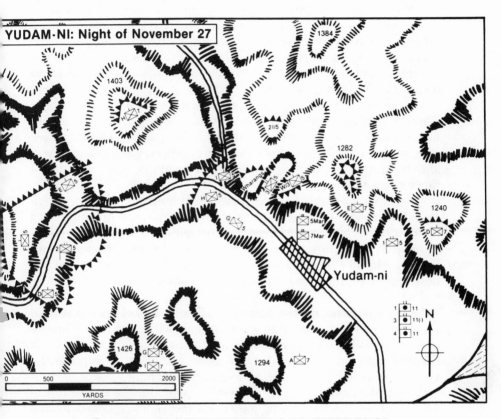

YUDAM-NI: Night of November 27

(See endpapers for GUIDE TO MAP SYMBOLS AND ABBREVIATIONS.)

of concussion stick grenades into the Marine lines while machine guns on the heights dominating the battlefield probed the night sky with eerie puffs of green tracer. Following this rude awakening by several minutes, a sustained mortar barrage caught many Marines in the open, on the move.

Massed PLA infantry, led by ranks of submachine gunners, tore into the Marine lines, the forwardmost three hundred of them driving a wedge at the point where Fox and Easy Companies were joined. Massively overpowering, and attacking without regard to casualties, the Chinese went right after the machine guns supporting the right Fox Company platoon, which was commanded by 1st Lieutenant Bernard Christofferson.

The keen odor of picric acid, the cheap explosive used by the Chinese in their concussion grenades, had rattled many of Christofferson's men, who thought they were being gassed. The line gave way, hurled back by the sheer mass of numbers. Christofferson was able to muster one thin squad for a counterattack: ten men against thirty times ten.

Aided immeasurably by 81mm mortar illumination rounds, which revealed each new Chinese effort as it was forming, Christofferson's platoon slowly re-formed, crept forward and held, eventually piling up seventy-five Chinese on the snow-covered slope. But there were too few Marines to win back all of the lost fighting holes, and the best they could do for the moment was contain the Chinese salient.

★

To the left, Sergeant Jim Matthews, Fox/5's rocket section leader, was just awakening from an evening nap when the first Chinese probes hit. Still a bit fuzzy from sleep, the battlewise noncom began fiddling with the laces of his shoepacs, intending to replace the sweaty liners lest his feet freeze in a nightlong fight.

Before Matthews could act, however, panic hit the center of the Fox/5 line as the battle was joined on the right. Spooked by the masses of Chinese they had seen on the heights that afternoon, a few riflemen shouted for everyone to pull back. Matthews and several other noncoms countered these screams with firm orders for everyone to remain on the line.

Jim Matthews yanked on his shoepacs and looked up at the illuminated heights across the way. He saw a swirling crowd of white-clad forms plunging headlong through deep snow into the intervening valley. Marine machine guns were raking the lines of unbalanced Chinese, but they could not begin to halt the wild onslaught.

Despite his earlier firmness in settling the men around him, Jim Matthews had to suppress his own urge to cut and run. But a detached sense of calm overcame him, and he passed the time stacking extra carbine ammunition on the large tabletop rock that guarded his position.

At length, Matthews saw several Chinese set up a mortar behind a rock pile on his left front. He called up his section's 3.5-inch launcher and ordered the two-man team to deal with the mortar, never dreaming that they might actually destroy it. The bazooka's first round hit the rocks, impelling loose stones and gravel into the bodies of the crewmen, killing them all.

Matthews was next joined by the company first sergeant, who was kept from lighting a calming cigarette when the chill night wind kept blowing out his pocket lighter. Matthews offered the top sergeant the use of his sleeping bag to baffle the wind. When he turned to help hold up the makeshift screen, the rocket sergeant was slammed back against the tabletop rock as a bullet gouged out his right armpit. He had been shot by an infiltrator hiding on the rear slope of the ridge.

Surprised beyond belief, and feeling the onset of shock, Matthews crumpled back against the tabletop rock as the departing first sergeant ordered nearby Marines to his aid. Matthews was immediately at the center of a furious and largely superfluous effort by his buddies to staunch the bleeding. One rescuer cut through the sergeant's parka and, incidentally, his leather belt, revealing the ugly, heavily bleeding wound. Matthews was bandaged and sent off down the slope, holding his trousers up and parka closed, not quite certain he could explain what had befallen him. not entirely sure where he should be heading.

★

Private First Class Ed Debalski, a 60mm mortarman who had been sent to the line to help plug a gap, had the PLA tactics doped out within thirty minutes. First there would be an attack by grenadiers, then a lull, then an attack by submachine gunners, then a lull, then another grenade assault.

Fighting desperately through the night, the nineteen-year-old Regular watched helplessly as Fox Company was thinned from an average of one two-man foxhole every five yards to roughly half that. In time Debalski was himself culled. The fifth attack caught the mortarman on the move, diving behind a low bump on the skyline. He took eleven grenade shards in his left leg.

Bleeding profusely, Ed Debalski was on the verge of succumbing to shock and pain as the Chinese sally was turned back. Weak and disoriented, he placed himself in the care of his best buddy, a Chicago Regular named Daugherty, a man with whom he had shared two years of prewar service but whose first name he had never learned. Daugherty led Debalski to the company sick bay and stayed with him as a corpsman applied temporary field dressings.

Unable to move under his own power, Debalski asked an officer to provide a man to help him, but the officer said that he had no one to spare. Hearing this, Daugherty offered to see his buddy to safety; he hauled Ed Debalski headfirst by his parka hood, using a communications wire to guide them down the hill. At one place, the two Marines froze in silence as a half dozen Chinese earned the right-of-way. In the end, Ed Debalski was seen safely to the battalion aid station.

"You're okay now, Ski," Daugherty said with a wave of his hand. "I've gotta get back up the hill." He left immediately, to die that night in the defense of his position.

★

Captain Franklin Mayer, the headquarters commandant, joined Hal Roise at the battalion command post and found the battalion commander coolly rattling off orders and suggestions as calls flooded in from all the line companies, Regiment, and supporting arms. Roise simply could not be rattled.

When Captain Uel Peters called to say that Fox Company was running low on ammunition, "Stretch" Mayer and his driver loaded a jeep, which the driver took right up behind the embattled company. Mayer made two more such trips during the course of the night.

Peters later called back to say that he was swamped with wounded and had no men left to carry them out. Stretch Mayer took three of his technicians and two stretchers and climbed the hill to Peters's command post. The rifle company commander could not stop expressing his appreciation for the ammunition Mayer had sent earlier, or for his coming personally to help with the wounded. He gave the headquarters commandant a quick rundown on the situation, then turned to the pressing business of running a night battle. Mayer and his men lifted two badly wounded Marines and started down toward the road in the brightening moonlight.

The load was too much for two two-man teams. Mayer fell twice in the dark, dumping the man on his stretcher painfully to the ground. Nevertheless, the team reached the battalion sick bay, where Mayer grabbed every man he could find and led them back for more wounded. Chinese infiltrators fired on the party during the second descent, but the bullets went wide of the mark.

Later, Mayer was sent off alone in the dark by Hal Roise to try to find out what was happening to How/7, to the right. He found a group of riflemen, who told him that many Chinese were on the road farther down. Mayer led these stragglers to his lines and reported back to Roise, who blew out a stream of cigarette smoke and said, "We can hold 'em," the same thing he had been saying to Regiment all night.

★

Captain Sam Jaskilka's Easy Company, on the battalion right, was caught in the same state of semi-preparedness as Fox/5.

Corporal Barney Baxter, a heavy-machine-gun crew chief attached to Easy/5's 2nd Platoon, had been scraping away at the frozen ground since sunset, trying to terrace enough of the hillside to properly position his .30-caliber water-cooled Browning. In three hours' time, he and his assistant had barely succeeded in making a six-inch dent, not nearly enough. Moreover, Baxter had never seen the ground he was supposed to defend, having been placed on the line well after dark. The gun's barrel was intentionally impeded by a stake on either side, a precaution against an excited gunner's traversing too far one way or the other and spraying friendly positions. Baxter, a former paratrooper with three Pacific campaigns behind him, had no desire to be involved in a fight that night, given all the things going against him.

First Lieutenant Ray Jorz, asleep when the first probes hit, had been transferred to the command of Jaskilka's 1st Platoon only after dark, following the evacuation of 2nd Lieutenant Ed Deptula. It is doubtful that as many as five members of the platoon even knew that Jorz was their officer.

Asleep beside Jorz was Platoon Sergeant Russ Borgomainero, who had been in temporary command of the 1st Platoon so often that the men naturally looked to him as their commander. Since Pusan, the platoon sergeant had seen at least four officers come and go. An old-time Marine, Borgomainero was really in his element in a fight. He had been a guest of the Japanese through the entire Pacific War and seemed intent upon making up for lost time.

Private First Class Rick Seward's fire team was in the rightmost Easy/5 fighting hole, about seventy-five yards up the side of Hill 1403. Arriving just at sunset, Seward and his two buddies had been a little surprised to find a number of fighting holes already dug, but they were thankful to be spared the task of contending with the rock-hard soil. Old campaigners, the three Marines cut tree boughs, with which they lined the hole of their choice. Seward stood first watch, turning the job over to one of his teammates at 2100. He had no more than removed his shoepacs when the first thin cries of Chinese bugles wavered up from the valley floor.

★

Ray Jorz was pulled from his sleep when a machine gun at the junction of the 1st and 2nd Platoons opened fire. The gun was in the 2nd Platoon line, so Jorz stayed in his bag until he heard the voice of Sam Jaskilka come over the telephone receiver he kept close to his ear. The captain ordered Jorz to silence the gun and get some riflemen out after what appeared to be several infiltrators. Jorz yelled the order into the darkness. The response was even more gunfire and simultaneous "Here they come!" cries from the slopes on either side, from across the draw Easy/5 was blocking, from everywhere.

The initial rush at the junction of Fox and Easy Companies severely mauled Jorz's 1st Platoon almost before he could get out of his down bag. Scrabbling uphill to see how his left squad was faring, Jorz found that the occupants of the high crown were Chinese, men who had driven Christofferson's Fox Company people in the first rush. The lieutenant recoiled and began doing his bit to stabilize the line.

Corporal Barney Baxter was instantly alert, thumbs on the trigger of his machine gun as soon as the gun to the left opened with long bursts. But Baxter was unable to see anyone in the limits of the stakes impeding the traverse of his gun. Ten minutes of heavy fighting went by before the strong voice of the machine-gun platoon sergeant demanded that Baxter open fire. The veteran gunner was unhappy with the order. He had survived some pretty tough fighting on the principle that machine guns never fire without a target. But he had his orders and cranked off short bursts without seeing a thing, certain he was firing into thin air. After ten minutes of such futile action, riflemen on either side of the gun bellowed warnings that Chinese were directly on the front. Baxter swung the barrel from the right and fired, hitting at chest height two Chinese no more than ten feet out. When the tracers hit the men, Baxter could see eerie expressions on their faces. Then they crumpled to the ground, engulfed again by the pitch blackness of the night. Barney Baxter, veteran of combat with Japanese and North Koreans, had seen his first PLA soldiers, and had killed them. But there was no time to reflect, for hundreds of their fellows were now within range, and

Baxter's only thoughts were for swinging the gun back and forth, spraying human forms in the thin, wavering light of his tracers.

When he awoke to an order to get forward to spot for supporting fires, Sergeant Jim Friedl, Easy/5's 81mm mortar forward observer, hit the panic zipper of his sleeping bag and grabbed his boondockers. Sacrificing precious seconds to bang ice from the sueded pigskin footgear, he laced them on the run, ordering his radioman to set up near the company command post and make contact with the battalion 81mm mortar platoon.

The scene at Sam Jaskilka's command post was pandemonium. Runners and officers were racing through, yelling at one another over the din of fire, waving this way and that. It looked from there as if friendly artillery was falling into friendly territory. The company gunnery sergeant singled out Jim Friedl and told him to get a barrage working to support Jorz's embattled 1st Platoon, holding the left side of the draw. Noting that Captain Jaskilka had relinquished the guns to battalion control, Friedl said that he could only try. Then he found the sound-powered telephone to 1st Platoon and held a hurried talk with Platoon Sergeant Borgomainero, who barely had time to converse in the midst of yet another Chinese rush on his position. Borgomainero said that he would send a man down off the slope to guide Friedl in.

While waiting for the guide, Friedl heard the artillery forward observer attached to Easy Company order all supporting arms to cease firing because, he believed, they were hitting friendly troops. Friedl grew livid, for he saw that the green lieutenant was facedown on the ground, not once looking up to see what was going on. Another officer booted the panicked man in the butt and ordered him off the air.

Borgomainero's guide found Sergeant Friedl and led him uphill to confer with the platoon sergeant, who was firing a BAR as fast as several loaders could smack fresh rounds into spent magazines.

All Jim Friedl needed was a quick look: Jorz's platoon had been shattered. But for isolated pockets, the original line had been overrun. Friedl made a dash back to his radio, grabbed his headset, and gained contact with the 81mm fire-direction center, pleading for at least one gun.

While the riflemen hung on by their toenails, one of the battalion's six 81mm mortars was assigned to Easy/5. But there was a major problem. The tube had to be turned to a new azimuth, and it was impossible for the gunners to dig the heavy baseplate into the solid, frozen earth. A mortar sergeant named Johnson planted his two-hundred-twenty-pound frame on the baseplate and ordered the crew to respond to Jim Friedl's directions.

Barney Baxter had been firing his gun nearly full tilt for over an hour, and it was getting to him. Shaking from a combination of fear, the freezing cold, and the cramping of his legs and body from crouching too long in one position, it was all he could do to keep from hiding under the gun. But the weapon was not troubled by the cold, as were many light air-cooled machine guns; all the heavies had antifreeze in their water jackets. Ammunition was no problem, though the carriers had to risk running into infiltrators on their many trips to the rear for replenishment. Remarkably, not one of the thirteen members of Baxter's section was hurt in the fierce grappling of two armies working at such cross purposes.

The crisis came quietly as Baxter was feeding in a new belt of ammunition. The belt feed lever came off in his hand. A little pin had been shaken loose, and the gun could fire only one round at a time. Baxter asked his assistant to rummage through the spare-parts kit to try to find a replacement, but the boy claimed there was none.

With his assistant manning the gun, and guarded by his carbine-toting squad leader, Barney Baxter moved to the parts kit to try to find a new pin by touch. There was a lull in the fighting, but there was no telling how long it might last, nor where the Chinese would strike next. Slowly, blindly, Baxter fingered each spare part, setting aside anything that might work. After an eternity of seconds, he found a smallish pin and thumbed it into place. The fit was loose, but the critical assembly seemed as if it would hold.

Within thirty seconds the nearest heavy machine gun quit firing, and the Chinese mounted another attack. By the barest of margins, Barney Baxter was able to sweep his gun across the entire line of the right platoon, which stood in the gravest danger of being overrun.

The right-platoon leader begged for illumination. With Sergeant Johnson firmly atop the 81's baseplate, Jim Friedl alternated heavy explosive for the left platoon with illumination for the right, allowing each to throw back successive assaults while Sam Jaskilka scraped up bits and parts of his company to push into the breach.

Stray tracer rounds or a shard from an 81mm shell ignited a farmhouse about two hundred yards up the draw at about 2330, ending the need for illumination on the Easy/5 front. The rebuilt line plugged away with increasing success at the oncoming Chinese.

The turning point came too late for one brave Marine. A Chinese infiltrator shot at Sergeant Johnson as he stood in the momentary flash caused as a round left the tube he was steadying. The big noncom was thrown onto his back, the shock of a bullet through the groin killing him within minutes.

To the rear, Lieutenant Colonel Hal Roise ordered his clerks, cooks, and specialists to form a defensive line around the command tents in order to withstand an assault by numerous infiltrators which, fortunately, never materialized.

On the front, Sam Jaskilka committed his reserve platoon to the aid of Ray Jorz's embattled 1st Platoon.

Despite the very best efforts of both companies, the gap at the junction of Fox and Easy Companies remained filled with Chinese, though very few of them were able to buck the containment and move into the Marine rear. A fearsome toll was taken on back-up units, which foolishly re-formed time and again in the light cast by the burning farmhouse. A pattern soon developed: each time a group of Chinese formed by the burning farmhouse, Jim Friedl's by-then-two 81s fired several rounds to break it up, then machine-gun fire dogged the heels of the survivors until they left the light. This went on until nearly 0100, by which time the farmhouse had been reduced to embers and the Chinese had taken pretty much all the losses they could afford.

Partway up the slope of Hill 1403, on the battalion right, Private First Class Rick Seward and his buddies had had to sit idly by as the remainder of Easy/5 fought for its life. Because the right flank was dangling, Seward's squad leader had ordered his riflemen to hold their fire, lest they reveal the extremity of the line and show the Chinese a way around. The precaution was frustrating for the men involved, but it paid off handsomely when the fighting in the draw became too costly and a strong Chinese force ascended the hill directly in front of the flank squad's short line.

In a noteworthy exhibit of discipline, the forwardmost fire team, holed up in a creek bed forward of the main line, caught the approaching PLA infantrymen before they had an opportunity to deploy from marching order to a skirmish line. The attackers were routed in a brief fight, and the flank remained secure.

★

Once Sam Jaskilka was certain that the Chinese had shot their bolt, he turned his attention to the well-being of his troops. The rigors of the cold were of prime concern after care of the wounded and maintenance of weapons, so Jaskilka passed the word that the troops could be sent to warming tents in rotating fifteen-minute shifts. Men remaining on the line were permitted to put their feet and legs in sleeping bags if doing so did not interfere with their ability to fight.

Sporadic fire and desultory attacks continued through the night. Fearful that the company command post was under attack by infiltrators, 1st Lieutenant Ray Jorz sent a runner into the draw to see if help was needed. Impatient when the man did not return immediately, Jorz hoisted himself to his feet and slid-walked down the slope to see for himself. A mortar round, presumably Chinese, dropped in on his immediate left and dumped him on the slope with fragments embedded in his left side and chest. Jorz, whose command of Easy Company's 1st Platoon had begun after dark, was evacuated to the battalion aid station before dawn.

At 0600, first light on November 28, Easy/5's 1st and 3rd Platoons mounted an assault to retake the ground lost at its former juncture with Fox Company. The dispirited Chinese who had held the salient for nearly nine hours put up brief resistance, then broke for the safety of their own lines. Many were shot in the back.

Roise's battalion had sustained moderate casualties, and it had held. Not so the isolated Marine company on the right.

CHAPTER
10

Captain Leroy Cooke's How Company, 7th, was a tired bunch of Marines by sunset on November 27.

When Roise's battalion had set off down the road west of town that morning, How/7 had been sent to scale and hold Hill 1403, the commanding height overlooking the vital road junction. The job had been accomplished quickly, and without incident, but each squad had been sent back down the steep hill to retrieve field packs the men had grounded on the valley floor. Late in the day nearly everyone — except for the lucky members of a reserve platoon which was left at the base of the hill — had to descend to the valley floor yet again, this time to collect water, rations, and reserve ammunition. Thus, by day's end, most How/7 Marines had climbed Hill 1403 at least three times. And, between climbs, each man had had to contend with digging fighting holes in the unyielding frozen ground.

Other problems that would beset How/7 that night lay in its deployment. The company was in direct physical contact with no other Marine unit. Roise's battalion was well to the left, and the remainder of the 3rd Battalion, 7th, was a mile to the south, across the road. Since Captain Cooke's mission included a defense of the road junction, only two rifle platoons, plus supporting arms, were on the heights. Hill 1403 was a big piece of ground, and Cooke did not have sufficient troops on the summit to form an all-around defensive perimeter. He had to place his two rifle platoons in line facing north, and his supports just down the slope to the rear.

As the late afternoon winds kicked up the dusty snow and flung it into the faces of the struggling Marines, Captain Cooke ordered outposts to advance to positions in front of the lines. This precaution was in no way the result of a warning from higher authority, nor even the result of the heavy fighting the company had witnessed all around its position during the day. Outposts were simply standard. One platoon leader, showing more compassion than sense, allowed his platoon's outpost to light a warming fire once it had gotten into place.

How/7 was set by sundown. The rigors of the day notwithstanding, the troops went about their business with the assured competence of men who had been together, fighting, for months on end.

★

In the half hour before 2200, several monitoring posts within the communications network serving the 3rd Battalion, 7th, noted that the phone line to Cooke's command post was dead. However, 2nd Lieutenant George Caridakis, commander of the battalion 81mm mortar platoon, had his own wire loop through to How Company, as well as to the How Company reserve platoon at the base of the hill; he would relay messages while the battalion communicator, 1st Lieutenant Earnie Stone, ordered a troubleshooting team to follow the wire outward from the battalion message center. Stone assumed that there would be a break in the line, and the team was expecting to work a quick splice and return once it had confirmed that Captain Cooke was back in touch with Battalion.

The line was not merely severed. It had been butchered. In a totally inexplicable lapse of both etiquette and common sense, members of a 5th Regiment unit had cut five-foot sections out of the link to use as guy wires for their pup tents. Earnie Stone had to order a wire team out in a hurry to reestablish the link before any danger befell the isolated rifle company on Hill 1403. Meantime, the alternate line from the 81mm mortars was employed to complete a tenuous circuit involving a relay to Battalion from the mortar fire-direction center.

Captain Cooke checked in moments before 2200, informing Battalion that How Company had been subjected to light probes by small PLA patrols during the whole of the preceding thirty minutes.

No sooner said than the Chinese mounted a massed assault against the two-platoon line atop the hill.

★

The Chinese struck the rightmost element of the right platoon. At least half the men were caught in their sleeping bags, as was a 60mm mortar crew. It was common practice for the troops to remove their footgear for airing whenever they settled into their bags, so the suddenness of the violent assault left many Marines in the open, shoeless. That resulted in devastating losses to instantaneous frostbite among that group of Marines.

While the right platoon leader sought to reestablish order in the midst of his breaking squads, the Chinese were held momentarily when Platoon Sergeant Walton Watson rallied the men nearest him and counterattacked the attackers, who were rifling abandoned field packs and ration cases. The effort nearly succeeded, but the stand fell apart when Sergeant Watson was shot to death.

In the moment or two purchased by Watson's death, Sergeant Kenneth Hoffie, a machine-gun squad leader, pulled a wounded gunner from behind his light machine gun and sprayed the dark forms along the former front. Though grievously wounded in both legs by a bursting hand grenade, Hoffie refused to relinquish the machine gun until members of his squad pulled him bodily down the slope to an aid station.

Despite the best efforts of individuals, the right platoon broke for the protection of the left platoon's position. One 60mm mortar tube was abandoned, as were a number of dead and injured Marines.

As the left platoon braced to take the brunt of the assault, a lone Chinese burpgunner infiltrated to the Marine rear and squeezed off telling bursts as he scrabbled from position to position to avoid detection. Second Lieutenant James Mitchell was running uphill from the company CP to help restore order when he was forced to dive for cover by a nearly fatal burst from the burpgun. Mitchell changed direction instantly, and took on the burpgunner, a Chinese captain, who was killed in the confrontation.

As soon as the extent of the attack on Captain Cooke's position could be determined, he was on the phone to the 81mm mortars, asking 2nd Lieutenant George Caridakis to fire into a small draw where the company 60mm mortars had been dispersed in the first Chinese assault. Because his wire had been looped through the How Company positions, Caridakis was able to receive directions from his own forward observer on the left and the How Company 60mm mortar officer on the right of the company line. Preregistered 81mm and 4.2-inch interdiction fires were placed on key approaches to the How Company position.

Leroy Cooke personally organized the men around him and stepped off to reclaim the better positions lost to the first onslaught. Cooke, a Baltimore Reservist, had been in command of How/7 for only two weeks. He had not quite gotten the hang of commanding a company, and had been overheard wondering aloud if he was ever going to get into the groove.

Leroy Cooke led to the lost crest of Hill 1403 the men who heard him thunder, "Let's go!" There, within a step or two of retaking the lost ground, Cooke was thrown from his feet. A bullet through the liver killed him in agonizing minutes. Command of How/7 was assumed temporarily by 2nd Lieutenent James Mitchell, who worked to consolidate the embattled perimeter below the crestline even as Captain Cooke's stiffening corpse was placed beside those of the men he had sought to retrieve.

Word of Cooke's death and How/7's state was passed down the hill by casualties and men who had broken and run.

Visibly shaken, the battalion commander, Lieutenant Colonel Bill Harris, offered command of How Company to 1st Lieutenant Howard Harris, who had returned to the battalion only that night after a two-week absence at the Division Hospital in Hamhung due to illness.

Howie Harris looked quite haggard despite his two weeks in the rear. Having signed on for the new war as the battalion adjutant, he had briefly commanded How Company during the Sudong fighting in early November, then had been incapacitated by a severe case of sinusitus. Technically, Harris had not been released to rejoin the battalion, but the ennui of the sterile hospital routine had driven the former enlisted Marine to sheer distraction, and he had left of his own accord.

Lieutenant Harris was the logical choice for commanding How/7 on Hill 1403. Though he had never seen the hill in daylight, he knew all of the officers and most of the men, and that counted for a great deal if he was to reassemble the unit to hold its position. He grabbed his helmet, begged a radio and radio operator, and set off on foot to cover the three miles to the base of Hill 1403.

It took Howie Harris the best part of an hour to negotiate three miles of darkened, unfamiliar ground. When he arrived at the base of the hill he quickly found the uncommitted How/7 reserve platoon. Though worn by the long, brisk hike, Harris immediately started up the steep, treacherous slope, pulling his radio operator and less than forty fresh Marines in his wake.

The embattled portion of How/7 was in deep, deep trouble. Most of the officers had been hit, some badly, and the men were fighting from isolated pockets mixed in with pockets of Chinese.

Howie Harris arrived at the main How/7 position well after midnight with about thirty-five men. But they were pretty exhausted people, having scrambled up the unlighted, frosty slope in −25-degree winds. The most popular addition was the radio, which had fresh batteries and good range.

After seeing to the redistribution of his limited manpower along a reasonable line, Harris contacted 2nd Lieutenant George Caridakis, who directed sundry 105mm howitzers, 4.2-inch heavy mortars, and his own 81mm mortars upon the slopes farthest from where Harris thought a pocket of Marines might still be holding out.

The infusion of additional troops and the imposition of order must have been felt by the attackers, for they withdrew briefly to take stock. In that time, while still rearranging his troops, Howie Harris looked down at Yudam-ni from his commanding position and was shocked to see an almost 360-degree circle of incoming and outgoing tracer. It was Harris's first inkling that How Company's fight was part of a much larger battle for survival.

★

Earlier, the battalion's supporting section of 75mm recoilless antitank rifles, bolstered by a section of water-cooled heavy machine guns, had set up beside the How/7 reserve platoon, erecting a row of pup tents on a flat by the roadway.

Following the first strong attacks on Hill 1403, George Caridakis's 81mm gunners were shaking down and stripping an Oriental man they had found loose in their lines when Lieutenant Colonel Bob Taplett, commander of the adjacent 3rd Battalion, 5th, arrived to identify the prisoner as his Korean interpreter. As Caridakis was releasing the interpreter to Taplett, a knot of Chinese appeared on the road between the mortars and the roadblock, but they were stopped by machine-gun fire. Taplett suggested that the mortars, antitank guns, and machine guns be moved to the safety of his battalion's lines. Caridakis, however, had just finished registering his mortars and supporting artillery, and he did not want to move to new positions from which he could not immediately fire in support of How Company.

Later, however, when Howie Harris drew off the supporting How/ 7 rifle platoon, the antitank section leader, Sergeant William Vick, pulled the remnants of his 75mm crews and machine gunners back to a better position by a stream bed. The pup tents the troops had earlier erected were left in place, quite frankly forgotten.

A full company of Chinese glanced off the edge of the fight atop Hill 1403 and streamed down the slope in the direction of the pup tents. Sergeant Vick was ready for them, ordering all guns to train on the approaching mass of infantry, but holding his men in check as the Chinese moved with great stealth upon the former campsite.

The attackers rushed forward on command, screaming to awaken and confuse reposing Marines, thrusting bayonets into what they thought would be bodies in the empty sleeping bags. Lost to confusion, the Chinese were mown down in windrows by the patient Marines under Sergeant Vick and those supporting the 81mm mortars. The machine guns and recoilless rifles took a horrendous toll as panicked PLA infantrymen collided with one another in final acts of total fear.

Vick's gunners killed at least one hundred Chinese with the opening salvos, but scores more were moving down the slope, and most of them turned to face the unsupported weapons crews, though they were supposed to be making for the soft rear echelon encampments throughout the northern end of the valley.

Vick held for moments, then minutes, dropping about fifty additional Chinese and keeping the rest from their duties. But the pressure became too great, and he had to abandon the ambush. Coolly, exhibiting the finest discipline imaginable, these Marines backpedaled across the stream bed, leapfrogging the precious guns in the direction of the bivouac of the 3rd Battalion, 5th Marines. They arrived safely with all their weapons intact, a remarkable feat.

Even more remarkable was the fact that the Chinese did not directly threaten or molest the vitally needed 81mm mortars nearby.

★

While the roadblock was being hit, the Chinese came back against How Company, beginning with the usual shower of concussion grenades. Howie Harris bellowed orders and encouragement.

The Chinese were all over the dwindling perimeter, too close and too intermingled to be dealt with in any way but hand-to-hand. The attackers, however, were more intent upon breaking through How/7 than in destroying it, and surprised Marines emerged from losing scuffles as their adversaries scrambled over the crest and descended toward the valley below.

Lieutenant Harris realized that it was the perfect moment to sweep the open areas with mortars and artillery. He yelled into the radio mike, only to find that his direct link with Item Battery, 11th, was down. He switched to his landline to the battalion 81mm fire-direction center and blurted a string of commands. George Caridakis, working through a patched link to the 3rd Battalion, 11th, (which relayed directives to the 1st Battalion, 11th) was able to direct many howitzers to "search and traverse in reverse," an odd-sounding order that spoke volumes about the critical situation on Hill 1403. A perfect salvo hit the Chinese assembly area on the forward brow of the huge hill, scattering screaming men in all directions.

The attacks against How/7 continued through the dark hours. At one time or another, George Caridakis probably called fires for every 105mm and 155mm battery in the valley of Yudam-ni. Though he maintained contact with the How/7 mortar officer, 2nd Lieutenant Bull Friesen, by way of a direct wire link, Caridakis permanently lost direct contact with Howie Harris sometime between 0300 and 0400. Memorable was Friesen's exclamation that the supporting rounds "must have eyes on them," they were hitting with such accuracy. After a time, however, Friesen told Caridakis that he and the other men holding the isolated east side of the hill would follow the wire to safety as soon as they could make a break.

After losing direct contact with the 81mm fire-direction center, Lieutenant Harris regained contact with Battalion. The battalion commander took the call.

★

Lieutenant Colonel William Harris had been commander of the 3rd Battalion, 7th, only since November 11, 1950. Perhaps unfairly, he had not yet received the full cooperation, respect, and trust of his subordinates.

The unit had been a two-company peacetime organization designated the 3rd Battalion, 6th Marines, when the Korean War broke out. As a major component of the skeletonized 2nd Marine Division, the unit had a complement of officers and men that can safely be described as the finest available — professional Marines who had been training together for over two years. Caught in the midst of a Mediterranean cruise, they had been shipped through the Suez

Canal to Japan, where a third rifle company and other reinforcing elements — about five hundred men — had been added to the rolls. The 3rd Battalion, 7th, had been committed to war along the Inchon-Seoul Highway, and it had proven itself the equal of the finest fighting formations anywhere in Korea. Unfortunately, as things turned out, they had been commanded by a major who was subject to relief when an influx of more-senior officers reached Korea after 1st Marine Division landed at Wonsan.

Ordinarily, though the loss of a respected, successful commander is always a sad event for all concerned, the assumption of command by Lieutenant Colonel William Harris should have been smooth. And it appeared it would be — until news of Leroy Cooke's death and Howie Harris's call reached the blackout tents in a small copse in the shadow of Southwest Ridge.

Bill Harris was a "service brat," a young man who had grown up in the Marine Corps. In fact, his father, Field Harris, was at that moment a major general whose 1st Marine Aircraft Wing was supporting 1st Marine Division in Korea.

Two years after being commissioned a Marine second lieutenant, Bill Harris had been trapped in the Philippines at the outbreak of the Pacific War. Following months of service on Corregidor under the threat and reality of Japanese bombings and shellings, he had fought valiantly for a night and a morning in command of a rifle platoon, then had been taken prisoner.

In a unique show of defiance, Harris and another young Marine officer had taken to the water that first night in captivity, and they had spent several months walking and swimming southward, hoping to reach Australia. It was an act of incredible bravery and initiative. In the end, though his partner did reach safety, young Harris was recaptured. He spent the balance of the Pacific War behind Japanese wire, where he saw thousands of his fellow captives die of a hundred illnesses and anguish resulting from the uncaring attitude of their Asian captors. Thus, Bill Harris's one prior experience in war had been almost bereft of the emotional satisfaction of the victor, the feeling that had shaped so many of his contemporaries in the Regular Marine Corps. More importantly, Harris lacked the solid combat command experience and style with which the Pacific War had imbued most of his contemporaries.

Whatever his background or personal traits — for such matters are usually worked out or worked through in the close atmosphere of a battalion command group in combat — Harris was seen by his subordinates as being a bit overbearing, too quick to make decisions on the basis of his schooling and without recourse to *their* hard, recent combat experience in the new war.

★

Upon hearing of Leroy Cooke's death from How/7 stragglers, Bill Harris had lost much of the ebullient good spirits he had maintained since joining the battalion. Several of the men who were with him saw immediately that something had gone out of the handsome, boyish-looking thirty-two-year-old battalion commander.

Now, as he spoke with Howard Harris in short, choppy sentences, the battalion commander was greatly distracted by a hubbub of activity in and around his own tent; the majority of the battalion headquarters people, officers and clerks, were moving to man positions along a hastily drawn firing line. The PLA infantry who had forced Sergeant Vick from his blocking position were mounting a drive upon the copse sheltering the battalion command center. Bullets were already thunking into the tent poles above the heads of the men who had to remain inside to run the show.

The troubled conversation between the Harrises was nearing an impasse; though the Chinese in the vicinity of the battalion command post moved off without mounting the feared attack, it was at that point that Bill Harris peremptorily ordered How Company to abandon the heights.

Howie Harris was under something of a cloud. Several of his colleagues in the battalion felt, fairly or not, that he had forfeited a key hill unnecessarily during his debut as a company commander at Sudong. That might or might not have entered into his strong rebuttal that he could hold Hill 1403 if given a chance. He asked Lieutenant Colonel Harris to give How Company more time and any assistance that could be spared. But the battalion commander stuck by his order; How Company was to withdraw from Hill 1403.

That was about 0400, November 28.

★

Howie Harris ordered a fighting withdrawal, leapfrogging fire teams while the wounded assisted one another down the frosty slope. It was hard, dangerous work, for the path was strewn with human and natural obstacles. In the confusion, Lieutenant Harris lost his radio operator, who wandered off and suffered grievous harm from the cold.

George Caridakis's fire-direction center continued to support How Company, often blindly, for what remained of the dark hours. At one point, the battalion mortar officer, speaking by phone with Captain Bill Earney, the battalion operations officer, asked for a time check. Earney replied that it was coming up 0600. Surprised, Caridakis asked when it was going to be getting light, and Earney directed him to look up into the hills to the east, where the sky was already changing colors.

Caridakis was almost afraid of what he would witness in the sunlight. It had been a long, hard night. Nearly two hundred Chinese dead were counted around the spot where Sergeant Vick's ambush had been sprung, which was a positive beginning. And a group of How Company stragglers was found holed up in a draw on the eastern face of the hill by a mortar-platoon wire team following its wire up the hill; the wiremen helped carry the dead and wounded to the road. Nearer the road north of the 81mm positions was evidence of Chinese casualties — blood, uniforms, equipment — but no bodies.

The bulk of How/7, able-bodied and injured, came in behind Roise's embattled 2nd Battalion, 5th, at about 1100 hours. Others, mainly individuals, were picked up by rescuers sent out by Battalion.

While tracing a phone wire to George/7, 1st Lieutenant Earnie Stone ran into a How/7 platoon leader who had been wounded in the ear and was in shock from the cold. Stone helped the man into his jeep and drove him to a field designated as the regimental aid station. The communicator was appalled to see that hundreds of injured Marines were being cared for in the open, without even tarps to keep the elements at bay.

Private First Class James Hester and Navy Corpsman Joseph Pancamo, manning the battalion's closed "cracker-box" ambulance, had been on their third run of the night (they had spent the entire day evacuating George/7's wounded from Southwest Ridge) when they were stopped at a Marine roadblock and warned that the area ahead was infested with PLA infantry. After a moment's hesitation, Hester, a shy, retiring mountain boy, blurted out, "There's still some wounded up there." He jerked the ambulance into gear and roared off. The bullet-riddled vehicle was found later at the base of the hill, but neither Hester nor Pancamo was ever seen again, dead or alive.

★

The loss of Hill 1403 was the 3rd Battalion, 7th's first real defeat in Korea.

Elsewhere around Yudam-ni, other Marine companies and battalions were under intense, critical pressure.

CHAPTER
11

The more Lieutenant Colonel Bob Taplett considered the position of his 3rd Battalion, 5th Marines, the less he liked it. He had experienced an unshakable sense of unease through the entire afternoon and early evening of November 27, from the moment he had first seen the ground his superiors referred to as an "assembly area" for his battalion.

Taplett had spent the whole of the previous five months staying alive, keeping his battalion viable. Possibly the most cerebral of the rifle-battalion commanders, the tall, dark-visaged Taplett had had his senses honed to an unimaginable precision, and those senses fairly clanged with alarm.

The ground wasn't right. There were three broad avenues into the battalion area, and there was no sign that anyone was guarding them. Taplett had been told by Regiment that a company of the 7th Marines was on Hill 1384, the dominant height to the northeast, but nothing could be seen of the company from the valley floor.

As the wan winter sun gave up its meager, heatless light, Bob Taplett asked his executive officer how he felt. Major John Canney, a former dive-bomber pilot who had been staying alive in Korea for as long as the battalion commander, shrugged: "I feel the same way you do, Tap." The battalion operations officer agreed, so the three officers set out up a deep draw in the direction of Hill 1384, toward the battalion weapons company's bivouac. The closer they got to Hill 1384, the less the three men were able to convince themselves that the height was occupied. Another call to Regiment produced a response that had by then become monotonous: "They're up there. Quit worrying."

Taplett asked to speak to the regimental commander, Ray Murray: "Ray, I got a real uneasy feeling that we're sitting out here all by ourselves in this so-called assembly area." But Murray had The Word from the staff of the 7th, and he could only offer more assurances.

It was about dark. The worried battalion officers, too good at what they did to overlook gut reactions, decided to act on their own. Taplett mouthed a few terse orders, and a platoon of Item Company was turned out of its warm down bags and sent scampering up the ridgeline to man an outpost line overlooking the draw. Another group was sent to man a block on the road running north through the bivouac.

The fact of the matter was that, but for these two groups, Taplett's battalion was completely vulnerable to attack. The troops were at twenty-five-percent alert, but their deployment was casual, based upon the overly positive situation report issued by the 7th Marines that afternoon.

Lacking hard data, and expecting to be committed to the attack down the road west of town in the morning, Taplett was loath to tire his troops unnecessarily by sending them off over rough terrain in the night. He was loath to do it, but he was no fool, and he decided on a middle-of-the-road approach.

Meantime, Weapons Company, which continued to occupy the deep draw leading to Hill 1384, reported strange noises from beyond its outpost line. There was nothing firm, but the troops were tense.

Bob Taplett ordered the battalion to fifty-percent alert and began pushing additional small units toward the heights.

★

How/5, the westernmost of Taplett's companies, was buttoned up tight. Most of the men were huddled in warming tents behind a thin shield of pickets. One of the platoon leaders commented that the tents had been subjected to some pretty rough handling on the road; there were numerous holes in the roof of his. No sooner said than the man recanted, for new holes appeared as he and fellow officers stared in amazement.

As urgent calls flooded the battalion switchboard, How Company manned a defensive line along a stream at the boundary of the battalion sector. While many How/5 troops chipped away at the solid, frozen earth, others tossed hand grenades onto the frozen surface of the stream to break a channel which would hopefully impede possible attackers.

At no point thus far had the 3rd Battalion, 5th, been directly challenged. There was evidence of fighting in the distance, but no word had come from any embattled unit, nor from Regiment. Lieutenant Colonel Taplett's sense of unease had long since passed into a state of full alarm. And well it should have, for Roise's battalion was thoroughly embroiled in combat, and the first shattering attack against How/7 had been beaten back at heavy cost.

Captain Hal Williamson, How/5's commander, was warming up in his tent with the company exec and first sergeant when he was called to the sector held by his 3rd Platoon. Knots of men could be discerned on the far side of the creek. Cautious, Williamson ordered machine gunners to train on the shadows and prepare to fire on command. While holding his trumps for as long as possible, Williamson gauged his chances, blurted a request for 81mm illumination, and nodded an order to his gunners the instant the first mortar round *thungged* from its tube. Groups of PLA infantrymen were caught motionless in the stark light.

The gunners opened fire, dropping Chinese soldiers in heaps on the bank of the creek. As the first illumination round faded, Hal Williamson directed one machine gun to fire into a pair of thatch huts, setting them ablaze. More Chinese were gunned down in the flickering light.

As the firing reached its peak Captain Williamson called Battalion in order to share the good news. Bob Taplett, who had just heard about the fight on nearby Hill 1403, warned Williamson to expect stragglers from How/7.

The warning unnerved the How/5 commander. With visions of hurt Marines falling before his guns, Williamson ordered a cease-fire. It was like flicking a switch. The entire line fell silent.

The first small groups and individuals from Hill 1403 began slipping across the stream. The wounded, often shoeless, Marines, were sent to the battalion sick bay while the able-bodied were ushered to the company warming tents to thaw out.

It was 0115. How/5's fight had ended, but the rest of the 3rd Battalion, 5th, was approaching its gravest crisis.

★

One of Bob Taplett's biggest headaches that migraine night was operating in an information blackout. He was getting no word from the 5th Regiment CP, which was getting no word from the 7th Marines, which could not properly assess the deteriorating situation. He was getting nothing from How/7, though his communicators were trying to get a line up the rear slope of Hill 1403. Stragglers tended to be on the hysterical side, so their stories had to be largely discounted. And there was little that Taplett could actually see or hear for himself.

Even as How Company was reveling in what its commander referred to on the communications net as a "turkey shoot," Taplett was moving vigorously to reorient his battalion from its original casual deployment to a tight defensive circle. He soon found that there was too much ground for a continuous line deployment to cover, so he contented himself with sending platoons and detachments out into the total darkness to cover what he hoped were key points on the unfamiliar hilly ground.

Item Company was broken up to outpost several commanding knobs and routes leading to the center of the battalion sector. How Company had its hands full by the boundary stream. George Company was deployed on How/5's left, facing southwest. A section of South Korean National Police, known as Wharangs, was sent to man a spur directly overlooking the command compound, which was located beside a walled Korean house set back against one of the sheer spurs leading up to Hill 1384. The battalion was vulnerable from every quarter, but the battalion commander had neither the troops to cover all the ground, nor sufficient knowledge of the terrain to be certain that he was covering even the most critical areas.

At 0115, just as How/5 was greeting the first How/7 stragglers, a small group of Chinese approached a Weapons Company outpost several hundred yards up the draw to the northeast of the battalion CP. The Marines killed at least one of the intruders and sent the others scrambling for safety.

At almost the same instant, the Wharangs and an Item Company outpost reported taking small-arms fire on the heights overlooking the command compound.

Taplett's battalion was being probed.

★

A telephone wire was run all the way up Hill 1403 to How/7 in the midst of the probes, and a hurried conversation brought Taplett confirmation that heavy PLA concentrations were moving around the How/7 position by the right flank. The Chinese, it appeared, were intent upon seizing the road junction behind How/7 and the 2nd Battalion, 5th. Taplett's battalion held that junction, so it was inevitable that the probes would broaden into a full-scale clash.

Within minutes of fathoming the enemy's intentions, Taplett received news from Item/5 that "many, many troops" were moving on its sector from the northwest, from Hill 1403. The Item Company outpost which made the sighting pulled back, and the Chinese were fired on. Recoiling, the probers moved to find a way around the strongpoint.

The next attack hit Item Company's 2nd Platoon, which had been sent to guard the ridgeline earlier in the evening. The platoon leader was tucked down in his sleeping bag, shoeless, unaware that trouble was close at hand. He had been awake all day and well into the night, and it was simply his turn to get some needed rest. When he spotted a small cluster of dark forms approaching from the northeast, he assumed that they were members of his own platoon. He quickly realized his error, leaped from his sleeping bag, leveled his carbine, and squeezed the trigger. The weapon was frozen, useless, so the lieutenant, in his stocking feet, raced to a machine-gun position to the rear. Surprised themselves by the encounter, the infiltrators sought cover behind a clump of trees.

There were several moments of silence, then two sharp whistle blasts. Two companies of PLA infantry charged, screaming, from both sides of the spur, bypassing the forwardmost Marine squad, making for the rear. The Chinese pushed aside all opposition and delivered a headlong assault upon the Wharangs, a tough, dedicated lot which had taken its lumps alongside Taplett's Marines since the summer fighting around Pusan.

The fight was by then taking place directly over the heads of the battalion command group. In fact, one Item Company Marine was thrown over the side of the spur and landed behind the operations tent. He was immediately interrogated by anxious staffers, who could hear much but see nothing.

Meantime, the Wharangs held the Chinese in check for anxious moments. Basing their defense around a light machine gun, the South Koreans clung desperately to their ground. Four of their gunners were shot in quick succession, and the remainder of the section was dispersed or dragged off. They bought only a few moments, but their sacrifice gave the battalion staff and headquarters troops a bare margin for survival.

★

In the hour between the arrival of the first How/7 stragglers and the collapse of the Wharangs at 0215, Bob Taplett had been carrying on increasingly heated exchanges with Regiment. Initially he had the opportunity to vent his spleen upon the operations staff. In time, however, he could reach only the regimental commander, Lieutenant Colonel Ray Murray.

One of the Marine Corps' most talented battalion commanders, Taplett might have been the least patient man in his position. It was evident that Regiment did not know what was going on, but Taplett felt he had the right to some answers, and, though he took all possible care in deploying his battalion, he continued to hold Regiment accountable for news.

Taplett had no idea that Regiment itself was under siege. Ray

Murray had no time to explain that he was personally in grave danger. While Taplett was trying to dope out the situation in his own sector, Murray had been run out of his command tent by heavy fire, presumably enemy, but possibly friendly. During the whole of his exchanges with the irate Taplett, the regimental commander was prone behind an earthen dike bordering a field north of the town. He had a single wireman as his staff, and a single telephone as his only weapon. Murray's command group had been dispersed under heavy fire, and the regimental commander had no way to assess or control the fighting by his battalions.

The 3rd Battalion, 5th, had been isolated and was on its own.

★

Tucked into the lee of the northern spur leading to Hill 1384, Taplett's command post was not particularly vulnerable to attack. But the peculiar circumstances of the night's unfolding confusion made it impossible for the battalion commander to seal the area. Having discovered the extremities of the rifle companies, the Chinese sought paths of least resistance, and found them. It is doubtful that they were intent upon attacking the battalion command compound *per se*. Their goal was clearly the road junction beyond. While the Marine rifle companies battened down for a watchful night, the battalion CP bore the brunt of the Chinese effort in that sector.

Minutes after Taplett had committed the last of his headquarters and weapons troops to a defensive line on the slope and at the foot of the northern spur, Chinese careered down from the heights. They hit right at the juncture of the weapons and headquarters positions, jarring the barely settled Marines from the line, opening a wide gap just to the north of the CP. Intent upon finding the road junction, the Chinese turned southward and headed straight for the command compound.

While the attackers fought through the darkened Marine lines, marauders on the heights dropped clusters of concussion grenades into the command compound. A key hit took out the message-center switchboard, which was tucked into a natural alcove, protected only by a single thickness of canvas tarpaulin. All of the battalion's wire communications were out.

As headquarters and weapons people fought to close the gap and subdue infiltrators, Bob Taplett clung grimly to his operations tent, trying to bring order from chaos. The battalion exec, Major John Canney, made frequent stops at the operations tent with updates on the situation. Major Bull Durham, the battalion operations officer, held a cocked .45-caliber automatic pistol in one hand and a phone in the other, and Taplett's personal radioman was kneeling beside the door, carbine at the ready.

Confusion was complete.

★

Taplett's ace in the hole was George Company. Across the road to the rear, George/5 was unmolested, a battle-hardened reserve that could be committed as soon as the battalion commander could sort things out sufficiently to give adequate directions. To ensure that the counterattack would be mounted properly, Taplett turned to 1st Lieutenant Charlie Mize, assistant operations officer, the man who had commanded George/5 all the way from Pusan until replaced by a more senior new arrival a few weeks earlier. Taplett and Mize had complete rapport, and only a few words were exchanged. Mize, a tough bantam cock of a combat Marine, gripped his carbine and took off across the dark, open ground, heading for George Company and the battalion's salvation.

In the meantime Major John Canney strained to rebuild the broken line of headquarters and weapons troops. Rushing from one side of the broken perimeter to the other under intense fire, the former pilot was felled behind the operations tent with a bullet through the eye, killed instantly.

First Lieutenant Hercules Kelly, the communications platoon leader, was tracing a line on his hands and knees, staring intently at the wire in search of a break, when he crawled through the darkened entryway of the besieged operations tent. There was a click and a dull metallic sheen just overhead, and Kelly found himself peering down the muzzle of a .45 held by Bull Durham. The two officers recoiled in horror, neither aware until after dawn that the pistol had fallen casualty to the cold and could not be fired.

As Herc Kelly strung his wire, enlisted communicators rewired the switchboard and patched lines through to Bob Taplett from Regiment and the rifle companies. It was uncomfortable, dangerous work. One wireman was shot through the head while running a line across exposed ground.

In the midst of the furious fight, the battalion sick bay, one of the most vulnerable installations in the area, continued to function as wounded from the battalion and nearby units were dragged in out of the cold. When the Coleman lanterns providing meager light were shot or blown out, the battalion's two Navy surgeons carried out critical, life-prolonging operations in the weak aura of hand-held flashlights while an industrious Marine stripped some communications wire and jury-rigged adequate illumination from a pair of head lamps and a battery commandeered from a parked truck.

Bob Taplett took a call from the regimental staff, which had just reconvened in its operations tent, and was ordered to mount an immediate counterattack in support of the embattled units to the right. He blew his stack, firing several tart verbal darts before clearing the line.

★

First Lieutenant Charlie Mize succeeded in getting across the beaten ground to the George Company command post, where he ordered the company commander to prepare to mount a counterattack directly across the battalion command compound and right on up the spur behind.

The Chinese had by then become a disorganized rabble. Denied access to their best objective, the road junction, the victorious PLA infantry milled about in apathy and confusion, allowing themselves to be contained and killed.

George Company's opening thrust was assured success.

As the headquarters and weapons people continued to clear the opposition in and about the command compound, George/5 stepped off smartly just after 0400, two platoons abreast. The sweep across the beaten zone was swift and effective. Second Lieutenant Blackie Cahill, recently returned from the hospital after recuperating from wounds suffered at Pusan in August, grinned from around a wad of chewing tobacco as he passed Herc Kelly, who emerged from the message-center tent to watch the show. A haggard, weary Bob Taplett quit the operations tent in time to cheer the attackers on, amazed and gratified by the alacrity of the young George Company officers and their spirited troops. The right platoon leader, 2nd Lieutenant Dana Cashion, was wounded in the foot by a concussion grenade, but he hop-hobbled after his Marines as they swept aside all contenders and mounted the steep slope behind the command post.

The Chinese were shattered, easy pickings for the reorganized Headquarters and Weapons Companies, which rooted them out and secured the CP in the wake of George Company's sweep.

The advancing George/5 platoons secured the site of the Wharang section's last stand and paused to wait for the sun. Then, resuming the attack under supporting fires from Blackie Cahill's platoon,

Cashion's recovered seven bypassed Item Company Marines, incorporated them into his platoon, and continued his rapid drive upon the topographical crest of Hill 1384.

On learning of Cashion's long advance, the battalion commander, proud though he was of the young platoon leader's élan, ordered Cashion and Cahill to consolidate on the spur, hundreds of yards to their rear, lest they be cut off beyond supporting range. It was as positive a note as could have been imagined for ending such a crummy night.

Action on Taplett's right front was going less well for a pair of isolated Marine companies.

CHAPTER
12

Nowhere did the element of luck come into greater play at Yudam-ni that night than in the case of the two orphan companies of the 2nd Battalion, 7th Marines.

Yudam-ni was seen by all higher headquarters as a temporary staging area. No strong hostile action was anticipated, and there was no strong central authority determining where this battalion or that company was to be placed. Too large to be defended by a continuous line, the valley of Yudam-ni was merely screened by fairly isolated pockets of Marines: How/7 to the northwest, Charlie/7 to the southeast, Dog/7 and Easy/7 to the east. Units of the 5th Marines caught on the "perimeter" just happened to be there when the fighting started. There was nothing wrong with the deployment; indeed, it was an adequate response of the solid combat experience of the planners to the latest intelligence data from higher headquarters.

The "orphan" companies of the 2nd Battalion, 7th, were orphans because of the way Marine divisions of the era were *not* built. They were not built for moving and victualing themselves over very long lines of supply. There was not sufficient motor transport in 1st Marine Division for moving so many men so quickly over so many road miles to a place like Yudam-ni. Owing to movement schedules worked out by harried motor-transport officers juggling conflicting priorities, it just happened that the 2nd Battalion, 7th, was split up for the longest period of time. On November 26, there were sufficient trucks to get two companies from Hagaru-ri to Yudam-ni. The remainder of the battalion had to await the vehicles that were bringing its relief up from the south on November 28. Thus, the two companies, about four hundred men, moved early and were attached administratively to Ray Davis's 1st Battalion, 7th, which placed them out of the way in the hills east of the long central valley of Yudam-ni.

★

Though composed largely of Reservists, Dog and Easy Companies, 7th, were considered first-rate combat units. They had been baptized on the Inchon-Seoul Highway in September, and they had been in steady action all the way up from Wonsan.

After arriving at Yudam-ni on November 26, the companies had been sent to outpost Hills 1240 and 1282, east of town, the former about one thousand yards east by south of the latter. The relative isolation of their positions was not lost upon the company commanders. Patrols were sent out to examine and cover the intervening ground through the first day and night. As with the other 7th Regiment units guarding heights on the periphery of the valley, the two companies of the 2nd Battalion, 7th, were to be aided in covering their ground by the guns of the 3rd Battalion, 11th, the regimental 4.2-inch mortars, and such other mortars and heavy armaments as could be brought to bear in an emergency. It was a standard solution to a standard problem.

During the night of November 26, an Easy/7 light machine gunner at the left extremity of the company line on Hill 1282 detected movement on the front. He tossed a grenade and bagged a Chinese infantry officer who had been busily plotting the company position when he met his end; strewn about the corpse was a plotting board, tape measure, and alidade. Papers on the dead man identified him as a member of the 79th PLA Division.

★

The bulk of Captain Milt Hull's Dog/7 stepped off late in the morning of November 27 to patrol the ground north of Hill 1240. After three hours on the go the point platoon ran into a dozen Chinese and dispersed them. The middle platoon then passed through the point and swung eastward toward the village of Kyo-dong-ni, on the shore of the frozen Reservoir.

The village had previously been burned out by marauding Marine fighter-bombers and was said to have been abandoned. The lead platoon, however, was hit by heavy fire as it crossed some low ground preparatory to entering the ruins. A strong Chinese force was entrenched on high ground north and west of the hamlet.

Four Marine Corsairs made runs on the village as the two lead Dog Company platoons deployed to deliver an attack. One platoon leader was seriously wounded at the outset, but the other pressed on as a second air strike swept in. The Chinese had the terrain advantage and superior firepower, and the Marines were pressed back. The point platoon leader was killed while attempting to make a stand.

Captain Hull informed his nominal superior, Lieutenant Colonel Ray Davis, that Dog/7 was under heavy pressure. Unable to do anything more constructive, Davis ordered Hull to return to Hill 1240 under friendly air and mortar cover. The Chinese chased Dog Company as far as they dared, then drifted back toward Kyodong-ni. In all, sixteen Marines were killed or injured.

★

Easy/7 had nowhere near as dramatic a day as its sister unit, but the troops were kept alert by almost constant sightings of white-clad Chinese all over distant ridges.

Initially, Captain Walt Phillips had only two platoons with which to defend Hill 1282. These were placed in crescent-shaped arcs at the summit, one facing northeast, the other northwest. The detached platoon, which had spent the day guarding the regimental command post, was returned in the early evening of November 27. This unit was placed in line on a low spur just to the south of the summit of Hill 1282, several dozen yards behind the lines of its sister platoons, almost like a tail protruding from the main body of the company. The company's three 60mm mortars were emplaced below the summit, between the two forward rifle platoons and the company CP. All light and heavy machine guns were deployed with the forward rifle platoons.

Though the troops received no official warning of an impending attack, they routinely set out trip flares along the entire front, and all weapons were registered upon every reachable approach to the company lines.

Milt Hull's Dog Company, on Hill 1240, was similarly vigilant, though its position was somewhat below the actual summit of the hill, possibly hidden from Chinese observers manning posts on the rim of hills to the east.

★

The 79th PLA Division was deployed to seize three of the four hills guarding the western side of the Yudam-ni base. It is evident, though not certain, that each of the division's three regiments was assigned an objective that did not appear to Chinese observers to have been occupied by American Marines: the rightmost Chinese regiment was to seize Hill 1384, *behind* which Taplett's battalion had come to rest in the late afternoon of November 27. The center Chinese regiment was to take Hill 1240, *behind* whose summit Milt Hull's Dog/7 had been camped since November 26. The leftmost Chinese regiment was to take Hill 1167, which was not occupied at all by Marines. Only Hill 1282, between Hills 1384 and 1240, was to be spared. The Chinese had had Walt Phillips's Easy/7 under direct observation since November 26; indeed, they had lost a mapping officer to Phillips's vigilant sentries that very night. It seems that the commander of the 79th PLA Division had decided to move into the valley of Yudam-ni against the least possible opposition, by way of the "undefended" heights.

The forbidding terrain knocked the Chinese plan askew. The regiment bound for Hill 1384 found its way, but the two southern regiments, attacking in columns of battalions deployed in columns of companies, veered northward. Thus, unoccupied Hill 1167 was not assaulted; the regiment bound for it moved on Hill 1240, and the regiment bound for Hill 1240 blundered toward Hill 1282. While this placed both Marine companies in danger, the Chinese advantage of freedom of movement was negated by the fact that the troops would be delivering their attacks across totally unfamiliar terrain, at night, against unanticipated opposition.

★

The first activity near Hill 1282 was noted at about 2200 hours, when several PLA squads approached the previously unoccupied rear spur and ran into 1st Lieutenant Bob Bey's 3rd Platoon. Light skirmishing ensued for about thirty minutes, in which time the probers were driven off at a cost of three Marines wounded.

Dog Company, to the east, was also lightly probed. The company commanders, communicating by phone, agreed to pull in their horns, and canceled the routine patrols that were to have covered the open ground between the ridges.

★

In late 1942, John Yancey had been a corporal with Carlson's Raiders on Guadalcanal. At twenty-four, the Arkansan had striven to be the best Marine in the Corps, and he had been awarded a Navy

Cross and a battlefield commission as a testament to his coolness under fire.

In late 1950, John Yancey was a thirty-two-year-old family man and the proprietor of a Little Rock liquor store he had built up between the wars. Older and wiser, he had volunteered to fight again in Korea, more out of a yearning for action than anything else. In that sense, 1st Lieutenant John Yancey, commanding Easy/7's 1st Platoon, was typical of many Pacific War veterans who had stayed in the Reserves in the late 1940s and who had been called to the colors from good jobs and fledgling businesses in the summer of 1950. But John Yancey was a certified hero, and the impulse to stand and fight was still very much with him.

The second round of Chinese probes unfolded directly in front of Yancey's platoon. They were light, as usual, and the Chinese recoiled upon contact, content to draw fire to learn the whereabouts of the rifle pits and supporting machine guns.

Yancey was not overly perturbed by the probes. He had ordered his gunners to hold their fire in order to avoid giving away their positions. It was business as usual, but only for a few moments.

The unearthly silence was replaced by the cadenced tread of thousands of sneaker-shod feet crunching down upon the thin film of snow. In the distance, above the sound of the crunching, Yancey and his men could discern the rhythmic chant of a single voice. Straining his hearing to the limit, the former Raider thought he heard the words, "Nobody lives forever. You die!" repeated over and over in heavily accented English. It was almost too bizarre to believe.

John Yancey cranked the handle of his sound-powered phone set and was answered in a whisper by the company exec, 1st Lieutenant Ray Ball. "Ray," Yancey warned, "they're building up for an attack. Get the 81s and give us some light, and then lay in on the ridge and work back toward us."

"There's a shortage of 81s," Ball revealed. "We can't give you many."

Yancey's platoon waited while the shadowy mass of Chinese peasant-soldiers stalked nearer. But for the crunching of feet on the snow, the only sound was that lone Chinese voice: "Nobody lives forever. You die!"

Index fingers lightly traced the outlines of triggers and trigger guards. Moments passed, and those fingers toyed with the first pull, then tensed and froze before squeezing through the final, firing, pull.

It was midnight.

The first trip flares burst, giving the illusion that the Chinese were motionless silhouettes. The picture that was burned into the retinas and memory cells of Yancey's Marines was unprecedented, horrifying.

The Chinese ranks stretched, endlessly it seemed, from one flank to the other. Each was a precise fifteen yards from the one in front, as far back as the eye could see. Leading the mass of white-clad infantry was a lone officer, who yelled over and over in heavily accented mission English, "Nobody lives forever. You die!"

John Yancey leaped to his feet and hurled a challenge at the Chinese officer, but his voice was lost in the din of the Chinese chants and the cacophonous bleats of whistles, bugles, and shepherds' horns.

"Lay it on, Ray," Yancey blurted into the phone to the company exec. He dropped the receiver and fired a full clip at the Chinese officer leading the attack.

As the Marine line erupted in gunfire, 60mm and 81mm mortar fire rained down on the Chinese, starting long and pulling closer to form a protective curtain. But the supply of mortar ammunition was limited, and the fire quickly abated. White-clad forms flitted between foxholes to assemble near the center of the company position, immune to fire from Marines who feared hitting their own.

Certain that Yancey's 1st Platoon was bearing the brunt of the attack, Captain Walt Phillips sprang from his command post and sprinted forward to take charge. He found John Yancey and his platoon sergeant leaping from hole to hole, shouting encouragement and distributing spare ammunition. Yancey could barely breathe because a grenade splinter had penetrated the bridge of his nose; his report was delivered amidst much hawking and spitting of the blood that trickled uncomfortably down the back of his throat.

While Yancey moved one way, Walt Phillips moved the other, shouting encouragement, seeing to the evacuation of the wounded, calling up his meager reinforcements from the company CP area. Though hit by bullets in an arm and a leg, Captain Phillips continued to stand his ground, an example to his troops.

First Lieutenant Bill Schreier, the company mortar officer, was directing his crews amidst exploding hand grenades and mortar rounds when he glanced up to see a half-dozen PLA infantrymen coming right at him. He snapped his carbine up and fired, stopping the attackers momentarily, until the simultaneous explosions of numerous grenades forced him to duck. Schreier next saw about twenty Chinese heading his way. His fire had little or no effect, so he trundled uphill to the company command post, where he found the wounded company commander.

Phillips and Schreier spent the next several minutes attempting to form a line around the command post. There were no more than ten Marines in the vicinity, and there was no cover. White forms were moving through the company area, and grenades were bursting in batches, like firecrackers. Schreier had the distinct impression that Chinese grenadiers were dragging baskets of concussion grenades through the line platoons, stopping now and again to hurl whole clusters of them. He felt a sting in his left leg as he fired his carbine steadily at the grenadiers, but he had no time to check for a wound. Two or three grenades exploded practically on top of the mortar officer, and he was wounded in the arm, wrist, and chest.

The Chinese attack faltered, then receded. In time, it was nearly quiet but for the desultory discharge of weapons that frightened men from both armies fired at targets, real and imagined. It seemed to Marines on the line that hundreds of dead and dying Chinese had been stacked up within ten feet of Yancey's line, and throughout the perimeter.

★

One thousand yards to the right of Hill 1282, across an open saddle the Chinese were using as a pathway into the center of the valley of Yudam-ni, Captain Milt Hull's Dog/7 was fighting a seesaw battle to hold Hill 1240.

The usual PLA probes were followed by vicious, tearing assaults upon Hull's line. The company commander had placed all three of his understrength rifle platoons in a single line, and all three were thrashed repeatedly by equally concentrated hammer blows. Two officers had been lost on the patrol to Kyodong-ni during the day, and two more were lost that night with a large and growing number of riflemen and gunners. In time, the repeated body blows dislodged the center platoon, forcing the entire company — all those Marines who could still move — into headlong retreat down the hill.

The rush was stemmed by sturdy, bull-necked Milt Hull, who placed his burly, twice-wounded body between his Marines and the rear. Slowly, Dog/7 re-formed under intense pressure, won back a few square yards of lost ground, then followed the determined company commander up the dark, slippery slope toward the summit.

The Chinese were caught by surprise, and allowed themselves to be forced from the newly won ground. But they rallied within minutes and stampeded to retake the summit of Hill 1240. About thirty of them sideslipped the fighting and established a machine-gun strongpoint in the Marine right rear. The last of Hull's officers was wounded, as was his best platoon sergeant. Milt Hull raged at the survivors, "Hold fast! It's only one gun, and it can't kill us all." The weapon was grenaded out of action, and the reinforced squad that was Dog/7 held.

★

Walt Phillips phoned Lieutenant Colonel Ray Davis at the first opportunity: "We broke up the first attack, Colonel, but we've taken a lot of casualties. We need some help."

There was no overall base commander at Yudam-ni, merely two coequal regimental commanders, each with his own set of problems. Homer Litzenberg was by far the senior to Ray Murray, but he had no mandate for taking command, and he did not. Murray, on the other hand, controlled the only viable reserve force in the valley, Lieutenant Colonel Jack Stevens's 1st Battalion, 5th, which was encamped in the shadow of Hill 1282. Stevens was, in time, ordered to mount a relief force to bail out the orphan companies on Hills 1282 and 1240.

The only officer in Stevens's battalion who had ever been on Hill 1282 was 2nd Lieutenant Nick Trapnell, a professional Marine who had been leading his platoon in constant action since joining Able Company, 5th, as a replacement on the Inchon-Seoul Highway. While establishing an outpost line between his battalion CP and the hill mass late that afternoon, Trapnell had been shown the awesome terrain by Captain Walt Phillips, with whom he had shared some prewar service. Phillips took pains to call Trapnell's attention to the numerous white-clad Chinese on distant ridges.

The night's action began for Nick Trapnell when one of his fire-team leaders crashed into the platoon's command post screaming, "They're coming! They're coming! There're *thousands* of 'em!" Terrified at the prospect of being caught on low ground in the dark, Trapnell immediately began gathering in the fire-team outposts he had strung across the open ground and, without instructions, reformed his platoon on higher ground. Closest to Hill 1282, Trapnell's platoon was the first of Stevens's units to be ordered to the aid of Easy/7. That platoon comprised no more than thirty-five men, probably a smaller number than the losses Easy/7 had already sustained.

The trek up the back of Hill 1282 was frightening, strange, confusing. Tracers passed overhead, but the reinforcements did not hear the sound until they were virtually on top of the beseiged summit. Unsure of the way, unsure if Easy/7 still existed, Trapnell's platoon stumbled upward, calling vainly into the threatening void, "Eas-ee Compan-ee! Eas-ee Compan-ee?"

★

John Yancey was speaking with the right platoon leader, 1st Lieutenant Leonard Clements, trying to coordinate a defense, when the Chinese approached through the almost-silent darkness. Before either man could react, a large hole appeared in the front of Clements's helmet, and blood spurted out. Though the two men and their wives were the best of friends, John Yancey did not waste one instant seeing how his fellow platoon leader fared, for it seemed obvious that the round through Clements's forehead was fatal. Yancey tore off to rejoin his thin platoon. In fact, although Clements had been knocked unconscious, he was not badly injured. The bullet had glanced off his head at an oblique angle and had spun about harmlessly in the helmet's liner.

The 1st Battalion, 235th PLA Regiment, tore back into Easy/7's line after a thirty-minute respite. Hard one-two punches beat at one flank, then the other. Marines were deafened by the discharge of bullets and the close-in bursts of their own and Chinese grenades. The line was thinned as more and more Marines were killed or disabled.

John Yancey was wounded again, seriously, when a grenade fragment holed the roof of his mouth. And Walt Phillips was cut down by machine-gun fire just as he thrust a bayoneted rifle into the frozen earth. "This is Easy Company," he roared an instant before the fatal burst hurled him to the ground, "and we hold here!"

First Lieutenant Ray Ball, the company executive officer, too badly injured to assume command of the company, propped himself up in a rifleman's sitting position beside his foxhole and fired his carbine with telling effect as his life's blood froze in expanding puddles beside him. In time, he fainted, and died.

Nick Trapnell's Able/5 platoon found its way into the position of the rearmost Easy/7 unit, 1st Lieutenant Bob Bey's 3rd Platoon. Bey had no idea as to the dire straits his company was in, so he suggested that Trapnell's thin platoon push off to the right to cover the open ground between Hills 1282 and 1240. Trapnell had not nearly enough men for the job, but he gamely led his riflemen into the void, dropping them off two at a time until he was alone on the dangling flank.

The next Able/5 platoon up the hill came in directly behind the engaged portion of Easy/7 and was cannibalized to flesh out Yancey's and Clements's embattled platoons.

The first news of the company's predicament reached Bob Bey when a squad leader and four riflemen from Yancey's platoon tumbled off the summit almost into the arms of Bey's platoon sergeant, Staff Sergeant Daniel Murphy. When he heard for the first time the full story of the fight higher up, Murphy rushed to Bey, repeated the gruesome tale, and requested permission to take every man he could find to help. Out of touch, unable to even hear the sounds of the furious battle because of strange breaks in the ground, Bey felt that he could spare no more than one squad and the platoon's corpsman, who volunteered to go along.

It wasn't much: Staff Sergeant Murphy, the corpsman, twelve 3rd Platoon riflemen, the five 1st Platoon stragglers.

As Murphy's group was breasting the summit, it slammed into a gaggle of Chinese which had just broken through at the center of the Marine line. The tiny group of Americans clawed their way over the beaten ground, overran the overrun company CP, and re-formed while the corpsman went to work on the wounded.

Walt Phillips was dead. Ray Ball was dead. Leonard Clements appeared to be dead. Bill Schreier was down with shrapnel in a wrist and a lung. The young officer commanding the reinforcing Able/5 platoon was severely injured. No one knew where John Yancey was, cut off somewhere to the left it was supposed. The company's senior noncoms were also missing. The rest was all up to Daniel Murphy.

The platoon sergeant bellowed for attention, rallying isolated Marines to his position by the CP. He redeployed those who came to him, moved a machine gun to better advantage, kicked ass, threatened, and prepared for the worst.

It was not long in coming. Masses of white-clad Chinese loomed out of the darkness and slammed into the Marines. Murphy doled out the last of the grenades and began dismantling BAR clips to eke out the last of the .30-caliber rifle ammunition.

★

On the far side of the gap, John Yancey counted nine men who could still fight beside him. Hoping to instill some confidence in nearly beaten men, Yancey hawked blood and gurgled the battle cry he had learned as a Marine Raider: "GUNG HO!" It means "Work Together," and it is spoken in the Cantonese mother tongue of most of the peasant-soldiers who were then trampling victoriously across the summit of Hill 1282.

"GUNG HO!"

Ten weary, wounded Marines lifted themselves to their feet, fixed bayonets, shuffled forward, their reedy battle cry cutting through the shrill night wind, their bayonets silhouetted in the firelight.

"GUNG HO!"

John Yancey went to his knees as a shadowy Chinese soldier fired a Thompson submachine gun full into his face. The impact of the only round to hit him popped the Raider's left eye out of its socket. The amazed platoon leader fingered the slimy orb back into place and crawled blindly up the blood-bespattered hillside.

"GUNG HO!"

The thin Marine line faltered, dissolved.

CHAPTER

13

Two officers fresh from the States chose the site from which Fox Company, 7th, would outpost Toktong Pass, the vital potential bottleneck between Hagaru-ri and Yudam-ni. Lieutenant Colonel Randolph Lockwood had been in command of the 2nd Battalion, 7th, for a bit less than two weeks, and Captain Bill Barber had spent even less time with Fox/7. Of the two, Barber had the greater combat experience, having been commissioned after two years of enlisted service in the Pacific. He had won a Silver Star at Iwo Jima. Randolph Lockwood had been a Marine since his 1936 graduation from the Naval Academy, but he had put off entering active duty until 1940 so that he could complete an advanced degree at Harvard. He had seen exactly one day's combat in the Pacific, at Pearl Harbor, on December 7, 1941. New to the battalion, neither man was yet accepted by the veterans they commanded.

It was the luck of the draw that brought Fox/7 to Toktong Pass on November 27. Lacking sufficient transport, Division had been forced to move the battalion's relief to Hagaru-ri piecemeal, and that meant that Lockwood's companies had to move to Yudam-ni in increments, depending upon the availability of transport. Between the time Dog and Easy Companies left Hagaru-ri on November 26 and Fox Company was relieved by elements of the 3rd Battalion, 1st Marines, on November 27, Division had decided to use Barber's seasoned troops to outpost the vital pass. While his company officers worked at scrounging transport at the growing division base, Bill Barber joined Lieutenant Colonel Lockwood for a jeep ride to find a suitable defensive position for the slightly reinforced rifle company.

While the two-hundred-forty Marines attached to Fox/7 waited in the cold by the newly started airstrip at Hagaru-ri, none knowing if he would walk or ride up the steep, tortuous grade to the top of the pass, Barber and Lockwood drove about seven miles into the mountains and tried to pinpoint the hill the company was to occupy. A difficulty arose from the maps, which had been adapted from Japanese materials. Often as not, details on paper failed to match up with details on the ground. The two officers passed Toktong-San, whose forty-seven-hundred-foot peak dominated everything within sight, then proceeded another mile up the twisting MSR before deciding that they had missed the objective. The jeep was turned and driven a mile back, at which point Barber and Lockwood agreed upon a position on Toktong-San's south shoulder, just north of the roadway. The site, a bit over seven road miles from the airstrip at Hagaru-ri, was marked by a pair of abandoned huts and a spring at the edge of a thick belt of stunted scrub pines.

A mile farther down the MSR, as they made their way back to Hagaru-ri, Barber and Lockwood were flagged down by a Marine warrant officer who was heading toward the pass. The three men chatted for a moment, in which time the warrant officer conveyed a sense of unease. He noted that North Koreans living along the road had been begging food from passing Marines for days, but that they were now running for cover every time Marines appeared. Even the children had stopped looking for handouts of chewing gum and candy. And the abundant game was nervous; deer were coming down from the wooded heights as if driven.

Lockwood and Barber left the warrant officer and found Fox/7 riding in nine trucks its officers had borrowed from How Battery, 11th, the 105mm howitzer outfit that usually supported the 2nd Battalion, 7th. Captain Barber rejoined his company, and Randolph Lockwood continued on to Hagaru-ri, where he rejoined his headquarters company and the remnants of the battalion weapons company.

★

Fox/7 was late arriving at the hill. It had taken a good part of the day to scrounge transport and get the troops and their gear loaded, and crowded road conditions had further delayed the unit. It was 1700 hours before the two hundred thirty-two enlisted Marines and corpsmen and their eight officers began trudging uphill to the ground selected by the battalion and company commanders for the company position.

Fox Hill, as it was to be known, was fairly well isolated from the dominating height to the northeast, Toktong-San. The hill rose sharply from the roadway, its lower slope banded by thick stands of dwarf pines and other scrubby growth. A nine-hundred-yard-long saddle curved northwest to east from the hilltop to Toktong-San, its steep sides falling away abruptly to the east and west. The best approach to the hill was from the peak, across the saddle, and this was covered by Barber's 3rd Platoon, amply bolstered by light and heavy machine guns. The 2nd Platoon was tied in on the left of the 3rd, and 1st Platoon was manning an isolated position well to the right. The company command post, aid station, and mortars were in the scrub overlooking the roadway, well downslope from the rifle platoons. A pair of 81mm mortars and the company's own three-gun 60mm mortar section were registered on avenues of approach well out of sight on the far side of the hill, and on the saddle to Toktong-San. A forward observer team from How/11 was unable to register the nearest 105mm howitzers for fear of hitting the heavy late traffic on the road. Because they were late in arriving, the troops were barely able to dig foxholes and gun emplacements before sunset, and no effort was made to erect warming tents nor even the company galley.

Fox Company was settled in by 2100, by which time half the men were asleep in their heavy down bags. The hill was brightly illuminated by a full moon, but the piercing cold wind reduced the ability of those men who were awake to concentrate on scanning the slopes and heights on all sides. It was in every way a mind-numbing chill.

The last big truck convoy from Yudam-ni passed, headlights ablaze, as did several lone vehicles. But all traffic ceased abruptly at an indeterminate and unnoticed moment after 2100. No one on Fox Hill knew or had any reason to think that the company was completely isolated, cut off by the Chinese regiments that had stolen down from the heights to sever the MSR.

★

Captain Ben Read, the veteran commander of How Battery, 11th, was probably the last man to get from Yudam-ni to Hagaru-ri that

night. He had been to the northern garrison to plan How/11's anticipated move the following day and had not been able to get away
until well after sunset. He had spoken briefly with 1st Lieutenant
Bob Messman, the King Battery commander who was made captive
on the road, and he assumed that Messman was right behind him.

Shortly after returning to his battery, Read was called by Lieutenant Colonel Carl Youngdale, the exec of the 11th Marines, who
wanted to know if Read had been contacted by a messenger sent
earlier in the evening by Major Fox Parry, commander of the 3rd
Battalion, 11th. Read said that he knew nothing of the messenger,
though he assumed the man was carrying written confirmation of the
movement plans he had worked out with Major Parry earlier in the
evening.

The messenger was dead. His jeep had made it over Toktong Pass
without mishap, but the driver had missed the turnoff into Hagaru-
ri and had proceeded down the road toward Koto-ri. Rounding a
curve, the jeep's lights had picked up ghostly white-clad figures on
a roadside embankment. The driver had braked to ask directions,
but the jeep was riddled by gunfire and sent careening into a ditch.
The messenger was killed by the first volley, but the driver grabbed
the dispatch case and went to ground. He hid for several hours, then
walked to Hagaru-ri.

It was plain lucky that the message was delivered late, at 0130.
Had Major Parry's orders reached Ben Read on time, he would certainly have sent nineteen heavy trucks laden with four thousand
rounds of the 3rd Battalion, 11th's reserve ammunition to Yudam-ni.
It is virtually certain that the convoy and its thirty-eight-man security detail would have been stopped on the road and captured or
destroyed.

When the artillery forward observer on Fox Hill, 2nd Lieutenant
Don Campbell, called in to request precautionary fire support, Captain Read had to convey the miserable news that ammunition was
scarce, and that the six-gun battery would respond only in the direst
emergency. Besides, the guns had not been registered and could not
be fired on Fox Hill until careful arrangements had been made.

Campbell took the news with equanimity, but expressed concern
over the sounds of heavy fighting and the occasional illumination
that he could hear and see far to the north. Worse, the cold was
ruining his radio batteries, and he was not certain that he would be
able to raise How Battery again if he needed to. Alternative links
were laid on, but radio contact between How Battery and Fox Hill
remained tenuous.

At length, Captain Read contacted his regimental commander, Colonel Jim Brower, to ask if he should move How Battery from its isolated position into the newly formed Hagaru-ri perimeter. There were Chinese out there, and plenty of them. But there were factors militating against such a move: Fox Hill was at the extremity of How Battery's range, and a move into the safer perimeter would place the hill beyond the range of the guns; the guns were emplaced in deep protective pits, and there was little chance that emplacements nearly as secure could be carved or blasted out of the solidly frozen earth within the perimeter; there were no approaches to the battery position that could not be adequately interdicted by the guns themselves or the battery's own security force, which had been beefed up by the thirty-eight men sent to guard the ammunition train. Colonel Brower left the decision to Ben Read, and Read decided to stay where he was. It was a vital decision, and a good one.

★

First Lieutenant Bob McCarthy, Fox/7's 3rd Platoon leader, inspected his lines at 0100 and came away furious with the results. Though he well knew the effect the cold was having on his troops, he had chewed out his squad leaders to get them to bring the riflemen to a proper state of alertness. Other troop leaders were having similar difficulties, though they were not as hard on their men as McCarthy felt he had to be on his. It was rounding 0200 when the platoon leader returned to his command post from a second inspection tour, in which he found the men bitching but well up to the task of watching out for themselves. Satisfied, Bob McCarthy pulled off his footgear and eased into his warm down bag, hoping to be able to sleep through to sunrise.

★

The Chinese hit Fox Hill just before 0230, and with a vengeance underscoring the importance their commanders placed upon severing the Yudam-ni garrison from any possible ground support.

Bob McCarthy was awakened from a deep sleep by a shout from his reserve squad leader: "Here they come!" It was the platoon leader's first news that at least a company of Chinese, all armed with Russian burp guns and American Thompson submachine guns, had already steamrolled across the saddle connecting Fox Hill with Toktong-San. The 3rd Platoon's two forward squads were all but overrun by the time McCarthy struggled out of his sleeping bag.

The thirty-five riflemen and machine gunners manning the forward positions put up an inspiring stand against utterly overwhelming odds. Fifteen of the thirty-five were killed as they stood to meet the unexpected assault, and nine others were wounded. A Marine whose machine-gun jammed shot six of the densely packed attackers to death with his pistol at point-blank range. The survivors held with remarkable tenacity as three corpsmen dragged the wounded to safety. Then the thin line collapsed. Three more Marines were lost, overwhelmed by the Chinese tide as the eight survivors crossed the open platoon bivouac to secondary positions held by the reserve squad and the tiny platoon headquarters team.

★

Within five minutes of the opening thrust across the saddle, a rocket-team member near the foot of Fox Hill detected a PLA column marching on the company command post. He shouted a warning, triggering a sharp exchange. Chinese grenades exploding amidst Fox/7's three 60mm mortars killed two gunners and wounded the section officer, the section chief, and six other gunners. That obviated the effective use of the tubes to ward off the main attack from Toktong-San. Two of the guns were saved, however, and moved uphill to get them out of immediate danger. They were soon responding to fire calls, but ammunition was limited, and the guns had not been precisely registered.

The company command group moved with the mortars to the open ground above the belt of stubby pines near the base of Fox Hill. Captain Barber called in every available clerk and technician and soon established a line behind an earthen bank. There was little more he could do to meet the challenges on the front, left, and rear.

★

As soon as Bob McCarthy's forward line had been chewed up and spit back, the direction of the Chinese assault shifted slightly toward the American left, going for 1st Lieutenant Elmo Peterson's adjacent 2nd Platoon, which moved reflexively to prevent the attackers from driving a wedge between it and the survivors of McCarthy's 3rd Platoon.

While Peterson shook his Marines from their sleeping bags, the Chinese were held momentarily by 3rd Platoon fire teams under Privates First Class Harrison Pomers and Gerald Smith. Pomers survived the blasts of three Chinese concussion grenades in his foxhole, never letting up his steady fire until a fourth stick grenade exploded on contact with his steel helmet and knocked him cold. Smith's four-man team was about to be overwhelmed when events in the 2nd Platoon sector brought unexpected salvation from the left.

★

Private Hector Cafferata, a nineteen-year-old Regular from South Jersey, was the biggest Marine in Fox Company, a veritable mountain of a man. He was good-natured in the tolerant manner of men of great physical stature, but he was constantly in trouble over minor infractions of the many piddling rules that make life in the military so memorable. He had been chewed out that day by a superior, and he was a little afraid of screwing up, at least until the latest incident had been forgotten.

Hector Cafferata was asleep in the foxhole he had dug with his best friend, Private First Class Kenneth Benson, when the Chinese streamed across the saddle from Toktong-San. Awakened by the sound of gunfire, he sat up, startled, as his fire-team leader and BAR-man were shot to death in the rightmost foxhole of the 2nd Platoon line. When the Chinese attack shifted to the left front to engage 2nd Platoon, Cafferata and Benson legged it to the right to join Gerald Smith's leftmost fire team of 3rd Platoon.

The two 2nd Platoon men came in firing. Cafferata dropped six Chinese with the first eight-round clip he fired, then dove into Smith's fighting hole to reload. The Garand rifle he had been carrying since Inchon failed him then, but he retrieved the weapon of a wounded Marine, who offered to reload abandoned rifles strewn about the fighting hole.

Hector Cafferata stood up to reveal his full, massive bulk to the Chinese who were about to overrun Smith's fire team and sweep away 3rd Platoon. Nerveless, he stood his ground, awing the attackers into meek acceptance of the death blazing from the barrels of the Garand rifles the anonymous wounded Marine passed up to him. The Chinese died, and the Marines took heart. Two grenades were scooped up by the big private and thrown back at the Chinese, but the third blew, tearing away a joint of one of Cafferata's little fingers. Then a satchel charge landed in the fighting hole. Everyone who was able to leaped to safety, but the wounded Marine who had been reloading rifles was killed in the blast.

To the left, Lieutenant Peterson was drilled through the shoulder. He took only a few moments out to have the gaping wound dressed, and returned to the fray as soon as the corpsman finished tying off the bandage.

Grenades continued to rain down on the fighting hole defended by Benson, Cafferata, and Smith's fire team. Benson fell victim to one, which blew up in his face as he attempted to throw it back; his spectacles were broken and his eyes were veiled in a deep red film.

Several other Marines took desperate swipes at the grenades with entrenching shovels, batting them back at the men throwing them.

Whistles and bugles pierced the roar of gunfire, and the Chinese tide receded. The two remaining 60mm mortars, far to the rear, found the range, butchering Chinese on the narrow saddle, flushing others into the gunsights of the survivors of McCarthy's platoon.

The Chinese probed and prodded through the few remaining hours of darkness. The remnants of 2nd Platoon were pulled back to defend the company CP area and the mortars. First Platoon was not threatened, though its flanking fire teams got into a brief fight as they were shifted to better advantage.

The remnants of McCarthy's platoon, plus Hector Cafferata, clung grimly to their tiny position. Private First Class Harrison Pomers, the fire-team leader who had been hit in the head by a bursting grenade, regained consciousness and resumed the fight as though nothing had happened to him.

Hector Cafferata stalked forward at daybreak to examine a mound of intertwined bodies. He peeled back the eyelids of a PLA soldier who seemed to be alive, but found the pupils rolled into the man's head. Shortly after he moved on, however, the huge private heard a shot and dove into a snowbank. Then, screaming oaths, he stalked back to the man feigning death. He nicked the Chinese soldier's cheek with his bayonet, but got no reaction. He shot the man in the leg, but got no reaction. He shot the man in the shoulder, bringing him to a sitting position. He shot the man dead.

Next, Hector Cafferata was stitched up the right arm by a line of machine-gun bullets. As he plummeted to the snow-covered ground, he saw fellow Marines move to help, but motioned them back with his good left arm. The big nineteen-year-old pulled himself to a sitting position, undid his web belt, and fashioned a sling. Then he rose to his feet and lurched unsteadily to safety.

It was 0730 when Hector Cafferata was dragged to the nearest aid tent. Only then was it discovered that he had fought for five freezing hours in his bare feet.

★

Twenty Fox/7 Marines were dead, sixteen of them from McCarthy's platoon. Another fifty-four were wounded, and three were missing. That is a casualty rate of thirty-two percent. Fox/7 had been engaged around a two-hundred-seventy-degree arc and had killed an estimated four hundred Chinese, mainly on the ground in front of 3rd Platoon.

First Platoon mounted a counterattack shortly after dawn to clear Fox Company's end of the saddle. Several Chinese were surprised and killed as they were setting up a light machine gun. Three 1st Platoon Marines seized the gun and its ammunition and chased other Chinese onto the saddle, dropping a score of them over the steep slopes.

★

The first night's fight ended there. A frustrated 2nd Lieutenant Don Campbell, the How Battery forward observer, placed an early call to his fire-direction center and arranged a detailed fire plan to screen the occupied portions of Fox Hill from further attack. Ben Read insisted, however, that none of his precious, finite supply of shells be used in registering the guns, a decision that rendered Campbell's plan academic and, at best, questionable.

The only outside help Fox/7 received in the wake of the crippling attacks came from a four-plane division of Royal Australian Air Force F-51 fighter-bombers and a pair of Marine Corsairs, part of a massive aerial effort aimed at sweeping the MSR clear of blocks and blockers. The larger effort fell far short of its goals, but the Chinese division around Fox Hill was kept at a respectful distance from the Marine defenders.

Fox/7 had ten rounds of 60mm mortar ammunition remaining, and barely a prayer of getting more. The one hundred sixty-three effectives and fifty-four wounded were six miles from the nearest friendly unit, and the only land routes in or out were sealed by at least a division of PLA infantry.

C H A P T E R
14

Seventh Infantry Division had been the last large American occupation unit in Japan to be sent to Korea. It had never been up to strength, and the long delay in getting it to Korea had deprived it of many of the trained professionals who had filled its ranks in the early months of 1950; the division had served, for a time, as a manpower pool from which other units bound for Korea had filled their ranks. While large numbers of Regulars had arrived from the States to undertake the Inchon-Seoul battles with the 7th Infantry Division, most of the new arrivals were recently inducted enlistees and draftees who had had the luck or misfortune to complete their basic training immediately prior to their shipment overseas. And approximately one in five of the division's line infantrymen was a South Korean, a man or a boy who had been dragooned into the service of his country by brute force.

Though the professionals who staffed and led the regiments and battalions had had to struggle with their mixed manpower bag, they brought their units through Inchon-Seoul with honor and acclaim. By the time 7th Infantry Division had been committed to the drive on the Yalu in northeastern Korea, it seemed a steady, seasoned combat force. Two of its regiments — the 31st and 32nd — had lost their colors to the Japanese in the Philippines in 1942, and both had been barred by tradition from service in the United States until they redeemed themselves. They had both done so in the Inchon-Seoul fighting, and that boost had helped prepare them for the next round of battle. Or so it seemed. For no amount of training and time spent in combat could have prepared any group of soldiers for the ordeal that was to befall the thirty-five hundred members of 7th Infantry Division who passed through Hagaru-ri on November 26 and 27, 1950.

★

A sizable portion of the heavy traffic that had caused and been effected by the numerous delays all along the MSR from Hamhung to Hagaru-ri had resulted from the movement of large increments of 7th Infantry Division to the vicinity of the Reservoir.

Lieutenant Colonel Don Faith's ragtag and bobtail 1st Battalion, 32nd Infantry, had begun relieving Ray Murray's 5th Marines on the east side of the Reservoir on November 26. It was joined on November 27 by the reinforced 3rd Battalion, 31st Infantry, two six-gun 105mm howitzer batteries of the 57th Field Artillery Battalion, a self-propelled antiaircraft battery, and the forward headquarters of the 31st Regimental Combat Team. Altogether, more than three thousand officers and men were moved through Hagaru-ri and on up the eastern shore of the largely frozen mountain lake formed by the dammed Changjin River.

They had started their two-day journey less than seventy miles from the Chosin Reservoir, from scattered positions by and on the road to the Fusen Reservoir. There were no lateral roads from one sector to the other, so the troops and their equipment had to be driven all the way down to Hamhung, where many stayed the night, then north the sixty-four miles to the Hagaru-ri cutoff. It was a grueling, bitterly cold journey, and it had thrown all the elements of the relief force into various states of organizational chaos, some seriously so. Valuable equipment, some ammunition, even some of the troops, had been misplaced in the rush to fill the void that was being left by the reassigned 5th Marines. No one weathered the journey in top physical condition, and the late arrival of some key elements prevented the organization from taking full advantage of the ample defensive options it might otherwise have enjoyed.

It would all have to be straightened out in the morning.

★

Private First Class Jay Ransone, an assistant squad leader with Able Company, 1st Battalion, 32nd, had had about the most exhausting day he could recall. And one of the most frightening.

The twenty-year-old Virginian, a proud product of the tradition-rich Tidewater, was about as thoroughly trained an infantryman as there was in 7th Infantry Division. In the year before the war Ransone had been a member of the small-unit-tactics demonstration team at The Infantry School at Fort Benning; he had helped indoctrinate wet-behind-the-ears lieutenants and had retrained very senior officers in state-of-the-art advances in infantry tactics. And he had been through serious combat during Inchon-Seoul. All that training and combat, coupled with a life in the outdoors, had made Jay Ransone one tough, knowledgeable infantryman.

He had been called out that morning by one of the company officers and teamed with a corporal he did not know and a pair of South Korean conscripts. The four had been sent vaguely to the north to see what they could see. No specific goals were set, no radio was provided, and no firm time to return was mentioned. The minuscule size of the patrol — far too small to defend itself under any circumstances — and the vagueness of the mission combined to strike fear into the heart of Jay Ransone.

Hours after leaving Able/32's advanced perimeter beside the Reservoir, miles from friendly units, the four-man patrol stumbled upon a find of indeterminate value.

The three North Korean civilians did not seem important when they were first encountered, but closer examination had revealed a fact that was startling only in its context. The three were a very old man, a very old woman, and a son in his late twenties or early thirties. North Korea was a war-torn waste, involved to the last man in its war with the West. All the healthy young men were soldiers.

All, it seemed, but the healthy-looking son of the two North Korean ancients stopped by a tiny American patrol on a nameless hillside in the middle of absolutely nowhere. The South Koreans questioned the young man, and seemed excited by his response. As they lacked a means of communicating with their allies, however, the two Americans decided to use the encounter as a pretext for returning to friendly lines.

The young North Korean was eager to please, and the Americans allowed him to lead the way through country he seemed to know well. Their trust seemed to come a cropper when they were fired on briefly from a lonely farmhouse, but the North Korean quickly led them around the hut and directly to the lines of Able/32.

It was dark when the tiny patrol reported in to the company command post. An interpreter was called in to question the captive, who eagerly gave out the news that tens of thousands of Chinese soldiers were in the hills around the Chosin Reservoir. Jay Ransone was dumb struck, but the officers did not seem perturbed, so, when he was sent back to his platoon, Ransone did not feel overly concerned.

Faced with the choice of digging into the frozen soil in the dark or unrolling his down bag on a flat beside his platoon sergeant's foxhole, Jay Ransone opted for the path of least resistance. He would have plenty of time to dig in in the morning.

★

At the moment Jay Ransone was crawling gratefully into his sleeping bag, several PLA divisions were padding silently out of the hills along a six-mile section of the road that ran up the east side of the Reservoir from Hagaru-ri. The defenses those divisions faced are best described as helter-skelter.

The American force east of the Reservoir was a mixed force, lacking organizational integrity. Its composition and order of battle had been determined solely on the basis of the starting positions its components had occupied in the Fusen Reservoir area; the 1st Battalion, 32nd, had been the rearmost 7th Division unit on the road to the Fusen, so it had become the first 7th Division on the road to the Chosin. It was the plan of the Army division staff to reorganize the 31st and 32nd Regimental Combat Teams around the nucleus battalions, the 1st of the 32nd and the 3rd of the 31st. Once the total force had been brought up, the advance on the Yalu River would commence. That night, in fact, most of the 2nd Battalion, 31st, was encamped in a village between the Fusen Reservoir and Hamhung; a company of the 1st Battalion, 31st, was in Hungnam; and elements of all remaining portions of both combat teams were strewn over one hundred miles of roadway between the Fusen Reservoir and the coast.

Don Faith's 1st Battalion, 32nd, was the northernmost of the American units east of the Reservoir, occupying a loose all-around perimeter just north of an eastward-jutting arm of ice.

To the south, Lieutenant Colonel William Reilly's 3rd Battalion, 31st, had gone into position astride the road. Reilly's companies were widely dispersed, with some elements on commanding heights and others on low ground dominated by unoccupied heights.

Able and Baker Batteries of Lieutenant Colonel Ray Embree's 57th Field Artillery Battalion were in separate battery sites beside the road, within Reilly's battalion area. Embree's command post, alongside Reilly's, was guarded by a mixed battery of self-propelled twin-40mm antiaircraft guns and half-track-mounted quadruple-.50-caliber antiaircraft machine guns. Though normally a supporting arm of the 31st Infantry, Able/57 was oriented in the direction of Faith's battalion of the 32nd. Neither of the six-gun 105mm batteries was reliably defended. No alert had been issued, and no more than the standard number of gunners had been told off for sentry duty.

About forty staff officers and clerks comprising the 31st Infantry's forward command group were occupying a tiny, isolated position between Faith and Reilly. A much larger headquarters had been established in a schoolhouse some miles to the rear. It comprised the regimental operations center, the regimental medium-tank company, the bulk of the regimental heavy-mortar company, communicators, medical personnel, and assorted special and service troops, about two hundred fifty mainly noncombatant troops in all. Additional headquarters and service troops were still on the road between Hagaru-ri and the schoolhouse operations center. These had been delayed to the passage of Marine units from the east side of the Reservoir to Yudam-ni, and they would be filtering forward through the night.

With the possible exception of Don Faith's forward companies, none of the Army units east of the Reservoir was on particularly good ground. Faith was, but the relaxed state of his command appreciably negated the advantage of terrain. Lieutenant Colonel Bill Reilly was obliged to cover more ground than could be covered effectively by a mere battalion, and what he did cover was not necessarily the best available.

Colonel Allen MacLean, the commander of the 31st, had worked tirelessly through the day to prepare for the arrival of much larger forces than actually did arrive. In the absence of any sort of warning

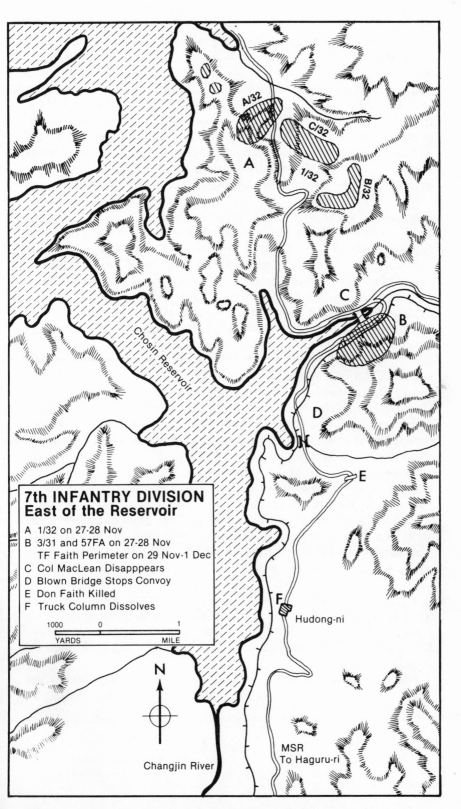

7th INFANTRY DIVISION
East of the Reservoir

A 1/32 on 27-28 Nov
B 3/31 and 57FA on 27-28 Nov
   TF Faith Perimeter on 29 Nov-1 Dec
C Col MacLean Disapppears
D Blown Bridge Stops Convoy
E Don Faith Killed
F Truck Column Dissolves

1000   0   1
YARDS   MILE

A/32

C/32

1/32

B/32

A

C

D

B

D

E

Chosin Reservoir

F Hudong-ni

N

MSR
To Haguru-ri

Changjin River

(See endpapers for GUIDE TO MAP SYMBOLS AND ABBREVIATIONS.)

as to Chinese intentions — or even proximity — MacLean assumed, fairly, that the major deficiency, lack of manpower, would be remedied during November 28.

Colonel MacLean, who had taken command of the 31st Infantry after the fall of Seoul, had spent most of the day shuttling back and forth between his forward battalions and his schoolhouse operations center. A tireless worker, he was in the throes of a very bad cold, and he had been admonished by his staff to get all the rest he could. He had acceded halfheartedly by taking short naps, but there was much to be done, and he insisted upon overexerting himself.

The colonel had been forward in the early afternoon to make a jeep reconnaissance with Don Faith north of the 1st Battalion, 32nd's positions. Faith was scheduled to make a limited advance on November 28, and MacLean had invited him along to help choose a defensive site. They drove as far as the spot where the Chinese had engaged in the midnight fistfight with the outpost of the 3rd Battalion, 5th Marines. There, the colonels viewed the remains of several PLA soldiers who had been killed in the fray.

After dropping Faith at his headquarters, MacLean had driven a few miles south to monitor the activities of the 3rd Battalion, 31st, and the 57th Field Artillery. As they were about as well off as they could be, the regimental commander continued on to his operations center and managed a short nap before conferring with Brigadier General Henry Hodes, the 7th Division assistant commander, who had been flown into Hagaru-ri by Marine helicopter and jeeped forward to the regimental operations compound. Hodes's mission was to acquaint MacLean and his staff with the X Corps plan for the advance on the Yalu. The precipitous departure by MacLean's command from the Fusen Reservoir had deprived the colonel of an opportunity to learn the details of its mission.

Late in the evening, perhaps as late as 2300, MacLean awoke from another nap and ordered his driver to take him to his forward command group, which was bedded down in a tiny village several miles north of the 3rd Battalion positions. He arrived before midnight.

★

The Chinese struck Able/32 with mind-numbing suddenness. First they rolled over several outposts, then they swooped down from the high ground overlooking the juncture of Able and Charlie Companies, which were joined on the roadway running through the battalion bivouac.

Private First Class Jay Ransone, asleep beside his platoon sergeant's foxhole, was instantly awake as the first trip flares caught the leading Chinese in motion through the Able Company line. The attack started that swiftly: Chinese were already passing between American and South Korean foxholes before many defenders were awake and responsive.

The first thing Jay Ransone saw in the flare light was a PLA attack upon a small security force occupying a line of fighting holes up-slope and at right angles to the left front. Masses of white-clad Chinese infantrymen overpowered the American soldiers, killing them all.

Screaming, hollering men attacked in response to atonal bleats of shepherds' horns and a cacophony of whistle blasts and bugle calls. Concussion grenades rained on American foxholes, and bursts from submachine guns caught yawning Americans and South Koreans in their faces and chests.

Asleep in a bunker in Able/32's command compound, Captain Ed Stamford, a Marine forward air controller who had been with Faith's battalion since Inchon, was awakened by the first flurry of gunfire and shouted warnings. Curious, and a bit frightened, Stamford pulled back the poncho that was shielding the entryway of the bunker, and looked right into the face of an Asian soldier. Terrified, the Marine airman dropped to a sitting position and pushed the muzzle of his automatic pistol into the intruder's moonlit face. The first round blew the Chinese soldier's head apart, but the man had already hurled a grenade into the bunker, wounding a Marine communicator.

Captain Edward Scullion, the Able/32 commander, was at Don Faith's command post, being briefed about a limited morning advance, when the Chinese struck. The confab broke up in a hurry, and Scullion made directly for his command post, where he learned that his 1st Platoon leader had been wounded in the knee by one of his own men. Captain Scullion charged toward the 1st Platoon sector on the company left, but was killed on the way by a Chinese grenade.

Individuals and small groups manning what remained of Able/32's line fought back reflexively while some of their comrades broke and ran or cowered helplessly in their holes. Jay Ransone fired at every passing shadow, though fearful that he was dropping friendly stragglers as often as he was stopping Chinese attackers.

Ed Stamford broke for the open at the first lull, but was driven into a fighting hole by a renewed Chinese assault upon the company command compound. Machine-gun fire broke up the attack, and Stamford organized what few men he could find to defend the CP.

The Marine airman was livid. Until that night he had merely been disdainful of the Army men and their South Korean "buddies." He had heard battalion officers complain about their inability to impress upon the troops the need to remain awake on sentry duty. And he knew that it was common for enlisted soldiers to complain about their sore feet — the result of having to butt kick the South Koreans into the line. Within minutes of assessing the situation that night, Ed Stamford became convinced that he had overestimated the fighting abilities of the battalion. His disdain turned to a mad pity. It was clear to the Marine airman that his survival depended mainly upon his ability to fend for himself.

When he heard of Captain Scullion's death, Don Faith ordered his assistant operations officer to assume command of Able Company. That officer, however, was shot to death by infiltrators before he could get to Able Company. Faith phoned the company executive officer and ordered him to take charge.

Ed Stamford crawled into the Able Company command bunker after a hurried trip to help reorganize 1st Platoon. He found the company exec silent and inactive. It was evident that the man had done nothing to organize a viable defense, nor had he so much as taken the time to learn the details of his unit's stand.

Furious, Stamford stalked from the bunker, unsure about how he should act. He was accosted in the entryway by the Able Company's heavy-machine-gun officer, who said, "Well, Captain, you're the next senior man. I guess you have the company."

Ed Stamford, an airman out of his element, had not considered taking command of the company, but the platoon leader's words galvanized him. He pulled the least-molested platoon from its position and sent it to sweep the company rear. The job was progressing well when the Chinese were seen massing before the vacated portion of the line. Captain Stamford pushed the platoon back into the gap, which it held with ease, then sent it again to grapple with the Chinese in the rear.

In time, making use of the good men Able/32 had to offer, Stamford managed to stabilize the company position and even made some headway against numerous infiltrators.

To the right of the roadway, along a front running from northeast to southeast, Charlie/32 was effectively neutralized in two successive attacks. The first pushed in the right and center platoons, and the second won the Chinese machine-gun emplacements on the high ground overlooking the company left, where it was tied in with

Able Company. Guns on the heights raked the farmhouse from which the company commander was directing the battle, forcing the command group to disperse. The Charlie Company commander, having lost effective control of his unit, moved to the front line and fought on as a rifleman.

Somehow Charlie/32 held.

Neither Baker Company nor the battalion command group was seriously molested that night, though there was nothing either did, or could do, to relieve the serious pressure on Able Company during the seesaw for its survival.

★

The 31st Infantry's Intelligence-&-Reconnaissance Platoon had been sent out early in the evening to outpost a wide draw to the northeast of the positions held by the 3rd Battalion, 31st, and the 57th Field Artillery Battalion. The entire unit was eradicated in an assault so swift and so overwhelming that it had not even an instant to contact any friendly unit by radio. The entire platoon simply vanished.

★

True to their established tactical doctrine, the Chinese sought to segment the American forces by mounting simultaneous assaults upon the front, center, and rear positions along the road from Hagaru-ri.

Awakened by a fellow officer, 1st Lieutenant Ed Magill, a veteran forward observer with Baker Battery, 57th Field Artillery, heard what he and other battery officers took to be far-distant automobile horns. Earlier that evening, while Baker/57 had been emplacing its 105mm howitzers, a crowd of North Korean civilians had come through on their way south. Highly emotional, and eager to be on their way, the civilians had told an interpreter that Chinese soldiers were bivouacked to the north. The artillery officers, assured by higher headquarters that there were no enemy units of any sort in the vicinity, entirely discounted the civilians' story. As Lieutenant Magill and his comrades listened to the distant horns, however, they became increasingly restive. One of the group finally suggested that the horns might be bugles. The sounds persisted, and the battery officers became quite concerned. Their doubts dissolved when the stable in which they were billeted was riddled by machine-gun fire from the heights to the east.

Forward of the artillery positions, screening the small valley in which the howitzers and the headquarters of the 3rd Battalion, 31st, and 57th Field Artillery had been set up, King and Love Companies, 31st, occupied dominating heights overlooking the road and a narrow concrete bridge across an arm of the Reservoir.

Because of the rush to get north, and the poor road conditions, King/31's tents and sleeping bags had not made it to the bivouac. The company commander had called in his officers and senior noncoms early in the evening and had told them that each platoon could keep a warming fire burning all night. The troops had been fed a hot meal, which helped a bit.

Sergeant First Class Ed Farley, King Company's 60mm mortar-section chief, was in the process of checking the scratch crews he had manning each of the three guns when he heard a sudden, unremitting fire to the rear, from the vicinity of Able Battery, the nearest artillery unit. Farley woke all the gunners, set most of them on a defensive line around the mortars, and dogtrotted back to the company CP, where his captain told him that the 57th Field Artillery was under attack.

First Lieutenant Ed Magill pulled on his frozen leather combat boots and scurried out into the cold with his fellow Baker/57 officers. The forward observers, who usually served the 2nd Battalion, 31st, had been called home to the battery for the duration of the move from the Fusen Reservoir. Unable to contribute more, they moved directly to the perimeter line to help beat back the first infantry attacks aimed at taking the guns.

Sergeant First Class Ed Farley no sooner got all his gunners positioned than the infantry platoons he was to support streamed down off the hill immediately in front of the mortar section's position. The riflemen had been severely mauled by the Chinese, and panicked Americans and South Koreans charged headlong for the rear. When he stopped and questioned one of the rifle-platoon sergeants, Farley found that he had virtually no one protecting his guns, that all of King Company had just fallen apart. Farley acted quickly. He called in the gunners he had earlier sent forward to screen the mortars, then leapfrogged the guns toward the rear, putting out as many rounds as his gunners could get off during frequent stops. Two of the guns and six crewmen were lost before the mortar section stormed across the small bridge into the Able Battery perimeter.

The gunners and straggling infantrymen were fighting the Chinese at close quarters. Several of the howitzers were temporarily overrun as the battle whipped across the battery area. Casualties among the gunners and their officers were extremely high. The 57th's executive officer was one of the many who were killed.

At least thirty King Company riflemen retreated all the way to the 3rd Battalion command post. A virtual rabble, they informed everyone in earshot that they were the only men to survive the dismemberment of their company. One of them happened to be the King Company commander, who was ordered to re-form the stragglers and rejoin the fight around the howitzers.

The rifle-battalion command post was itself fired on through the night. One of the casualties was Lieutenant Colonel Bill Reilly, who took a round in the leg but refused relief offered by his executive officer.

Love Company, on a hill overlooking the northeast corner of the artillery perimeter, held despite furious assaults by massed PLA infantry.

The Chinese continued to apply severe pressure against the Able Battery perimter through the night, and Baker Battery had several heart-stopping assaults with which to contend. Though they lost some important high ground, the riflemen and gunners in the central sector slowly built up their positions and held the Chinese to their initial gains.

★

Captain Harvey Galloway, the 31st Infantry's regimental surgeon, had spent the hours since dusk pondering the reasons why his serial of the medical-company convoy was proceeding with its headlights full ablaze. A veteran of armored combat in Europe, Dr. Galloway had never advanced at night with lights shining, though it was true that he had never been driven along narrow mountain tracks as treacherous as the MSR.

Lights or no, Dr. Galloway's medical-company vehicles managed to miss the turnoff into the schoolhouse compound that was serving as the 31st Infantry's operations center. It had been a cold, grueling drive from the Fusen Reservoir, and the lead driver must have been thoroughly exhausted, too tired to watch for a turnoff about which he might well have known nothing.

It was dead on midnight when Harvey Galloway noticed that his jeep was falling well behind the truck directly in front of it. Before he could say a thing to the driver, however, the jeep's headlights caught the movement of a log being speared across the roadway by Chinese bushwackers. The driver braked suddenly, then was shot in the arm as machine-gun fire sprayed the length of the small column. Dr. Galloway took rounds up his right side: one in the leg, two in the arm, one in the brain.

Fully conscious, and aware of just which parts of his body were affected by the brain shot, Galloway felt only relief as the injured driver threw the jeep into low-low gear and ground forward over the impeding log. He soon outran the Chinese fire and sped to the command post of the 3rd Battalion, 31st, where the badly wounded surgeon was given rudimentary first aid and set aside, to survive or die, as luck would have it.

The following vehicles were trapped, and there were precious few men aboard who had been trained to fight. Casualties were frightful.

Captain Clifton Hancock, the medical-service officer in charge of the medical-company convoy, nearly missed the ambush because he had been attending to the company mess truck which had broken down outside of Hagaru-ri. He had found the regimental operations center, but was sent on to catch up with the rest of the medical-company convoy. His jeep drove into the fight, headlights ablaze.

Hancock jumped to the roadway as his driver simultaneously braked and doused the lights. There he found several enlisted soldiers and the company first sergeant, who briefed him. One of the men, who had played possum for a time, said that he had seen Chinese soldiers shooting the wounded at the head of the column. Another man noted that the firing had abated as soon as Hancock's light came into view. But it was clearly picking up again.

The captain and the able-bodied troopers got the vehicles at the rear of the column turned, gathered in all the wounded they could find, and roared off to the regimental operations center. In all, a dozen men reached safety.

One of the men awakened by the clamor of Clif Hancock's return was Brigadier General Henry Hodes, the 7th Division assistant commander. Upon hearing the medical-service captain's story, Hodes asked that the 3rd Battalion, 31st, be ordered to dispatch a relief force; he had no idea that Reilly's battalion was under attack, so could not understand why the urgent message went unacknowledged.

The scene in and around the operations center was, given the circumstances, fairly unreal.

The regimental commander, Colonel MacLean, had been there for most of the evening, but he had departed in just enough time to miss being caught on the road when the Chinese closed in. The executive officer was in Hamhung with the regimental rear-echelon Command of the operations center and — in the absence of word of or from Colonel MacLean — command of the regiment was in the hands of the Regimental Operations Officer, Lieutenant Colonel

Barry Anderson. While General Hodes was the senior man anywhere near the Reservoir, it would have been unusual for one of his
rank to intercede in what then appeared to be the routine operations
of a subordinate command.

Barry Anderson, who was seen by his subordinates as being a
rather overbearing individual, had just been promoted lieutenant
colonel. Considering that he had served with the regiment for well
over a year, he had made himself thoroughly unbearable during the
previous week by chastising the many subordinates who had made
the natural error of addressing him as "Major," the title by which he
had been known until only a week earlier. Anderson always acted
in a decisive, correct manner when there were seniors present, but
he did nothing — nothing at all — this night despite the presence of
the assistant division commander.

Though units a few miles to the north were being severely mauled
by a determined enemy, men like the still-shaken Clif Hancock
were left to their own devices. Captain Hancock spent the rest of the
night in the schoolhouse courtyard, warming himself before a blaze
in a fifty-five-gallon fuel drum; no one suggested that he spend it
otherwise. As far as Hancock could tell, no one else seemed the least
bit anxious about being isolated in a school compound with no
strong infantry force standing guard.

The Chinese did not molest Lieutenant Colonel Barry Anderson
that night, and he did nothing to molest them.

★

Battles east of the Reservoir raged and ebbed through the long
cold night. Men died. Others broke.

PART FOUR

November 28

CHAPTER
15

No sunrise could ever have been more ardently prayed into being by so many men-at-arms as was the sunrise that slowly lighted the battlefield that was Yudam-ni.

As the hooded light of dawn brightened, the carnage that greeted the eyes of attacker and defender alike was appalling, utterly, unmistakably appalling. Pyres burned at odd spots around and along the narrow perimeter. Blood and human viscera lay everywhere. Here and there, blood feuds raged hot and deadly. Elsewhere, a numb, numbing silence descended upon the living as the dead were identified and mourned.

Corporal Barney Baxter rose stiffly from behind his heavy machine gun on Easy/5's line and stretched his cramped legs and back muscles. Nearby the wailing of a horribly mutilated Chinese soldier was stilled when a nervous Marine, unable to bear more of the horrid screaming, pulled a .45-caliber pistol from his belt and stalked forward into the killing ground to fire a single round into the dying man's head. Barney Baxter witnessed the killing, and felt only a faint revulsion.

The dawn was not quite beautiful, but men who had been so close to death in the night reveled in its heatless light. The clouds of the previous day had broken up to reveal a stunning blue sky. Inevitably, Marines not encumbered with carrying off the wounded or fixing up foxholes kindled little cook fires and began frying foul brew for their intimate coffee klatches.

Barney Baxter warmed his innards over such a tiny fire, then ventured to the front to see what he could see. A veteran of combat on Choiseul, Guam, and Iwo, Baxter had long since become inured to the sight of death, though he was thankful to be spared the smell of it by the deep-freeze atmosphere that pervaded the butchering ground. What he saw that morning, however, shook him anew.

Picking his way just twenty-five or thirty yards into the field of fire covered only by his one heavy machine gun, Baxter stared at the corpses of more Chinese soldiers than he could have counted. Mainly he saw young boys who looked as though they were sleeping. Others had been torn apart by bullets and hand grenades, and lay now in pools of crimson ice and ribbons of gray-brown bowels. The oddest realization of all was how very many of the dead lay in neat rows, almost ranks, mown down side by side in attacking files, comrades soldiering in death.

Unable to bear more than a few moments gawking at the dead, Baxter shuffled back to his gun, which needed careful attention. He noted that many of the Marines who had been avid collectors of memorabilia in previous fighting had forsaken such activities this pallid morning.

★

The fighting around the valley of Yudam-ni did not end with the dawn. Most particularly, it did not end on the eastern perimeter, where remnants of Dog and Easy Companies, 7th Marines, remained locked in combat with the last of their attackers.

It was by merest coincidence that elements of Charlie Company, 1st Battalion, 5th, a reserve unit from the Salt Lake City area, reached the summit of Hill 1282 as the last-gasp counterattack by the last organized elements of Easy/7 was being turned aside by the Chinese victors of the nightlong mauling match.

Originally deployed to support Taplett's 3rd Battalion, 5th, a bit to the north of Hill 1282, one platoon of Charlie/5 had been sent at midnight to Hill 1240 to help Dog/7. The remainder of the support company was sent in the traces of two Able/5 platoons that had begun their ascent of Hill 1282 much earlier.

The bobtailed company hurriedly picked its way across the broken moonscape, stopping stragglers and wounded Easy/7 Marines to ask directions and learn more about the nature of the fighting. It was tedious work, and it took Charlie/5 a good two hours, until 0430, to get within range of the killing ground at the summit. The point man, Captain Jack Jones, knew he had arrived when he was greeted by a long burst of machine-gun fire.

Jones made contact with Staff Sergeant Dan Murphy about one hundred yards below the summit of the hill. By that time Murphy's small group of Easy/5 riflemen had been pushed onto a spur to the right of what had been the company main line. A little farther on was 2nd Lieutenant Nick Trapnell's unengaged platoon of Able/5. Murphy was at that point attempting to re-form about twenty Easy/7 Marines for a stand across the center of the spur. He told Captain Jones that he thought other Easy/7 people were on the far side of the summit, possibly with survivors of another Able/5 platoon that had followed Trapnell's up from the valley floor hours before.

The main body of Charlie/5 could not have been operating under worse conditions. Not one of the men had seen the ground in daylight, and not one knew the effect supporting fire might have upon friendly troops who might or might not be hiding or holding isolated positions indeterminate distances beyond an enemy force of unknown size. Charlie/5 had already taken casualties from the heavy fire that had raked the single file of men on the approaches to the summit, and the darkness had thrown the organization into a state of mild chaos.

Time slipped away. Captain Jones deployed his two rifle platoons. Charlie/5's 60mm mortars were sited, and firm communications were established with the battalion 81mm mortar platoon in the valley. Word was received that friendly aircraft were on the way from Yonpo, the big coastal air base, but they would not be on station until first light. Captain Jones opted to wait until he could see what he was doing.

Sunrise was an omen. One of the first things Marines in the valley and on the ridges saw were flights of Marine Corsair fighter-bombers and Navy AD Skyraider attack bombers.

As Charlie/5 waited pensively while friendly aircraft made repeated runs on the Chinese-held portions of the summit, Nick Trapnell's platoon of Able/5, which was guarding the rear approaches, was treated to an incredible display of airmanship. Lying on their stomachs a foot or two below the spur's razor spine, Trapnell and his riflemen watched what they might have taken for a blue-painted shark's fin whizzing by from left to right. It was the wing tip of a Marine Corsair scraping off its load of napalm to fry Chinese soldiers on the reverse slope.

As the last of the attack aircraft pulled up and away, Captain Jones led Charlie/5 against a company of the 1st Battalion, 235th PLA Regiment. Fifty Chinese armed with submachine guns and hand grenades stood to receive an assault, forcing the attacking Marines to charge uphill into the face of a murderous fire.

Marines closed to within arm's length of the defenders and fought as brutal a hand-to-hand struggle as had characterized all the fighting that had thus far taken place on Hill 1282. The 1st Battalion, 235th PLA Regiment had been ground to dust during the night. The fifty men holding the summit were all that remained, and they were blown to the winds by Charlie/5 and the last Easy/7 Marines under Staff Sergeant Murphy. The last fresh platoon of Able/5 arrived up the rear slope to complete the job and pry through the rubble to sort out the dead and wounded.

First Lieutenant John Yancey emerged from the dead. He was bleeding from untreated shrapnel wounds across the bridge of his nose and in the roof of his mouth. His jaw had been shattered by a .45-caliber bullet, and one eye was whirling crazily in its socket. The former Marine Raider requested relief from the first Charlie/5 officer he could find. Then, quitting the battle, John Yancey led thirty-five walking-wounded Marines slowly down the defile toward the valley.

★

The fight to wrest victory on Hill 1240 was going less well.

Daylight found twice-wounded Captain Milt Hull in tenuous possession of the lower slope with sixteen Dog/7 survivors. Chinese from the 3rd Battalion, 236th PLA Regiment, were firing from every direction and mounting limited assaults on Marines who stood back to back to meet them.

The only reinforcement that could be spared to retake Hill 1240 was 2nd Lieutenant Harold Dawe's 3rd Platoon of Charlie/5. The platoon had been dispatched from the vicinity of Hill 1384 at 0400, but had been delayed repeatedly as it struggled across the jumbled terrain in pitch-darkness.

Dawe's platoon was hotly engaged far short of Hull's position by numerous unseen Chinese. Fighting an uphill battle, Dawe missed Hull's tiny enclave and had to backtrack. When the two groups combined, they mustered less than fifty men, many of whom were wounded and all of whom were exhausted. Still, bolstered by Milt Hull's unrelenting determination, the small force fought its way clear to the summit of Hill 1240 against diminishing odds. Gaining a good position on the northeastern spur, however, Lieutenant Dawe spotted very large groups of PLA infantry massing for a counterassault. He had no communications with supporting arms, and very little hope of holding, but he was in as strong a position as he could manage by the time the Chinese struck at 1100. It was clearly a losing proposition, however, and all the Marines on Hill 1240 backpedaled off the summit to a more defensible position one hundred fifty yards downslope. They held there, harassed by the Chinese, but not seriously threatened.

★

Care of the wounded was, by far, the most serious problem facing the shocked Marine battalions in the valley of Yudam-ni.

A few of the wounded were flown out aboard helicopters, the only aircraft that could land. That was an ordeal in itself, but vastly preferable to remaining within the embattled Yudam-ni perimeter to be treated or passed over by a medical delivery system that was being overwhelmed.

Sergeant Jim Matthews, the Fox/5 rocket-section chief whose armpit had been gouged out by a sniper's bullet, had spent a harrowing few hours of the night getting to the sick bay of the 3rd Battalion, 11th. There, most of the wounded had to sleep on the bare, frozen earth, though several managed to flake out on stretchers. A stove was kept burning until a severely misguided soul made off with the fuel. The twelve-man pyramidal tent, which reeked with the rank odor of an abattoir, had dozens upon dozens of men in it. Jim Matthews received no treatment, though he was certain that men had who were hurt more seriously than he was.

When it was light enough for him to find his way around, Matthews shuffled into a long chow line, from which he was able to see innumerable wounded Marines stretched under a tarpaulin out on the bare ground. As the line moved slowly forward, orderlies moved among the reposing wounded and brushed the rime of wind-whipped snow from their faces. Here and there, dead men were pulled out from under the tarp and stacked like cordwood on a growing pile.

The scene was so ghastly that Jim Matthews found himself incapable of reacting strongly one way or the other.

★

Though dawn came to thousands as welcome respite from the travail of the surprise night assaults, there was much work to be done if the Yudam-ni perimeter was to be held. Fortunately the sun also brought out a steady stream of Marine, Navy, and Australian aircraft from bases near the coast and carriers at sea. And that, more than anything else, forced the Chinese to proceed with caution.

Still, very serious fighting continued well into the new day, particularly on and about the rim of hills to the east and southeast of the central village.

C H A P T E R
16

Charlie/7 was mousetrapped during the night in a roadside draw about three miles up the MSR between Yudam-ni and Toktong Pass.

The company's position was well known to the 1st Battalion, 7th, which had eaten its Thanksgiving dinner there on November 25. The feeding of nearly one thousand Marines had resulted in a vast, bizarre litter of turkey carcasses on and by the roadway. The hill, 1419 on official maps, would be known evermore to Lieutenant Colonel Ray Davis's troops as Turkey Hill.

Charlie/7 was short a platoon, which had been kept back to guard the regimental CP. Because the company lacked adequate manpower to provide an all-around defense, Captain John Morris placed his truncated company on a crescent-shaped line in a deep draw giving out onto the MSR on Turkey Hill's northwest slope. The position had been used earlier in the week by two batteries of the 3rd Battalion, 11th, and was riddled by bulldozed gun emplacements and command and sleeping holes. Morris deployed the bulk of his Marines within the former artillery position, then sent a reinforced squad farther up the hill to guard the draw from the rear.

★

The Chinese struck Charlie/7 at 0230, November 28, five hours after the first massed assaults careered into stronger Marine positions in and about the valley.

Though Charlie/7 Marines heard heavy gunfire from the valley for most of the night, the Chinese caught the right platoon by surprise. The right center was quickly driven in, and only the immediate commitment of the reserve squad and several mortar gunners prevented a permanent rift in the line. The Chinese were chased from the Marine fighting holes they had taken, but at heavy cost to the defenders.

The Chinese then shifted farther to the right, but were driven back.

Pressure soon began mounting against the understrength left platoon. The company radio was disabled, leaving only the forward observer's radio for communication with the outside. First Lieuten-

ant Joe Glasgow, George Battery's senior representative with Char-
lie/7, used the link to good advantage by placing small 105mm
concentrations on staging areas on all sides of the company. Glasgow's precision work was hampered, however, by the effect of the
sub-zero weather on the guns. Sluggish lubricants quadrupled the
time it took to get a gun back in battery each time it was fired, and
frozen propellants and fuses resulted in numerous shorts, overs, and
duds. Gunners in the valley did everything they could to support
Charlie Company, but that was very little indeed.

The company mortars made up the difference. One of the 60s had
a cracked baseplate and should not have been used, but the situation
was critical, and one of the gunners held the tube in his hands while
others chucked in rounds as fast as they could.

There were not enough riflemen, so Captain Morris stripped the
machine-gun and mortar sections, then committed nearly all of his
headquarters people. The line held, but barely. In two hours of
close-in grappling, all of the headquarters troops were killed or
wounded, as were several gunners and a significant portion of the
understrength platoon they had been sent to stiffen.

The seesaw struggle raged unabated past sunrise.

Oddly, the new dawn found Marines on the unassailed right extremity of the line fast asleep. They had not been molested for hours,
so their platoon leader had allowed about half of them to remove
footgear and crawl into sleeping bags. These men were caught flat-
footed — and barefoot — for the second time in five hours.

Private First Class Walker Merell, a twenty-year-old Ohio Reservist who had served with the company mortars until a week earlier,
when a tiff with the section officer had resulted in his transfer to a
rifle platoon, awakened to a torrent of fire from Chinese positions on
the high ground to his rear. Merell leaped from his sleeping bag and
yanked on his frozen shoepacs amidst a shower of bullets that was
snapping off twigs and chopping up the scrubby ground cover just
over his head. Before he could lace his slippery shoepacs, however,
Merell was driven from his fighting hole, forced to tuck his rifle
close to his body and roll away downhill.

Coming to rest on his back, Merell saw several Chinese flit across
a break in the skyline. He steadied his rifle and got off only one
round before a bullet penetrated his right shoulder and upper arm,
damaging the radial nerve, forcing him to release his heavy weapon.

Merell heard a Marine downslope yell, "I'm hit!" and yelled back,
"So am I!" The other Marine complained anew: "I'm hit again. I'm
hit in the other arm!"

Walker Merell rolled farther downhill in the hope of finding some cover. A burp-gun bullet spanged against the frozen earth, its steel jacket thudding into the Ohio Marine's left forearm. When the fire slackened a bit, Merell staggered clumsily to his feet and dogtrotted to a deep hole near the center of the perimeter. He could feel nothing below his right shoulder, did not realize that his right glove had slipped from his immobilized right hand, exposing the insensate fingers to the freezing cold air.

Charlie/7 was saved by the sun. Alerted to the company's plight by Joe Glasgow's calls for artillery support, Ray Davis got word to senior tactical air coordinators that air support was vitally needed in the vicinity of Turkey Hill.

When Walker Merell glanced downslope toward the MSR, he could see four Australian F-51 fighter-bombers sweep in low over a farmhouse compound the Chinese were using for a command post and rallying point. The Aussies, popping into view across the mouth of the draw long after the roar of their dives rolled across the ground, dropped silvery canisters of napalm on the Chinese massing by the farm buildings. Great billows of dark, oily flame mushroomed skyward, incinerating the attackers. One by one, the Aussies pulled up and roared off toward Yudam-ni, a few seconds' flying time farther on.

And so it went. The squad that had been sent to guard the uphill end of the draw had not been heard from since the company command radio had been damaged. Captain Morris called for a volunteer to guide the squad to the main position. Corporal Curtis Kiesling scaled the boulder-strewn hillside and disappeared from view for a few anxious moments. "No sign of them," he called as he swung into view and moved to the left to continue the search. A Chinese machine gunner caught Kiesling as he worked around a rock outcropping, and he tumbled into the draw, dead.

It was a hard decision, but Captain Morris ordered that further efforts to locate the lost outpost were beyond acceptable risk. The main body of the company was in dire straits: short on all types of ammunition, lacking reliable communications, burdened with casualties that, by 1000 hours, topped fifty wounded and fifteen killed.

★

It took guts to release the balance of Ray Davis's 1st Battalion, 7th, to save Charlie/7, and the guts it took belonged to Homer Litzenberg. Releasing Davis meant uncovering the southern sector of the perimeter that had been forming along the rim of the valley since before sunrise. There was no question but that a rescue effort would be mounted, though Litz would have been forgiven some wavering and waffling. The decision was made without hesitation, however, and Lieutenant Colonel Davis was free to leave as soon as head-quarters and service troops could be moved to cover the gap in the line.

First Lieutenant Gene Hovatter's Able/7 moved first. The company was to march as far along the MSR as it could manage, then swing into the hills to the west as soon as it ran into trouble. The attack would be delivered cross-country until Able/7 had passed beyond Turkey Hill. At the same time, 1st Lieutenant Joe Kurcaba's Baker/7, still a little rocky from being ambushed in those same hills the previous afternoon, was to follow Hovatter down the MSR, then drive along the slopes to the east. It too was to pass beyond Turkey Hill and link up with Hovatter south of Charlie Company's perime-ter. Both companies would then contract against the Chinese sur-rounding Morris's troops. If all went well, Davis had the option of moving on to relieve Fox/7 at Toktong Pass, but he had to be back in Yudam-ni no later than dusk, no matter what.

It was, given the circumstances, a sanguine plan. Far from merely relieving Charlie Company, Davis's mandate envisaged the destruc-tion of a large PLA force, quite possibly the same force that had bested each of his companies on three successive days. The battal-ion commander's incredible sangfroid was his unit's most important edge.

Considering the fury of the night attacks and the numbers of PLA infantry known to be in the area, the initial thrust by the main body of the 1st Battalion, 7th, met surprisingly little opposition. The lead Able Company platoon managed to hike a mile up the road before long-range machine-gun fire forced it to move to the left. Breasting the first rise off the road, the same platoon surprised the crews of two machine guns as they were getting ready to ambush the relief force on the road. A quick, sharp fight claimed the lives of all the Chinese gunners, but it also brought the wrath of fresh Chinese units down upon Able/7.

Forced by the Chinese to move under fire across the steep hills and deep draws west of the MSR, Able Company slowed to a crawl. Baker Company deployed on the lower rises to the right of the road-way, but it was hampered by snipers and long-range machine-gun fire and could not move much faster than its sister unit.

Meantime, Charlie Company's position was deteriorating. The Chinese maintained steady pressure and inflicted additional casu-alties. Without a reliable radio, Captain Morris was unable to direct close air support, nor was he able to provide any directions for the sister companies as they ground slowly toward him through the hills. Ray Davis spent a good deal of his time urging his riflemen forward and ordering up air and artillery support, but no amount of nail-biting or fury could move the battalion faster.

The hours dragged by. It was clear that Davis would not be able to relieve Fox/7 at the Pass; it was becoming doubtful that he would even have Charlie Company safely away by the dusk deadline.

At length, Able/7 was stopped by a Chinese company occupying the last finger ridge between itself and Charlie Company. Heavy support could not be used to soften the Chinese position for fear of dropping overs upon Morris's troops.

The ball dropped into the hands of Able/7's mortar officer, 2nd Lieutenant William Davis, a seasoned veteran who had been over the ground enough during the preceding week to have the ranges memorized. The trick was to lay rounds upon the steep reverse slope without placing overs into the tiny Charlie Company enclave just behind. The two operable guns began on the left, then slowly walked fire to the right, toward the roadway. Two rifle platoons attacked in the wake of the fire, shaking the Chinese loose, rolling them up from left to right.

The assault was a classic. Marine riflemen followed hard upon the bursting 60mm rounds, grappling with the slower Chinese. One of the Able Company riflemen, a giant black Marine known as "Ivan the Terrible," unhooked a long-handled axe he always affected, swung it in long, sweeping arcs, crushed skulls and severed vital appendages. The few Chinese who tried to stand soon broke and ran. As the Marines gained the summit of the finger ridge, they paused to take careful aim at the backs of the fleeing enemy, who surged onto ground that could be reached by Baker Company from across the road.

A division of Corsairs roared out of the evening gloom and blasted the scattering Chinese with guns and rockets.

Lieutenant Davis ordered one of his 60s forward. Its crew fired a white phosphorous round by line of sight, hitting a knot of Chinese scrabbling into a wooded area. One of the Corsair pilots mistook the splash of white phosphorous for a marker round and planted a napalm tank in the midst of the Chinese, killing as many as forty.

While the assault companies cleared pockets of Chinese around the draw, the detached Charlie/7 platoon arrowed into the lines of what had been the bulk of its parent unit and got right to work moving the dozens of dead and wounded toward the MSR. In all, fifteen of the defenders were able to walk out unassisted. Only four of the fifteen Marines manning the detached outpost in the rear of the company position returned.

Trucks from Yudam-ni were driven into a turnaround carved out five days earlier by artillery bulldozers, and the wounded were rushed straight to the overcrowded casualty clearing stations in town.

Private First Class Walker Merell, who had been shot through the shoulder at sunrise, did not receive even rudimentary first aid until nearly midnight. Because his arm had been left insensate by the wound, Merell had not been able to feel — and had been too excited in the course of the battle to see — that the fingers of his gloveless right hand were severely frostbitten. He and other wounded Marines were led into a darkened tent and left to find space on the packed, straw-covered earthen floor. The lucky few who habitually carried snacks in their pockets had their only meal of the day. Others, like Walker Merell, did not.

C H A P T E R

17

The Yudam-ni garrison's most significant characteristic on the morning of November 28, 1950, was that it was not a "garrison" at all.

There was a force comprised of two Marine regiments and the bulk of three artillery battalions. No one person was in charge of the whole, nor did any one person have a clear mandate to take charge.

The two regiments and their supports had divergent missions. The 5th Marines was to advance up the road to the west and link up with 8th Army — an organization which had ceased to be an effective fighting force two days earlier. There was no longer any reason for the 5th to attack westward, and it could not do so. But no one at X Corps knew there was no reason, and the stunning effect of the nightlong battles took most of the day to crystallize into a definitive realization that Yudam-ni was the end of the road.

The 7th Marines was in Yudam-ni to hold the valley and rest. The two battalions and two companies of the regiment arrayed around Yudam-ni could not have held the valley themselves against the People's Liberation Army divisions on the high ground. It was evident by first light that the 7th was in serious straits, but it took time before a solution could be perceived. Most of the time was spent getting around to the conclusion that a solution was required.

No organization was in control, not even Division. The commanding general, O. P. Smith, had no idea how deeply involved were his forward regiments, and his senior staff was scattered over sixty-four miles of mountain roads, moving toward a consolidation at Hagaru-ri, but not yet moved, not yet consolidated, not yet able to function. Division did not know a thing about the gravity of the situation at Yudam-ni, nor, yet, did the 5th and 7th Regiments.

★

Nowhere is the slow dawning of reality better illustrated than in several late-morning radio exchanges involving Lieutenant Colonel Hal Roise, the bluff, combative commander of the 2nd Battalion, 5th.

After seeing to the consolidation of his battalion's position on the north side of the road leading west from Yudam-ni, Roise called in his staff and set it to work preparing for the day's advance into the Taebeks. The 2nd Battalion, 5th, had fought and won a fierce night battle, but it had no inkling as to the severity of Chinese attacks elsewhere around Yudam-ni. The battalion had seen a lot of confusion that night, and it was mightily surprised at the number of Chinese it had bested. All in all, the battalion was tough, resolute, and ready for more.

Captain Sam Jaskilka, Easy/5's commander, reported to Hal Roise with all the necessary statistics. Basically, the report said: We don't have bullets. We're out of hand grenades. Medical supplies are short. We need food. The troops are worn out and some key people have been hurt or killed. What are my orders?

Roise's reply rocked the company commander back on his heels, releasing a flood of emotion dammed up through the night and morning: "Re-form and attack!" Jaskilka smiled through a film of tears and nodded confirmation to the men around him: Re-form and attack!

But, when Roise passed a summary of his battalion's condition along to Regiment, he was told to stand by for further orders. A while later, he was given a set of map coordinates and told to move the battalion. A quick check revealed that the new position was to the *rear*. Roise asked if an error had been made. No, no error; the battalion was to move to positions screening the northern end of the valley of Yudam-ni and prepare a defensive position.

Hal Roise was astounded.

★

Two men were responsible for the simple plan that made the valley of Yudam-ni defensible. Colonel Homer Litzenberg, the senior Marine in the valley, took charge. And Major Hank Woessner, Litz's operations officer, wrote the plans and orders. Woessner's plan, issued at about noon, was, in a word, realistic.

Charged with defending as large a piece of ground as possible against as large an enemy force as was imaginable, Woessner's first priority was to give ground and consolidate his limited resources.

Roise's battalion, holding a line of low rises on North Ridge, was not in physical contact with any other Marine unit, a condition brought on by the loss of Hill 1403 by How/7 during the night. Both of Roise's flanks were dangling, and the battalion had to be brought into firm contact with units on either side. That meant relinquishing North Ridge to the Chinese and pulling the 2nd Battalion, 5th, back to a line stretching from the MSR north of town to Hill 1426. At the same time, Lieutenant Colonel Bob Taplett's 3rd Battalion, 5th, was ordered to withdraw from positions on Hill 1384 and shift back to cover the ground from Roise's right to the far side of Hill 1282. Lieutenant Colonel Jack Stevens's 1st Battalion, 5th, which had been fragmented in order to stabilize the Marine positions on Hills 1282 and 1240, was pulled to its right and sent into positions centering on Hill 1240. That meant that a unified, integrated 5th Marine Regiment was covering half the perimeter on a continuous line around the northern end of the valley.

The 7th Marines had about as much ground to cover as the 5th, but it had to do so with fewer companies, four of which had lost numerous casualties in the spectacular night fighting. How/7 was down to about one hundred effectives, and Dog and Easy Companies barely mustered that number when taken together; the fate of Charlie/7, trapped three miles up the MSR at Turkey Hill, still hung in the balance.

Lieutenant Colonel Bill Harris's 3rd Battalion, 7th, was tied in on Roise's left, charged with defending the ground between Hills 1426 and 1100. Ray Davis's 1st Battalion, 7th, which spent the entire day extricating Charlie/7 from the Turkey Hill fight, was to fill in between Harris's left and Hill 1276, overlooking the MSR south of town. All that remained, then, was to fill a gap between Davis, on the southwestern line, and Stevens, on the eastern line.

Well before noon, Major Woessner hit upon the idea of restoring the 7th Marines to its typical three-cornered configuration by forming what he called a "2nd Provisional Battalion." This unit comprised the remnants of Dog and Easy Companies, 7th, which had been so brutally handled during the night and early morning. The new unit, which was initially filled out with some headquarters and special troops from the 7th Marines, was placed on a short arc on the southwestern curve of the perimeter. Its left was initially tied in with Stevens's battalion, but its right dangled well short of the MSR, where it was to tie in with Davis's battalion. George/7 was detached from Harris's battalion and shifted to Davis's left to plug the gap. That still left a mighty thin line of infantrymen in the sector, so Major Fox Parry's 3rd Battalion, 11th, the artillery unit nearest the provisional battalion, was ordered to provide troops to screen a short stretch of the line between Stevens's right and the provisional battalion's left. The provisional battalion was placed in the able hands of Major Hal Roach, who had become Litzenberg's logistics officer when replaced two weeks earlier by the more senior Bill Harris as commander of the 3rd Battalion, 7th. Though Roach had no staff, he drew heavily upon the good will of many of Harris's staffers.

A good deal of ground and several dominating heights had to be sacrificed, but the result was a compact perimeter that could be manned adequately by the troops on hand. Manpower deficiencies in rifle units were to be made good by drafts from service and support units, primarily the three artillery battalions. These provided provisional rifle platoons, some of which were formed on a fairly permanent basis, while most appeared for brief periods in response to specific needs.

★

Two factors contributed to the successful consolidation at Yudam-ni on November 28. The first was Lieutenant Colonel Ray Murray's decision, in the absence of orders, to abandon his regiment's drive to the west. It took Murray several hours to sift through enough data to arrive at the decision, and he preferred a "postponement" to an outright cancellation. But it was obvious to all, once the news was in, that the 5th Marines had no business advancing an inch beyond the valley of Yudam-ni.

The second factor leading to the successful joint tenancy was an at-first tacit agreement by the regimental commanders to coordinate and integrate the defense. Since neither had a clear mandate to take charge, both allowed the conventions of rank to move them toward a solution. Homer Litzenberg, at 47, had been a Marine since 1922 and an officer since 1925. Ray Murray was 37, a member of the Basic School Class of 1936. Litz was a very senior full colonel, Murray a very senior lieutenant colonel. They did not know each other well, having met for the very first time in September, on the Inchon-Seoul Highway.

Withal, Litzenberg was reticent about exerting complete control. Some think he did not want the responsibility, but there is nothing in his character to give that impression. After being contacted by Colonel Litzenberg, Murray had the distinct impression that the older man's offer to establish a "joint command" was a courtly gesture, and highly complimentary. By day's end, the two regimental command posts had been set up side by side, and staffers from each regiment were working alongside or in firm contact with their opposites in the sister regiment. For all that, however, it became clear early on that Litz and his staff would dominate.

It was hoped by many that Division would send an officer senior to both regimental commanders, thus relieving them of the added burden of negotiating rather than commanding.

★

The better part of three artillery battalions — sixty-seven percent of the 11th Regiment's guns — was emplaced near Yudam-ni by nightfall on November 27. Their orientations reflected their differing missions. Lieutenant Colonel Harvey Feehan's 1st Battalion, 11th, was pointed westward to support the expected drive by the 5th Marines in that direction. Two batteries of Major Fox Parry's 3rd Battalion were aimed southwest and south to support the 7th Marines' sweep to clear the hills rimming the valley. And Major Bill McReynolds's 4th Battalion, the division's 155mm general-support battalion, was scattered in all directions to cover the entire valley and its environs with long-range fires. Until the Chinese attacks began, there was no need to coordinate the battalions. And, until dawn, there was no opportunity.

At first, no one gave much thought to coordinating the artillery. Harvey Feehan, the senior battalion commander, made no attempt to bring Parry and McReynolds under his control. Fox Parry, who was marginally junior to the recently promoted Feehan, was less reticent than Feehan about expressing his opinions.

Fox Parry was 32, the son of a Philadelphia judge, the product of several fine private schools. He had played lacrosse and wrestled for Navy, and had graduated from Annapolis in early 1941, a member of the academy's first accelerated wartime class. He had put in for the Marine Corps simply because the Basic School had been located at the Navy Yard adjacent to his native Philadelphia; his class, however, had been the first to train at Quantico, in Virginia. Initial combat for the tall, solid, athletic Parry had been at Guadalcanal, where he rose from forward observer to battery commander. He later served at Okinawa, and had been in combat with the 3rd Battalion, 11th, all the way up from Inchon. He was one of Homer Litzenberg's most trusted confidants.

When Parry realized that no plan for integrating artillery coverage for the entire perimeter would be forthcoming from Feehan, he boldly approached Litzenberg and suggested the formation of an artillery groupment incorporating all the guns under one commander. Litz readily agreed, and called the three artillery battalion commanders to his tent to discuss the matter. In the end, of course, Feehan was given command, but it was clear that Fox Parry had the colonel's ear. It was a fairly blatant political act, but it got the ball rolling.

Many of the guns had to be moved. One of McReynolds's batteries had been under Parry's command for weeks and had gone into position with Parry's 105s. It had to be moved across the valley. Other guns merely had to be turned, though a great deal of bulldozing and blasting was required for even the simplest of moves.

The forward observers from the 105mm batteries remained with the rifle companies to which they were normally assigned, and they remained in touch with their own fire-direction centers. However, because the alignment of the guns did not match the deployment of the rifle units, fire-direction centers from any given battery stood a good chance of having to control the fires of a strange battery or two. It was an imperfect arrangement, but superior to the alternatives.

Despite the look of the artillery plan on paper, there were serious deficiencies that could not be overcome by a command accommodation. The most serious was the shortage of ammunition. Parry had been prevented from moving four thousand reserve rounds from Hagaru-ri, and he had fired a good deal of what he had had on hand during the night. Feehan had more rounds on hand than Parry; he was willing to share, but he also had more guns than Parry, and his stocks were limited in any case.

The second greatest problem, which helped ameliorate the ammunition shortages in a most negative way, was the effect of the cold upon the guns. Lubricants became sluggish, and it took as long as three minutes for recoil mechanisms to bring a gun back into battery.

These conditions combined to defeat the purpose of modern artillery, which is designed to place masses of fire upon relatively defenseless enemy infantry. The more rounds the artillery can put out in the least amount of time, the better it is doing its job. Often as not, a critical call for massed artillery would bring forth a desultory four or eight rounds. The gunners were as frustrated as the infantry by the limitations imposed by supply and nature.

Many of the rounds that were on hand were also affected by the cold. The solid propellants became unreliable, so range became a matter of luck. That meant overs that would not hit the enemy, and shorts that would maim or kill friends.

Many Marine positions on the eastern perimeter were on the reverse slopes of steep hills also occupied by PLA units. Artillery support had to be handled with surgical precision under such conditions, and the most appropriate technique was high-angle fire. Parry's battalion was not in the best position to support the units on the eastern rim, but his gunners had been handling high-angle missions all the way up the MSR, while Feehan's crews had little experience, if any, with the technique.

McReynolds's 155s presented a whole other set of problems. Because of their range, the 155s did not employ forward observers. Often as not their spotters were airborne. There was no airstrip at Yudam-ni, so there was no reliable spotting available for the 155s. Even if there had been aircraft available, most of the fighting was expected to take place at night when aerial observation was impossible. It was evident from the outset that McReynolds's battalion would be cannibalized first to provide needed infantry fillers.

It was most evident by the end of November 28 that the artillery would not play a significant role in the defense of Yudam-ni.

★

The shifting of thousands of Marines across the breadth of the valley did not go entirely as planned. The Chinese were fairly active despite the availability of American air support.

Following the stalemate achieved on Hill 1240 by the tiny remnant of Dog/7 and Dawe's platoon of Charlie/5, the 1st Battalion, 5th, was ordered to secure the hill with a fresh company. Lieutenant Colonel Stevens chose Baker/5, which had not yet been in action at Yudam-ni. This unit moved up the hill and relieved the beleaguered Marines there, but daylong fighting could not win it the summit of the hill mass. Artillery and air support could not budge the Chinese from bunkers they had quickly installed, and Baker/5 finally had to move back one hundred yards in order to dig in safely for the night.

Item/5, which was shifted from Hill 1384 to Hill 1282, where it relieved elements of Able/5 and Charlie/5, was forced to dig in under sporadic mortar and gunfire throughout the afternoon, and several probes had to be turned back. How/5, holding the approaches to Hill 1384, was fired on all day from the heights, but suffered no losses.

The withdrawal from North Ridge got the 2nd Battalion, 5th, and the 3rd Battalion, 7th, away from close contact with the Chinese, and the intervening valley served as an excellent buffer. There was almost no firing in that area during the day. Likewise, the southern line was not molested despite the absence of Davis's battalion.

★

No one believed that the Chinese would absent themselves during that second long night at Yudam-ni.

C H A P T E R

18

Much was done but little was resolved east of the Reservoir on November 28.

The intense fighting began letting up around dawn, though it was to be a hard, bloody day for the Army units scattered along the road.

Marine Captain Ed Stamford turned command of Able/32 over to an Army officer at sunrise and returned to his familiar role, calling strikes for the umbrella of Marine Corsairs that appeared over Lieutenant Colonel Don Faith's perimeter before first light. Chinese strongpoints hard by American lines were marked by rifle grenades and smoke, then blasted and riddled by bombs, rockets, napalm, and .50-caliber machine guns. A battery of Chinese 120mm mortars was sent packing by the air support and counterbattery by Faith's own 81s.

Both sides, it appeared, had suffered equally from the cold and confusion of the long night battle. Private First Class Jay Ransone ventured from his foxhole to see what he could see along the largely abandoned Able/32 line. He found a demoralized Chinese burp gunner alone in a captured foxhole. When Ransone leveled his rifle on the passive captive, the man pulled a fistful of family photos from his green quilted tunic and made entreating noises. Ransone was astounded to see that his prisoner was shod in flimsy canvas tennis shoes and cloth puttees.

Well to Ransone's right, elements of Charlie Company were battling furiously to retake a commanding knob from the Chinese. First Lieutenant Richard Moore's platoon mounted repeated attacks under Marine air support, and recovered a good deal of ground. But the knob overlooking the juncture of Able and Charlie Companies remained firmly in enemy hands. The attacks petered out when the battalion sergeant major was shot to death and Lieutenant Moore was hit square in the forehead and knocked cold by a spent machine-gun bullet. Charlie/32 had to content itself with a reverse slope defense, out of the line of fire of the many machine guns the Chinese had deployed on the key knob.

Far from having any thoughts about adhering to his orders for the day — the 1st Battalion, 32nd, was to have mounted a limited advance to the north — Don Faith had some early doubts that his battalion could even hold. Able Company, in particular, had lost many officers and noncoms, and many South Korean conscripts had simply melted away. Though the situation became stable, it would have been critical but for the air support.

★

Lieutenant General Ned Almond's two-place helicopter whirred in over the hills and touched down on a frozen rice paddy beside Don Faith's command compound at about 1400. The X Corps commander, bulked up in a new parka and pressed snow pants, flashed a huge smile as he stalked briskly into Faith's command post to ask detailed questions regarding the night battle and the condition of the battalion.

Anxious to give his report, Faith told the general that his battalion had been attacked during the night by elements of two PLA divisions. Almond, however, refused to give credence to the report. As other officers looked on and listened, he told Faith, "That's impossible. There aren't two Chinese Communist divisions in the whole of North Korea!"

After speaking for some time with Faith, the corps commander ambled back into the sunlight, where he reached absently into his parka pocket and withdrew a handful of Silver Star medals. Indicating that he would award one to the battalion commander, General Almond suggested that Faith call upon two of his subordinates to share in the goodies.

Don Faith was a general's son, and a West Pointer. He was a battle-hardened paratrooper, and he had served as an aide-de-camp to General Matthew Ridgway in Europe. He was one of the most promising young field officers in X Corps. If he did not screw up or die, Don Faith was assured of one day wearing stars upon his shoulders. His reaction to Almond's suggestion was totally out of character.

Worn down by the night's struggle, and seriously put off by the corps commander's falsely ebullient demeanor, Faith laconically called over the first two men he set eyes on. It was clear to observers that the colonel had no stomach for the general's game. One of the medals went to a platoon leader who had been wounded during the night, an officer who happened to be perched atop a water can beside the command post. He was, nevertheless, a decent choice for a Silver Star. The second man was a mess sergeant who happened to be walking by. The wounded lieutenant and the astounded mess sergeant were ordered to stand at attention while Faith called upon a dozen clerks, drivers, and walking wounded to act as witnesses. The battalion commander braced, accepted the award, and shook the general's hand, as did his two confused and embarrassed subordinates.

Unable to let the matter rest, the immaculately turned out general delivered a brief pep talk to the haggard, scruffy, battle-weary men in the rice paddy: "The enemy who is delaying you for the moment is nothing more than remnants of Chinese divisions fleeing north. We're still attacking and going all the way to the Yalu. Don't let a bunch of Chinese laundrymen stop you!"

Almond next pulled a map from his pocket, spread it out on the hood of a jeep, and held a quick conference with a fuming Don Faith. Then, without ever explaining where those Chinese divisions had come from, nor what had caused them to flee, Almond walked briskly to his waiting helicopter and sped from sight.

Don Faith tore the Silver Star medal from his parka and threw it to the ground.

★

About the only boost Faith received on November 28, aside from adequate air cover, was the arrival in his perimeter of Colonel Allen MacLean and the forward command group of the 31st Infantry.

Unmolested during the night, MacLean had stuck to his original command center during the morning, trying to re-establish contact with his 3rd Battalion and the schoolhouse operations center to the rear. He had been able to do neither, nor could scouts find a way into the 3rd Battalion lines. In the end, MacLean had elected to drive forward to seek the protection of Faith's battalion.

Colonel MacLean's arrival removed much of the onus of command from Don Faith's shoulders, a burden he was eminently equipped to handle but was by far better off without. There was little MacLean could do, but whatever happened would be his responsibility.

★

Lieutenant Colonel Bill Reilly's day started off just so-so. The commander of the scattered 3rd Battalion, 31st, emerged from the night fighting with a minor leg wound and an unrelenting confusion. Neither he nor any of his colleagues quite knew what had hit them. Marine air had forced the Chinese back early, but weak attempts to regain some of the crucial heights came to nothing.

Reilly's first order of business was stabilizing his position, counting noses, and consolidating his own battalion and the truncated 57th Field Artillery Battalion. The best ground, it appeared, was that which Able Battery and King Company had held in desperate night fighting. All of the infantry units were consolidated there, as was Baker Battery, which had spent the night laagered ("circle the wagons") several hundred yards to the south.

Bill Reilly was in his command tent sweating out preparations for renewed night fighting when he was interrupted by the whirr of helicopter blades and the news that the corps commander had arrived. Before Reilly could protest, he was lined up with several other men and presented with a Silver Star by Ned Almond. The ceremony was duly recorded for posterity by a *Stars & Stripes* cameraman (the photo was to be captioned a week later with Don Faith's name), then Reilly was treated to the general's ebullient brand of war reporting, getting much the same pep talk as had his colleague to the north.

Several of the more seriously wounded soldiers were brought out of the sick-bay tents and stuffed into escorting helicopters. One of the injured was Lieutenant Colonel Ray Embree, the commander of the 57th Field Artillery Battalion; he had been hit in the legs during the night fighting and, while not in critical condition, it was felt that he would do a lot better in the hospital at Hungnam. Another of the badly wounded was the 31st Infantry's Regimental Surgeon, Dr. Harvey Galloway, whose brain wound needed immediate attention if he was to survive. It was inevitable that the high proportion of officer evacuees would cause some dissension in the ranks.

Almond whirled off before sunset. He was due at a conference at GHQ-Tokyo, in Japan, and had a plane to catch at Yonpo. Bill Reilly hobbled back into his command tent and set out to make up the lost time.

★

Only one effort was made that day by rear units to reopen the road to the embattled battalions east of the Reservoir.

Brigadier General Henry Hodes, assistant commander of 7th Infantry Division, had little to go on. Communications with forward units were desultory, where they existed. It was nevertheless clear to Hodes that the road north of the operations center had been severed, though he had no idea who had cut it, nor in what strength.

The idea for a relief expedition mounted from the operations center would have been ludicrous but for the presence there of Captain Robert Drake's 31st Medium Tank Company, a smart-looking, hard-fighting outfit equipped with World-War-II-vintage Sherman M4 tanks. Also, following the withdrawal of elements of the ambushed medical convoy, a mixed bag of combat troops had been halted at the operations center. In time it was even learned that a portion of the 31st Heavy Mortar Company, a 4.2-inch outfit, was also encamped beside the school compound.

Captain Drake was placed in command, and anyone who wanted to join in was free to do so, which was a pretty bizarre way to run a very serious rescue operation.

The tanks set off in column of platoons at 1000 hours, surrounded by a very mixed bag of detached infantrymen, clerks, some artillerymen, cooks, technicians, communicators, whomever. Captain Clif Hancock trailed the motley column in one of the ambulances he had recovered from the medical convoy ambush after midnight.

The head of the relief column clanked forward two miles before drawing fire in the vicinity of the ambushed medical convoy. The lead tank triggered a mine, and the column was stopped as the tankers tried to push the damaged vehicle from the roadway.

It was a neat trap, for the tanks could not pass along either side on the steep verges without running the risk of sliding down out of control into an adjacent cornfield. Clif Hancock's ambulance, the last vehicle in line, was also fired on, and the medical company's first sergeant was killed.

The 75mm tank guns were turned on Chinese emplacements uphill to the right and downhill to the left, as were all infantry weapons. But the column was firmly pinned, and the slugging match that ensued could have had but one outcome.

It was a weird battle. Clif Hancock, at the tail end of the column, helped administer first aid to the wounded, and even made several trips to the operations center to drop off injured soldiers and collect medical supplies. A number of the men who started out with the tanks simply quit and walked back to safety, passing volunteers and adventure seekers who were pressing forward to join the fight.

One late arrival was Captain Martin Hoehn, the 31st Infantry's forty-six-year-old Catholic chaplain. Hoehn had volunteered for the Army at the outbreak of World War II and had won a Silver Star at age 40 while serving with the artillery in France. Adamant in the face of convention and direct orders from the senior chaplain at GHQ-Tokyo, Marty Hoehn insisted upon wearing a .45-caliber pistol every day he was in Korea.

When Father Hoehn finally heard about the medical convoy ambush of the previous night, he commandeered an ambulance and set off in the direction of the firing, hoping to become involved in rescuing wounded survivors.

Overtaking the tank-infantry column, Father Hoehn succeeded in getting as far as the roadside command post established by General Hodes and Captain Drake, the tank company commander. Hoehn had seen a good deal of fighting since 1942, and he was impressed mainly by Hodes's inability to control the fight or reach a decision as to tactics. The priest pressed on when the general was forced by enemy fire to make for a clump of trees several yards off the roadway. Hoehn's ambulance soon came abreast the damaged point tank. A tank retriever was off the road to one side, likewise damaged and immobile. And several riflemen were on guard nearby, but not firing.

Determined to reach the unfortunate survivors of the medical convoy ambush, Hoehn jumped from the cab of the ambulance and inspected the narrow space between the damaged tank and the impassable verge. It looked wide enough. The priest walked backward down the road, directing the ambulance driver with subtle hand motions. The bulky vehicle was nearly through the gap when a single shot rang out and drilled the driver through the hip.

Marty Hoehn clambered aboard the still-moving vehicle and brought it to a halt before it fell over the steep verge into the cornfield. One of the nearby riflemen volunteered to turn the ambulance and drive it back to the operations center, but not forward. Unable to talk anyone into advancing with him on foot, and realizing that he would be helpless and useless alone in the event there were living Americans at the ambush site, the fighting priest backtracked down the stalled column, evading friendly as well as enemy fire, stopping now and again to succor the needy wounded.

The rate of fire from the roadbound tanks diminished as more and more of them began running dangerously low on 75mm and machine-gun ammunition. Although Captain Drake passed back and forth along the column in an effort to cheer his troops on, the advance could not be restarted, and the slugging match could only result in greater losses. As the afternoon sun waned and sank, most of the infantry and support troops left to return to the operations center. Several tanks had run out of ammunition, and these also moved to the rear. Captain Drake was loath to leave his four disabled vehicles to the enemy, but he finally concluded that he had to save what he could. Everyone who was still afoot mounted the surviving tanks, which sped to the rear as the last rays of the heatless sun folded into the nearby hills.

The attack had accomplished nothing.

C H A P T E R

19

Major General Oliver Prince Smith was a quiet, austere, deeply religious Texas-born Californian. A 1916 graduate of the University of California at Berkeley, he had applied to the Marine Corps for a commission that year. There was a war in Europe, and young Oliver Smith was looking for an adventure. Perversely, he was shipped to Guam in the Pacific following his training, and the experienced man he replaced went to the war. Over succeeding decades, the scholarly officer built a reputation based upon his exceptional intelligence. He was alternately a student, a teacher, a leader of men. Still, he remained a captain for seventeen years, though he was a major for only two. As a junior lieutenant colonel, O. P. Smith commanded a rifle battalion sent to Iceland. It is significant to note that that battalion was expected to be among the first American units to fight in Europe against the Nazis, an expectation that remained unfulfilled.

Following rotation back to Washington, Colonel Smith served on the Marine Corps Plans and Policies Staff, then commanded the 5th Marines on New Britain. He was promoted brigadier general in 1944 and served as assistant commander of 1st Marine Division at Peleliu. He served at Okinawa as deputy chief of staff for 10th U.S. Army.

Early in 1948, the spare, silver-haired general was named Assistant Commandant of the Marine Corps. Two years later, on the eve of war in Korea, probably only one step away from retirement, he was sent to San Diego to command 1st Marine Division, the only unit with which he had ever served in combat. O. P. Smith rebuilt the peace-shattered division in under a month, then sent it ashore at Inchon, commanded it at Seoul, and oversaw its advance into North Korea.

Early on the morning of November 28, 1950, Major General O. P. Smith donned his heavy parka and climbed aboard a two-place helicopter for the sixty-four-mile flight from his division headquarters at Hamhung to the division forward base at Hagaru-ri. He had heard reports of heavy fighting at Yudam-ni, and he had been in direct touch with the command posts of the two regiments in the mountain valley on the far side of Toktong Pass. But short of going forward to see for himself there was little Smith could do to help out.

★

O. P. Smith was not a demonstrative leader, nor was he given to taking overt, direct charge in situations where responsible subordinates could act. He rarely gave an order, but always pointed in the direction he thought things ought to be heading. He liked self-reliant subordinates, and he saw to their advancement in his own quiet way. It would have been out of character for this general to take personal charge at Yudam-ni, but it would have been better for his division if he could have done away with the joint command that was just evolving there.

Normally, the forward force would have been placed under the command of the assistant division commander, Brigadier General Eddie Craig, an absolutely marvelous combat leader who had commanded a regiment at Bougainville and the "fire brigade" at Pusan. But Craig was in the States, having been granted emergency leave on November 25 to be with his dying father. He would be called back to Korea, but would not rejoin the division in time to influence the outcome of the Yudam-ni fighting. Craig's absence left a serious void in the division's senior command, but it was a void that could have been adequately filled by the veteran officers who comprised the top echelon of 1st Marine Division.

While the full meaning of the night battles at Yudam-ni would not be adequately assessed for days, it was clear by the time O. P. Smith arrived at Hagaru-ri that his forward regiments were in serious straits. Homer Litzenberg was a trusted subordinate, but he had his own regiment to run, and it would have been unfair to burden him with the command of a two-regiment-plus field force. That would have overburdened his regimental staff, which would have had to double up on duties.

There were two men subordinate to Smith and senior to Litz who might have been sent forward. The Division Chief of Staff, Colonel Gregon Williams, held the third-ranking billet in the division, but he was a staff man with neither recent combat nor troop command experience. Moreover, Williams was a key member of the commanding general's inner circle. He had accompanied Smith to Hagaru-ri, but Smith opted to keep Colonel Williams by his side. The Deputy Chief of Staff, Colonel Ed Snedeker, would have been an ideal commander at Yudam-ni. He had been a valuable communications and staff specialist early in the Pacific War, and had commanded the 7th Marines at Okinawa. But Snedeker was in Japan, caught by the suddenness of the Chinese onslaught, serving with a special study group. He would not be free to fly to Korea for days.

So no one senior to Colonel Litzenberg would or could be sent forward to take charge at Yudam-ni.

★

Two factors seriously disrupted the ability of Division to control events in the forward arena on November 28. First and foremost, Division did not yet have any real inkling as to the gravity of the situation. Unalarmed, it had no reason to act with dispatch. More importantly, Division *could not* react with dispatch.

Most of the division staff — the subordinate officers and experienced staff technicians who did the real work — was scattered over sixty-four miles of road between Hungnam and Hagaru-ri. Many were stalled at Koto-ri, the next town south of the division base. There were rumors abroad that the road had been cut north of Koto-ri, and several men who had set out from there were not yet accounted for. The only staff section head who was slated to go forward from Hungnam during the next several days was Colonel Alpha Bowser, the division operations officer. Bowser was considerably junior in rank to Litzenberg, and by far too valuable to General Smith to be detached from the division command group. He was to spend most of November 28 at Hamhung, flying forward only when he had confirmation that a functioning operations center had been established at the division forward base.

★

Al Bowser at forty was a light-complexioned man of medium height and build, a chipper, cheery go-getter known throughout the Naval Service as a future general. A native of western Pennsylvania, he had attended the Naval Academy, graduated high in his class, and had selected the Marine Corps to the lasting bafflement of the Navy officers who had been his mentors at Annapolis. A Marine since 1931, Bowser had trained during the prewar years as an artilleryman, and he had been sent time and again to attend or teach the highly technical courses that were the province of the artillery.

Despite a burning desire to command a battalion in first combat, Al Bowser had been tapped as assistant operations officer of 3rd Marine Division in mid-1943, and had planned the Bougainville landings late that year. A relatively junior lieutenant colonel, he had become the division operations officer in the midst of that first grinding campaign. Later, however, he had insisted upon being demoted and given an artillery battalion, which he commanded at Guam and Iwo Jima.

By a strange turn of fate, Colonel Bowser had been relieved as operations officer of Fleet Marine Force, Pacific, on the eve of the Korean War, and had assumed his duties with 1st Marine Division just in time to oversee the rebuilding of the command. Al Bowser was the man most responsible for the indescribably intricate task of planning the flawless Inchon landings, and for orchestrating the day-to-day grind up the Inchon-Seoul Highway by a division that trained in combat. He was thought by many to be the best man the Marine Corps had to fill the job he filled. His own feelings were characteristically modest: He had commanded a Marine combat battalion in combat, and everything that followed was gravy.

The adjective most often used to describe Al Bowser is "brilliant."

★

Al Bowser left Hungnam in the middle of the afternoon. He had heard of events far to the north, but the news was garbled and incomplete. He ordered his pilot to land at Koto-ri, where he spoke with the commander of the 1st Marines, Colonel Chesty Puller, no doubt the Corps' most combative officer. Puller seemed in control of the local situation, and the Koto-ri base had not been molested, so Bowser flew on. His helicopter was fired on several times, an unusual breach of ironbound Chinese fire discipline. On the ten miles of roadway between Koto-ri and Hagaru-ri, Bowser and his pilot counted nine unmanned roadblocks and spotted several abandoned American vehicles.

Bowser's arrival at Hagaru-ri galvanized the staff effort at the forward base. The colonel was not overly surprised when he read late reports describing the Yudam-ni situation. He had been forecasting rough times for weeks, and he had been primarily responsible for the unusually slow pace of Litzenberg's advance from Hagaru-ri during the preceding week. But he had expected to receive some warning from X Corps or higher headquarters. Strongly mistrustful of the Army's intelligence service, he had engineered a trip to Tokyo by the division intelligence officer, Colonel Bankson Holcomb, who was even then monitoring theater intelligence data at GHQ-Tokyo. Colonel Holcomb, however, had been stonewalled by MacArthur's senior staff and had not been able to issue anything more substantial than vague warnings to his fellow Marines.

Still, there had been warnings. The Division Air Officer, Major Mike Wojcik, had been telling Al Bowser for weeks that "something" was out there. Wojcik was a highly experienced aerial observer, and he had been given a helicopter practically as his own. He had failed to turn up any hard evidence during his many flights over the Taebek Plateau, but he could not stifle the visceral sensation that "something" really was out there. Mike Wojcik and Al Bowser and several thousand fellow Marines found out what "something" was, but late.

Denied permission to fly to Yudam-ni to see for himself, Bowser spent the late afternoon and evening hunched over his field desk, studying radio reports from all over the division area, working out plans and more plans as more and more-detailed news — and more and more-detailed rumors — flooded in.

★

All the concerns of the previous weeks had been borne out. While the PLA armies caught the bulk of 1st Marine Division in better positions than it would have been occupying at any time before or after, the first blow fell just when Division was least capable of initiating and controlling a cohesive effort.

The division forward base at Hagaru-ri had some more-pressing problems to work out.

CHAPTER

20

Hagaru-ri. November 28, 1950.

It had all the aspects of an Old West gold camp: its isolation, its barrenness, the speed with which it had been claimed and built up by succeeding waves of lean Americans.

Each day for a week, Hagaru-ri had grown until it had become so filled that its meager space and resources had been utterly overwhelmed by the continuing influx of men and the matériel of modern warfare.

In a week's time, Hagaru-ri had gone from being an obscure mountain-road town — its only important characteristic was the road net branching off northeast and northwest around the reservoir whose southern extremity touched the northeastern end of town — to becoming a vital headquarters and supply base supporting the drives of first one and then two American combat divisions.

Nearly three companies of Marine engineers, and a company of Army engineers, had been sent to Hagaru-ri in the days before the Chinese offensive began, and they had gone to work with a fury, egged on by the deep onset of winter weather and the quickening pace of the drive on the Yalu. One entire company, with all its modern, heavy construction equipment, had been turned loose on a long piece of relatively flat ground, its objective being the completion of a landing strip large enough to handle modern cargo aircraft. Elements of a second Marine engineer company were at work constructing the forward base. And the bulk of a third company was a few miles north of the town, stripping an enormous sawmill complex of needed lumber supplies.

An advance detachment of the 1st Marine Service Battalion had arrived to assume control of the burgeoning dumps, and the headquarters of the 11th Marines, the artillery regiment, was developing a new fire-support center. Army and Marine communicators were planning to turn the base into a major forward communications center. Heavy equipment was on the way from the sea, including enormous long-range transmitters and relay boosters. The commander of the 1st Marine Tank Battalion had already been up from Hamhung to plan the installation of his unit's repair and base facilities, and the commander of the 1st Marine Engineer Battalion had accompanied him to find places along the MSR that would have to be widened and buttressed to support the advance of the wide, heavy tanks beyond the Hagaru-ri road junction.

And, of course, the headquarters of 1st Marine Division was in motion toward Hagaru-ri. Division had already apportioned most of the permanent buildings in the town, and a sea of tents belonging to the headquarters battalion was being erected, chiefly at the northern end of town.

Several thousand men — a nearly uncountable assemblage — were scattered over the flat, frozen alluvial bowl nestled among the high peaks of the Taebek complex. For the most part, the men comprised bits and parts of units, mainly advance detachments of an American corps whose movement through the stark mountains was impeded by a thoroughly inadequate road net.

★

The leading elements of Lieutenant Colonel Tom Ridge's 3rd Battalion, 1st Marines, had arrived during the night of November 26, following a precipitous and strenuous move in the dark that had made most of the battalion senior staff highly anxious. It was too dark to deploy the two advance rifle companies to replace Dog and Easy Companies, 7th, which had moved to Yudam-ni early in the day, so the growing base was, for all practical purposes, undefended only twenty-four hours before the commencement of the PLA Second Phase Offensive. (The third company, George/1, had been held up well to the rear because there was not enough transport available; it was not expected to rejoin the battalion before November 28.)

Ridge's battalion was a good one. One of the two companies at Hagaru-ri and many of the headquarters and weapons people had served with the battalion at Camp Lejeune (when it was designated the 1st Battalion, 6th). The entire battalion had been in intense combat on the Inchon-Seoul Highway and had acquitted itself with notable esprit.

After speaking at length with senior members of Lieutenant Colonel Randolph Lockwood's 2nd Battalion, 7th, Lieutenant Colonel Ridge took it upon himself to order a survey of the defenses on the morning of November 27. He had his operations officer and weapons company commander, Majors Joe Trompeter and Ed Simmons, walk the entire perimeter in the hope of finding an adequate way to defend the large and growing base with a truncated rifle battalion.

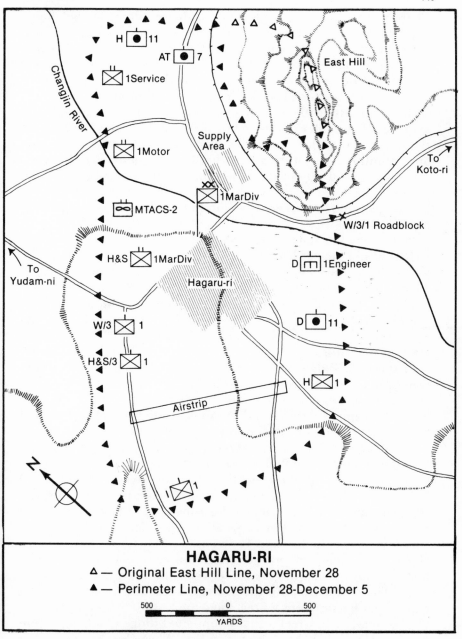

HAGARU-RI

△ — Original East Hill Line, November 28

▲ — Perimeter Line, November 28-December 5

500   0   500

YARDS

(See endpapers for GUIDE TO MAP SYMBOLS AND ABBREVIATIONS.)

There was yet no solid evidence of Chinese intentions, but Ridge and his senior subordinates had already discussed the ethereal "something" that had been attacking the viscera of so many Marines in days past. There was certainly enough doubt in the air to warrant Ridge's cautious frame of mind. What Trompeter and Simmons learned was something less than confidence-inspiring.

Hagaru-ri sits in the center of a bowl of hills several miles in diameter. The center of the bowl is flat, but the valley floor begins sloping upward at increasingly steeper grades outside the core town. Several hill masses jut from the otherwise flat valley floor between the town and the rim of the bowl. One — a high, jumbled mass of ridges — overlooks the town from the east, just across the stone bridge spanning the frozen Changjin River, which bisects the valley floor.

The survey yielded a careful professional analysis by the two majors: it would take at least two regiments of infantry to defend the valley. Tom Ridge had two reinforced companies and a six-gun 105mm battery. A reverse slope defense, which would require a deployment near the crest of every hill along the rim of the bowl, was clearly out of the question; it would require a four-mile line and necessitate the deployment of Ridge's troops at the rate of one man every seven yards.

In the end, Ridge, with the eventual concurrence of Division, elected to cover the most-exposed sectors with the most troops — all close in toward the town — and to cover the remainder of the perimeter with supporting fires and, in a pinch, drafts from service and support units. That was the best of a bad set of choices.

Based largely upon conversations between his senior staffers and senior members of the 2nd Battalion, 7th, and incorporating intelligence estimates and the eyeball analysis by Majors Simmons and Trompeter, Lieutenant Colonel Ridge decided to deploy his two rifle companies on pretty much the same ground formerly held by Lockwood's battalion. Item/1 went into positions on the western curve of the perimeter, and How/1 tied in on Item's left to cover about half of the southern perimeter line, to a point adjacent to a finger of low, swampy ground between the town and the frozen river. The sector fronting the swampy area was to be left undefended but for supporting fires, though the six 105mm howitzers of Dog Battery, 11th, which usually supported Ridge's battalion, were emplaced directly behind the frozen bog. When George/1 arrived, it would be deployed on the hill mass east of town (eventually named East Hill). The ground north of town was assigned to the various service and support units bivouacked in that area; these units would see to picketing their sectors at night, or to defending them in the event of attack. For the moment, there was no overall defense commander, and no one to oversee a coordinated effort. That would be left to Division once the forward command post had been fully established.

Ridge's troops spent the day moving into their defensive sectors, though little effort was made to improve upon the defenses established during the preceding week by the 2nd Battalion, 7th. Each company did make use of the ample lumber supply to fashion solid skeletons for twelve-man pyramidal tents, which would be used on a rotating basis to thaw out the troops.

But for the enormous effort expended in developing the airstrip, base facility, and division forward command post, November 27 passed uneventfully at Hagaru-ri. The only unit to engage in any sort of combat during the night was Captain Ben Read's How Battery, which was involved in the sporadic delivery of high explosives to the vicinity of Fox Hill. Most of the men at Hagaru-ri knew nothing of the desperate fighting to the north.

★

Lieutenant Colonel Randolph Lockwood awoke early on November 28 and proceeded in excellent spirits to prepare his headquarters and weapons companies for the trip to Yudam-ni, where they were to join Dog and Easy Companies. Lockwood had not an inkling that two of his reinforced companies had been shattered in the night, or that Fox/7 was firmly trapped on the slopes of the hill he and Bill Barber had scouted the previous afternoon.

The small convoy proceeded northward along the MSR for about a mile. At the top of the first long rise, where the road dipped into a small valley before climbing to the next, higher, line of hills, Lockwood paused to eyeball the remains of a Sherman tank lying on its side in the middle distance; the American medium tank had not been there when last he passed that way, so Lockwood paused for a precautionary sweep of the terrain with his binoculars. In a saddle about one thousand yards distant, starkly silhouetted against the sky, was a line of evenly spaced dots. They appeared to be the heads of men, sticking up from behind the saddle. Before he could react, Lockwood and the leading elements of his convoy were taken under rifle fire. The headquarters company moved to the left of the road, uphill, and deployed to return the fire. At the same time, the Weapons Company people moved to the right, deploying across the jumbled, rising ground on that side of the roadway. These moves were countered by Chinese moves to the left and right. Each time one side extended to the flanks, the other countered with an attempt to secure its position against a flank attack. The Chinese had the advantage of numbers, elevation, and cover, but the maneuvering, countermaneuvering, firing, and counterfiring went on for hours. Though friendly aircraft passed overhead throughout the day, Lieutenant Colonel Lockwood was unable to secure their support.

In time, as the short winter afternoon drew to a sulky close, Lockwood decided to withdraw. No one had told him what lay ahead, but it was clearly more than his small command could handle. The convoy was turned and run back to Hagaru-ri.

★

Rumor-fueled speculation was rampant among the several thousand men comprising several large units and numerous splinter groups around the central hamlet. Much of the information was circumstantial and of a negative nature, evidence of absences rather than of occurrences:

★   Lieutenant Colonel Al Creal, the 1st Marine Division signals officer, was to meet with the commander of the division radio-relay platoon in order to discuss placement of vital relay boosters. The platoon leader set out from Koto-ri at 0800, but never arrived for his meeting with Creal at Hagaru-ri.

★   A small convoy of division headquarters personnel was never heard from after leaving Koto-ri right behind the missing radio-relay platoon leader.

★   A messenger from the 1st Signal Battalion was ambushed on the way south to Koto-ri and returned to Hagaru-ri to report the incident.

★   A routine patrol mounted to the southwest by Item/1 ran into a PLA infantry company, which was dispersed with mortar and artillery fire a few miles from town. The Marine platoon proceeded until it ran into a second PLA force, then returned to the perimeter.

★   Three Marine heavy tanks and a How/1 platoon were ambushed within sight of the perimeter by fifty Chinese. The Marine force prepared to deliver an attack, but withdrew when observation aircraft reported that three hundred additional Chinese were deploying to launch a flank attack.

★   A steady stream of reports from airborne observers, including the division operations officer, attested to a growing number of abandoned vehicles and roadblocks on the MSR between Hagaru-ri and Koto-ri.

★

There was, in time, no question but that the division base was surrounded and in growing, if not extreme, peril. But the news was restricted largely to the upper echelons. Most of the very large number of small, mainly noncombatant, units strewn across the valley had no inkling that there were Chinese in the vicinity.

Warrant Officer Butch Reynolds's radio-repair platoon learned that something was amiss as it was building its shop. A Marine was on the roof of the shed at about 1400 hours, tacking down the last of a roll of burlap insulating material, when he yelled down to Reynolds, "Hey, Gunner, I might be crazy, but it sounds like a lot of bees buzzing past me up here."

Reynolds realized at once that the reports of distant rifles were being whipped away by the high wind that was gusting across the valley floor. He ordered the man off the roof and deployed his platoon around the building, wondering why no one had warned him to be on guard. The Marine who had been on the roof clambered to the ground and complained to Reynolds as he rubbed the circulation back into his chilled limbs, "Hell, wouldn't you know they'd wait until we finished building the hut!"

★

Lieutenant Colonel Tom Ridge had been on the regional communications net from the first hint of trouble. As evidence mounted, he saw a clearer need to secure the entire valley against possible attack. Conversations with 1st Regiment headquarters at Koto-ri convinced Ridge that his George/1 would not be arriving before the next day. No one had any idea as to precisely what units were strewn in and about Hagaru-ri, but it was evident that few of them had an immediate combat potential. In a radio conversation with Al Bowser before the colonel left Hamhung, Ridge suggested that an overall defense commander be appointed. He also requested that George/1 and any other combat units caught on the MSR be given top priority in drawing transport and road clearance.

Later in the day, after Colonel Bowser had arrived at Hagaru-ri, he called to appoint Ridge defense commander of the entire base. The task was given a dramatic shove only ten minutes later when a Chinese 76mm mountain gun fired a round into Ridge's CP, killing the battalion logistics officer and wounding the Weapons Company supply sergeant.

Ridge called a conference of troop commanders in the middle of the afternoon. It was only three hours until sunset, and everything would have to be done in that time. His staff was overwhelmed by the task of inventorying personnel around the base, not to mention organizing them to man an all-around defense, so Ridge appointed Lieutenant Colonel Gus Banks, the service-battalion commander, to oversee the northern perimeter. Banks was a good choice. An austere former Raider with a good combat record, he would whip his noncombatants into shape with a legendary iron hand. Officers were sent out to list the designations and strengths of all units in the area, and others were set to organizing the many small units and detachments into provisional fighting formations. Tom Ridge and his senior battalion officers took care of planning and briefing. It was with some disappointment that Ridge received the news that crack Marine combat engineers would remain at work on the vitally needed airstrip — only about one-quarter complete that afternoon — until or unless the perimeter was actually assaulted and breached.

All but one of the roads leading into town were defended directly by Marine heavy-weapons and tank units under the direction of Major Ed Simmons, who was both Ridge's Weapons Company commander and supporting-arms coordinator. Most of the more vulnerable portions of the line were given to Marine combat or combat service units. But the desperation of the moment was evidenced strongly by the placement of units which, in normal circumstances, would never have been used on a combat perimeter line: elements of the X Corps Signal Battalion were assigned with other noncombatant Army units to the vital, dominating summit of East Hill; Marine Tactical Air Control Squadron 2, a unit comprised entirely of Marine airmen and communicators, was given a sector of the long western line; Dog Battery, 11th, was placed without any infantry support behind the frozen bog east of town; How Battery, isolated and unsupported by infantry, remained in its deep gun pits on the far side of East Hill, trapped there by the need to support Fox/7 at Toktong Pass at the extremity of the guns' range.

While it did mitigate the cause of some deep fears, a final intelligence assessment pointed to the southern portion of the perimeter as being the area most likely to be hit in strength; East Hill was also a likely Chinese objective. It was for this reason that How and Item Companies, 1st, were kept on the southern line; George/1 would replace the Army and Marine noncombatant units on East Hill the moment it arrived. If it arrived.

★

The efforts of How and Item Companies to dig in on November 28 were frenetic. Neither company had done much to improve its defenses on the quiet 27th, but there was no stopping either unit once elements of each tasted Chinese gunfire on the 28th.

Members of 1st Lieutenant Joe Fisher's Item/1 managed to beg or steal several bags of C3 plastic explosive from the engineers at work on the airstrip adjacent to the company line. Small bits of the plastique were stuffed into empty ration cans, yielding crude shape-charges useful for breaching the first foot of frozen topsoil. The results were weapons pits and foxholes of a quality far exceeding any others held by Marines in North Korea that day.

How/1 had less luck or cooperation. Captain Clarence Corley, the company commander, had been stymied in his efforts to secure even a few long-handled shovels. There was a lot of frontage to cover, so the best efforts by all hands resulted in a barely adequate network of defenses. Corley's 3rd Platoon, which was to occupy the center of the three-platoon front, lost precious hours because of the fruitless patrol action it fought south of the perimeter, within sight of the company line. Corley was also troubled by the intelligence data collected at grave risk by two South Korean counterintelligence operatives. During a meandering walk through the surrounding hills they had picked up word that How Company was to be subjected to — of all things — a Chinese cavalry charge at 2200 hours that night.

The troops improved their fighting holes until nearly dusk, when they were fed in shifts at mobile company kitchens. One rifleman in four was put on alert at dusk, then half the men went on alert several hours later. As it came up 2200, Fisher and Corley had all hands ready to counter an assault.

There had been snow off and on all day, the troops were downright miserable, and the barbed wire in front of the line was nearly covered by the snow. There was dead silence.

Captain Corley ran a phone check every fifteen or thirty minutes while his headquarters troops routinely rotated watches. All automatic weapons were test-fired in shifts to prevent or discover freezing.

Light mortar and artillery fire, particularly white-phosphorous rounds, began falling around the Marine positions at about 2200. Corley first thought the fire was friendly, but small arms opened minutes later. The captain was amazed at how close the Chinese had been able to get to his line without being detected, but he reacted swiftly, scrambling his headquarters group, issuing a general warning over the battalion communications network.

Bugles, whistles, and grenades blared, tweeted, and burst to life as the Chinese rose like wraiths in the snow and stampeded against the center of the How Company line, against 2nd Lieutenant Wendell Endsley's ill-prepared 3d Platoon. The clash was brief and violent. Lieutenant Endsley was killed, and the 3rd Platoon was pushed backward with extremely heavy losses.

The way to the rear was open. All that stood between the Chinese and the interior of the Hagaru-ri perimeter was the How/1 command post and the company's mobile kitchen. The company 60mm mortars were pumping out rounds as fast as they could be put into the tubes while machine guns in the quieter 2nd Platoon sector, to the left, fired across the rear of 3rd Platoon's former positions to catch what Chinese they could reach in enfilade. Second Lieutenant Harvey Goss — a high-strung, overly aggressive young man who had commanded 3rd Platoon until he had been relieved by Lieutenant Endsley several days earlier — gathered up five enlisted men and tried to stem the Chinese tide. He was killed before he could do any good.

The Chinese stemmed their own tide. In an egregious display of greed the successful attackers swarmed over the warm mobile company kitchen and paused to fill their bellies. The attack faltered, providing Corley's troops with the edge they needed to survive.

At grave personal risk, the How/1 exec, 1st Lieutenant Horace Johnson, ran to the battalion CP to beg for reinforcements. He got about fifty enlisted Marines and 1st Lieutenant Grady Mitchell, who had served with How/1 until drafted a few days earlier to become assistant battalion operations officer.

Johnson took about half the men and returned to the company command post to report to Captain Corley and organize a sweep against the left shoulder of the breach in his company's line. Lieutenant Mitchell, who was to mount a coordinated sweep against the right shoulder of the breach, led his troops through a confused melee that had flared up in and around the Item/1 sector. Many of his troops, sent to save How Company, were drawn into Item Company's fight, and only a few actually slammed into the Chinese behind the How Company position. Grady Mitchell was killed.

First Lieutenant Harrison Betts, the How Company machine-gun officer, was unloading reserve ammunition at the company command post when the Chinese struck. A white-phosphorus round took out many of the men near Betts, but he emerged unharmed to organize and lead about thirty Marines in a sally against a native house occupied by scores of Chinese. Two more white-phosphorous rounds injured all but eight of Betts's men, who continued to advance under heavy fire. Lieutenant Betts himself was wounded as he closed on the house, but he kept going, leading his troops into the fray, evicting the Chinese in a bloody brawl.

Clarence Corley exchanged information with Joe Fisher, whose Item Company had been hit hard. Then he turned his full attention to sealing the breach in the center of his line and organizing a clearing operation.

A jeep laden with urgently needed 60mm mortar ammunition overshot the company position and was abandoned by its badly shaken driver in Chinese territory. Second Lieutenant Ed Snelling, the How/1 mortar officer, ran into the Chinese fire and recovered the vehicle and its trailerful of precious ammunition.

How Company was barely hanging on.

The scene was appalling. Captain Corley's jeep had been set afire in the first clash, and the flames were casting eerie shadows over the battleground. Dead and wounded Americans and Chinese were hopelessly intermingled, and neither side was able to extricate itself sufficiently to muster a telling blow against the other.

Alone, Clarence Corley held the mound on which he had placed his CP tent, now reduced to tatters. Somewhere nearby, Harrison Betts, the wounded machine-gun officer, was leading roving forays against Chinese who had been trapped by several disorganized but partially successful Marine counterthrusts. The company mortars fired without pause, and detached reinforcements — many of them Marine and Army noncombatants — trickled in, adding to the confusion but gamely going over to the attack when called upon to do so.

Several hours of stalemate ensued. How Company's telephone net was knocked out, forcing the company commander to rely upon runners, who moved messages at unbelievable personal risk. With the help of his exec, Lieutenant Johnson, Corley slowly put the pieces back in place. He was determined to mount a counterattack to sweep his company area, and it only remained to be seen if he could get the attack organized. He spoke to Ed Snelling, his mortar officer, who warned that the guns might hit friendly troops as easily as they might hit Chinese. Corley replied that he had to take the risk. Then the big Louisiana captain made a speech to all of his men who could hear him. He called them yellow, unfit, cowards. He challenged them to show they really had the stuff to be Marines. Fired up, they rose, yelling and cheering, and went to work.

The fight was brief, and shocking. The confused, tattered Chinese remnants turned and ran.

★

The Chinese hit Item Company's left platoon at the same moment they first lashed out at the adjacent How Company line. Penetrations were minimal, however, and, though the fighting was exceptionally hot, the Chinese were held back from the airstrip, which was directly to the rear.

Hours of profitless fighting ensued before 1st Lieutenant Joe Fisher, 1st Marine Division's junior ranking company commander, ordered his men to set two Korean houses afire. The Chinese seemed drawn to the flames, where they were picked off by the dozens and scores as they waded into a cross fire laid on by the machine guns of two Marine heavy tanks that had been sent to support Item Company.

★

Chinese who had breached Corley's line moved on the vital airstrip, firing on Marine engineers who continued to work under floodlights despite the fighting on the perimeter. Second Lieutenant Robert McFarland, of Dog Company, 1st Engineer Battalion, organized a scratch team of heavy-equipment operators and mounted a vigorous sweep of the construction area. Several engineers were injured, but McFarland drove the intruders away, and work on the airstrip was resumed.

The medical clearing station operated by Charlie Company, 1st Medical Battalion, was also right behind the Item/1 line, and it drew its share of the fire. The surgeons and their dedicated corpsmen continued to work despite the hazard of being hit by the numerous machine-gun bullets that bored through the plywood walls.

Lieutenant Colonel Carl Youngdale, exec of the 11th Marines, received a frantic call from the exec of Dog Battery, which was holding a portion of the perimeter line adjacent to How/1. The man said that American .50-caliber machine guns sweeping the rear in search of infiltrators were firing on the howitzers. Youngdale knew that he could not get the machine guns to cease firing, nor could he afford to evacuate the Dog Battery sector until the friendly machine-gun fire ceased. He told the younger officer to keep firing unless the friendly fire really got dangerous, to which the man replied, "Well, that last burst went between my legs. Is *that* close enough?" Impressed by the humor in the battery officer's voice, Youngdale blurted back, "No! Keep firing!"

A short time later, coming up midnight, the Dog Battery gunners were engaged by Chinese light artillery on the heights. It was imperative to neutralize those guns, for the tightly packed perimeter could be blown away if even one round hit any of the numerous fuel and ammunition dumps. Captain Andy Strohmenger, the Dog Battery commander, organized an unusual response.

Five of the Dog Battery 105s were silenced while the sixth howitzer was run out one hundred fifty yards in front of the line to act as a decoy. The Chinese immediately spotted the lone piece and attempted counterbattery. Strohmenger quickly ran an azimuth and computed the range, then ordered all his howitzers into counter-counterbattery. At least two Chinese 76mm mountain guns were destroyed, and two others were forced from the heights.

★

The most serious threat to the security of the Hagaru-ri base came from the direction of East Hill, the dominating ground which Tom Ridge had not been able to get adequately manned during the day.

During the late afternoon, Major Ed Simmons was overseeing the development of a roadblock in the shadow of East Hill by a ten-man detachment of machine gunners from his own weapons company. He was approached by the lieutenant commanding a platoon of X Corps communicators. The young Army officer had been given a portion of East Hill to defend, but he confided to Major Simmons that doing so was well beyond his ken. The major asked the lieutenant if he was willing to work under the direction of the Marine gunnery sergeant who would be commanding the roadblock, and the lieutenant gratefully agreed. The gunnery sergeant used his Army reinforcements to hold a knob overlooking the roadblock and leading up to East Hill. It was the best that Simmons could do to cover that sector of East Hill.

A short time later, Simmons got into the middle of a flap between the elderly, unaggressive Army captain commanding Dog Company, 10th Engineer Combat Battalion, and the younger, more aggressive captain who served as the company's executive officer. The older man did not want to be drawn into combat with his one hundred sixty-seven inexperienced, untrained construction troops, ninety of whom were unreliable South Korean conscripts. On the other hand, the younger man was eager to help the Marines defend the base. It was Simmons's position that the point was not debatable. The construction engineers were to pass through the Army signal platoon on the knob and continue on up toward the crest of East Hill. Marine service troops would be coming up the far side of the hill to cover the left half of the ridgeline. To lend some infantry expertise to the

Army engineers, Simmons offered to send his weapons-company executive officer, Captain John Shelnutt, an old-time enlisted Marine who had been complaining for weeks that he was not seeing nearly enough combat.

In all, Simmons was able to arrange for defense of the right half of East Hill by about two hundred fifty noncombatant soldiers armed with their light infantry weapons, four .50-caliber machine guns, five .30-caliber light machine guns and several bazookas.

★

The first act near East Hill unfolded when, at about midnight, a full company of PLA infantry in marching column walked right into the guns of the ten-man Marine roadblock at the base of the hill. The block had been moved from its original position at dusk, back about one hundred yards to the far side of a swale. If Chinese observers had seen the withdrawal, they might have concluded that the Marines were abandoning the sector. Whatever the reason for approaching in column rather than deployed for battle, the Chinese company was taken by surprise and hacked to bits by the Marine machine guns.

★

Several hours after sunset, Simmons received a radio call from Captain John Shelnutt, complaining that he had been unable to locate the Marine service troops who were supposed to be occupying the left half of the ridgeline. Simmons called the service battalion headquarters, but was told that the service troops were definitely on the hill. He told Shelnutt to keep extending the line to his left until he made contact. But successive conversations brought the same news: the Army troops on the right half of the hill were unable to find the Marine units on the left. Finally, at about midnight, two hours after the Chinese had mounted their assaults against How and Item Companies, Captain Shelnutt told Major Simmons that he was in the center of the ridgeline and that there was absolutely no sign of anyone from the service battalion. Unable to do more, Simmons told his exec to turn back his left flank for the night, that things would be straightened out as soon as it was light, and that he would try to fill in the gap with artillery and mortar fire if it was needed.

The collapse was so swift that few weapons or men got into action. The Chinese rammed home an assault on Shelnutt's left, unseating the Army combat engineers in that sector in a flash. When Captain Shelnutt moved left to stabilize the collapsed stretch of the line, the engineers in the center gave way.

Ed Simmons soon heard that American and South Korean troops

were streaming off the hill at about 0200, November 29, and he immediately tried to place a call to John Shelnutt. He was able to raise Shelnutt's radioman, Private First Class Bruno Podolak, who informed the major that Captain Shelnutt was not there. Simmons asked to speak to one of the Army officers, but Podolak told him that there was no Army officer around either. Fearing the worst, Simmons gave the young radioman a spirited pep talk, telling him that he was a Marine and that he should take charge. But it was too late for that sort of heroics.

Captain Shelnutt was dead. Simmons was not able to raise Podolak again by radio and presumed him to be dead also.

Several Army engineer officers managed to stem the retreat of their company, and a new line was established two hundred fifty yards behind the ridgeline at about 0230.

Private First Class Podolak went to ground. Miraculously, he remained on the ridgeline, reporting Chinese movements and helping to register artillery and mortar fire.

About the only thing between the Chinese and the supply dumps at the base of East Hill was Captain Ben Read's How Battery, which, with Strohmenger's Dog Battery, had for some time been firing into the gap between Captain Shelnutt's left flank and the supposed position of the Marine service troops. Three of Read's guns were turned to bear directly on the slopes of the adjacent hill, and the Chinese who ventured into view were ground to dust by direct fire. Masses of men charged the three 105s, which heaped mounds of viscera and bone upon the frozen hillside.

★

The PLA division responsible for taking Hagaru-ri had not mustered sufficient strength to ensure the success of its mission. Proper exploitation of any of the breakthroughs managed by the assault battalions might have defeated the Marine defenders, but the Chinese really simply underestimated the strength and the will of the defenders. The base was by no means secure as the first rays of sunlight brought forth powerful aerial support, but the garrison was intact, able to fight on.

The danger to the Hagaru-ri base remained acute, however, for the Chinese lodgment on East Hill had not been reduced.

PART FIVE

November 29-30

CHAPTER
21

East Hill. November 29.

The bid to hold Hagaru-ri would be determined on East Hill, the jumbled mass of steep slopes and narrow ridgelines overlooking the crowded Marine base straddling the frozen Changjin River.

Dawn of November 29 found a battalion of Chinese and one Marine radioman on the commanding ridgeline. The Marine, Private First Class Bruno Podolak, of Weapons Company, 3rd Battalion, 1st, had installed himself in a deep hole when the Chinese overran the thin line of Army construction engineers which had been left to hold the hill. He had been firing off brief, whispered radio flashes through the long night, telling listeners at Lieutenant Colonel Tom Ridge's embattled command post that the Chinese were moving fresh troops and several 76mm mountain guns up the reverse slopes to cement their hold on East Hill.

Tom Ridge knew from the start that he would have to wrest the heights from the Chinese or face the possibility that their light mountain guns there would be able to fire directly into his crowded perimeter. Just below the hill, isolated on the far side of the Changjin River, was the main ammunition dump, a fantastic target for Chinese gunners. And two packed-to-the-walls hospitals were operating in clear sight of the hill, as was a company of Marine engineers bent upon making the new airstrip operational. Everything in the American perimeter could be directly observed and fired on from East Hill.

Ridge's mobile reserve, put together the previous evening from the bits and parts of nearly *sixty* separate Army and Marine special and service units, was down to about twenty men. All the rest had been fed into the night battles. Given time, Ridge knew that he would find men to rebuild his reserve. But there was no time. Hours before sunup, Ridge called aside his battalion executive officer, Major Reginald Myers, and told him to take the last reserve contingent and lead an assault against the Chinese holding the center of East Hill. Ridge would feed fresh troops to Myers as quickly as they could be found.

Myers led the way through the crowded perimeter, first by road, then along a narrow ditch, the only protection that could be found to shield the small party from plunging fire from the heights. True to his promise, Ridge sent small groups to Myers as the major painstakingly forged a combat force from disparate elements of numerous combat and noncombat organizations. Several 105mm howitzers were freed from other pressing missions and re-layed against the Chinese-held heights, their fires monitored and directed by Private First Class Podolak.

As the hours of darkness threatened to give way to light, Major Myers passed The Word among his officers, now numbering six. There were just over three hundred men on hand, as mixed a bag as could be imagined, or dreaded. All were to crawl up the icy slope to a ripple Myers designated as the line of departure. As soon as the 105s stopped firing and mortars cut in, the entire force was to move up and out in a single massed frontal assault, the only tactic Myers dared employ with so disorganized an assault force.

It took forty-five minutes for the solid mass of Americans and South Koreans to crawl up the steep, slick slope to the line of departure. Fortunately, morning mists obscured the deployment, but it also forced Myers to waste precious time on the exposed slope until it was clear. New snow lay ahead and behind, sure to result in painful falls for heavily laden men, a real cause for fear among the troops.

Corsair fighter-bombers came on station at 0930. Working under the precise direction of forward air controllers — grounded Marine aviators with an enormous stake in the outcome — the aircraft peeled out of their circling formations and roared down upon East Hill to deliver rockets and napalm, and 20mm and .50-caliber machine-gun fire. One Corsair emerged from its dive trailing smoke. The pilot spun her around and pancaked onto the ground, sliding out of control in front of How/1's lines. To the accompaniment of cheering Marine riflemen, the pilot threw back his Plexiglas canopy, disengaged his restraining harness, scrambled to the ground and sprinted to the safety of the Marine line. Friendly light machine guns fired into the damaged aircraft, setting it ablaze.

Even as the fighter-bombers continued their runs, Reginald Myers ordered his officers to get the ground attack started.

Sliding and slipping, losing one step for each two they took, Myers's troops surged upward. The terrain was broken by deep furrows and pointed outcroppings, and the troops quickly became channelized into Chinese fire lanes, sustaining heavy casualties or

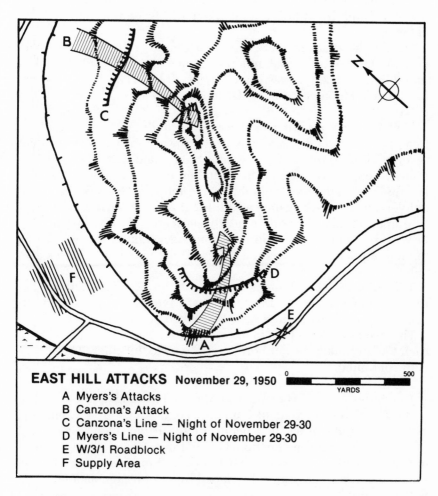

EAST HILL ATTACKS November 29, 1950

A Myers's Attacks
B Canzona's Attack
C Canzona's Line — Night of November 29-30
D Myers's Line — Night of November 29-30
E W/3/1 Roadblock
F Supply Area

(See endpapers for GUIDE TO MAP SYMBOLS AND ABBREVIATIONS.)

bogging down. The first ranks, nevertheless, passed Bruno Podolak's hiding hole, and he rose to join them in the attack. First Lieutenant Robert Jochums, a Marine engineer battalion staffer leading forty-five Marine engineers and clerks, was shot through the foot, but he hobbled painfully uphill, forcing his troops forward at the forefront of the assault.

Most of the attackers were driven to ground or hit by massed rifle fire, mortars, and several mountain guns. Bruno Podolak took a round in the back, but was spared by his radio pack, which bore the full impact. He kept going for far longer than anyone expected him to participate.

Peeking and squeaking in short spurts, a diminishing core of extremely determined Americans drove toward the crest. Less than seventy of the three hundred made it to the top with Major Myers. Below, Tom Ridge ordered his battalion communicator to take the last reserves to the foot of a draw to the left of Myers's position and deliver a flank attack against a Chinese unit applying the most pressure upon Myers. This group nearly succeeded, but was pinned by heavy fire from distant Chinese emplacements. A second group, formed of phantoms it seemed, followed the first, but its attack also failed.

Miraculously, the 76mm guns the Chinese had pushed up the reserve slopes were used only against Myers's and subsidiary attacks. No rounds were fired into the packed perimeter below.

The two forces stood toe to toe atop the forward slope of East Hill, each too unthinkingly stubborn to give way to the other. The blood-bath continued.

★

Two miles north of Hagaru-ri, on the road leading up the east side of the Reservoir, the bulk of Captain George King's Able Company, 1st Engineer Battalion, had been quietly, if pensively, sitting out the night's and morning's action. Cut off from Hagaru-ri by two miles of unimproved roadway and what appeared to be several Chinese regiments, King's engineers had stood by to withstand an attack that never materialized.

The engineers had been sent a few days earlier to exploit the vast holdings in cut lumber stacked all around the sawmill in the tiny mountain town. Now Captain King's only desire was to get his men and vehicles back to the relative safety of the Hagaru-ri perimeter. The Chinese took no action against Able/Engineers, probably did not even know the company was behind them.

If the Chinese were not looking at George King, he was certainly looking at them, and directing the odd artillery salvo against what he saw. The sport was interrupted two hours after sunrise by a call from Division; King was to send a patrol to a nearby town. The company commander called Warrant Officer Bill Downs, a 30-year-old equipment maintenance expert whose career in the Corps had begun in 1938, and ordered him to lead twenty men. While the troops were preparing to mount out, King and Downs walked to some high ground and had a look at the nearby objective, which was teeming with at least several hundred Chinese. King called the patrol off right then; he reported to Division, and was directed to pack up and return to the main perimeter.

It was a crazy thing to do, charging back through massed Chinese battalions, but it would have been crazier to stay put, at the mercy of a totally unpredictable enemy. The engineers, more dedicated to the preservation of their equipment than most other Marines, carefully struck their tents and stowed all the company's loose effects. All the vehicles were lined up on the road between enormous stacks of cut lumber. Bill Downs counted nineteen vehicles, including several bulldozers and a road grader. Someone even remembered to feed diesel fuel into the cooling systems of each vehicle to ward off the effects of the − 25-degree freeze.

Captain King gave the signal to move out, and Able/Engineers roared off down the road. Ten vehicles passed completely through the enemy before the Chinese tumbled to the gamble and turned their guns on the Marines. The rear vehicles were riddled, though no one was injured. A dump truck slid to a wheezing halt, blocking the road, keeping the tail of the column from safety. A sergeant jumped to the roadway and stretched a tow cable from the vehicle ahead to the damaged dump truck. The entire column chugged into friendly lines at about 1100.

Far from receiving accolades for the daring escape, or even a rest, Captain King's engineers were put to immediate work. The company headquarters section, under Gunner Downs, was ordered to construct a camp and pitch tents. And the rest of the bobtailed company (2nd Platoon was at Yudam-ni) was sent to East Hill.

★

There were sixty Marines and sixteen Army men left at the deepest point of penetration atop East Hill, and many of them were wounded. Below, scores of other Marines and soldiers were pinned behind outcroppings and in shallow cuts all the way to the base of the ridge.

First Lieutenant Nick Canzona, a veteran of all the fighting since

Pusan, was ordered to take his 1st Platoon of Able/Engineers straight up the back of East Hill and report to Major Myers. After completing an exhausting climb with most of his platoon intact, Canzona was ordered to return to the base of the hill. The engineers were the last viable force in the perimeter, and they were to be used to deliver a flank assault in Myers's support.

Canzona's platoon rushed to a line of departure about one thousand yards northeast of the point where it came off East Hill. Moving by a predetermined route, two engineer squads pushed up a spur on a nearly vertical slope. Canzona had zero support, not even a radio. He did have one light machine gun and the infantry weapons and hand grenades he and his troops were packing.

The twenty engineers made it to their immediate objective, but were held there by sheets of machine-gun fire. Only Canzona and two men had room for fighting back. The light machine gun was passed forward and set up, but it would not fire. One of the men was hit, and rolled off the flat, unconscious.

The engineers clung to the crest while a second machine gun was painstakingly packed up the sheer slope. Lieutenant Canzona sent a runner to the nearest radio at the foot of the ridge to plead for mortar support. The response, after a long delay, was two rounds of 81mm.

Frustrated by the lack of support, Canzona left his perch in the late afternoon to beg information from Captain King, who was attempting to guide events from the base of the hill. King told Canzona to pack it in. There was no point being stuck atop the hill after nightfall. But that left Nick Canzona doubly frustrated. He was certain that a mere platoon of Chinese was barring his way, and he knew that that small obstacle could be cleared by a brief mortar or artillery barrage. But there was no such support to be had. The situation was desperate, and there were not enough guns to cover all the danger spots.

The engineers reluctantly withdrew.

★

About five hundred yards from Nick Canzona's perch, Reginald Myers was growing more desperate by the moment. The lengthening afternoon shadows were an omen. Myers, too, knew that he could not maintain his precarious position during the night. He had been waiting all day for reinforcements which were supposed to be on the way up from Koto-ri, only ten miles to the south, but the many promises and assurances he had received through the long day had come to nothing. In the end — past the end — Myers decided to risk holding through the night, a task he considered impossible, but a gamble he knew in his heart of hearts that he would have to dare.

Had he known more about the fate of the expected reinforcements, Major Myers would have been even less sanguine about his abysmally poor chances. There had been a tragedy of the first magnitude in the making on the MSR between Hagaru-ri and Koto-ri.

C H A P T E R

22

Bemused by the setting, Captain Charlie Peckham reluctantly checked his pistol and grenades at the door, strode across the crowded room to a table festooned with a clean red-and-white checkered tablecloth and was served a delicious hot breakfast by freshly scrubbed Korean waitresses. All the other men in the large, airy room were dressed in Class-A uniforms and murmuring the urbane profundities of rear-area warriors. Charlie Peckham, out of place in his odd assortment of field clothing, looked every bit the combat infantry officer he was. The best meal he had had in weeks — or would have for three long years — went down a little hard. The infantry captain could not relate to the unreal clubbiness of the X Corps Officers' Mess at Hamhung, and he longed to be back with his troops, Baker Company, 31st Infantry.

Peckham had fought his way up the Inchon-Seoul Highway in September, and he and his company had just completed a week-long motorized reconnaissance mission up to the Yalu. Alerted for a move to a rest area at Hungnam, Peckham's battalion commander had rewarded Baker/31 by sending it to the rear to find a bivouac area and stake a claim; the rest of the 1st Battalion, 31st, would follow in a few days.

Baker/31 had spent the previous day, November 27, setting up a camp at Hungnam, but had been ordered to move to Hamhung. Peckham had commandeered a Korean freight train for the company and had driven ahead to meet with his regiment's liaison officer at

Corps to get further instructions. After breakfast, which was the liaison officer's treat, Peckham staked a new claim and went to work. No sooner done than he was told to stand by for a new directive.

The news, when it came, was not good. Corps staffers told Peckham there were reports that the MSR had been closed by unknown, unspecified enemy units, and that Baker/31 was to draw transport and move north to help clear the road. The company commander would receive clearer orders along the way. His immediate objective was Koto-ri, where he was to report to the commander of the 1st Marine Regiment, which was headquartered there.

★

Colonel Lewis Puller — the Marine Corps' incomparable "Chesty" — had been seething for days over orders that were keeping his 1st Marines shackled to the MSR. Puller was an unusually, perhaps abnormally, aggressive combatant, who never relished being behind any other Marine when combat was in the offing. He had been a legend, an authentic character, for nearly three solid decades, and the aging tiger clearly desired to fight what could well be his last battle in his usual combative style, in the attack.

Based with his regimental headquarters at Koto-ri, which was guarded by the reinforced 2nd Battalion, 1st, Puller had received word on November 26 from his rear battalion — the 1st, based at Chinhung-ni, the railhead town at the foot of the Taebek Plateau — that it had been lightly engaged but had failed to achieve solid contact with unknown enemy forces.

As uncertain as anyone about the quality of intelligence summaries from X Corps, Puller authorized his 2nd Battalion commander, Lieutenant Colonel Allan Sutter, to mount several deep patrols on November 27.

A motorized platoon-strength patrol from Easy/1 drew fire from about twenty-five Chinese west of Koto-ri late that morning. The attackers were routed, leaving two of their wounded to be taken captive. The Marine platoon dismounted from its trucks and gave chase, but was stopped by about two hundred Chinese manning emplacements on commanding ground. Gunfire was exchanged until late in the afternoon, when the outnumbered Marines withdrew with their prisoners. The captives stated under interrogation that they were members of a PLA division that was assembling west of Koto-ri.

Charged with keeping the MSR secure, Colonel Puller seized the opportunity to plan more aggressive patrols over a far wider area.

On November 28, while Charlie Peckham was packing away his

breakfast at Hamhung, a Marine outpost on a hilltop northeast of the Koto-ri perimeter was fired on by Chinese across the way. The outpost was first reinforced, then evacuated under an umbrella of Marine Corsair fighter-bombers.

Chesty received his first definitive orders from O. P. Smith at 1100 hours. The division commander, who had just established his Division Forward CP at Hagaru-ri, directed that the 2nd Battalion, 1st, mount a clearing operation directly up the MSR. By that time, airmen passing along the road had reported spotting abandoned American vehicles at roadblocks between the two villages. Dog Company, 1st, was dispatched aboard trucks at 1330, charged with meeting a tank-infantry force that Division said was heading south to link up with 2nd Battalion. (The second force, comprising a platoon of How/1 and three heavy tanks, had already been defeated within sight of the Hagaru-ri perimeter.)

After covering less than a mile of the ten-mile stretch between the towns, Dog/1 was engaged by numerous Chinese dug in on higher ground east of the roadway. The fighting was heavy. A Fox/1 platoon was sent up late in the day to provide an extra punch, but mounting casualties and negligible gains convinced the 2nd Battalion operations officer, who was running the sweep, that he had taken on more than he could overcome. The Marine force pulled back to Koto-ri with the help of its air cover.

★

By the time Dog/1 returned to Koto-ri, the tiny encampment had become a vast vehicle park. All traffic from the rear had to be stopped, and a plethora of units and parts of units had gathered in mind-boggling profusion. George/1, on its way to reinforce the Hagaru-ri garrison, had been stopped, as had the last serial of trucks carrying 1st Marine Division's Forward CP. Charlie Peckham's Baker/31 arrived after dark, as did 41 Royal Marine Commando, a two-hundred-fifty-man light infantry force attached to 1st Marine Division to bolster its reconnaissance capability. And there were scores of trucks brimming with Army headquarters and service troops and their equipment and baggage. No one knew how many men there were within the confines of the perimeter, nor exactly which units were represented. All of the transients were eager to be moving on, to rejoin their units. More, it was said, were on their way from bases to the rear.

As many of the transients as possible were put under canvas that night. Most had to feed themselves, and many went hungry.

Few of the transients had clear-cut missions, but Captain Charlie

Peckham drew one. As commander of an experienced infantry company, he reported directly to Chesty Puller, who told him that Baker/31 would be used to break through the PLA roadblocks and lead the way to Hagaru-ri, which seemed to have come under attack itself that bitter cold night.

Colonel Puller's headquarters was given the thankless task of organizing the transients into a convoy that would be able to defend itself and break through on the MSR in the morning. The senior combat officer among the transients was the commander of 41 Royal Marine Commando, Lieutenant Colonel Douglas Drysdale, the most spit-and-polish man any of the American Marines had ever seen. Drysdale was placed in command of the mixed combat units, though few of his new surordinates received that tidbit of news.

★

Dawn, November 29, found the Chinese in possession of the heights west of Koto-ri. While Fox/1 peppered the opposition with small-arms fire, Easy Battery, 11th, and the garrison's mortars were re-laid to bear on the road north. Then, as Baker/31 moved to begin clearing the roadway itself, the Royal Marines and George/1, bolstered by the 1st Marine Division Reconnaissance Company, deployed to attack the first hill mass east of the road. Word arrived that a heavy-tank company was on its way from the south, so Lieutenant Colonel Drysdale postponed the assault to await the tanks.

After a harrowing, exhausting morning spent traversing the icy, narrow, twisting road from Chinhung-ni, the main body of Captain Bruce Clarke's Dog Company, 1st Tank Battalion, stopped off beside the 1st Regiment CP to beg fuel. Puller's supply people could produce fifty gallons per tank, more than enough for the short run to Hagaru-ri. As soon as his command had refueled, Captain Clarke ordered his 1st Platoon leader, 1st Lieutenant Paul Sanders, a veteran mustang with nine years' active service behind him, to proceed from town to support the assault by 41 Commando and George/1. Sanders conferred briefly with Lieutenant Colonel Drysdale, who assigned him a common radio frequency and a small infantry support team. Then Sanders's five-tank platoon moved up the road to a position from which it was able to fire down the long axes of the enemy-held ridge.

The Royal Marines and George/1 delivered a spirited attack, bolstered by skilled close air support. The tanks fired on suspect areas along the ridge, and seemed to account for several Chinese strongpoints. In time, however, Sanders lost radio contact with Drysdale and had to secure firing. When he looked back to see how the convoy

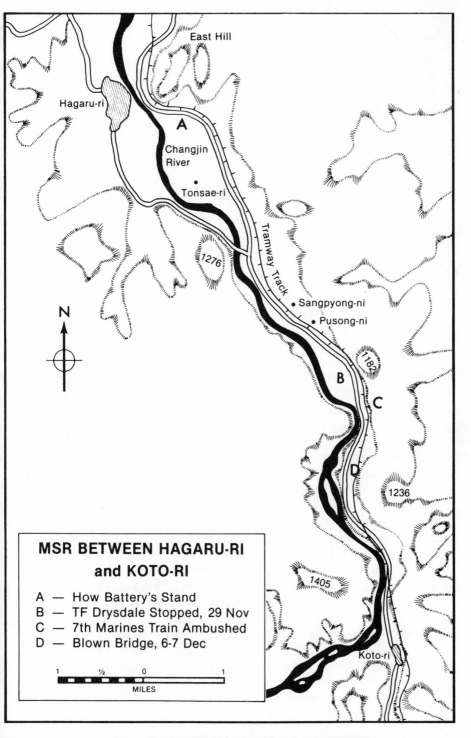

East Hill

Hagaru-ri

A

Changjin
River

Tonsae-ri

Tramway Track

1276

N

Sangpyong-ni

Pusong-ni

1182

B

C

D

1236

1405

MSR BETWEEN HAGARU-RI
and KOTO-RI

A — How Battery's Stand
B — TF Drysdale Stopped, 29 Nov
C — 7th Marines Train Ambushed
D — Blown Bridge, 6-7 Dec

Koto-ri

1   ½   0   1

MILES

(See endpapers for GUIDE TO MAP SYMBOLS AND ABBREVIATIONS.)

was faring, the tank officer was surprised to see that it had fallen far behind. However, he could not see Baker/31, which had advanced out of range. Sanders next queried headquarters, which ordered him to proceed slowly up the MSR with the remainder of Dog/Tanks and the heavy-tank platoon of the 5th Marines' Antitank Company following in his traces.

The Royal Marines and their American colleagues eventually reduced the Chinese strongpoint on the ridge overlooking the road just north of Koto-ri. George/1 moved down to the roadway and climbed aboard its trucks, and the Marine reconnaissance company hiked back to Koto-ri to help man the defenses there. Forty-one Commando deployed between the roadway and the skyline, screening the first elements of the long vehicle column.

It was a misty morning, and snow flurries were whipped into the faces of the attackers each time they dismounted from their vehicles to return fire. Marine Corsair pilots, based aboard Navy light carriers cruising off the coast, were willing enough to answer calls for close air support, but the shifting mists and the high, jumbled terrain forced many to pull up before they could get as near as they would have liked to their targets.

Progress on the roadway was agonizingly slow, and very costly. In the vanguard, Charlie Peckham maneuvered Baker/31 with great care. Behind, Captain Carl Sitter's George/1 maneuvered against numerous Chinese who had been driven briefly to ground by Peckham's company.

Tank Lieutenant Paul Sanders became a radio-relay operator because of freak atmospheric conditions. Stations at Koto-ri and Hagaru-ri could not pick each other up, but Sanders could converse with both on his tank's radio set. For a time, his was the only viable link between the bases, so he was privy to much disheartening news: the serious attacks of the night before had left Hagaru-ri's defenders severely shaken, uncertain about their prospects for holding out. Their pleas, more than anything, kept the advance from Koto-ri going despite stiffening opposition and mounting casualties.

As the point inched doggedly forward, Douglas Drysdale's native aggressiveness got the better of his judgment. Charlie Peckham had been conducting an exemplary advance against serious odds, but he was a methodical man — perhaps a bit more so than the worsening situation warranted, and certainly more so than the sanguinary Drysdale could bear.

It was well past noon, and Peckham was directing the loading of his lead platoon's truck following the reduction of yet another roadside strongpoint. Suddenly Peckham heard the roar of tank engines — an absolutely unmistakable sound — and he turned in time to see the lead vehicle as it surged on by. The next vehicle was a jeep bearing Lieutenant Colonel Drysdale, who yelled above the din, "Let's move forward!" Peckham demurred, noting that he had wounded and would not advance until they had been seen safely away. Drysdale heard Peckham out, responded with a smiling "Tally ho!" and took off down the road, drawing the tanks and Captain Sitter's George/1 in his wake.

Drysdale's impatience, brought on, perhaps, by desperate-sounding radio messages from Hagaru-ri, played havoc with the deployment of his mixed combat units, and it wrecked the tenuous cohesion of the noncombatant mixed units in the transport column.

For a time, a headlong stampede threatened to stall the long column in a massive traffic jam. The many "soft" vehicles — trucks, jeeps, ambulances — were easy pickings for Chinese gunners firing pre-registered mortars from the heights, and the convoy was soon fragmented by stalled vehicles and the smoking remains of burning trucks and jeeps.

Technical Sergeant Carl Hanson, a San Francisco Reservist serving as the 2nd Battalion, 1st's "atomic warfare specialist," spent most of the afternoon huddled in the confines of a canvas-covered 6x6 truck. Hanson, a combat veteran of five Pacific campaigns, had been forced by the ennui of his non-job to volunteer for every task he could find. This day, November 29, he had heard that fighting men were needed to help guard the convoy, so he had volunteered again. Far from seeing any fighting, however, Hanson spent the day on the bed of his closed truck, mixed up with a bunch of strangers who knew as little about the ten- and fifteen-minute delays as he. Hundreds of men in scores of other vehicles were similarly in the dark, and more and more of them were succumbing to Chinese fire from the heights.

★

Charlie Peckham was nearly beside himself with frustration. The move forward by Drysdale and the tanks had fragmented Baker/31. Unable to move back in the column, the infantry captain allowed himself and the remnants of his lead platoon to be pushed forward. He requested permission to withdraw, but was denied. He asked for ammunition to replace the morning's heavy consumption, but was again denied. At length, Baker/31's lead platoon was stopped in its tracks by a burning ammunition truck that had sealed the roadway. A knot of American and British Marines in the charge of Major John

McLaughlin, the senior Marine X Corps liaison officer to O. P. Smith's headquarters, was working to help several injured and wounded men and to clear the roadway. Unable to proceed, Charlie Peckham called his troops onto the road and deployed them in roadside ditches to protect the wounded and return fire at the Chinese on the heights.

★

The last cohesive unit to enter Koto-ri from the south was Captain Bruce Williams's Baker Company, 1st Tank Battalion, which arrived at about 1500 following many minor delays. Captain Williams set his crews to refueling and reported to Colonel Puller. As commander of the regiment to which Baker/Tanks was normally attached, Puller commandeered Williams's 2nd Platoon to remain at Koto-ri. The balance of the company moved out at about 1600 hours, separated from the tail of the convoy by less than three miles.

Bruce Williams was an experienced combat veteran with twelve years in the Corps, and he was not at all happy about being sent off alone with eleven tanks and his company's twenty-three soft vehicles. He had surveyed the MSR a week earlier, so he knew better than most that there was almost nowhere that a heavy tank could safely turn around or pass another vehicle. Being at the tail of the column, once he caught it, meant remaining at the tail of the column.

Baker/Tanks moved off cautiously, catching fire from the numerous Chinese who had been bypassed by the leading wedge of infantry and the main body of the convoy.

★

First Lieutenant Paul Sanders, commanding the lead platoon of Dog/Tanks, continued to relay disquieting messages from Hagaru-ri to Colonel Puller. The garrison ahead was counting heavily upon being reinforced; all news of adversity on the MSR was countered with renewed pleas for fresh troops. General Smith ordered Lieutenant Colonel Drysdale to get through *"at all costs."*

While the combat units at the head of the straggling, struggling column had a slim opportunity to comply with Smith's directive, the prospects of the more than one hundred soft vehicles comprising the main body were becoming grimmer by the minute.

The eventual loss of every radio in the column to gunfire assured loss of control, and that resulted in crumbling discipline throughout that long, fire-swept afternoon. Unable to advance, numerous drivers simply turned their vehicles around in vain attempts to breast the tide. For a time, ambulances filled to capacity and beyond were getting through, but even they were stopped as the roadway and verges were sealed by greater and greater snarls.

★

Late in the afternoon, at a narrow defile about five miles north of Koto-ri, the lead tanks approached a sharp right bend in the road. Several houses comprising tiny Pusong-ni could be seen through the view slits and periscopes of the buttoned-up tanks. It was clear that the Chinese were in positions enfilading the roadway. Paul Sanders saw a number of them taking cover along the bank of a frozen water-course to the left. High Explosive rounds were fired through the houses, and machine guns were put to work on the stream bed. The choke point was passed, but dead ahead was a bridge, and it had been demolished.

It was getting dark, and colder. Sanders had no maps, and no idea what lay ahead. He radioed his company commander, Captain Bruce Clarke, and was told to make way for the rear platoon, which would try to bypass the blown bridge. The maneuver was accomplished with great difficulty, convincing Captain Clarke that, while tanks might get through, soft vehicles would be sitting ducks. He reported as much to Lieutenant Colonel Drysdale, who sent his adjutant forward to have a look; the British lieutenant was wounded before he could find Clarke. At the same time, sheets of gunfire from the heights wounded George/1's machine-gun officer and Lieutenant Colonel Drysdale. Command of the vanguard group passed to George/1's Captain Carl Sitter, who ordered his troops to deploy and return the fire.

As the troops were jumping down to the road to join the fight, a scream of "Grenade!" sent everyone ducking for cover. Private First Class William Baugh went for the grenade, smothering it with his body. Baugh was mortally injured, but the men around him were untouched.

By then, it was dark. Paul Sanders had to crack open his tank's turret hatch and peer out in order to direct his driver along the tricky, slippery roadway. He gave wrong directions once, and the tank slithered out of control into a roadside ditch. It took considerable effort to regain the roadway. Disdainful of the ribbons of tracer rolling down from the heights, the tank platoon leader stood fully erect for a better look, and spotted two Chinese moving up from behind to score a quick kill. Sanders fired his .45 in anger for the only time in his long career and he felled both attackers, an amazing feat.

Farther on, Sanders's tank slipped from the roadway once again, blocking it. There was no way to maneuver out of the ditch, so Sanders climbed down through the gunfire and stretched a tow cable. Then he strode to the next tank back and banged for several long moments on the driver's hatch before it was opened. After voicing some strong emotions at the driver, the platoon leader ordered that the tank close on his own stranded vehicle. The tow was successfully completed, and Sanders returned to his exposed turret perch to guide his platoon through the next series of adventures.

Feeling its way along the darkened, fire-swept road, the heavy-tank company edged toward the first Marine blocks guarding besieged Hagaru-ri. One of the heavies was knocked out by an antitank grenade and had to be shoved into a ditch to clear the roadway. Paul Sanders passed through the friendly roadblock almost before he realized he was home free. Immediately, he felt his engine seize and die. He had run out of fuel right on the dime.

(When one of the tanks inadvertently crushed one of the jeeps owned by the gunners manning the roadblock, the gunnery sergeant in charge called his commander, Major Ed Simmons, to complain. Simmons, like most infantrymen, had developed a strong organizational bias, and an all-too-typical paranoia regarding other friendly units. He told the gunnery sergeant to "slip a rocket" to any tank that damaged any more of his equipment.)

Next up was George/1, which paused beside a small tent encampment, believing it to be in friendly hands. It was not, having been abandoned the night before in the face of the first Chinese attacks. A grenade landed in one of the troop trucks, wounding everyone aboard. All hands quickly remounted the trucks to be driven briskly through the weapons company roadblock by 2000 hours, after ten and one half hours on the move. George/1 was immediately ordered to East Hill to help man the line.

The rapid, sudden, last lunge by the tanks and Captain Sitter's company left the bulk of 41 Commando holding the bag. The Chinese quickly surrounded the two hundred odd Royal Marines and proceeded to whittle away at their diminishing positions.

★

Miles to the rear, Captain Bruce Williams, of Baker/Tanks, had been inching forward with the bulk of his company since 1600 hours. Now it was dark, and the tanks were highly vulnerable to a determined attack by infantry and sappers. Williams was deeply concerned. He advanced on foot about ten yards ahead of his point tank, rounded a curve and laid eyes on a disaster that took his cold-numbed mind minutes to comprehend. The road was securely blocked by wrecked and burning vehicles, and there was no way for the tanks to bypass the carnage. Then heavy mortar fire opened and began falling perilously close to the tank company's fuel and ammunition trucks.

One look was enough. Captain Williams ordered his company to turn around and head back to Koto-ri. All he could accomplish on the MSR was the destruction of Baker/Tanks.

★

The horned head of the column had lurched to a modicum of safety, and the armored tail was groping its way back toward Koto-ri. But the soft body of the column was pinned to the road in several places, squirming like a dying serpent, wholly at the mercy of the Chinese vivisectionists on the heights.

It would be a long, dark night.

C H A P T E R

23

Captain Bill Barber's Fox/7 was hanging on at Toktong Pass. Barely.

On the morning of November 28, following the brutal night-long fighting in which Fox/7 had held its hill against unbelievable odds, the badly hurt company had drawn protection from the squadron of Australian F-51 fighter-bombers based at Yonpo. It had taken some ingenuity to patch a relay to the RAAF pilots through the air-control squadron at Hagaru-ri, but the Chinese were soon suffering grievous harm under the guns of the daring Aussies and, later, familiar Marine Corsairs.

The day was spent registering How Battery (based at Hagaru-ri), digging in, and caring for the numerous wounded. There was an air of expectancy throughout November 28, but news that evening that Lieutenant Colonel Ray Davis's 1st Battalion, 7th, had been turned back at Turkey Hill went down hard with the troops.

Marine four-engined transports put in a bid to resupply the tiny enclave. Most of the drop fell by two houses at the base of the hill, near the MSR. The company supply sergeant went out immediately to retrieve the goods, but was shot through the leg as he was cutting away the parachute lines from the first bundle. The company machine-gun officer ran down the slope to retrieve the fallen sergeant, but he had his leg broken by a round fired by the same sniper. A fire team from 1st Platoon rushed out to flush the sniper while the company exec organized a team of volunteers to race the goods back up the hill, a task accomplished without further incident.

All the wounded who were able crawled from the warmth of their down bags at sunset, picked through a pile of discarded weapons that had been stacked by Bill Barber's command post, and went to the lines to beat off expected attacks.

★

The Chinese returned in strength at 0200, November 29. A mortar round immediately killed one 3rd Platoon Marine and injured two others.

Private First Class Bob Ezell, a light-machine gunner whose squad had been moved across the perimeter during the day to support 3rd Platoon's defense of the saddle leading to Fox Hill from Toktong-San, was startled by the sudden onset of the attack. Together with his buddy, Private First Class Jerry Triggs, Ezell grabbed two hand grenades and pulled the pin from the first one. Then, to be certain the cold had not affected the mechanism that ejected the arming spoon, he pulled the spoon away from the grenade and heaved it with all his might. The two gunners used up their four grenades in a hurry as the Chinese breasted the slope and moved right on through.

Though its guns were urgently needed to support Hagaru-ri's defense that night, How/11 managed to answer a quick call from Fox/ 7's forward observer, 2nd Lieutenant Don Campbell. The salvo discouraged the Chinese on the saddle from following the first increment of about fifty riflemen through the Marine line.

Bob Ezell and Jerry Triggs fired their Garand rifles as quickly as they were able to, which was not very quickly at all. The cold made the cartridge ejectors seize up, and the two men had to crank back the levers in order to eject each empty and insert the next round into the breech. Cold hands prevented smooth loading of new eight-round clips.

The initial penetration was quickly sealed off, and a machine gun was turned on the infiltrators. A Chinese bugler made a great racket until he was shot dead by an unappreciative Marine.

As soon as How Battery stopped firing, Private First Class Lloyd O'Leary, the most senior mortar gunner still on duty, set a curtain of

60mm and 81mm rounds across the saddle, keeping the Chinese on Toktong-San at bay.

Corporal Tom Ashdale, whose 3rd Platoon squad had held the Chinese back the previous night, was wounded, and two of his men were killed. Ashdale, however, returned to the fight as soon as he had had his wound dressed.

The Chinese on Fox Hill were held firmly between 2nd and 3rd Platoons, but they were feisty. While Bob Ezell was squeezing a fresh clip into his balky rifle, a Chinese soldier on the other side of an eight-foot-high boulder dropped a grenade between Ezell and Jerry Triggs. Their gear absorbed most of the blast, but the two gunners were thrown from their fighting hole. Ezell knew that he had sustained a bad wound in one leg, but lost consciousness before he could react.

Third Platoon had to pull back to cover on its right. First Lieutenant Bob McCarthy, the platoon leader, was moving right, toward 1st Platoon, when Captain Barber arrived to check the line. Both officers were immediately hit in their legs by a burst of machine-gun fire. McCarthy was taken to the sick bay, but Barber plugged the hole in his leg with a wad of handkerchief and continued to hobble about, encouraging his troops with cheers and advice.

Private First Class Bob Ezell came to, realizing at once that he was surrounded by Chinese. He lay still, breathing quietly into the hood of his parka, holding his eyes half open to see what was going on. After some minutes, a Chinese soldier sat down between Ezell and his buddy, Jerry Triggs, and began looting the two "bodies." Ezell felt his gloves being slipped from his hands, then went limp as the enemy soldier fumbled for his wristwatch. The man then took the gloves from the unconscious Triggs and moved on.

The battle waxed and waned through the night. Bob Ezell heard an American voice suggest that mortars be fired into the rocks in which he lay doggo. "There're Marines up here," he ventured. The voice of a member of Ezell's squad cut through the night, asking if it was, indeed, Ezell: "Can you move?"

"I don't know. I'll try." He was able to roll over onto his belly and pull himself downhill through the snow with his arms; his legs would not function. Reaching the tree line, he told his buddies that Jerry Triggs was still in among the rocks; then Ezell was carried to the sick-bay tent.

Third Platoon's new commander, Staff Sergeant John Audas, a professional who had seen first combat at Guadalcanal as a rear-seat gunner aboard a dive bomber, led a spirited counterattack at dawn against the infiltrators who had been pinned by 2nd Platoon. The Chinese gave ground quickly, wounding two Marines as they scattered across the saddle and disappeared, leaving most of their number dead.

A nose-count revealed that Fox/7 had lost five killed and twenty-nine wounded during the second night's attack.

Fox Company's only hope lay in its being massively reinforced or relieved. There was no way Bill Barber could withdraw when over half his troops had been wounded or killed.

Help was on the way.

★

Major Warren Morris, known to everyone as "Lefty," had enlisted in the Corps as a private in 1940. He had served as a platoon leader at Guadalcanal, and at Tarawa he had led an assault company in which he and every one of his officers had been wounded in two days of combat. He had come to Korea leading a five-hundred-man casual detachment used to fill out the Regular battalion that became the 3rd Battalion, 7th, when it arrived in Japan from the Med. Morris had stayed on to serve as the battalion exec during Inchon-Seoul and the drive north from Wonsan.

When Lefty Morris was told that he would be leading an effort to free Fox/7 from its isolation at Toktong Pass, he was elated. When his old friend and contemporary, Major Hank Woessner, told him how his force was to be comprised, Morris's elation flagged a bit.

It was risky to leave too large a gap in the Yudam-ni perimeter line, so Woessner had recommended to Colonel Litzenberg that a company be drawn from each of several battalions on the southern line closest to Toktong Pass, and placed under Major Morris, who would draw a scratch staff to help him direct the effort. The plan called for Morris to advance down the MSR to the pass, link up with Barber, and pull back to Yudam-ni unless he was dead certain he could hold the pass open long enough to allow the reinforcements to get through from the south or the withdrawal of the Yudam-ni garrison to Hagaru-ri.

Litz bought the plan and left Woessner and Morris to make the arrangements.

The Composite Battalion, as it came to be called, was assembled at the CP of the 1st Battalion, 7th, at sunrise, November 29. It consisted of 1st Lieutenant Joe Kurcaba's Baker/7, which was hiking back up the MSR for the third time in three days; Able/5, which was replaced on Hill 1240 by a mixed bag of artillerymen and clerks;

George/7, which had not been in action since its brutal hill fight on November 27; a section each of 81mm mortars from the 1st and 3rd Battalions, 7th; a section of 75mm recoilless antitank rifles from the 7th Antitank Company; and several communicators from the 3rd Battalion, 7th. Morris's entire staff was Captain Bill Earney, operations officer of the 3rd Battalion, 7th.

The plan was simple: Baker/7 would attack down the left side of the MSR, while George/7 would move on the right; Able/5 would be reserve. The mortars and recoilless rifles would leapfrog along the roadway while the companies on either side pushed the Chinese back from the road. Marine Air and several 105mm howitzers would be on call if needed.

★

The Composite Battalion jumped off from Ray Davis's CP at 0800, proceeding slowly along the road, which rose endlessly toward Toktong Pass. There was no opposition whatsoever for the first seven hundred fifty yards, at which point the leading elements were engaged by mortars and machine guns to the left and right. Major Morris dismounted from his command vehicle in the center of the road and directed his rifle companies to move to the hills. An observation plane arrived to scout the Chinese positions; its pilot dropped written notes in grenade canisters.

Chinese gunners on the heights were in plain view, planting their aiming stakes with infuriating deliberation. Morris called his two 75mm recoilless rifles forward, and these were used with telling effect. As time passed, however, the Composite Battalion commander feared that he would run out of 75mm ammunition, so he had the guns secure in favor of calling fire from the 105s back in the perimeter.

The attack ground steadily forward, but slowly. Major Morris and Captain Earney were worried about being channelized on the roadway, which was rising steadily through a narrowing defile.

On the heights to the left, Baker/7, with 1st Lieutenant Woody Taylor's 1st Platoon in the lead, was experiencing almost zero opposition. Second Lieutenant Joe Owen, the company mortar officer, was firing steadily at targets spotted by troops in the vanguard. Ammunition began running dangerously low, so Owen placed a standing order for as much as could be packed up the steep slopes to his advancing 60mm section.

Taylor's platoon tipped the crest of a steep ridge shortly after 1300 and looked into the valley on the far side. It was crawling with PLA infantry, at least a battalion. Taylor called his supporting machine guns forward and quickly deployed his men along a secure firing line.

On the roadway, Lefty Morris and Bill Earney read a hastily scrawled message that had been dropped moments earlier by the observation pilot. A very strong Chinese force had been spotted to the right of the MSR and a second, larger, force was maneuvering through adjacent valleys to the left. Major Morris placed a call to Colonel Litzenberg, who ordered the Composite Battalion to break contact and return posthaste to Yudam-ni.

On the heights, Joe Owen was putting out 60mm rounds as fast as they could be dropped into the muzzles of his mortars. On the line, Woody Taylor's platoon was killing Chinese by the dozens. A runner from the company commander arrived and told Taylor to withdraw, that a superior force was massing for an attack against the company left and rear. Joe Owen was told to cache all his reserve ammunition and move to the roadway as fast as he could.

The quickest way back to the road for Taylor's platoon was straight down a steep wall which, fortunately, was interspersed with out-croppings and ledges every fifteen or thirty feet. The platoon dropped nearly five hundred feet in all and formed with the remainder of the Composite Battalion, which withdrew quickly under an umbrella of air and artillery support.

The Chinese resisted the battalion's retrograde movement in strength at a point midway between Hill 1542 and Turkey Hill, but the entire force managed to get by and file into the perimeter none the worse for wear.

★

On Fox Hill, Captain Bill Barber ordered his men to lay out the brightly colored parachutes that had fallen with the supplies dropped by Marine cargo aircraft the day before. More Marine transports flew over the tiny enclave at 1030 and placed more ammunition and supplies right on the money. A little while later 1st Lieutenant Floyd Englehardt landed his two-place helicopter atop Fox Hill and dropped off a critically needed load of radio batteries despite heavy fire from the Chinese atop Toktong-San, just across the way.

An afternoon supply drop by Air Force C-119 Flying Boxcars landed over five hundred yards to the west. Immediately, 1st Lieutenant Elmo Peterson, twice wounded in previous action, led a group of volunteers through the lines and reached the supplies without incident. However, as soon as the Marines started cutting away the parachute lines, they were sprayed with heavy gunfire. The company mortars went into action, as did the 3rd Platoon. The company mortar officer, 2nd Lieutenant Joe Brady, who had been painfully wounded in one arm the first night, clutched a pair of 81mm rounds under his good arm. A former Dartmouth football star, Brady ran for a touchdown, followed by the remainder of the supply detail.

The insertion of needed supplies into the shrinking perimeter, and the good results obtained by several morale-building combat patrols, did not alleviate the ripple of depression that passed quickly through Fox Company when it was learned that Fox Hill had to be held for yet a third night.

Another depressing realization was that air-dropped supplies that had fallen into Chinese hands could be and were being used against the company, particularly 81mm mortar rounds, which could be used in Chinese 82mm mortars.

But the supplies that reached Fox Company had materially improved the lot of the troops, particularly the wounded. Large quantities of wool blankets and several air-dropped stretchers insured that most injured Marines would not have to sleep on the cold earth. Still, it was a harrowing experience for the men whose injuries kept them down. Private First Class Bob Ezell, whose gloves had been pulled from his hands by a Chinese looter, would have lost his fingers to the cold but for the compassion of a wounded buddy who, though his own hand had been injured, massaged Ezell's to keep the circulation going.

It was dead certain that Fox Company would face renewed attacks before help could arrive.

C H A P T E R

24

Strangely, though the three PLA armies surrounding the 5th and 7th Marines had vast numerical superiority over the Yudam-ni garrison, they made no serious bid to destroy the Marines. They had allowed the garrison to consolidate its position on November 28, and they undertook no threatening action during the night of November 28–

29 to push in any of several tenuously held positions around the circumference of the Yudam-ni perimeter.

Most of the fighting on November 28 had occurred between Marine and Chinese units that happened to remain in close proximity following the bloody fighting of the first night. Those same units snarled and raged and lashed at one another through the long second night, but neither side tried seriously to severely damage the other.

The Chinese passivity — it was for them to act or remain passive — continued through to the morning of November 29.

Still, incidents did occur. And men still died.

★

Baker Company, 5th Marines, had moved up to Hill 1240 on the morning of November 28, following the heroic stand by Dog/7's Captain Milt Hull and no more than sixteen of his bloodied command. Though fresh, Baker/5 had been pretty much unable to move the Chinese from the positions they had won on the hill, which was partly a result of the impossible terrain, but largely a result of the dogged determination of at least that one unit of PLA infantry.

Somehow, the Chinese had gotten possession of a bunker-centered strongpoint — either the bunker had already been on the hilltop, or it was very quickly installed following the ejection of Dog/7 during the first night's fighting. Constant sorties by Baker/5 Marines on November 28 had run into terrifyingly accurate grazing fire from the bunker and outlying positions, and the company had suffered bloody repulses, gaining nothing. Chinese mortars emplaced on the reverse slope and on hills farther to the east had supported Chinese sallies the night of November 28–29, but Baker/5 had proven the worth of its own defensive efforts, and the Chinese had been repulsed. The best support that could be mustered for Baker/5 that night had come from the regimental 4.2-inch heavy mortars, whose fire could not be accurately assessed by the artillery forward observer who called it, for it invariably landed on the far side of the jutting razorback ridge, and no Marine was high enough to observe the shells as they landed. Similarly, air strikes called at dusk and dawn could not be observed from the ground, though the pilots claimed to have hit numerous targets.

The only way that Baker/5 could be certain of clearing the crest was to mount a successful infantry assault.

Second Lieutenant Austin Jenson's 1st Platoon mounted the direct assault with 2nd Lieutenant Ed Morris's 3rd Platoon providing a base of fire. Jenson was killed leading his troops, who were turned back after achieving almost zero gains. The Chinese threw in a counterattack on the heels of the withdrawing platoon, but Morris's platoon was able to hold the line. As the day wore on, the company 60mm mortars, the battalion 81mm mortars, and the regimental 4.2-inch mortars were registered and fired, often against targets on the forward slopes, often within yards of Ed Morris's forward platoon.

Baker/5 wasn't winning any new ground, but it wasn't losing any either. And that was something.

★

The next Marine-held hill north of Hill 1240 was Hill 1282, which was partly in the possession of Lieutenant Colonel Bob Taplett's 3rd Battalion, 5th.

Taplett had had an odd visitor his first night in position behind Hill 1282. One of his outposts had captured an Asian man it found lugging through no-man's-land an enormous valise filled with freshly printed yen notes. The man claimed to be a South Korean intelligence agent who had made his way, at grave personal risk, to assist the American Marines. He was sent to Regiment after he tried unsuccessfully to provide a satisfactory explanation for having such a fortune in his possession. Bob Taplett chalked the experience up to the already-accepted weirdness of the war.

While Item/5 traded grenades and mortar fire all day with Chinese dug in just over the razorback ridge, How/5 established several blocking positions on the valley floor, covering the narrow draws running to the north-northeast and northeast.

Toward dawn on November 29, Marines at a listening post a short way up one of the draws detected movement on its front by about sixty Chinese, and alerted the nearby blocking force they were screening. All hands at the blocking position were awakened to man a section of machine guns, BARs, and a full complement of infantry weapons. At first these Marines thought they heard the troops from the listening post withdrawing to safety in the murky light, so they held their fire.

The listening post had been withdrawn to friendly lines, but by an alternate route. The only men in front of the How/5 machine guns were Chinese.

The intruders walked right up to the muzzle of the forwardmost machine gun before they could be identified. The gunner was belted across the helmet by the first Chinese soldier, and knocked aside. The assistant gunner recovered quickly, grabbed the gun's trigger and spread the intruder across the mouth of the draw along with seventeen other Chinese. The machine gunner who had been coldcocked hurt mainly in his pride.

The fighting on Hill 1282 was a stalemate. Bob Taplett did not really desire the reduction of the Chinese on the reverse slope, for covering the entire ridgeline would have stretched his ability beyond the limit. Because it was supported by enfilade positions to the right and left, Item/5 was fairly secure from being thrown from the hill.

Item/5 Marines could not see the Chinese on the far side of the razorback crest, and the Chinese could not see them. The battle, conducted with the liberal use of hand grenades, was as hairy a fight as could be imagined. The skipper of Item/5, Captain Harold George Schrier, was a former Marine Raider, the man who had placed the *first* of two American Flags atop Mount Suribachi on Iwo Jima. When George Schrier told Bob Taplett that Hill 1282 was his toughest fight, Taplett was simply awed. Item/5 expended over one thousand grenades in a one-hour period on the morning of November 29.

Adding to the uniqueness of the Hill 1282 fighting, Marine Corsairs had to attack the Chinese on the reverse slope by flying directly at the Item/5 lines.

Casualties mounted steadily. Schrier's company had to be augmented by a provisional platoon of gunners from Charlie Battery, 11th, while a similar platoon from Able Battery went to George Company.

Toe to toe with the enemy, Taplett's battalion was being slowly bled dry.

★

The boldest Chinese effort of November 29 unfolded in front of the 2nd Battalion, 5th, which had dug in the previous day on and around Hill 1426 at the northeastern end of the new perimeter.

After adjusting his positions in the morning, Captain Sam Jaskilka, Easy/5's commander, called his 81mm forward observer, Sergeant Jim Friedl, to the crest of the hill and ordered him to re-register the company 60s and his section of 81s. The impact area was in a broad valley fronting the hill.

Starting from the right, from which he could see barely half of the high-walled valley, Friedl was dictating his first set of coordinates when he was called to the left to observe some enemy movement. As the veteran gunner slithered around an obscuring knob, he was stunned to see a Chinese battalion massing in full view in the left half of the valley.

"I'll need all the guns," Friedl blurted through his hand mike to the 81mm fire-direction center.

"What?" went the reply. "You must be joking. No way!"

Friedl called for Sam Jaskilka, who called the battalion commander, Hal Roise, as soon as he had had a look at the Chinese in
the valley. The guns were Roise's weapons of opportunity, and only
he could release all six of them to the control of a single forward
observer. Captain Jaskilka outlined the situation, and Roise gave
him the guns.

Jim Friedl called for High Explosives. "All guns, search and traverse."

Six 81mm rounds *thungged* from six mortar tubes and arched high
over Hill 1426. They were on target. The guns fired continuous
search-and-traverse box patterns, scything great swaths through the
Chinese formation. The dent in the battalion's ready ammunition
supply was enormous. The Chinese were well beyond the range of
Roise's small arms and machine guns, but they remained passively
within the range of the 81mm and 60mm mortars plugged into Jim
Friedl's radio net. There was sheer butchery for a time, but the
depletion of ammunition made it look for a time as though many
Chinese might escape.

Two things saved the game. First, in the great American tradition
of the cavalry arriving in the nick of time, Air Force transport planes
swept in over the valley of Yudam-ni, dropping great hulks of cargo
suspended from brightly colored parachutes. By a lucky turn of fate,
the crates that landed closest to the 2nd Battalion, 5th, included a
planeload of 81mm mortar ammunition, which was rushed to the
gun pits by jeeps streaming parachutes behind. The new cases were
broken open and the new rounds were fed directly into the hungry
muzzles of the guns under Jim Friedl's direction.

As the transports droned northward away from the Yudam-ni before turning back over the mountains toward home, Lieutenant
Colonel Tony Eisele banked his Corsair away from the beehive
holding pattern over the valley and answered the call of a forward
air controller on Hill 1426. Eisele, who had drawn first blood over
Guadalcanal in 1943, was the temporary commander of VMF-212
out of Yonpo, and he was eager to avenge some of the sights he had
seen on the MSR on the way to Yudam-ni that day. He roared over
the hill and fired his F4U-5's four 20mm cannon at the ranks of
Chinese which had broken on the valley floor and were now scrabbling up the steep ridge to the east. As mortar rounds arched across
his line of flight, Eisele streaked toward the ground.

Every third round from his wing-mounted cannon was High Explosive, and each of them flashed brightly upon impacting against
the frozen ground. As Tony Eisele reached the ridgeline at reduced

speed, he saw one explosive round hit a Chinese soldier in the thigh. As he pulled his Corsair over the ridge, the airman saw that the infantryman was still clinging to the ridge with his hands; the injured leg was dangling from a single strand of flesh or a tendon.

Lieutenant Colonel Eisele formed up with the rest of his four-plane division and undertook a second run, noting that there were numerous bodies at the foot of the ridge. His third run, and several that followed, accounted for diminishing numbers of Chinese in the scrub and deep snow on the reverse slope of the ridge he had first attacked.

After using the last of his ammunition, Eisele re-formed his division and highballed to Yonpo for a bath and a hot meal.

★

A meal — any meal, hot or cold — would have been fine with Private First Class Walker Merell, who had been wounded on Turkey Hill the day before. So would some medical attention for his shoulder wound have been fine with the twenty-year-old Ohio Reservist as he lay on a stretcher on the packed earth floor of an overcrowded, charnel-smelling hospital tent in the middle of the Yudam-ni perimeter. But in the full day since he had been brought back from Turkey Hill, Merell had had only a few soda crackers and a cursory medical examination by a very tired Navy corpsman.

The feeling in the fingers of Merell's right hand had been gone for most of the day.

★

Sergeant Jim Matthews was airborne, and a badly wounded Marine on a litter was screaming in his ear.

Matthews had been wounded in the dark on the morning of November 28 as he helped hold the Chinese away from Fox/5's hilltop position. After a day of wandering about the hospital area, he had heard that penicillin was among the medical supplies dropped by Air Force cargo transports. He had received no antibiotics for his wound, so he ambled over to the aid tents to beg a shot.

The tent was warm and cozy, and Matthews really hated to leave when a corpsman told him to come back in a while, after the cargo crates had been unpacked. The cold air hit Matthews before he knew it, and he collapsed unconscious halfway out of the tent.

The next thing he knew several strangers were cramming him into the seat of a two-place helicopter while others stuffed a litter half in and half out behind him. Forced to kneel the whole way to Hagaru-ri, the Michigan-bred Reservist passed the most terrifying moments of his life as the man on the litter screamed and screamed in his agony.

★

But for sporadic firing up and down the Yudam-ni line, particularly along a sector manned exclusively by gunners of Major Fox Parry's 3rd Battalion, 11th, the Yudam-ni garrison passed the quietest night of its existence.

In the darkened headquarters tents the commanders of the 5th and 7th Marines, and their senior staffers, decided to contract the perimeter some more on November 30, and prepare for the expected order from Division to evacuate the valley and head south through Toktong Pass to Hagaru-ri.

CHAPTER
25

The Marine Corsairs completed their runs on several large Chinese maneuvering elements at 1730, November 29, and flew from sight, leaving Lieutenant Colonel Don Faith's battered 1st Battalion, 32nd Infantry, to face another night with worsening prospects for survival.

Once darkness had set in over Faith's perimeter, several riflemen from each platoon were detailed to fetch food from the galleys that had been set up around the battalion CP, but it was so cold that the hot food froze before it could be carried to the men who had been manning the line through the day's incessant fighting.

Two days of effort had failed to dislodge the Chinese from a knob overlooking the juncture of Able and Charlie Companies, but plenty of good men had been killed or injured taking the fight to those particular PLA soldiers. All that could be spared to hold the Chinese on the knob at bay were two heavy machine guns and a five-man squad of riflemen.

The Chinese struck at about 2230, hitting several segments of the weakened perimeter at the same moment. First Lieutenant James Campbell, a platoon leader with Dog/32, the battalion weapons company, heard a shout and saw several shadows run from the knoll held by the five-man squad. He counted five figures passing his fighting hole in the dark, and he shot the sixth. Then he ordered one of his two machine guns to displace to cover the gap, at which instant a mortar fragment knifed through his cheek and lodged in the roof of his mouth. Campbell remained with his gunners, who held the Chinese to their initial gains through two hours of heavy exchanges.

Captain Hugh Robbins, the 31st Infantry's personnel officer, rushed to Don Faith's CP with Colonel Allen MacLean as soon as the perimeter was attacked. Faith was in control, but as the staffers of the 31st listened to his exchanges with officers and noncoms holding the line, it was evident that the 32-year-old battalion commander was reaching the limits of his patience and endurance. At length, Faith ordered all nonessential personnel from the tiny room, telling them to find weapons and man a defensive position outside.

Unengaged, Hugh Robbins idled away the midnight hour watching mortar shells exploding all around and within the perimeter. Lovely chains of tracer flew to and from the perimeter, winking merrily through the blackness. Shadowy figures passed continually through the CP hut, and the line of stretchers outside the aid station continued to grow. . . . In time, the volume of firing subsided.

Captain Bill McNally, MacLean's regimental communicator, was called into the command post, but returned after only a few moments inside. He told Captain Robbins that the colonel had decided to withdraw Faith's battalion in the morning and attack down the road to achieve a junction with Reilly's 3rd Battalion, 31st, some miles to the rear. That was at 0200.

As many men as could be spared from the lines were pulled back to unload all the battalion's vehicles, regardless of what was aboard. All the wounded had to be loaded, and there was barely room enough for them. Colonel MacLean rejected the suggestion that the abandoned gear and files be burned, for fires would alert the Chinese that the battalion would be attempting a breakout.

It was snowing like mad, which helped muffle the preparations more than it hindered work. Drivers began getting the frozen engines going, which was no mean task. As each truck or jeep was started, it was moved onto the road in no particular order. Hugh Robbins had to crank his jeep's frozen engine by hand.

Colonels MacLean and Faith had agreed to withdraw the fighting units in rotation and fight a slow rearguard action until everyone was on the move. Charlie and Baker Companies were to advance along the ridgelines on either side of the road while Able Company guarded the rear. As soon as the first combat units were withdrawn, however, the plan fell apart; everyone rushed into position at once.

The fire from the Chinese on the heights was horrendous.

First Lieutenant James Mortrude, who had taken command of Charlie/32 when its original commander had been wounded that night, could hear plenty of activity down on the road, but he could see nothing in the darkness, which at least prevented the Chinese from taking decisive action.

The situation changed dramatically at first light as Chinese gunners aimed at the slow-moving column on the road.

Marine Captain Ed Stamford was standing by at sunrise to direct the first flights of Marine Corsairs against Chinese emplacements overlooking the road at the end of an icy inlet that was barring direct access to Reilly's perimeter.

From his position at the head of the column, Stamford could see tiny figures at the tip of the frozen inlet. They appeared to be packing mortars and machine guns as they galloped through the snow. A mortar flashed in the early morning light as the first of Faith's troops occupied the nose of a ridge on their side of the inlet. Stamford requested permission to call in the Corsairs, but Faith and MacLean both hesitated, fearful that the distant figures might be Americans.

The three officers watched for a few moments more, then Faith told the Marine airman to call a strike against a Chinese maneuvering element closing on Able Company's rear guard. The Marine forward air-control team pulled out of the column, which started up again as soon as the Corsairs began hitting the mortars to the front and the attackers to the north.

While Faith quickly moved two companies forward, 1st Lieutenant James Campbell, who was still carrying a Chinese mortar shard in the roof of his mouth, was sent up the ridge with two heavy machine guns and a 75mm recoilless rifle. As soon as the guns were set, Campbell ordered them to commence firing at the Chinese roadblock, which by then had stopped the vehicle column. From his high vantage point, Campbell could see the small perimeter of the 3rd Battalion, 31st, and two batteries of the 57th Field Artillery Battalion. Beyond that were hundreds of Chinese. Campbell directed his machine guns to keep firing at the roadblock on his side of the inlet, but had the longer-ranged recoilless rifle engage the enemy south of the friendly perimeter.

What happened next on the road is somewhat open to speculation. It appears that a small detachment of infantry crossed the stone bridge from friendly lines, either to guide the convoy in or to assist in the reduction of the roadblock. There was a flurry of firing, which looked from the point of the column to be friendly troops around the bridge engaging Faith's maneuvering elements by the ridge.

Colonel MacLean, who had shown signs of being under severe strain during the latter portion of the withdrawal, jumped to the roadway and slid down the bank onto the ice, heading for the bridge. Americans nearby thought he was trying to stop unidentified troops across the inlet from firing on friendly troops by the ridge. He was waving his arms frantically.

Several men at the point of the motor convoy distinctly saw MacLean's body jerk four times, an indication that he had been hit by machine-gun fire. Nevertheless, the burly colonel bulled his way to the far side of the inlet and disappeared from view. He never reappeared.

His maneuvering elements now in position, Don Faith mounted a quick assault on a Chinese company that appeared to be preparing to mount an attack on the perimeter across the ice. The Chinese were quickly dispersed. The force manning the roadblock was engaged next by two of Faith's companies, and it fell apart, clearing the approaches to the stone bridge. The motor column dashed through, drawing the infantry units in behind. The recovering Chinese slammed the door behind the last of Faith's command.

★

If Don Faith expected the move to improve the lot of his battalion by joining it to Reilly's, he was in for a sad revelation. The 3rd Battalion, 31st, had been about as brutally fought out as the 1st Battalion, 32nd. Ed Stamford noted, in fact, that unburied bodies were strewn all about the tiny perimeter, and that long stretches of the line, presumably the quieter zones, were mighty thinly held. Still, Reilly's command had a few things going for it, chiefly the better part of two 105mm firing batteries and a battery of mechanized antiaircraft artillery, including 40mm self-propelled guns and halftrack-mounted quadruple-.50-caliber machine guns.

These last had gotten forward late on November 27, and they had been instrumental in keeping the Chinese from overrunning the tiny perimeter. They had also proven themselves a mixed blessing for Lieutenant Colonel Bill Reilly.

During the general reorganization of the perimeter the day before, November 28, the quad-.50s had been placed directly behind the centrally located command compound. Ordered to test-fire his weapons, one of the gunners had taken aim at Chinese emplacements on the ridge beyond the CP. The first burst of thumb-sized steel-jacketed projectiles had riddled the command post. Bill Reilly, who had been lightly wounded by grenade fragments during the first night's fighting, was felled with a round through a leg and another in a foot. The battalion communicator took a round in the cheek which tore away his jaw. The same burst totally destroyed the battalion's radio gear.

A very high proportion of officers had been killed or wounded. Checking for comrades in the overcrowded aid station, a chastened Captain Hugh Robbins found the battalion logistics officer dying from his wounds, as was a fine rifle-company commander with whom he had served in Japan. The commander of the regimental medical company, Captain Henry Wamble, lay on a stretcher, barely able to speak above a whisper because of bullet holes in both his lungs. Wamble showed Robbins an automatic pistol he was hanging on to in order to avoid captivity, one way or the other.

Don Faith was commander of the combined force — which, according to convention, he named "Task Force Faith" — from the instant he reached the friendly end of the stone bridge. And he took over with a burst of manic energy that transformed the deepening spirits of both groups. Hugh Robbins was appointed task-force logistics officer, and Captain Bill McNally, the 31st's communicator, was put in charge of all communications. The perimeter was divided up among the six small rifle companies, and all the heavy weapons were combined and redistributed.

High on the agenda was contacting rear headquarters to say that Task Force Faith had been formed and that supplies of all types were urgently needed, as was a quick relief.

There was no word on the relief, but Air Force cargo transports put in a late-afternoon appearance, dropping a high proportion of their parachute pallets into the perimeter. Unfortunately the Chinese benefited from stocks that were dropped well behind their lines during the third supply attempt of the day.

Captain Ed Stamford found that the Air Force control team assigned to Reilly's battalion had been ineffective after the loss of the senior controller the previous night. He immediately set up his radio on the best vantage point he could find and was directing Marine Corsairs against Chinese gun emplacements the whole time the infantry and weapons were being reshuffled.

In the end, the only factor that might have ensured the integrity of Task Force Faith was a breakthrough by friendly forces from the south. One local effort was made during the day, but the highest authority — GHQ-Tokyo — had all but written off Task Force Faith as an unrecoverable debit.

★

There was hope that morning at the 31st Infantry's schoolhouse operations center, four miles south of Reilly's perimeter: hope that the troops mustered there could open the road and help Reilly break out; hope that Marines from Hagaru-ri would march to Reilly's and Faith's rescue; hope that the uncommitted 2nd Battalion, 31st, would be sent through Hagaru-ri from Hungnam to spearhead the drive; hope against hope.

In the utter confusion of the day, the Chinese investing Hagaru-ri neglected to sever the road between the Marine base and the 31st Infantry's operations center at Hudong-ni. Captain Clif Hancock, the 31st Medical Company's motor-transport officer, made a trip down that road to carry a load of wounded to one of the Navy medical companies set up near the growing airstrip. On the trip back, Hancock led five or six trucks loaded with medical supplies and ammunition, and two jeeps full of Marine escorts returned to their base late in the day, all without incident.

Some reinforcements trickled through to the operations center, though not nearly as many as 7th Infantry Division's Brigadier General Hodes had hoped for.

For a brief period early in the day it seemed as though the headquarters force and the 31st Tank Company would mount a new attempt to clear the road to Reilly's perimeter, but the force was stopped only a short distance north of the schoolhouse compound by Chinese units on the way south to attack the operations center.

Fighting flared inconclusively through the day. A composite infantry company supported by elements of the 31st Tank Company attacked northward at 0900, but it was stopped where the previous day's effort had been stopped. At least two PLA battalions occupying the heights on either side of the road inflicted serious casualties upon the American force, which was withdrawn at about 1600 hours. Two medium tanks were destroyed and an officer killed when an armored platoon tried to blaze a cross-country route around the Chinese blocking positions on the road north of Hudong-ni.

The Chinese pressed closer to Hudong-ni through the day, advancing cautiously along the ridges overlooking the village despite the seemingly accurate fire of a snub-nosed self-propelled 105mm howitzer that had been driven from Hagaru-ri early in the day. Several combat patrols sent into the hills to monitor or impede the

Chinese advance became embroiled in serious fire fights, and several American officers and riflemen were killed or wounded before the patrols were withdrawn.

Captain George Rasula, the 31st's assistant operations officer, fell into an exhausted bout of restless sleep about midafternoon, the first sleep he had had in days. A Regular with combat experience at Peleliu in the Pacific, Rasula was clearly on "automatic," for he awoke behind an earthen mound beside the schoolhouse, having nodded off inside the building. Dusting himself off, Rasula went back inside and happened to catch the end of a worrisome radio exchange between Lieutenant Colonel Barry Anderson, the regimental operations officer, and Brigadier General Hodes, who had gone back to Hagaru-ri to beg reinforcements from O. P. Smith.

The Marine division commander had patiently heard Hodes out, but had remained firm in his conviction that stripping Hagaru-ri of troops would endanger everyone's chance for survival. If Hagaru-ri fell because it was undermanned, Smith reasoned, its garrison and all the troops to the north would succumb in time to the Chinese.

Unable to hold against mounting pressure from the Chinese in the hills, Barry Anderson's small headquarters force had only one real choice, and that was to pack up and head for the safety of the Hagaru-ri perimeter. Word was that the 2nd Battalion, 31st, had been cleared by X Corps to advance up the MSR to Hagaru-ri. Anderson's group would be on hand there to bolster the battalion and guide it back to rescue the now-combined force to the north. All Task Force Faith had to do was hang on for a day or two longer.

Anderson's group moved out late in the afternoon of November 29. Captain George Rasula was particularly impressed by the air of utter confusion attending the move, which seemed to him more a headlong flight than a deliberate withdrawal.

All the supplies and ammunition that could not be loaded aboard motorized transport were stacked around the schoolhouse and doused with gasoline. Most of the medical supplies Clif Hancock had brought from Hagaru-ri earlier in the day went into those pyres. The last tank in the rear guard fired one round into the stacked crates, and they went up along with the schoolhouse in a great gout of fiery smoke.

Arriving at Hagaru-ri without incident, the Army men were assigned tasks by the Marines who were running the base. Most of the able-bodied men were organized into provisional infantry platoons and sent to guard the northern end of the perimeter, which intelligence operatives claimed was due to be assaulted that night. Clif

Hancock and the 31st's fighting chaplain, Father Marty Hoehn, were detailed along with all the medical company personnel to help care for the hundreds of wounded soldiers and Marines in the over-crowded hospital tents by the growing airstrip. The remnants of Captain Robert Drake's 31st Tank Company were doled out along the vulnerable northwestern curve of the perimeter, a most welcome addition.

There was nothing for the men of the 31st Infantry to do at Hagaru-ri but wait and hope and, if need be, fight for their lives.

C H A P T E R

26

Over six hundred Americans and South Koreans were trapped on the MSR between Koto-ri and Hagaru-ri, and the majority of them appeared doomed. There was the smell of defeat in the air that long, bitterly cold night of November 29–30, 1950.

Of the nine hundred who had started out from Koto-ri on the morning of November 29, only about two hundred had arrived at Hagaru-ri by midnight. The rest were scattered along several miles of the road in at least six separate groupments, isolated by Chinese strongpoints and impassable snarls of wrecked and burning vehicles of every description.

★

The northernmost enclave was manned by about two hundred Royal Marine Commandos under the wounded Lieutenant Colonel Douglas Drysdale. Its prognosis was better than that of units to the south, for 41 Commando was one mean light-infantry team led by some of the most dashing and dedicated officers in North Korea. The impeccably dressed Drysdale and his senior officers conducted a spirited defense, forbidding the Chinese to fragment their bloodied unit. Casualties were very heavy, particularly among the officers, but the Royal Marines inched along toward Hagaru-ri. The bulk of them, including many wounded, passed through the first Marine roadblock a few hours after midnight, where, despite a severe wound in his right arm, the courtly Drysdale returned Marine Major Ed Simmons's salute with an even snappier salute of his own. When they counted noses, the Royal Marines found that fully one half of their original complement of two hundred fifty were killed, wounded, or unaccounted for.

That left about five hundred men still out on the MSR.

★

The rearmost unit was the bulk of Captain Bruce Williams's Baker Company, 1st Tank Battalion, which turned itself around after dark in the hope of dashing back to the safety of the Koto-ri perimeter. While the tanks and the company's soft vehicles were turning, an unarmed Marine lieutenant, identifying himself as a member of the 1st Marine Regiment staff, approached from the south and asked to be taken to the company commander. The man had set out from Koto-ri hours earlier with his jeep driver, who had been killed when the lone jeep was stopped by several Chinese on the darkened road. The lieutenant, a large, robust man, had been captured by the Chinese, but had fought clear with his fists and had run about a mile before coming upon the tank company. The story put Captain Williams on alert against Chinese strongpoints that had been bypassed during the day's fighting.

Baker Company's five-tank 3rd Platoon had the vanguard, with 1st Platoon trailing the soft vehicles. The company commander's weasel — a tracked amphibious jeep — was overturned while maneuvering, and the driver's hip was shattered. Captain Williams had this vehicle righted and attached by cable to the next-to-last tank in the column, then ordered the company to move out. If opposition was encountered, all guns were to be fired to the right and left and the block was to be overrun at maximum speed.

They had gone only a mile when extremely heavy concentrations of machine-gun fire shot away every external antenna of the lead platoon's tanks. The vehicles behind 3rd Platoon were stopped by the fire, but the tanks, cut out of the radio net, barreled right on through to Koto-ri. That left Baker/Tanks's 1st Platoon and soft vehicles stopped on the roadway, unable to proceed.

★

Five hundred Americans and South Koreans, segmented with their vehicles in five major concentrations, were trapped along several hundred yards of roadway running through the defile just south of Pusong-ni, about halfway between Koto-ri and Hagaru-ri. The northernmost group was under the command of 1st Marine Division's Assistant Logistics Officer, Lieutenant Colonel Arthur Chidester, until he was shot through both legs while directing traffic in a vain attempt to turn back. Command fell to Major John McLaughlin, who found that he had about one hundred thirty-five men under his direct control, including Captain Charlie Peckham and the remnants of a Baker/31 platoon. McLaughlin also counted a section of Marine military police under Warrant Officer Lloyd Dirst, a score of Royal Marines, assorted headquarters types, and a large and growing contingent of wounded.

About two hundred yards south of McLaughlin's position, two understrength platoons of Baker/31, with several Marine stragglers, were holed up in a roadside ditch. Thirty yards south of them was a small group under Captain Michael Capraro, a San Francisco newsman serving as 1st Marine Division's public information officer. With Capraro was O. P. Smith's aide-de-camp, Captain Martin Sexton, several staff officers, and about ninety-five enlisted technicians and clerks, many of whom were veterans of combat in the Pacific War.

The southernmost group comprised about forty-five men under the 1st Marine Division Motor Transport Officer, Major Henry "Pop" Seeley.

A fifth, very small, group under the Marine division's personnel officer, Colonel Harvey Walseth, had turned itself around after dark and commenced a slow fighting withdrawal toward Koto-ri. Walseth, who had been in tanks in the Pacific, was wounded in the arm just before his group ran into the rear of Baker/Tanks, which had been stopped on the roadway. The Walseth group bypassed the stalled tankers on the fly and kept going until, about a mile short of Koto-ri, its vehicles were blocked by a tank with a damaged track. Colonel Walseth walked the rest of the way with his companions.

Technical Sergeant Carl Hanson, the atomic-warfare specialist who had volunteered to accompany the convoy that morning, spent some time in a roadside ditch with a group of strangers before deciding to hike back to Koto-ri. Hanson had been a squad leader at Guadalcanal, Tarawa, Saipan, and Tinian, and had volunteered for duty at Okinawa even though he could have been rotated home. He had a knack for coming through unscathed, but this night he really outdid any previous accomplishments by leading two fellow Marines all the way back to Koto-ri without drawing so much as a warning shot. It was a grueling, bitterly cold walk, but the three passed through Marine roadblocks almost without alerting the guards. Hanson walked straight to his tent and sacked out, sleeping through until dawn.

★

Captain Charlie Peckham commanded the only viable infantry increment in the northernmost enclave, but even he was not particularly enthused by the quality of the troops, many of them panic-stricken South Korean conscripts who blew off the bulk of their ammunition firing at phantoms.

First Lieutenant Barrow Turner, executive officer of Dog/Tanks, had landed in the middle of Major McLaughlin's enclave entirely by accident. He had started north well before the tank platoons of his company had even reached Koto-ri, but his jeep had become ensnared in many traffic jams on the MSR through the day, and he had been unable to drive forward to join his unit. The Thompson submachine gun Turner was packing was one of the few automatic weapons available to Major McLaughlin, and Turner used it with telling effect whenever the Chinese ventured down from the heights.

Warrant Officer Lloyd Dirst, a reliable Old Salt leading a military police section, was one of the coolest, most collected men in the McLaughlin enclave. He strode up and down the road, pipe in hand, barking curt commands, leaving steady, organized soldiers and Marines in his wake. When he heard troops firing too much precious ammunition, he gently admonished the offenders, telling them that they had only to fight through to daybreak to draw the awesome support of Marine Air and, hopefully, ground reinforcements. In the end, however, Gunner Dirst was shot through the head and had to be placed in a roadside ditch to await treatment by Charlie Peckham's overworked company medics.

The hero of the hour was clearly Major John McLaughlin, who left no doubt as to who was in command, nor how the defense was to be conducted. As the hours of fighting passed and ammunition supplies dwindled, the Marine staff officer collected rounds from the dead and wounded and personally distributed them to the men who seemed most composed. The few able-bodied officers in the enclave — Peckham, Turner, and several others — were glad to be working under a man as rock-steady and coolly determined at John McLaughlin.

Sometime after midnight the remnants of the two Baker/31 platoons that had been trapped south of the McLaughlin enclave managed to work their way into the larger perimeter, a welcome reinforcement despite the panicked condition of the troops and the limited supplies of ammunition they brought with them.

★

Captain Michael Capraro, the newsman, took a forthright and aggressive stance as the confusion mounted among his small group. Far from waiting for the Chinese to pry his men out of their defenses, Capraro asked for volunteers to go into the hills to scout and attack Chinese strongpoints. There were no takers, so the newsman moved out alone under heavy fire. But the enemy was too strong to fall prey to a one-man counterattack, and Capraro returned at length to deploy and redeploy his small force to meet a constant stream of Chinese sallies. At one point, voices from the Chinese lines called upon Capraro to surrender his men in return for good treatment. After a few insults had been exchanged, the Chinese mentioned that there were three regiments deployed on the heights, and that continued resistance was pointless. Capraro roared back a curt "Hell no!" and continued to direct his troops to meet renewed assaults.

★

Several miles to the south, a platoon of Baker/Tanks and the company vehicles were embroiled in heavy fighting that had engulfed them as soon as they had been stopped by sheets of Chinese machine-gun fire.

Captain Williams had an impossible dilemma to sort out. Tanks are extremely vulnerable to infantry, particularly in the dark. As he had to laager his vehicles, he was denied use of his 90mm turret cannons, which could not be fired because their muzzle blasts would have knocked the pins from under every man standing anywhere nearby when they were fired. The tankers had a preponderance of .30-caliber air-cooled machine guns, which were deployed to excellent advantage, and many of the more acquisitive crews had bolstered their authorized personal weapons with additional firepower. Ammunition did not pose a major problem as the company had its supply trucks along.

The rearmost tank took a 3.5-inch bazooka round, probably from a captured weapon, right through the engine compartment. It had to be towed into the laager.

Bruce Williams made all the right moves: the laager was contracted into an area two hundred feet long by thirty feet wide, though that meant abandoning several vehicles which had been stalled at the head of the column; a sick bay was established in the lee of the tanks; Koto-ri was called and, after some haggling, artillery was registered on either side of the road. The artillery registration alone caused the Chinese to become considerably less aggressive. But it did not stop the infrequent massed infantry assault, which was met with some impressive firepower. Captain Williams had the opportunity to fire his pet Ithaca .12-gauge shotgun at ranges of a mere twenty feet; his biggest problem was reloading, a task that required the removal of his gloves and resulted in some pretty numb fingers.

Troopers armed with light carbines found their weapons completely unreliable in the sub-zero chill, and they ditched them in favor of Thompsons and Garands whenever those became available from the injured. The American hand grenades also proved unreliable, as did, fortunately, whole showers of Chinese fragmentation and concussion grenades.

Captain Williams knew for certain that he could hold until dawn if only he did not use up his ammunition. In that respect he was in charge of the only group of men on the MSR so blessed.

★

Charlie Peckham, holding the southern end of the McLaughlin enclave, was down to handing out rifle bullets two and three at a time. His driver had been carried off to the roadside ditch, dead or dying, he knew not which. And a number of his South Korean fillers had drifted off to mesh with the surroundings. In time, he counted less than a dozen effectives under his command, and he knew that Major McLaughlin, in charge on the northern line, was not much better off.

Two Marines turned a jeep southward and roared off in the hope of begging fresh ammunition at Koto-ri. It was a brave, foolish attempt, and the two were captured almost immediately. When they were prodded up the hill to join a group of Americans who had already been captured, a Chinese political officer who spoke good English asked the captives if one of their number would act as an intermediary in a surrender plea. Sergeant Guillermo Tovar, a military policeman, asked Major James Eagen, the wounded 1st Marine Division assistant supply officer, if he should act. Eagen gave his permission, and Tovar stood up.

The Chinese fire slackened as Tovar was led to Major McLaughlin's enclave.

"Major McLaughlin! Major McLaughlin," Tovar called into the quiet darkness.

"Who's there?" the major called back.

"Sergeant Tovar. I'm a prisoner. The Chinese want to talk to you."

McLaughlin paused to consider his response. "Come in and be identified."

There was a brief wait, then Tovar passed through the American line.

McLaughlin spoke to Tovar for a moment, then followed him up the railway embankment. Three Chinese were standing on the tracks, ready to parley. If McLaughlin surrendered, they promised, the wounded would be returned to friendly lines. Major McLaughlin said that he wanted an opportunity to discuss the offer with his officers. The Chinese assented.

While McLaughlin was on the railway embankment, another Chinese officer, accompanied by an American GI who had been captured earlier, approached Charlie Peckham. The Chinese officer told Peckham that he would be well treated if he surrendered. Peckham gave the man a pack of cigarettes and asked him to take it to his superior; if the Chinese commander gave up, Peckham vowed, he would see that the Chinese troops were fed and well treated.

Major McLaughlin dropped down into the roadside ditch filled with his wounded and found Lieutenant Colonel Arthur Chidester, whose condition was deteriorating. He explained the Chinese terms to the colonel, who asked, "Do you think we can trust them?"

"It's a chance we'll have to take if we decide to give up."

"How much ammunition left?"

"Not much," McLaughlin revealed. "Not more than two clips per man."

Chidester responded in a hushed tone, "I don't see what else you can do, Mac."

They talked on for a few moments longer, deciding in the end to give in, and to pass word down the road to Major Seeley, whose small group was undoubtedly in similar straits.

While Chidester and McLaughlin were reaching their decision, the Chinese officer who had taken Charlie Peckham's cigarettes returned with a message from his superior: If the Americans failed to lay down their weapons within fifteen minutes, a full regiment would roll over the enclave. Peckham reached the same conclusion as had Chidester and McLaughlin. He asked for time to get word to all his troops, then set all hands to destroying their weapons.

First Lieutenant Barrow Turner, the tank company executive officer, got The Word from John McLaughlin as the major strode through the line to resume the negotiation. Much to the annoyance of the Chinese, McLaughlin insisted upon getting word through to Pop Seeley. They agreed to allow Sergeant Tovar to carry a verbal message. McLaughlin took the military policeman aside and told him, "Contact Major Seeley. Tell him to come up and talk with these people. Take your time."

Tovar walked off into the night, shouting Seeley's name. He was to find the motor transport officer and tell him to stall around for as long as he could; there was a chance that the entire force would be saved at daybreak, less than an hour hence.

Several more rounds of palaver ensued between McLaughlin and the Chinese political officer, during which McLaughlin averred, "We are not surrendering because you beat us. We are surrendering to get our wounded cared for. If we can't get our wounded evacuated, we will fight on."

★

A case of stomach cramps probably saved Pop Seeley's life, and they weren't even his cramps, but his driver's. The enlisted Marine had been left at Koto-ri to recover from some vile illness, and Major Seeley had driven north that morning at the wheel of his own jeep. Major Jim Eagen, the division assistant supply officer, had been riding in the right seat, the side on which the Chinese had been deployed above the MSR.

When Seeley's jeep had finally been stopped at dusk, he had naturally exited to the left, climbing down into the protection of a roadside ditch. Jim Eagen had gone to the right, joined a group of Marines on that side of the road, and moved north as the firing from the heights increased. Eagen had been wounded and most of his group had been captured early. Pop Seeley had been spared to organize the forty-five men he found scattered along the ditch near his jeep.

After driving off a group of burp-gun-firing Chinese who attacked from across the road, Major Seeley's group had moved west from the roadside ditch to the protection of the bank of the frozen Changjin River, which paralleled the MSR. From there, Seeley's men could see shadowy figures amongst the burning vehicles on the road, Chinese moving through the flames to mount repeated assaults against Pop Seeley's enclave.

The serious nature of the situation was hours dawning on the division motor-transport officer, who assumed from the start that a relief expedition would be mounted from Hagaru-ri or Koto-ri at first light. Meantime, the Chinese were being held back; the greatest threat seemed to come from the dank sub-zero chill. A noncom was told off to check the troops constantly for any sign of frostbite, to remind all hands to keep their limbs in constant motion. The ammunition supply was another constant worry, for the many head-quarters people under Seeley were not carrying as much ammunition as was normally allotted to full-time riflemen.

When Seeley heard a voice yelling his name in the dark, he ordered his troops to cease firing. Sergeant Tovar approached and talked Seeley into accompanying him into a field on the east side of the road. There, he told the major what was going on, and about Major McLaughlin's desire to stall for as long as possible. Farther on, the two Americans were met by two Chinese, who spoke no English, but nevertheless got their message across loud and clear: Seeley was to have his troops put down their weapons and come in with their hands up. As the exchange was winding down, Major Jim Eagen, who had been carried down from the heights, spoke out of the darkness and asked Seeley to come talk.

Seeley found Eagen lying on the bare ground, both legs swathed in bandages.

"How are you, Jim?"

"They got me in the legs, Pop." Then Eagen told Seeley everything he knew about McLaughlin's situation and the Chinese offer. He also urged Seeley to surrender, having seen the Chinese setting up heavy mortars on the road. This was Seeley's first real inkling as to size of the PLA force. But he felt it was worth waiting until dawn, which might produce needed help.

Seeley gave it one last try. "What do you think of this surrender business?" he asked.

"We've got the wounded to think of," Eagen replied. "They can't live out here very long in this weather."

The Chinese, by this time highly impatient, interrupted the exchange. It was clear to Seeley from their hand signs that they wanted his decision. He asked Eagen to do anything he could to stall, then turned and walked back to his enclave by the riverbank. He told Sergeant Tovar to return to Major McLaughlin with a plea to stall while he and his troops dug in more securely; he was not going to give in.

By that time, the Chinese were already at work disarming Mc-Laughlin's people, only forty of whom were capable of putting up further resistance in any case.

★

Upon returning to his enclave, Pop Seeley was approached by Warrant Officer Dee Yancey, the division assistant ordnance officer, who reported that he had reconnoitered the river, finding that it was solid ice, and that there appeared to be no Chinese fire coming from the far shore. Yancey suggested, and Seeley agreed, that the group ought to abandon its position at the riverbank by daylight. So, once the wounded were prepared for the move, the entire group started west, across the river, heading for a ridge it hoped would provide better cover. Two men who had earlier crawled behind a log to sleep had frozen to death.

Crossing a field beyond the river, Seeley's group, which had been joined for the breakout by Captain Michael Capraro's contingent, found two Marines who had been lost on patrol three days earlier. Both had been seriously injured, but had saved themselves by crawling into a cache of raw wool they found in the field. They were carried along with the other wounded as the group struggled up the ridge, clambered over the top and turned south toward Koto-ri at an agonizingly slow pace.

Daybreak found Seeley's group out of sight of the Chinese on the MSR. But as the men moved down the slope toward the river again, they heard voices and Chinese bugles to the rear. Gunner Yancey, who had suffered painful shrapnel wounds in both legs and back, dropped behind the rest of the group and, as the first Chinese came over the ridge, adjusted the sights on his Garand rifle. An old Marine Corps team shooter, he quickly dropped the two Chinese point men while the remainder of the American group scrambled down the slope and made for the river. The Chinese patrol went to ground, and Yancey followed his countrymen.

★

Captain Bruce Williams decided to pull up stakes at sunrise. The dead and wounded tankers were placed in trucks, many of which had to be towed at the ends of stout ropes; one truck would have to make the trip to Koto-ri on its brake drums. As the preparations were being completed, the first of Pop Seeley's men, attracted by the sound of idling tank engines, began filtering in. Seeley himself rushed up to Williams as the convoy was pulling away, cautioning the tank-company commander to turn his guns on the Chinese that Gunner Yancey had temporarily halted. But the Chinese never reappeared, and the rest of the trip to Koto-ri was utterly uneventful.

★

True to their word, the Chinese began assembling the wounded Americans, South Koreans, and British after they had disarmed the survivors and, typically, stolen every scrap of food they could winnow out of the pockets and packs of the men facing an uncertain future in captivity. (Most of the wounded were, in fact, returned to American lines; some, including Military Police Warrant Officer

Lloyd Dirst, eventually succumbed to their wounds. Lieutenant Colonel Arthur Chidester and Major Jim Eagen were not repatriated with the other wounded, and no one ever saw either of them again.)

The able-bodied enlisted men were soon led off into the hills, but the officers were kept behind. Captain Charlie Peckham found himself walking down the road between solid ranks of PLA infantrymen, who just stared at him as he walked. Peckham was convinced that he was to be shot, and he prayed for a quick, clean end. However, he was met by a Chinese colonel who shook his hand and told him, through an interpreter, that he was a good soldier who had killed many Chinese soldiers that night.

As Peckham walked down the road with the Chinese colonel, he realized that he had forgotten to rid himself of his personal weapons, a .45-caliber automatic pistol and a trench knife. He matter-of-factly took the side arm from its holster and stripped it down, throwing the parts over the heads of the Chinese soldiers lined up by the side of the road. No one made a move to stop the Army captain, who got rid of everything that could possibly be of value to his enemies. He was certain, in the end, that the Chinese colonel was according him a very high honor by allowing him to destroy his weapons rather than surrender them.

★

First Lieutenant Barrow Turner and most of the other officers were led directly into the hills and placed in a tiny Korean farmhouse. There they met 1st Lieutenant Bob Messman, the Marine artillery officer who had been taken on the road from Yudam-ni two nights earlier.

Charlie Peckham spent two full days standing on a frozen watercourse beside the MSR before his guards led him into the hills to join the other captive officers, a total of thirteen, including Lieutenant Messman.

★

Of roughly eight hundred fifty men involved in the tragedy on the MSR, about one hundred fifty escaped that night and one hundred sixty-two are officially listed as killed or missing. Another one hundred fifty-nine were wounded and repatriated, by one means or another, to friendly lines. Over three hundred Americans were marched off to prison camps. Of these, eighteen escaped the following spring, including Technical Sergeant C. L. Harrison, who had been taken by the Japanese at Wake Island and who had just arrived in Korea when ordered to Hagaru-ri. About two dozen Britons from 41 Commando and several dozen American soldiers and Marines went to ground in the hills, cut off from friendly bases, but determined to await rescue. It would be quite a wait.

CHAPTER

27

The light two-place Marine helicopter breasted Toktong Pass and made straight for the valley of Yudam-ni, hovering for only an instant above the combined headquarters of the 5th and 7th Marine Regiments before gingerly dropping the last few inches to the ground. As the pilot leaped out to secure the machine, the passenger, bundled up against the frigid air of the open cockpit, shook himself erect and stretched his hand toward those of the field officers who had come out to greet him. It was a happy reunion, for Lieutenant Colonel Joseph "Buzz" Winecoff had grown up in the Marine Corps with many of those regimental staff officers.

Buzz Winecoff was Assistant Division Operations Officer for Plans, Colonel Al Bowser's right-hand man since the evacuation a few days earlier of Bowser's former plans chief, a victim of pneumonia. Winecoff was on a personal reconnaissance at Yudam-ni, the first senior division staffer to get there from Division Forward. It was, in the eyes of the regimental staffers who met him, a welcome but seriously belated arrival. It was November 30, after all.

Following the amenities, Lieutenant Colonel Winecoff was given over to the care of Major Hank Woessner, Litz's operations officer. Woessner and Winecoff were friends and had been neighbors while both were on pre-war duty at Camp Lejeune. They were able to get right down to business.

Before getting much of an assessment from Hank Woessner, Buzz Winecoff outlined an astounding proposal. Corps, he said, had talked Division into sending the 5th and 7th Marines over the mountains to relieve pressure on the collapsing 8th Army by mounting an assault against the PLA's inland flank.

Woessner thought he was dreaming as he listened to Winecoff's presentation. Then he reacted strongly. He pleaded with Winecoff to have a good look around, to see the serious straits into which the

Yudam-ni garrison had been plunged, to get as good a feel for the situation as he could. Then he must return to Division and make O. P. Smith and Al Bowser see the light: Yudam-ni was the end of the road; it had to be evacuated, immediately . . . sooner . . . right away!

Buzz Winecoff reboarded his helicopter about midday, seething with the outlines of a blockbuster report he knew he would have to deliver to superiors he had been serving for only a few days. He prayed they would listen.

★

Of course Al Bowser listened to Buzz Winecoff. He had had more than a vague suspicion that the Yudam-ni commanders would want out as quickly as possible. That is why he had sent Winecoff in the first place, to hear and see and feel and, above all, think. He would have gone himself, had wanted to go more than anything he could imagine. But O. P. Smith had been loath to risk his operations officer on a risky helicopter ride, and Buzz Winecoff had been tapped in Bowser's place.

Al Bowser knew that things at Yudam-ni were bad, but he did not know *how bad* until he saw how so experienced a man as Winecoff had reacted to what he had seen. Winecoff came back from Yudam-ni a shaken man.

All the talk of pitching in to help 8th Army had come from higher up, from Corps and, most certainly, from GHQ-Tokyo. That was out of the question. It was time to formulate a plan to save what could be saved.

★

Corps was not making sense. Beginning on the afternoon of November 29, after issuing no plans or directives for two critical days, X Corps issued a series of plans and directives and recommendations that were so at variance with one another and with objective reality as to render them utterly meaningless.

The suggestion that the Yudam-ni garrison attack overland into the flank of the Chinese destroying 8th Army came *after* a Corps directive authorizing the 7th Marines to attack southward to clear the MSR as far as Hagaru-ri.

First Marine Division had anticipated that last directive by several hours when, at 1545, Division Forward had contacted Colonels Litzenberg and Murray to order the 5th Marines to assume full responsibility for Yudam-ni in order to free the 7th for the road-clearing operation. Until Buzz Winecoff returned to Hagaru-ri, however, no one had a reasonable solution for the plight of the 5th, which could not possibly have held alone for any length of time.

Except for the silly order involving the rescue of a multi-division field army by two Marine regiments, Corps had made the vital intellectual connection: the MSR had to be opened between Yudam-ni and Hagaru-ri before anything else could take place. The fact that Corps got around to saying so before 1st Marine Division did made General Smith's lot that much simpler, for he had previously issued an order to that effect, and would have stood by it no matter what Corps came up with.

True to form, O. P. Smith withheld specific recommendations, leaving the details entirely to his regimental commanders and their staffs.

★

As far as Homer Litzenberg was concerned, the *final* decision to evacuate Yudam-ni had been made on the evening of November 29, following the withdrawal of the second abortive effort to rescue Fox/7 from Toktong Pass. He had anticipated the Corps and Division directives regarding clearance of the MSR by the 7th Marines, having ordered his staff to formulate a plan for occupying Fox Hill with at least a battalion from the Yudam-ni garrison, a diminution of the infantry force that virtually assured the need to totally evacuate the valley of Yudam-ni.

Major Fox Parry, commander of the 3rd Battalion, 11th, and Litz's artillery advisor, was on his way back to his quarters after checking on his battalion's stretch of the perimeter line when he decided to make a courtesy call on the the colonel. Striding toward Litzenberg's tiny personal tent, Parry was a little surprised to hear muffled voices coming from within. The tall, husky major eased through the drawn flaps and saw that Litz was sitting on his cot, speaking with Lieutenant Colonel Ray Davis, who was on the cold earthen deck with his knees drawn up to his chest. Parry was about to withdraw, but the colonel motioned for him to take a seat on the deck beside Davis.

The two were discussing a bold plan aimed at relieving Fox Company. On the following night, after a full day of preparation, the entire 1st Battalion, 7th, was to scale Turkey Hill and dash overland across the trackless, snow-covered wastes to attack the rear of the PLA division besieging Fox Hill. If successful, Davis was to go into position on and around the hill and await the arrival of the remainder of the 7th Marines, which would launch its clearing operation at dawn on December 1. Litzenberg seemed confident that the 5th

Marines would be ordered to withdraw as well, and he said he thought someone at Division or Corps would get on the stick in time.

★

Momentum was gained through the whole of November 30.

Brigadier General Henry Hodes, assistant commander of 7th Infantry Division, established a temporary command post next to the 1st Marine Division Forward CP, the better to coordinate activities in behalf of Task Force Faith. Later in the day, Major General David Barr, the 7th Division commanding general, arrived by helicopter to confer at length with O. P. Smith regarding the help the Marines might provide Faith.

Smith and Barr had first met in Japan during the planning phase of the Inchon operation. Both were combat officers, and they had taken an initially cautious liking to each other. Numerous meetings before and during the landings and subsequent drive toward Seoul had cemented a working relationship that would have been severely taxed by Smith's unshakable conviction that he could not — as opposed to *would* not — help Faith with the forces then under his immediate control. Dave Barr said he understood, but asked that a plan envisaging the availability of larger forces at least be considered.

Barr flew north to Faith's position later in the day, and had a shocking view of a shocking situation. On the way out, he brought the badly wounded Bill Reilly, who was flown from Hagaru-ri aboard an Air Force C-47, one of the first to use the dangerous airstrip since its opening a few hours earlier.

Ned Almond arrived still later in the day, packing a plan for the relief of both Yudam-ni and Task Force Faith.

Whereas O. P. Smith and Dave Barr got along very well, O. P. Smith and Ned Almond shared a mutual loathing dating from their very first meeting in Japan before Inchon. It was a matter of chemistry, but it was close to getting out of hand.

Almond had won permission from GHQ-Tokyo to withdraw X Corps to the base at Hungnam-Hamhung, but he was forbidden to commit any elements of the fresh 3rd Infantry Division to ease the burden of the two divisions then locked in combat with the PLA. He authorized O. P. Smith to abandon Yudam-ni and to draw its garrison back to Hagaru-ri, at which point one Marine regimental combat team would mount an attack up the east side of the Reservoir to rescue Task Force Faith.

General Smith did not object to this plan, but he reserved final judgment until he had had an opportunity to assess the capabilities of the regiments *after* their return from Yudam-ni.

Almond next conveyed a mild order that 1st Marine Division abandon any notion that it might hold Hagaru-ri through the winter; the division was to proceed as quickly as possible to the sea the moment Task Force Faith had been brought safely within its lines. Stressing that speed was of the utmost importance, Almond promised — with the concurrence of Major General William Tunner, commander of the Far East Air Force Cargo Command — that the Marines would be resupplied by air. General Smith could, if he chose, burn or otherwise destroy as much of his equipment as he thought he must in order to facilitate the withdrawal.

Losing patience with General Almond's ebullient presentation, O. P. Smith exploded in a characteristically quiet way: "I think, General," the Marine division commander enunciated from between clenched teeth, "that my command is perfectly able to bring its equipment out intact."

Unmindful of the snub, Almond left Generals Smith and Barr to work out details. The two agreed that no plans could be formulated until the Yudam-ni garrison had gotten safely to Hagaru-ri.

★

Far to the south, Marine Major General Field Harris (whose son, Bill, was the commander of the besieged 3rd Battalion, 7th) was ordered to concentrate the bulk of his 1st Marine Aircraft Wing at Yonpo, the fighter base near Hungnam. Several Navy aircraft carriers were called to stations off northeastern Korea to bolster Harris's wing. The first Marine squadrons sent from Wonsan to bolster the Australian and Marine squadrons already at Yonpo flew up by way of the Reservoir, delivering the strongest air attacks against the Chinese to date.

In Tokyo, and at sea, top naval commanders exchanged orders and plans: the United States 7th Fleet was to concentrate around Hungnam and prepare to evacuate X Corps and several South Korean corps from the port city. If all went well, the evacuation would take place under the guns of the fleet, including those of the battleship *Missouri*.

★

Shortly after midnight, November 30, as the troops on the line experienced the lightest night activity to date, the staffs of the 5th and 7th Marines turned their attention from defense to regroupment. If Yudam-ni was to be evacuated by one or both regiments, the area under Marine domination would have to be contracted and strengthened. The first moves would give ground at the northern end of the perimeter. That would give the 5th Marines a tighter, stronger area to hold if, indeed, the regiment would have to hold alone. At the same time, the 7th Marines would be that much closer to its objectives, Toktong Pass and Hagaru-ri.

Giving up dominant hills was no easy task, particularly when the numerically superior enemy held some dominant hills of their own.

The first move was made by Lieutenant Colonel Hal Roise's 2nd Battalion, 5th, which was deployed across Hill 1426, on Southwest Ridge. While holding his right flank steady at its juncture with Taplett's 3rd Battalion, 5th, near Hill 1282, Roise had to swing his left flank nearly a mile to the east and anchor it on Hill 1294, overlooking the MSR.

Lieutenant Colonel Bob Taplett's 3rd Battalion, 5th, maintained its positions astride Hill 1282, and Lieutenant Colonel Jack Stevens's 1st Battalion, 5th, remained in place in the vicinity of Hill 1240. The immediate benefit of Roise's move was shortening the perimeter line sufficiently to squeeze out the 3rd Battalion, 7th. As things stood at that point, Lieutenant Colonel Bill Harris's battalion would be used to spearhead the drive down the MSR while Lieutenant Colonel Ray Davis's 1st Battalion, 7th, moved east from Turkey Hill the following evening, December 1.

Marine Air was on station in stronger numbers than at any previous time, and all the Marine artillery batteries were fully manned and ready to stem the tide if any attack was launched to take advantage of the perimeter's temporary weakness. Surprisingly, though the maneuvers were conducted in broad daylight and in plain view of the Chinese, no attempt was made by the besiegers to attack the besieged.

★

By the end of the day, November 30, Colonel Litzenberg and Lieutenant Colonel Murray had both been informed that the entire Yudam-ni garrison was free to fight back over the MSR to Hagaru-ri. As always, tactical plans were left entirely in the hands of the regimental commanders and their staffs.

Major Hank Woessner and his opposite number in the 5th Marines, Major Larry Smith, spent nearly the entire day perfecting the attack plan.

It was already a given that Davis's battalion would march overland to relieve Fox/7 at Toktong Pass. The 3rd Battalion, 7th, which had already been squeezed off the line, would open the MSR by securing Turkey Hill and Hill 1542, then attack southward to link up with

Davis's battalion at the pass. Taplett's 3rd Battalion, 5th, would escort a column comprising all the garrison's soft vehicles right behind Harris. Flank security for the vehicle column would be provided by provisional companies and platoons drawn from headquarters and artillery units. In order for Taplett to withdraw from Hill 1282 while Harris was already in the attack, Roise and Stevens would have to provide a moving screen, pivoting southward and refusing their flanks near the MSR south of town, which was to be abandoned. The shrunken perimeter would be made to shrink still farther during the day as Stevens's battalion followed the vehicle column. Roise's battalion would be rear guard.

The artillery would leapfrog firing batteries southward, one or two at a time, keeping vanguard and rear-guard infantry units within range at all times.

The 4th Battalion, 11th's 155mm ammunition was to be fired up or destroyed during the course of December 1, and the battalion would not be resupplied. Priority resupply of 105mm ammunition was ordered; the lighter 105mm rounds could be air-dropped in greater numbers and stood a good deal less chance of being damaged than 155mm rounds, though the loss rate for November 29 and 30 had been over forty percent. Except for tractor and equipment drivers, the entire 4th Battalion, 11th, was to be cannibalized to provide provisional infantry platoons.

An enormous amount of equipment and supplies would have to be abandoned to make room on the available rolling stock for the wounded, both those who had already been hurt, and those who would inevitably be hurt during the withdrawal. It was with the greatest reluctance, in fact, that Colonel Litzenberg ordered the interment of eighty-five dead officers and men by Navy chaplains in a field near Yudam-ni.

Work continued at a frantic pace through the night.

★

Fourteen miles to the south, there was considerable doubt that the 5th and 7th Marines and their supports would have a base to which to return. The Hagaru-ri garrison had a very bad November 30, and the night that followed was far, far worse.

C H A P T E R
28

The night of November 29–30 passed more quietly at Hagaru-ri than anyone had dared dream it might. For a change, Marines took the war to the Chinese. Thanks entirely to data brought in by several South Korean line-crossers, Marine Air and artillery were able to zero in on Chinese assembly areas, particularly on the far side of East Hill, where Major Reginald Myers's thin assault force was awaiting its fate. The air strikes were delivered by Marine night fighters, the first time in the campaign that they had been employed with such total effectiveness, the result of ideal tactical intelligence.

The Chinese did not attack at all that night.

On the morning of November 30, as soon as Captain Carl Sitter's George/1, fresh from the terror of the MSR, could be mustered at the base of East Hill, it was sent into the attack.

After splitting his company into two attack elements, Captain Sitter closed on the lines to which Myers's troops had withdrawn after dark the previous night. On the left, 3rd Platoon, bolstered by 1st Lieutenant Nick Canzona's 1st Platoon of Able/Engineers, was to attack across the nose fronting the Chinese defenses overlooking the Marine perimeter. Sitter was to lead his 1st and 2nd Platoons uphill obliquely from the right, hooking at the crest to take the Chinese by the flank. The 3rd Platoon of Able/Engineers would be the reserve.

Progress was initially slow, the result of hundreds of feet having pounded the snowy mantle on the slope to a slick shine. As the Chinese poured fire from the heights, hurting the road-weary company more than it had ever been hurt, Carl Sitter ordered both engineer platoons to follow his left rifle platoon around the Chinese right while he pushed on with the remainder of George/1.

Both attacks failed in the difficult terrain as George/1 and the engineers slowed to a standstill in the face of a growing volume of fire from the heights. Realizing that East Hill would not soon fall to George/1, Lieutenant Colonel Tom Ridge, the base defense commander, approved Carl Sitter's suggestion that the company dig in along a line containing the Chinese salient at the summit.

As soon as the Marines on the ground had backtracked to viable

positions, Marines in the air dug up a good deal of East Hill with
rockets, bombs, and machine-gun fire.

The matter rested there.

★

The most important event to take place in the life of the Hagaru-ri
base occurred at 1430 hours on the afternoon of November 30. As
hundreds of Marines, soldiers, and sailors looked on from vantage
points throughout the crowded perimeter, an Air Force C-47 twin-
engined Dakota transport circled the valley and let itself down from
east to west on the forty-percent-complete airstrip. The heavily
laden transport bounced and lurched over the rough surface, and
the crew was a bit surprised to find that the second half of the
runway tilted upward at a five-percent grade. The landing, however,
was a success, and the first cargo was unloaded to the accompaniment of cheers from everyone who could see. Turnaround time was
thirty minutes. Starting at the uphill end of the strip, the Dakota,
loaded with twenty-four seriously wounded soldiers and Marines,
roared off at full power and climbed away for the fifteen-minute run
to Hamhung. The next two Dakotas took out another sixty casualties,
but the fourth plane of the day collapsed its landing gear on impact
and skidded to a metal-rending halt; the cargo was salvaged, but the
hulk had to be destroyed in order to clear the vital runway.

Medical service facilities were springing up throughout the X
Corps rear. The 1st Marine Division hospital, manned by two Navy
clearing companies, was already in service at Hungnam, as was an
Army evacuation hospital. An Army MASH unit was also in the process of pitching tents, and the hospital ship *Consolation* was due to
dock at Hungnam within days. In Japan, where numerous 8th Army
casualties were already arriving from northwestern Korea, Army and
Navy hospitals were geared up to full war capacity.

The most optimistic result of Hagaru-ri's new air capability was
the decision by O. P. Smith to fly in as many replacements as possible. The rear areas had hundreds of combat-trained Marines to
offer up, some from rear headquarters and service units, others fresh
from the States or Japan, and still others who had become available
after recuperating from wounds or illness incurred earlier in the
war. Once the worthiness of the airstrip had been proven, a call
went out to Marines in the rear, and volunteers were gladly accepted
as long as transport was available.

★

Not all the wounded would be flown out soon. Not very many, in
fact, for Hagaru-ri had been filling up for days with casualties of its

own and others flown laboriously from Yudam-ni aboard two-place helicopters.

Sergeant Jim Matthews, of Fox/5, had thought he had the war licked when he was lifted out of Yudam-ni on November 29, but his first full day in Hagaru-ri was a weird, nightmarish sort of experience.

Left entirely to his own devices, Sergeant Matthews had checked in at Charlie/Med — Charlie Company, 1st Medical Battalion — and received a change of battle dressings and some medication for the wound in his armpit. Then he had been turned loose, a Marine alone and unfettered in a crazy place.

His first impressions of the Royal Marine survivors of the ambush on the MSR was one of awe. He had never seen combat infantrymen so completey squared away. All were clean-shaven, and their gear was in perfect order. One entire schoolhouse building near Charlie/Med was filled with injured Britons, and even they looked as if they were taking good care of themselves.

After touring the sights in the town, Matthews fell into a building that had been comandeered by members of the 1st Motor Transport Battalion. He had heard there was room to bed down in their mess hall, and they allowed him to stay. He shared some coffee with an impeccably-turned-out British color sergeant, but the warmth from the coffee got the pain in his shoulder going, and Matthews passed out in the middle of their conversation.

Another new companion, a Marine warrant officer, had taken a sliver of shrapnel in the eye. He was in terrific pain, but put up a great front. He also happened to be the best scrounger Matthews had ever seen. Throughout that first day, Matthews never saw the man without an armload of booty, usually food, and usually too much food. Once the warrant officer asked Matthews if he liked fruit juice. "Yeah, I like it," Matthews allowed, keeping up his end of what, to him, was an idle conversation. The older Marine produced a can of fruit juice and left it with Matthews, then rose to collect another armload of booty from outside.

Late in the day, a group of newcomers arrived, and Matthews was pleased to see that it included some buddies from his old Reserve outfit. After chewing the fat for a time, Matthews mentioned that he wished he had a pipe and some tobacco. One of his old buddies remarked that he thought he knew where he could get one. He left, and returned within the half hour carrying a can of tobacco and a bent cherrywood pipe with an aluminum bowl. Trying the tobacco,

Matthews was moved to comment, "Hey, this is pretty good. Where'd you get it?" The reply: "Oh, off a dead gook."

Puffing contentedly away, Matthews learned that Chinese infiltrators could be seen running up and down the village streets most nights. Usually, they climbed into chimney flues or eaves of the houses to take potshots at Marines in the streets. The motor-transport people, out for a little sport, usually found a "snuffy" (a "sucker") to draw fire from their infiltrators, then burned whole buildings down with white-phosphorous grenades scrounged from the ammunition dumps.

Quite a life, Matthews thought as he idled away the afternoon. Quite a life!

★

The last night of November began quietly. Marines along the lines of 1st Lieutenant Joe Fisher's Item/1 reported hearing bugle calls at 2015, followed an hour later by a green flare. About two hours later, however, at 2330, small Chinese patrols started probing Fisher's line for weak spots.

In the two days since the Chinese had last attacked, How and Item Companies had completed some impressively elaborate preparations. Machine gunners scrounging through the dumps for spare parts had hit upon a cache of .50-caliber machine guns and ammunition, and at least four of these awesomely destructive weapons had been placed along the lines. Concertina wire had been spread along the entire front, and there was no end of trip flares and booby traps. The latter usually involved an armed grenade stuffed into an empty tin can which was hung on the wire; a severe enough jolt to the wire would upend the can, freeing the grenade to flip its arming spoon and explode. Sandbagged foxholes and weapons pits provided maximum protection. And the line was backed by Marine and Army heavy and medium tanks, pre-registered 60mm and 81mm mortars, and artillery.

The Chinese attacks against Item/1 built up enough momentum in several places to close on the Marine line, but quick response by special reaction forces — chiefly Royal Marines and some technicians — prevented the attackers from exploiting their gains. In one case, a Marine squad leader who had run out of ammunition resorted to the rarely used cold steel of his bayonet to pry several attackers loose.

The hot reception by Item/1 cost the Chinese scores of dead and wounded for two Marines killed and ten wounded.

To Fisher's left, engineer Warrant Officer Bill Downs was whiling away the night in the How/1 CP when a 76mm mountain gun zeroed in on the straw-and-lath shack. Several rounds passed straight through the flimsy walls and struck in among the battalion 81mm mortars, about fifty yards to the rear. Several howitzers from Dog Battery, 11th, adjacent to How/1, were ordered to engage the Chinese gun, but it was too deeply in defilade, and the 105mm shells were wasted.

Warming to their work, the Chinese gunners proceeded to step up the pace of their firing, alternating white phosphorous with High Explosives. The American 81mm crewmen were taking severe casualties while the men in the How/1 command post were kept busy brushing volatile, smoldering white-phosphorous dust from their bulky clothing. At length, the 81mm-section chief said that he would try to reach the Chinese gun, and he was told to get right to it. The Chinese gun ceased firing after three mortar salvos. How/1 was not hit by infantry attacks following the withdrawal or destruction of the 76mm gun, but Item/1 remained in action until dawn.

★

The night's action on East Hill began when two thoroughly shaken Marine engineers who had been manning a listening post barreled into the main line, screaming both parts of the sign-countersign password combination for the night. Right on their heels were several hundred dark forms, cascading down the slippery, snow-covered hillside.

As the Chinese closed on the engineers holding the Marine left, intense mortar concentrations landed on the center George/1 platoon, threatening to pulverize it. While the center platoon was pinned in place by the mortar fire, the George/1 platoons on either side were knocked askew, pivoting back to form a deep V centered on the center rifle platoon. George/1's contact with the engineer platoons on either flank was severed.

Just to the left of George Company, the 3rd Platoon of Able/Engineers was butted all the way to the foot of the hill, suffering the loss of fourteen of twenty-eight effectives. The tide was stemmed by fire from Army and Marine service troops holding a secondary line to the rear.

When the Chinese won their bid to reduce the Marine line on East Hill, they moved into positions which could be effectively reached by How Battery, 11th, which was just the other side of the knob. Observers behind the lost line called the shots, walking a devastating 105mm barrage up and down the Chinese-held portion of the hill's forward slopes, butchering the momentarily victorious PLA infantry. Reinforcements, including a pair of heavy tanks, were rushed in from quiet sectors.

Lieutenant Colonel Gus Banks, the 1st Service Battalion commander, paraded his portion of the line, hurling oaths and epithets at his ragtag elements of Army and Marine "noncombatants." He ordered his men to crack open several drums of gasoline, which were set ablaze to light the battle-scarred slopes. The illumination was the charm. As he looked on from the door of his command post, nearly a mile away, O. P. Smith watched with imperturbable calm as the Chinese on the East Hill were eradicated in the bright firelight.

Pressure on George/1 and its supports had become so intense by 0100 that the 3rd Battalion, 1st's Intelligence Officer, 2nd Lieutenant Richard Carey, was ordered out with every available man from the battalion CP. Carey, who had served earlier as a platoon leader with George/1, loaded his scratch team up with as much ammunition as could be shouldered and moved through the flickering light to find Captain Sitter. The reinforcements arrived in time to prevent the destruction of Sitter's squad-sized 1st Platoon, Lieutenant Carey's old command.

Later that dark morning, Tom Ridge had to send a group of Royal Marines to the base of East Hill to further bolster Sitter's dwindling company. After securing George/1's left flank, the British commandos mounted a counterassault which secured much of the ground lost during the initial clash.

Marine Air arrived at 0900, as the morning mists were burned away by the weak sun, and drove the last of the Chinese back to their former positions atop East Hill.

Hagaru-ri had held for yet another night. And for one day more, it was bound to be a beckoning beacon for the Yudam-ni garrison. Unexpectedly, it became the haven for a disintegrating Task Force Faith.

PART SIX

Breakout

CHAPTER
29

Task Force Faith was dying

The consolidation of the 1st Battalion, 32nd, and the 3rd Battalion, 31st, had no appreciable effect upon the prognosis of either of them. It just put more American and South Korean soldiers in one place to be whittled away at the whim of the Chinese commander charged with clearing the east side of the Reservoir.

The first night the battalions were joined, the night of November 29–30, the Chinese mounted assault after assault all around the perimeter. They killed many of Don Faith's troops and sent dozens more into the charnel houses that served as rudimentary aid stations.

If help was going to be coming, Don Faith knew, it had better be coming damned fast.

The arrival of Major General Dave Barr, the 7th Division commander, had caused morale to soar for just as long as it took the general to step from his helicopter and pull off a glove to shake hands with Lieutenant Colonel Faith. Barr, who was known throughout the Army for his bluff honesty, pulled no punches, telling Faith right off that the Marines were utterly unable to mount a relief of the perimeter any time soon, maybe never. If Faith wanted to see his command to safety, Barr warned, he had better plan on handling it himself. It is to Barr's everlasting credit that he broke the news with a tear in his eye. There was no fanfare attending the division commander's visit, and he left following the brief, visibly painful discussion.

Don Faith assembled several key officers and gave them the news: the bloodied task force would, if it survived the night, break out for Hagaru-ri in the morning, December 1.

★

As he had the night before, Private First Class Jay Ransone, of Able/32, made his peace with his Maker, laid the tools of his trade within easy reach, and prepared to die in the defense of the stone bridge leading into Faith's perimeter.

Ransone's foxhole buddy was a South Korean conscript, a young man who could neither speak nor comprehend English beyond sim-

unts and oaths. The two of them were right in the
ajor route into the perimeter, and they had fought
first night there screaming mutually unintelligible ad-
other. The Chinese had launched wave after wave at
, right down their throats. And they had held.

During the day, they had been harassed by sheets of fire from the
heights directly across the ice-covered inlet that shielded most of
Faith's battalion from direct assault. Time and time again, men in
the foxhole next to Ransone's were hit, but the foxhole was always
re-manned. The only thing that had saved Ransone was a huge boulder that shielded his position from at least part of the Chinese fire.
Finally, on the second night, the South Korean lifted his head once
too often to have a look around. As Jay Ransone screamed in his ear,
warning him to keep down, the Korean took a nearly spent slug
smack between the eyes. Ransone stopped firing only long enough
to bandage the bloody wound and hoist the babbling man from the
foxhole. An instant later, he was firing his Garand rifle as quickly as
he could get rounds off. A Chinese soldier atop the boulder dropped
two grenades into Ransone's foxhole. There was hellfire and brim-
stone boiling up all around, but Ransone was uninjured, and he kept
firing. The Chinese soldier dropped down into the hole, and Ransone blew him away, pausing only long enough to make room to rest
his elbows on the foxhole's parapet. And he kept firing, all night
long.

★

The Chinese were mounting their most determined attacks to date
upon the Faith perimeter, clearly anticipating a decisive victory. For
the first time, at dawn, they actually penetrated the perimeter line
in force, and seized a small knob within the American defenses.
Faith had used up most of his reaction forces plugging other holes,
so he had to call his Dog Company commander to see if any heavy
weapons people could be spared to mount a sweep of the hill. First
Lieutenant Robert Wilson, a machine-gun platoon leader, volunteered to lead the assault.

Lieutenant Wilson managed to assemble about two dozen able-
bodied men, each of whom had only a few rounds of ammunition
and an average of three hand grenades. Carrying a Thompson submachine gun taken from a dead Chinese soldier, Wilson formed his
little band of weapons specialists and led it toward the hill as the
new sun cast an anemic, misty light across the battleground. As he
neared the objective, Wilson took a slug in the arm and was knocked
from his feet. He grasped the tommy gun in his good hand, picked

himself up and ran forward to resume the lead, tossing off a brave "That one bit," as he trudged resolutely forward. Then Robert Wilson was pitched backward with a killing shot to the forehead. The sergeant who took command was killed within minutes, as were several of the men he was leading. The Chinese lodgement, however, was reduced in some very tough close-in fighting.

Emboldened by the lack of American air support, which could not penetrate the thick morning mists, the Chinese persisted in their attacks well past dawn. First Lieutenant James Campbell's 75mm recoilless rifle, guarding the road that bisected the American perimeter, was assaulted by two Chinese platoons which approached by way of a deep roadside ditch. Campbell, who had been wounded several times in preceding days, rushed Corporal Robert Lee Armentrout forward to cover the recoilless rifle with his heavy machine gun, which had been damaged during the night by a round through its water jacket. The gun jammed after only a few moments' use, so Armentrout sent his assistant gunner to beg a replacement. The last operative gun in the section was rushed forward, and Armentrout killed at least twenty of the assailants, stemming the assault.

A short time later, Lieutenant Campbell was reassuring a battalion staffer that all was well when a Chinese mortar round landed only ten feet away, putting a lie to the assessment, felling Campbell with numerous shrapnel wounds in his left side. Helpless, Campbell had to be dragged beneath a nearby truck, then to a nearby aid station which was overflowing with injured soldiers. The lieutenant was left outside with three dozen other injured men for a half hour, at which point Don Faith came by to beg anyone who could to help man the lines against the persistent Chinese attacks. When he got no response, the harried, frustrated task-force commander berated the wounded men, accusing them of being, of all things, lazy. That stirred a few brave souls, including James Campbell, who crawled twenty yards along the railroad embankment with a carbine in tow; the carbine had but a single round in the chamber. The fearless machine-gun officer, however, had had enough, and collapsed into a foxhole, from which he was rescued and carried back to the aid station for treatment of his wounds.

★

Task Force Faith was indeed dying, and Don Faith knew that better than anyone. He was well below the bottom of the barrel. His air support, once the mists cleared, was a single Marine Corsair, which expended its payload with telling effect before it roared off for Yonpo. The wounded were dying, or soon would be. Most of the medical supplies allotted to Faith's own 1st Battalion, 32nd, had been lost in the dash to join Reilly's battalion, and the little that had remained was nearly expended. The combined force had been under unremitting infantry attack or incessant mortar fire for over eighty consecutive hours. Some of the troops were nodding off in the heat of battle! Frostbite casualties were mounting, and the tough core of wounded soldiers willing to resume the fight was rapidly diminishing.

Denied even the prospect of relief, and clearly in danger of being overrun, Lieutenant Colonel Don Faith, one of the finest battalion commanders the Army had, decided that it was time to throw in the towel. After discussing the matter with his senior subordinates, Faith passed the news: the combined forces would break out and run for Hagaru-ri as soon as possible.

Coordinating successive air strikes through his forward air controller, Captain Ed Stamford, Faith hoped to hold the Chinese at bay long enough for his infantry to penetrate the ring of attackers and lead the vehicle column out. The heavy-mortar company and two artillery batteries were ordered to fire all their ammunition on choice targets, then destroy the guns.

Staff officers, clerks, and drivers were set to work warming up vehicle engines and destroying nonessential gear while medics moved the wounded from the aid stations.

Chinese 120mm heavy mortars were particularly effective in taking out the men and vehicles gathering in the center of the thoroughly dominated American perimeter. Captain Hugh Robbins, who had become the task-force supply officer, was on his way to the command post of the 57th Field Artillery Battalion when one of those big rounds landed within three feet. He was wounded in an arm and a leg. Captain Bill McNally, the task-force communicator, was felled by the same round.

From his vantage point aboard the truck in which he had been placed facedown, Hugh Robbins watched gunners destroying their guns and drivers jabbing bayonets into the tires of vehicles that could not be made to start. And supplies, carefully hoarded over the past five days — was it only *five* days? — were doused with gasoline and set ablaze.

First Lieutenant Ed Magill, commanding Baker Battery, 57th, fired off the last of his ammunition and saw to the placement of thermite grenades in the tubes of his silent howitzers. Then, rounding up his gunners, he reported to Don Faith and was placed on the flank of the vehicle column.

The wholesale destruction occurring in the American perimeter alerted the Chinese in the hills to the impending breakout, and the offensive was redoubled despite the arrival of Marine fighter-bombers.

Making his way to the head of the slowly forming column, Don Faith placed 1st Lieutenant James Mortrude's platoon-sized Charlie Company, 32nd, in the vanguard, to be followed by a self-propelled twin-40mm antiaircraft gun and a halftrack mounting quad-.50 machine guns, neither of which had any ammunition for their otherwise fearsomely destructive weapons. The remnant of Able/32 was next, and was in turn followed by the head of the soft-vehicle column.

When Faith paused before Able/32 to deliver his final instructions, Private First Class Jay Ransone was surprised to see that the West Pointer was turned out in flawlessly ironed parka and snow pants and flawlessly shined boots. There was no question but that Don Faith looked every inch the leader of a crack, winning force of soldiers. Moreover, Ransone was certain that the little pep talk Faith used to close out his instructions was directed at him, and him alone. The Virginia rifleman was determined to do his all for the battalion commander.

The exodus began at 1300, much later than anticipated. Marine Captain Ed Stamford called in a low air strike, aimed at placing napalm on a Chinese emplacement only twenty yards from the point. The very first napalm canister was released a hairsbreadth too soon, and the leading twin-40 and several dozen Able/32 riflemen were engulfed in a stupendous, hideous wall of flame. Seared, unrecognizable forms of men shriveled up and sank to the roadway.

Though the tragedy was followed by highly successful pinpoint napalm drops, Task Force Faith had been thrown into chaos. The structure and discipline that had been maintained to that point, despite the severe buffeting at Chinese hands, became unglued. And, because of the loss of key staff and troop officers and many seasoned noncommissioned officers, there was also no way to bring things fully back to order.

First Lieutenant Mortrude gathered a dozen riflemen from the point platoon and stalked off down the road, dispersing twenty Chinese who were throwing a block across the path of the column.

No provision had been made to place combat troops on the high ground, so the seventy-two vehicles and hundreds of footborne soldiers had to run a gantlet of observed, plunging fire from the heights.

The only chance the wounded in the trucks had lay in a quick, steady move.

That chance had already been obviated. Hobbling down the road on a throbbing wounded leg, Lieutenant Mortrude came upon the hideous spectre of a blown bridge only two miles from the perimeter. Strangely, there were no Chinese in the vicinity, so Mortrude dropped heavily to the frozen earth and told his men to take a break. He was joined a short time later by what had been a platoon of Able/32, Private First Class Jay Ransone included. Unable to account for the delay of the vehicle column, the Able and Charlie Company groups coalesced and crossed the wide gully that had been spanned by the blown bridge. Pushing south and east to reconnoiter, the American infantrymen were fired on by Chinese on the heights, and everyone went to ground. While idly pondering all the reasons why the vehicle column had not yet come into sight, Lieutenant Mortrude was knocked unconscious when a spent slug spanged into his steel helmet. Assuming that the officer had been killed, the other soldiers in the group withdrew to the bridge.

★

It was midafternoon before the head of the vehicle column had fought as far as the blown bridge. Senior officers moved to the scene of destruction to assess the situation and their chances, and a decision was quickly reached. All available men were set to the task of clearing a path across the stream bed while a halftrack was moved to the head of the column. Infantry was sent to the left and right to secure the ground dominating the bridgesite, and the halftrack was hooked up to the first truck and sent across the cleared gully. The movement was excrutiatingly slow, but the straining semi-tracked vehicle succeeded. The first truck was unhitched and driven a short distance down the road while the halftrack went back for the second of the seventy-two wheeled vehicles.

Captain Bob McClay, personnel officer of the 3rd Battalion, 31st, was limping down the road on a painfully wounded leg when he was stopped by Major Harvey Storms, his battalion's nominal commander. The Chinese had established a base of fire on the ridge to the right, and Storms was forming an assault group to clear the skyline. McClay followed Storms despite his leg wound. The group made it halfway up the ridge before the Chinese turned their fire against it. McClay was about five yards behind Storms when the first bullets whistled through the struggling skirmish line. Storms was stitched by the machine-gun fire and felled. McClay could do nothing more than watch as the major's body rolled and rolled and rolled to the foot of the slope. The survivors trudged on and cleared the Chinese position following a brief fight, then followed the ridgeline southward to where it intersected the road above the blown bridge.

First Lieutenant Ed Magill, leading a provisional infantry company composed largely of his own Baker/57, was ordered across the gully to assault a hilltop machine-gun emplacement that had the towing operation under direct fire. Working carefully through wind-whipped snow, Magill pushed his troops upslope as quickly as possible. With the help of some nearby riflemen, the gunners destroyed the Chinese emplacement and moved on to occupy the summit of the ridge. Within moments, however, a misdirected Marine Corsair strafed and rocketed the newly won position. In the absence of further orders, Magill pulled his troops into a defensive deployment and watched the struggle below.

Slowly, painstakingly, under the patient guidance of 1st Lieutenant Hugh May, Faith's motor transport officer, the halftrack pulled wheeled vehicles through the gully during the long, fire-swept afternoon.

Captain Hugh Robbins watched with mounting concern as soldiers beside the road were felled by fire from the heights. Steaming pools of blood from the unattended dead and dying men in the open formed slushy red puddles all along the slowly moving column. And yet it registered on Robbins that most of the uninjured men in the killing ground had words of cheerful encouragement for the men in the trucks.

Later, the driver of Robbins's truck panicked and raced headlong into the gully, jostling the screaming wounded as he plowed across mounds and into ruts. The engine died and could not be restarted, so Captain Robbins watched as other vehicles streamed by under their own power. At length, the halftrack passed a tow and Robbins's truck was pulled clear of the gully and restarted.

Captain Bill McNally, who had been wounded alongside Hugh Robbins, had taken refuge in a ¾-ton radio truck, and had even managed to stretch out across the top of the built-in radio. Late in the afternoon, McNally was asked by a young soldier with a leg wound to trade places; the boy could not stretch out in the over-crowded vehicle, and his leg was hurting something awful. McNally assented. Not twenty mintues after he had hunkered down in the bed of the truck, McNally pulled his head in as hundreds of rounds from the heights pounded into the vehicle, riddling the boy atop the radio. Bill McNally's mind went blank.

As the afternoon wore on, Hugh Robbins noted that the troops

became increasingly reluctant to brave the burgeoning Chinese fire
to wrest key positions on the skyline. Officers and sergeants were
ignored or even reviled when they ordered and begged and pleaded
with men to get themselves going. Here and there, lone riflemen
and small groups bestirred themselves and mounted the slopes, but
they merely replaced men who had had enough and were dropping
down to the road for a rest. In time, the Chinese were able to move
along the skyline with impunity, in clear view of the many men who
would not raise their rifles.

A wide-eyed South Korean leaped aboard Robbins's truck, dropping onto a painfully wounded young American, who screamed in
agony. The Korean was so crazed that he did not recognize the threat
implicit in the carbine that Robbins shoved into his face. Robbins's
snarling finally bridged the gulfs of language, culture, and fear, and
the South Korean vaulted to the roadway.

Captain Robbins left the truck at length and, despite his injured
leg, joined an infantry lieutenant for a quick confab. The two decided to get going over a nearby hill. They rallied about twenty
soldiers to their cause and traded the terrifying known for the terrifying unknown, lost from the outset.

★

The Chinese were waiting for the head of the vehicle column at a
hairpin turn only a half mile from the blown bridge. The infantry at
the point moved forward under Don Faith to clear the block, and it
looked as though they might succeed until newly placed guns on
the heights stalled them in their tracks. Faith, who had pulled a
blanket around his shoulders to ward off the cold, stalked back along
the re-forming column, ordering able-bodied soldiers to join the assault. When he arrived at his own jeep, he jumped into the back and
latched onto the handles of the .50-caliber machine gun mounted
there, squeezing off long bursts at the Chinese guns on the heights.
The American point, forced to withdraw through intense fire, suffered grievously.

Aided by orbiting control pilots, Captain Ed Stamford moved his
fighter-bombers through the air in intricate displays of virtuosity. A
bid by the Chinese to close on the rear of the column, north of the
blown bridge, was shattered by timely and accurate air strikes
guided by the Marine air controller. And numerous machine-gun
emplacements on the heights were strafed, bombed, rocketed, and
napalmed to submission.

It became obvious to Stamford, as the afternoon wore on, that
discipline was wavering. Able-bodied men were less and less in-

clined to join sweeping operations. The large South Korean contingent, fearing particular reprisals at the hands of their fellow Asians, and never wholly integrated into their American units, began leaving in increasing numbers, hoping to blend in with the natives of the area. Few of the American soliders blamed the South Koreans, and many frankly and openly wished they could do the same.

When his radioman was hit, Captain Stamford opted to backpack his own radio, an instrument that was made to be jeep-loaded, not man-carried. It was, he felt, his only option.

★

Private First Class Jay Ransone, of what had been Able/32, was driven from the road into a cornfield by the intensity of the Chinese fire that reached down from the heights. He made his way to the center of the field and was soon joined behind a corn shock by more than twenty other men. Bullets were falling like rain. Fearful of drawing even more fire because of the size of the crowd, Ransone turned to the man beside him, a dental officer, and said he thought they all ought to disperse. As he spoke, five bullets hit Ransone and his equipment: one through his canteen, one through his ammunition belt, one through his bayonet scabbard, one through his parka, and one through his right arm, chipping the bone. A sixth bullet took the top off the dentist's head.

As Ransone rushed back to the road, he saw for the first time a line of four American medium tanks on the roadway in the middle distance. At first he thought the tanks were coming to the rescue of Task Force Faith, but he soon realized that they were derelicts. Indeed, they marked the farthest penetration of the abortive attack from the 31st Infantry operations center on November 28.

Ransone had his first real inkling of the degree to which control had been lost when he regained the roadway. He came upon his own company commander and an artillery forward observer who had served with Able/32. The young Virginian asked the infantry officer to check the wound in his arm, but the officer brushed him aside and dogtrotted down the road. The artilleryman, however, stopped and peered at the wound. "I don't think you were hit bad, soldier. You just got shot through the arm. I see where the bullet went through. You must not be hit very bad." Ransone never forgave his company commander for the slight, but he would hold the artilleryman forever in high esteem.

★

Marine Air units based at Yonpo had been sending an endless stream of Corsairs north to support Task Force Faith, but it was clear that the fight was going badly. When Major Ed Montagne and Captain Tom Mulvihill, of VMF-212, were asked if they would undertake a dangerous mission in support of Faith, both readily agreed, for they had been drawn emotionally to the plight of Task Force Faith while supporting the mixed unit over the preceding days.

The air-supply people had come up with experimental parachute canisters crammed with small-arms ammunition, which, if proven successful, could be dropped in great numbers and with great accuracy from fighter aircraft. Montagne and Mulvihill had one desperate chance to prove the delivery system in combat that very afternoon.

The squadron armorers, unused to the canisters, had a very hard time mounting them on wing bomb racks of the two fighters, and the late afternoon slipped away as Marine combat pilots over Task Force Faith radioed increasingly depressing news to their base. In time, however, the canisters were secured and the pilots, including several escorts, were called to their Corsairs.

The mission got off to a shaky start when one of the airmen accidentally touched the rocket-firing knob on his joy stick and sent eight armed 5-inch rockets streaking across the airdrome, narrowly missing a refueler truck.

The Corsairs roared down the runway and highballed toward the Taebek Plateau.

On the ground, Captain Ed Stamford single-handedly called dozens of strikes against targets in the hills. Aerial observers helped where they could, but the greatest burden was in the hands of "Boyhood-One-Four," as Stamford was known on the air.

Ed Montagne and Tom Mulvihill arrived as the sky was graying over at dusk. Both men could see the desperate battles on the ground as they roared above the roadway to get their bearings. Burning vehicles lay in profusion, and masses of PLA infantry could be seen preparing for killing night assaults. Every time Ed Stamford opened his mike to speak, the airmen could hear the staccato of small-arms fire in the background.

The two ammunition-laden Corsairs flew out over the Reservoir to descend. The air was filled with weaving fighters and the trails of rockets, so flying was extremely perilous, even among these practiced airmen.

As the dusk gloom deepened, Tom Mulvilhill could see colored tracer weaving back and forth between the ridges and the road: green Chinese tracer inbound, and yellow American tracer outbound. It was eerie, and quite beautiful in its way.

Ed Stamford took only a moment out to speak with Montagne and Mulvilhill, directing them to make their runs straight up the road. The two pilots tried a practice run at only twenty feet, agreeing that they would have to proceed more slowly on the live runs. By going flat out up the road, they were assured of getting their payloads into friendly hands.

The live runs were made from the rear of the column toward the front at under one hundred knots. Tom Mulvihill had time to think of how utterly hopeless was the plight of the men on the ground, but he continued through a wall of tracer to his release point.

The drops were perfect, and Mulvihill and Montagne pulled up and around to join the line of Corsairs awaiting targets for their rockets, bombs, and guns.

The evening shadows closed across the snow-encrusted hills, and the shadow of doom fell in upon Task Force Faith. Men in the air listened, awestruck, when Ed Stamford, their grounded brother, began coming apart. The desperate edge that had been growing in Stamford's voice rose octave by octave while he rattled off directives to the orbiting fighter-bombers. There appeared a frantic quality in his voice, and the orders grew less and less precise. With the night closing in around him, Stamford admitted that his cause was hopeless. He broadcast his last message kneeling upon the slope of a ridge overlooking the fire-swept roadway: "This is Boyhood-One-Four. I am destroying my radio."

One by one, the chastened Marine airmen expended the last of their payloads and reluctantly turned their Corsairs for Yonpo. Captain Harry Henneberger, of VMF-312, delayed his departure, watching fires pool along the roadway. He was just leaving when a division of Marine night fighters arrived on station, but Henneberger knew that there was little they could do without Ed Stamford's pinpoint direction from the ground.

After firing a .45-caliber bullet through his radio, Stamford threw away his cumbersome binoculars and made his way down to the road, regaining the whole of his composure by the time he got there. Alone, but game for a fight, he turned south toward the head of the column and trudged forward to see if he could be of any help.

★

The general flow of warm bodies continued in two directions. Men nearer the head of the column formed a stable nucleus and continued doggedly to overcome opposition. Men farther back had been drifting off toward the Reservoir and hoped-for safety since the late afternoon.

Shortly after sunset, before all of his vehicles had been towed across the gully, Don Faith called upon his senior subordinates to lead infantry attacks against the Chinese positions overlooking the hairpin curve. Captain Erwin Bigger, the Dog/32 commander, had been blinded in one eye by a mortar sliver earlier in the day, but he reported to Faith with about one hundred troopers, as did Major Robert Jones, Faith's intelligence officer. Several dozen other injured but able officers and men formed up under Captain Bob McClay and moved to rescue as many men as they could from the stalled vehicles to the rear.

The attack against the roadblock was sent in without any preparation, and its momentum carried it through the Chinese, but with heavy losses. As Ed Stamford moved forward to join the attack, he met Don Faith, who was lurching painfully toward the rear; he had been very badly wounded by grenade fragments in the attack. Moments after passing Stamford, in fact, he collapsed and had to be assisted to his jeep. And shortly after that, the thirty-two-year-old West Pointer refused evacuation aboard the last rescue helicopter, giving his place to a wounded rifleman.

★

The last solid core of Task Force Faith remained on the roadway under the nominal direction of Major Robert Jones. Smaller groups moved off into the hills in all likely directions. Many were never heard from again.

First Lieutenant Ed Magill lacked communication with higher authority so he led the remnants of Baker/57 from the heights and made for the ice.

After clearing the road and rescuing some of the wounded in the rear of the column, Captain Bob McClay's group headed west in search of the Reservoir.

Captain Hugh Robbins's group of twenty paralleled the roadway on the west side of a screening ridge. At length, the group regained the roadway well to the south and ran into a much larger group led by Captain Earle Jordan, commander of Mike/31, the 3rd Battalion's weapons company. Jordan was in favor of attacking northward against the Chinese rear, right up the road. Robbins, like many of the wounded, did not feel up to the exertion, but he voiced his approval of Jordan's plan and agreed to remain in position to await the outcome. The sound of heavy firing ensued, but Robbins's group could neither see anything nor affect events. Many stragglers joined Robbins in small groups, pairs and individually, and the milling crowd had all the earmarks of panic in the making. After a time, in which the fighting to the north seemed to intensify, Robbins decided to pull up stakes lest he have more trouble on his hands than he and his fellow officers could control. The mass of men set off toward Hagaru-ri.

Captain Bill McNally regained his senses while shuffling rapidly along the shore of the Reservoir. The last thing he could recall was the sound of the gunfire hitting his radio truck, and the vision of the bullet-riddled corpse of the boy who had replaced him atop the built-in radio. He had not even known that he was capable of walking under his own power until he found himself on the ice among a small group of refugees. McNally had no idea where he was going. Just that it was south.

Private First Class Jay Ransone climbed down from the ridge west of the roadway and padded cautiously to the shore of the Reservoir, where he found that he was only twenty-five feet from a machine-gun emplacement manned by five Chinese soliders. As he lengthened his stride, the young Virginian saw that the gun was pointed right at him, but the crew was clearly engrossed with some sort of mechanical problem. Other forms loomed from out of the darkness, all making a beeline for the ice, as the five Chinese grabbed their rifles and took off after Jay Ransone. Weaponless, Ransone ran, passing a South Korean soldier, who was butchered where he stood by the bayonet-wielding Chinese. Ransone next dropped from the shore to the ice and faced the problem of running across the slick surface in galoshes. He looked back and saw the Chinese on the shore, yelling epithets, waving their rifles, but neither pursuing nor firing. Though he risked his life, Ransone sat down to pull off the galoshes, which he tossed aside as he regained his feet. There was little to commend the leather soles of his combat boots over the rubber soles of the galoshes, but he had given up all other options. He struggled on until lack of sleep and general, terror-induced exhaustion got the better of him. He collapsed, unconscious, upon the ice.

★

Don Faith bled into his parka and upon the floor of his jeep as his senior staffers and troop leaders sought to regain some momentum along the road. Slowly, then with greater force, the sum total of his exhaustion, his body's fight against the cold, and the trauma of his wounds, carried Faith into a deep coma. One of the Army's most promising young field commanders died quietly beside his unknowing driver.

★

Only several dozen relatively able-bodied men remained to protect and guide the wounded who had been trapped aboard the last vehicles. According to several of the survivors, the Chinese had cut off the vehicles trapped on the north side of the blown bridge and, after an orgy of looting, had drenched the wounded in gasoline and set the trucks ablaze.

Three 2-½-ton trucks at the head of the column had been shot up during the fight to sweep the roadblock, and these had to be cleared of the wounded and rolled out of the way. The able-bodied searched for a half hour to find men who had been hit in the fighting after dark, and the result was that the surviving trucks had to be packed two-deep with moaning, agonized human beings.

Major Jones was able to find about one hundred fifty men who could still shoulder weapons, and he placed these on the front and flanks to guard the jammed vehicles.

Captain Erwin Bigger's group of less than one hundred men had cleared much of the opposition on the heights to the right, but had been prevented from returning to Jones's group by a Chinese force that had closed on its rear. Unable to win a fight, Captain Bigger led his men west and south to the Reservoir, and out onto the ice.

First Lieutenant James Campbell, the machine-gun officer who had been wounded and blasted at regular intervals during the past three days, stayed with Major Jones because he had not the strength to go it alone. Undaunted, Campbell secured a loaded carbine and clung to the side of a truck with five other men, ready to carry on the good fight if he had to.

The fifteen surviving trucks, surrounded by a loose gaggle of men, continued to inch southward until stymied by a pair of burned-out American medium tanks, which securely blocked the roadway.

While those who were able struggled to construct a bypass around the tanks, combat patrols ranged far forward. The going was very easy for the next several miles, all the way to Hudong-ni, where the 31st Infantry's operations center had been until two days earlier. There was much elation as the column approached the village, for it was known to be within two or three miles of Hagaru-ri.

The lead truck, which had gotten several hundred yards ahead of the column, was fired on by Chinese soldiers in the village. The driver was killed, the truck ran out of control and overturned, and the wounded were spilled onto the ground.

The small but cohesive force was destroyed at this point, for Major Jones opted to lead many of the men to the right, to follow the railroad embankment southward. It was closer to the ice and, above all, less likely to be blocked.

About one hundred men remained in the vehicles. Most of them were badly injured. An artillery officer took charge and placed a weapon in the hands of every man who could handle one. Fire from the vicinity of the village continued without much effect, so the column inched forward. After going only a short distance, however, several of the officers and men got into an argument. Some wanted to force their way through the village while others wanted to wait until morning in the hope that a rescue column would be sent from the nearby Marine perimeter. The column stood in place for over an hour, by which time the more aggressive officers and men had prevailed. The column ground forward again well past midnight.

★

First Lieutenant James Campbell, who remained with the last of the vehicles as they approached the sawmill town almost within sight of Hagaru-ri, was certain he was meant to die that night. As the column proceeded along the road and into the village, the first three trucks were sprayed at point-blank range by machine-gun fire. Campbell, who was aboard the third truck, scrambled to the ground and let himself down an embankment on the right, into a small field. He could see only the silhouettes of the trucks above him, and the winking of gunfire. He had a carbine with a thirty-round banana clip, and he fired twenty-seven rounds while braced against the embankment. The injured weapons officer saved the last three rounds, and turned his attention to one of the trucks, which was on its side in the field. A body with an arm torn off lay beside the truck, and a man in the truck was pounding on the side to attract attention. Many wounded men were in the field, moaning and wailing. Looking to the road, Campbell saw a Chinese soldier hurl a white-phosphorous grenade into one of the trucks farther back.

The driver of the fourth truck drove forward and pushed the three stalled vehicles over the embankment into Campbell's field, which was soon littered with screaming, agonized, crawling men and dark, inert, human forms. Campbell fired his last three rounds at a Chinese machine gun and headed for the railroad embankment, where he dove into a culvert to escape.

After crawling through the culvert, Campbell came upon a man who could not walk, and two other soldiers joined them. Campbell and the others dragged the injured man to the shore of the Reservoir, where they were joined by still other soldiers. The Americans stayed close to the shoreline and moved onto the ice, which was rough-surfaced enough to keep them from slipping. When they arrived at a native house, a South Korean with the group asked directions, and was told that American jeeps had been patrolling the road until two days earlier, that the road led directly to the American base at Hagaru-ri. There was some feeling that the locals might be lying, but Campbell thought he recognized the surroundings and talked the others into following his lead.

★

Marine Sergeant Brad Westerdahl, a member of the intelligence section of the 2nd Battalion, 7th Marines, was manning an outpost on the ice north of the Hagaru-ri perimeter when the first knots of straggling, struggling GIs began appearing from the north and east. Within a short time, dozens of injured and frostbitten Americans and South Koreans were passing through Westerdahl's position and others nearby. Some of the wounded should have been dead — like the man who staggered up to Westerdahl holding his guts in the crook of his arm — but they lived because of a desire so deep as to be inextinguishable.

Jay Ransone came to aboard a Marine truck. He had been pulled unconscious from the ice by rescuers who happened to find him sprawled where he had fallen in the night.

Ed Magill identified himself in response to a sharp challenge by a Marine sentry but, before he could move, the artillery officer was urgently entreated to remain rooted to his spot; he had penetrated halfway into a minefield and had to be led to safety by a volunteer guide. Magill was taken to a Navy casualty clearing station beside the runway to have his bullet and shrapnel wounds treated.

Bob McClay's group arrived late enough to be met on the far side of the minefield by Marine guides who had been sent forward for just such a happenstance meeting. McClay limped in on his wounded leg and was led to town to receive hot food and medical care.

Hugh Robbins's group had numerous close calls after heading away from the first roadblock, but they made it to the ice and had achieved something of a group high when ordered to "Halt!" in a clear, American-sounding voice on the approaches to the Marine perimeter.

Robert Jones and his sizable contingent were driven from the railroad embankment by machine-gun fire well before dawn. The group splintered, but most of the men took to the ice and survived the trip to the Marine outpost line without further incident.

Ed Stamford was taken twice by the Chinese, but managed to escape and evade them both times. Getting home among Marines was something special for the grounded aviator.

The group led by James Campbell moved cautiously along the road from the sawmill town and came upon a Marine tank before dawn. Campbell was seen safely to a hospital tent by sunrise.

Bill McNally did not reach Hagaru-ri at all that night, but he did avoid capture and further injury. Joining a group that elected to remain close to the shore of the Reservoir, he had to go to ground in a farmhouse with several of his companions when it became light enough for Chinese patrols to be a threat. In the end, McNally's safe return was postponed for only a day, during which time he had the opportunity to sample the gastronomic pleasure of dog soup, which was provided by the ancient couple hosting his stay.

★

Forty or more Americans were trapped at the sawmill town. With them was Captain James Connor, the 31st Infantry's Protestant chaplain, who could have walked to safety had he so desired. Neither Connor nor any of the men known to have been with him were ever accounted for, though there are reports that all were doused with gasoline and incinerated.

★

The hero of the hour was Lieutenant Colonel Olin Beall, the grizzled Old Salt commanding the 1st Marine Motor Transport Battalion. Upon receiving word of the arrival of the first refugees from the collapse of Task Force Faith, Beall got trucks and crews out onto the ice, scouring the southern end of the Reservoir for the hundreds of soldiers who had managed to elude the Chinese to that point. Beall personally drove two miles onto the ice, then walked even farther to test the surface, to see how far he could safely run his heavy trucks. He was fired on several times, as were a number of his crews, but he persevered. When he thought too many people were seeking too much danger, the motor transport commander snarled at them to keep back. One of his helpers, a stranger before that morning, was an American civilian named LeFevre, a Red Cross employee who could not resist the lure of fellow Americans in peril.

North Korean civilians driving bullock-powered sleds and carts brought in numerous Army survivors through December 2, and well into the week. These people, particularly, had everything to lose by their actions, but they persisted, often in the face of extremely perilous circumstances.

Marine helicopter pilots lifted many wounded men from the ice, and Navy and Marine combat pilots voluntarily prolonged their tiring missions to search farther afield than could men on the ground. Sometimes those aircraft kept Chinese soldiers at bay while rescuers on the ground performed heart-stopping extrications under blazing guns.

★

Of the one thousand fifty-three men who had been attached to the 1st Battalion, 32nd Infantry, a week earlier one hundred eighty-one had been accounted for by December 4. Others — but not many — were found to have been evacuated before a records-keeping system had been put in place. The 3rd Battalion, 31st, and 57th Field Artillery Battalion did not fare much better.

C H A P T E R
30

Lieutenant Colonel Bill Harris's 3rd Battalion, 7th, was not the unit it had been a week earlier, when it led the way into Yudam-ni. But no unit that had come to that mountain valley town was anywhere near the same as when it had arrived.

The battalion commander himself had changed, and changed back. A week earlier, Bill Harris had been a cocky, combative newcomer with a lot of gaps in his career that needed filling. He had done well in his first weeks of combat, but the spectre of being captured as he had been at Corregidor had seriously influenced the thirty-two-year-old son of a Marine general, and his staff had had to ease him through a period of emotional nightmare. With the seizure of the initiative in planning on November 30, Harris's spirits had surged upward, though he was still a chastened soul.

Harris's was a much smaller battalion than it had been on November 27, but so were all the other units at Yudam-ni. It was about the most rested unit of its size in the perimeter, and that accounted somewhat for its being chosen to lead the way down the MSR to seize two commanding heights, between which the soft body of the long column would have to pass in order to reach Toktong Pass and Hagaru-ri.

The simultaneous seizure of Hills 1542 and 1419 (Turkey Hill) was a tactical nightmare, particularly for a battalion comprised of relatively unsupported understrength rifle companies. Both of the "hills" might be more properly defined as "hill masses," for both were vast topographical entities jumbled into ridges and meadows and slopes extending over many square miles. Harris was obliged to deploy but one understrength company against each, with a third company in reserve. Neither of the assault companies would be in a position to support the other, nor was the reserve company — a hybrid composed of artillery and service troops and known as "Jig" Company, replacing George Company, which was attached to the 2nd Provisional Battalion — of a strength or quality to support both units.

Speed was of the essence that first day of December, 1950. At the same time that Harris's battalion would be going into the attack on either side of the MSR, battalions to the rear would be disengaging from contact with the Chinese at the northern and southern ends of the perimeter, and other battalions would be providing thin infantry lines to screen the chaos of reorganization that would be progressing daylong at the center of the shifting, shrinking perimeter. If Harris took too long at his task, units lined up on the road might be attacked while off balance and unable to adequately defend themselves. The planners had put as much slack time in the schedule as they dared, but Harris had no time to lose.

★

Leaving the battalion's thinly manned vehicle column on the MSR at the southern end of the deflated perimeter, Harris and his staff set up a command post in a ravine about a mile south of the old perimeter boundary and west of the roadway. Item/7 moved on Hill 1542, the same ground on which Baker/7 had been ambushed on November 27. How/7 drew Turkey Hill and "Jig" Company was well to the rear.

The move began at 0900 when an Item/7 patrol moved straight down a draw toward Hill 1542 to see what it could see. The patrol drew fire as soon as it stepped inside the range of Chinese weapons on the heights, and it withdrew to report. Captain Bill Earney, Harris's operations officer, groaned inwardly, for he viewed the minor action as the precursor of a time-consuming, bloody, repulse.

There was no air or artillery available to prep the objective, and the battalion's supply of mortar ammunition was low, precluding even local fires in all but the direst of circumstances. First Lieutenant Tom Sullivan's 2nd Platoon of Item/7 had to mount its initial attack straight into the teeth of the waiting enemy.

The first opposition came from three Chinese burp gunners holding forth in a single foxhole. While the platoon deployed and carried out a textbook advance, Private First Class Pete Orozco took it upon himself to go after the burp gunners, and he single-handedly overcame them, then shot a fourth Chinese soldier who was running away to the south. Tom Sullivan's platoon moved rapidly forward, followed by the remainder of the company, and seized the knob that was its immediate objective. The first casualty of the day was a heavy-machine gunner who was shot and killed as he prepared his weapon to support the upcoming series of sweeps.

The next objective was a numberless ridgeline about a mile to the south and east. The intervening ground comprised a short, steep drop, then a long, exposed climb. Chinese machine guns on the distant ridgeline had perfect fields of fire and excellent visibility.

After waiting for air and artillery support that did not materialize, the Item Company commander ordered Tom Sullivan's 2nd Platoon to lead the way again. Screening his opening move behind the eastern slope of a ridgeline running south toward the objective, Sullivan made initial rapid progress. Fire from a knob to the left, however, soon slowed the platoon and killed one Marine. When the fire suddenly intensified, the entire company went to ground amidst frantic calls for air and artillery support.

Hill 1542 was an impossible objective for so small an assault force as Item/7. The large mass was a profusion of peaks and fingers of the same altitude or higher. Chinese positions which could reach probing lines of Marines were as far away as Sakkat-San, and numerous Chinese had clear shots from, it seemed, all sides. The ground was too jumbled to be neutralized in any orderly fashion with the troops on hand, and the utter absence of artillery or air support — which was needed elsewhere — added to the general futility of the job. Most attempts to break through were met by flanking or, worse, enfilade fire from Chinese positions that could not be effectively reduced.

George/7, released from duty with the 2nd Provisional Battalion at about 1500, was rushed to the aid of Item Company, and some small amounts of artillery fire were placed on the nearest objectives. It was 1800 hours before George/7 reached positions approximating those of its sister company, and the rapid onset of darkness, coupled with the depletion of the ammunition supply, was making for a desperate situation. With approval from Battalion, the Item Company commander decided to mount a night assault against the most critically needed objective on his front.

Still leading, 1st Lieutenant Tom Sullivan's 2nd Platoon of Item/7 moved rapidly forward in the darkness, covering ground that had been denied it through the long day. Suddenly a challenge cut through the night, rooting Sullivan's platoon to the spot. Long moments of silence passed. Sullivan's platoon remained frozen, hoping to bluff through. The only movement was on the part of the Chinese soldier who had issued the heart-stopping challenge. He proved, unfortunately, too good a target for one of the American riflemen to pass up, and was dispatched by a single round that kicked up a horrible fuss in which one Marine was wounded severely in the legs.

Tom Sullivan was about to lead his men into the attack when he was ordered to return to his line of departure to dig in for the night. Easier said than done, for Chinese maneuvering elements had gotten between the assault platoon and the company rear. The troops had to fire on the run. Another of Sullivan's men was hit, and he died of his wounds later in the night.

While it did not achieve its mission — the reduction of the Chinese holding Hill 1542 — Item/7, bolstered by George/7, had succeeded in screening the MSR from direct assault or direct fire from the heights.

★

How/7 had been having a miserable time to the left of the MSR.

Badly depleted during its losing fight on Hill 1403 the night of November 27–28, How Company, 7th, was at least well rested after three inactive days. But it had not been adequately bolstered, and it was really too weak to contend seriously for a piece of ground the size of Turkey Hill.

Chinese machine guns, supported by large numbers of riflemen and mortars, were dug in on the four finger ridges by which How/7 had to advance upon the summit of its objective. It became evident early on that the attack would simply pulverize the attacking unit, so reinforcements were called forward.

Lieutenant Colonel Ray Davis's 1st Battalion, 7th, which was to have advanced over Turkey Hill after it had been secured by How/ 7, knew the ground as well as any unit at Yudam-ni. Charlie/7 had been mousetrapped on the hill on November 28, and Able and Baker Companies had both fought successively across the ground on November 28 and 29. Inasmuch as it was already deployed to exploit the seizure of the hill, and because its vital overland march to relieve Fox/7 at Toktong Pass might be driven seriously off schedule by How/7's failure, Davis's battalion was the natural choice for going into the attack to secure its own line of departure.

The battalion had stripped down to barest essentials, leaving most of its heavy equipment and weapons with its vehicle train on the MSR. It was, in fact, almost wholly composed of riflemen, and supported only by its own light machine guns and 60mm mortars.

Davis's battalion moved from its position near Hill 1276 at 1100 on December 1, and arrived at the foot of Turkey Hill about noon. While 1st Lieutenant Gene Hovatter's Able/7 advanced up the thickly wooded slope to come even with How/7, Marine Corsairs — the first air support of the day — plowed up the ground ahead with liberal doses of 20mm cannon fire, bombs, rockets, and napalm. Hovatter's skeleton 60mm mortar crews fired with telling effect, destroying one Chinese blocking position after another. The fighting was fierce, and casualties mounted swiftly as How and Able Company Marines wriggled up the overgrown forward slopes. First Lieutenant Howie Harris, the How Company commander, as well as key line and staff noncoms were hit and had to be dragged down to the road. But the attackers pressed forward under heavy air support. As the afternoon wore on, it looked increasingly as though the objective would be taken and the 1st Battalion, 7th, would be seen safely on its way into the wilderness backing the MSR.

★

With the outcome so long delayed at the initial points of contact with the enemy, there were bound to be revisions in the carefully honed plan that served as the basis for the breakout.

Lieutenant Colonel Bob Taplett's 3rd Battalion, 5th, which was to lead the vehicle column from the perimeter following the seizure of Hill 1542 and Turkey Hill, had begun a carefully staged, intensely intricate disengagement around Hill 1282 at 0800.

The move had actually begun with the redeployment of elements of the adjacent battalions on November 29 and 30. Because the perimeter had been steadily contracted over the previous two days, there was no chance that the abandonment of Hill 1282 would come as a real surprise to the Chinese. The only thing that Taplett could do was put on a show that would confuse the Chinese as to the time and manner in which the company holding the hill was to be withdrawn.

The plan, which was the work of Taplett's assistant operations officer, 1st Lieutenant Charlie Mize, called for George/5, on Hill 1282, and How/5, covering several draws to the north, to simultaneously disengage.

George Company, which had relieved Item/5 on Hill 1282 only a day before, was relatively fresh, and the nearest of Taplett's rifle companies to full strength. George/5 and the Chinese were engaged almost to the last man, though neither side was in direct physical contact with the other across the sharp razorback ridge running the length of Hill 1282. Combat was in the form of incessant exchanges of grenades and mortar fire, and patrol action. The objective of the withdrawal plan was to bluff the Chinese into deploying to stand off an attack by George/5 when, in fact, the Marine company pulled away from the hill.

Second Lieutenant Hank Ammer, an artillery forward observer from the 1st Battalion, 11th, and Taplett's two forward air controllers, held all the keys. Ammer was tied in with 1st Lieutenant Art House's 81mm mortar platoon, which had been registered through the previous four days on key Chinese positions all along the rear slope of Hill 1282.

As the bulk of George/5 prepared to take its leave, the forward air controllers ordered predesignated divisions of Marine Corsairs to begin execution of a prearranged plan. The aircraft lined up to the east and roared in at low level along flight paths that would take them directly over the Marine perimeter. The first was a dummy run, intended to get all Chinese heads in the vicinity firmly beneath ground level. As the planes roared over, Lieutenant Ammer blurted an order to Art House, whose six 81mm mortars fired as many rounds as possible while the Corsairs re-formed to the east to begin their first live run. The moment the first mortar rounds started hitting the reverse slope of the ridge, George/5 pulled up stakes and slid down toward the road, where other units had formed an infantry screen. The air strike was followed by a concentrated mortar barrage, which was followed by another air strike.

The timing was one-hundred-percent perfect. George Company clambered off Hill 1282 as though it was on maneuvers. All that was left on the abandoned ground was a profusion of booby traps that would keep Chinese engineers busy for a week.

Taplett's intermediate mission was holding the heights south of Yudam-ni and west of the MSR secure against Chinese attack while the huge vehicle column continued to form on the roadway. Later, when the column was fully formed, the 3rd Battalion, 5th, following the 3rd Battalion, 7th, would lead it from the valley.

As soon as Bob Taplett's troops were deployed, he surveyed the area around his position with the engineer officer responsible for booby-trapping the former Marine positions and a bridge leading out of town. The two were talking when a call on Taplett's radio told him to clear his present lines, form the battalion on the road, and report to the joint regimental command post for detailed orders.

What Bob Taplett found on the way to the CP was distinctly not to his liking. The roadway was jammed with artillery trucks, howitzers, and regimental vehicles of every type. He had a hard time just getting his nimble little radio jeep through, and cringed at the thought of having to transit the congested area with his battalion's heavy trucks.

Upon arrival at the joint command post, Taplett was directed to Colonels Litzenberg and Murray. Litz issued verbal orders: after Harris had seized Hill 1542 the 3rd Battalion, 5th, was to pass through the 3rd Battalion, 7th, and lead the attack.

Taplett took his leave and decided to press on to Harris's command post to discuss the passage of lines in detail. It was a tricky maneuver under the best of circumstances, and the congested road conditions had Taplett worried.

In fact, upon passing the joint command post, Taplett's jeep was stopped cold by the traffic, which happened at that point to be composed of Harris's vehicle train. Furious, Taplett jumped to the ground and stalked off, chased by his radioman, who had to pack his heavy radio.

Taplett found Bill Harris in his CP below Hill 1542, directing the twin assaults, and he tore a piece off him for having blocked the road. The two exchanged some ideas about how a battalion train should be operated, then calmed down to discuss their options in light of the 3rd Battalion, 7th's unexpectedly slow progress.

This was where Taplett's high intellect, and an animal cunning developed during five months of heavy fighting, really paid off. He weighed all the odds, and gauged all the times and distances. He took the view that daylight was a crucial factor because of air support and observation, and that there wasn't much of it left. He had Bill Harris convinced in under thirty minutes that the two should seek permission for Taplett's battalion to advance down the MSR even while Harris's companies were still fighting for control of the heights — and not, as ordered, *after* Harris had achieved success. Though he could not forecast the ultimate reduction of Chinese units overlooking the MSR, Harris, backed by his staff, assured Taplett that he could keep the enemy from severing the road.

Taplett placed a call to the joint command post and managed to get Lieutenant Colonel Fred Dowsett, exec of the 7th Marines, on the line. Dowsett heard Taplett out with distracted impatience — there was a lot going on at the joint CP — and said, "Sure, do what you think is right." It was as close to a brush-off as Taplett had ever received, but he seized the opportunity and returned to his rifle companies to get them ready to spearhead the drive from Yudam-ni.

★

Major Hal Roach had some serious problems to think through during the early afternoon of December 1. Formerly commander of the 3rd Battalion, 7th, and officially the logistics officer of the 7th Marines, Roach had been given command of the 2nd Provisional Battalion, 7th, on November 28. And it was the new responsibility that had him in a quandry.

The battalion had been built around the shattered remnants of Dog and Easy Companies, 7th, which had been formed into a composite unit (Dog-Easy/7) on November 28 and sent to guard the southeast corner of the original perimeter. At various times over the past several days, Roach had been given, and had relinquished, nominal command over a company of the 5th Marines and George/7, which he happened to have under his control on the morning of December 1.

The battalion, filled out by a few platoons of artillerymen, which came and went, was something of a losing proposition. It had no staff other than Roach and a radioman, and its permanent component had been brutally handled during the first Chinese attacks. Esprit had been built somewhat when Roach had allowed several of his men to retain scarves they had cut from green silk parachutes "damaged" in air drops; the device, in fact, had spread through the whole unit. Roach had taken positive steps to build upon that fragile identity when, on November 29, he rejected his unit's assigned radio call sign in favor of one that won immediate approval among his troops: Damnation. The battalion had been known from that point on as Damnation Battalion.

When Colonel Homer Litzenberg had first agreed to allow Ray Davis's battalion to attack overland across Turkey Hill to rescue Fox/7 at Toktong Pass, he and his planners had decided to send Roach's Damnation Battalion in Davis's traces, but by way of a more circuitous track.

The matter was discussed at length and Roach, a fiercely combative troop officer, had agreed to take on the mission. But he had his doubts. The unit, after all, was a hodgepodge; it had no staff, nor any organic heavy weapons, and its permanent cadre was the remnant of two defeated rifle companies. Above all, the mission was extraordinarily dangerous, for Damnation Battalion would have to cut its ties with units to the rear and advance alone and unsupported across miles of trackless wastes held by a more numerous enemy.

When the 1st Battalion, 7th, was called out before noon to drive an assault up Turkey Hill, Damnation Battalion followed. But Hal Roach drove to the joint CP and begged an audience with Litz and Fred Dowsett. The three men spoke for a few moments, which was all the time it took for Major Roach to convey his apprehensions. Litz gave a moment's thought, undoubtedly considering Roach's combative nature and the clear implications of his desire to be relieved of the mission. The colonel nodded a final nod, ordering Roach to dissolve Damnation Battalion and return to his chores on the regimental staff.

George/7 was returned to Bill Harris's control, the artillerymen and service troops were doled out to other infantry formations, and Dog-Easy/7 was placed under the nominal control of Taplett's 3rd Battalion, 5th, which was by then moving through the perimeter to its line of departure.

★

As soon as Taplett's 3rd Battalion was withdrawn from Hill 1282, the remaining battalions of the 5th Marines moved quickly to establish the final screening positions from which they would move in support of the withdrawing regimental and artillery trains.

Baker/5, which had been toe to toe with the Chinese on Hill 1240 since the morning of November 28, had serious difficulties withdrawing to the base of the hill. While a division of Corsairs lowered a curtain of steel between adjacent Charlie/5 and the Chinese on its front, Baker/5 did not draw air support quickly enough, and it received heavy fire from its former positions almost as soon as they were abandoned. A good portion of the company was forced to go to ground on very unfavorable terrain. A communications breakdown prevented the air support that was available from being put to good use, nor was there any way to control artillery support. First Lieutenant John Hancock, the Baker/5 commander, quickly deployed all available machine guns, which suppressed much of the Chinese gunfire. As the situation stabilized, Hancock leapfrogged his guns to cover withdrawing infantry increments. In time, communications were reestablished, and air and artillery were brought to bear in great force and with telling effect.

Once clear of the enemy, the 1st Battalion, 5th, which would have

to travel light in undertaking its task to scour the hills on either side
of the MSR, discarded all nonessential gear. The men were given
wide latitude in what they could retain or leave for destruction. John
Hancock, the Baker/5 commander, went so far as to discard his helmet. But he built esprit by sporting his "pisscutter" overseas cap,
which he had been carrying in his pack since Pusan.

★

Major Bill McReynolds's 4th Battalion, 11th, had been discarding
gear and firing off ammunition for two full days in order to lighten
its load. The battalion had already provided a large proportion of its
manpower for infantry fillers, and it was to be further cannibalized
during the afternoon of December 1.

The long-range 155s were employed through the morning, harassing known Chinese supply routes. And sixteen villages in the vicinity of Yudam-ni were bombarded in the hope that Chinese command
posts would be dispersed, and in the sure knowledge that the
Chinese would be denied shelter in the buildings that were demolished.

The battalion shut down at noon, when the guns were hooked to
their tractors and placed on the road. All remaining ammunition was
destroyed, as was some very expensive optical equipment, for there
was no room aboard the few trucks remaining under the battalion's
control (most having been assigned to carry wounded Marines).

Two infantry platoons and a platoon equipped with eight light
machine guns were sent to bolster the 2nd Battalion, 5th, in screening the withdrawal. The remainder of the battalion, divided into
provisional infantry platoons, was sent to protect the hospital convoy, which would be put together in the late afternoon.

★

The five 105mm batteries (How/11 was at Hagaru-ri) had been
resupplied by air to the extent possible, and had been spared some,
but by no means all, the burden of providing infantry fillers for the
trek to Hagaru-ri. In general, the five six-gun batteries were to be
dispersed through the column in such a way as to ensure that all
units on the road and in the hills could be reached by at least a few
guns at all times.

Inasmuch as their firing batteries could not be controlled from a
central location, Lieutenant Colonel Harvey Feehan and Major Fox
Parry, and the bulk of their staffs, were to travel with the regimental
command groups. The completely self-contained batteries were
well used to caring for themsleves, and the mission they were facing
was fairly routine from an operational standpoint. Since Parry's bat-

talion had covered the advance of the 7th Marines from Hagaru-ri to Yudam-ni, the job of the artillery was eased considerably because the best battery sites had already been surveyed and, in some cases, used. Several, in fact, presumably still had gun pits ready and waiting.

As with all other units, the 105mm battalions had to abandon a lot of otherwise useful gear. Parry's battalion was short fifteen heavy trucks, which had remained at Hagaru-ri when the MSR had been closed. Other vehicles were drawn off to provide transport for the wounded. So, like all the other battalions, the artillery was going out lean and hard.

★

The hundreds of wounded were lean, but they were by no means hard. Utterly overwhelmed by the inflow, particularly during the unstable first night and day of heaviest fighting, the medical system had balked and all but run down.

Private First Class Walker Merell, who had been wounded on Turkey Hill the morning of November 28, was loaded with three other litter patients aboard an ambulance jeep on the morning of December 1. He had yet to receive anything more than rudimentary first aid from a corpsman, and he had had no food, other than a few crackers and some cocoa, in all that time. He had lost the feeling in his right fingers two days earlier, and he deeply feared the possibility of succumbing to his relatively minor wounds in the right arm and shoulder simply because of the weather.

Private First Class Ed Debalski, who had served with the Fox/5 mortar section until his legs were peppered with grenade shards the night of November 27–28, received about as much attention as Walker Merell. However, he remained in better condition than Merell, and was one of the many casualties who asked to be armed for the trip out. Although this was the first occasion on which so many Marine wounded had to be armed in order to help protect themselves, the men who were crammed aboard the casualty trucks felt a boost in morale when they were given the option of packing small arms; they felt they had a contribution to make, and that their training and experience were being put to good use. Somehow, the Marines managed to turn a negatively charged situation into a psychological plus.

Sergeant Bob Oldani, who had won a Silver Star for his actions as a member of George/7 on November 27, was a casualty to the cold. Despite his very best efforts, which included a long overdue trip to the hospital on November 29, Oldani had succumbed to frostbite of the feet and was unable to walk. In that respect he was in far better condition than men who had been maimed in the fighting. What shocked Oldani was the overcrowding aboard the evacuation trucks. His own truck held dozens of men. The first layer was placed on the bed of the truck, then cut timbers were run through the slats of the siderails to provide support for succeeding layers. Depending upon the eagerness of the men detailed to load the wounded, three to five layers could be crammed aboard a single vehicle. Oldani, in the middle of his truck, and thus unable to get out without hurting several other injured men, had just enough space to turn over.

No one was going to travel in comfort. Least of all the wounded.

★

The Yudam-ni garrison was made one-hundred-percent mobile during the afternoon of December 1. With some notable exceptions, all units assigned specific missions achieved them in roughly the time and sequence allotted. Several missions were scrubbed, and several were altered or added.

What was of overriding importance was the fact that the long vehicle column and several thousand men were slowly on the move by the late afternoon.

No one quite knew what lay ahead.

C H A P T E R
31

Lieutenant Colonel Bob Taplett's 3rd Battalion, 5th Marines, jumped off down the MSR at 1500 hours, December 1.

Following his meeting with Lieutenant Colonel Bill Harris earlier in the afternoon, Taplett had called together his staff and company commanders and worked out plans based on the changed orders and a changing situation. Since the battalion would now be fighting its way southward — as opposed to following another unit which would have had to do the bulk of the fighting — it drew some important support, including 1st Lieutenant Wayne Richards's 2nd Platoon of

Able/Engineers, and, most important, the only tank at Yudam-ni, D23, which was fully crewed and armed thanks to several helicopter flights from Hagaru-ri during the past few days.

Captain Hal Williamson's How/5 was to take the lead, supported by D23. Next would be Captain George Schrier's Item/5, then Captain Chester Hermanson's George/5. The engineers would be placed near the front of the column to help clear numerous reported roadblocks.

The troops would be traveling light. All hands were ordered to secure their sleeping bags to their belts or across their shoulders. Cans of fruit cocktail and dry K-rations were stuffed into the large cargo pockets of their parkas, and dry socks and felt shoepac liners were placed beneath undershirts, next to the skin. Packs were placed on the battalion trucks, and ammunition was crammed into pockets and web belts.

The battalion moved out of the perimeter as soon as it was ready. How/5 proceeded several hundred yards along the roadway, until it came even with How/7, which was still struggling up Turkey Hill. When everyone was set, Taplett ordered Hal Williamson to move out. It was nearing 1500 hours.

Hard to believe, but the tank and the point platoon drove rapidly forward nearly fourteen hundred yards without encountering so much as one shot fired in anger. Then How Company ran into the first of the Chinese roadblocks and ground to a halt as the carefully integrated defenses put out an enormous volume of fire.

Ordering his radioman to stay put, Hal Williamson moved forward with his company gunnery sergeant and a runner to see what he could see. As he spoke to the point platoon leader, Williamson saw the gunney and the runner continue to press forward toward D23. They got only a few yards before the runner a Pusan veteran, was shot dead by machine-gun fire.

Leaving the lead platoons deployed on either side of the road, under cover, Williamson and his gunnery sergeant returned to pick up the radioman. There, they found Captain George Schrier, the Item Company commander, waiting to hear The Word.

Following a brief discussion, the two veteran company commanders decided that both their units should be deployed off the road to deliver simultaneous attacks against Chinese strongpoints on either flank. Williamson got on the horn and asked to speak with Bob Taplett.

Taplett was, at that moment, having difficulties of his own. As soon as he heard the firing begin ahead, he had bounded toward his radio jeep to find out what was going on. With him was his good right hand, 1st Lieutenant Charlie Mize, and an operations sergeant. The three were caught flat-footed on the snow-covered verge of the roadway by a quick mortar concentration. Going down in a tangle of arms and legs, the battalion commander bottom-most, the three were unscathed but severely affected by concussion. They meandered back to Taplett's radio jeep in time to receive the call from Hal Williamson. Shaking the dazed feeling from his head, Taplett listened to Williamson's proposal about deploying off the road, and gave the plan his blessing.

How Company was already pretty well to the right of the roadway, so Captain Williamson pushed it up on the slopes on that flank while George Schrier deployed Item/5 against the Chinese on the left. Both companies moved quickly and subdued the opposition on the immediate front, though Schrier was held from taking the core of resistance on his side of the road until after 1930 hours.

It was by then well after dark, and at least −20 degrees. The troops on both flanks were pretty well exhausted from the rigors of the climb and the brief, intense fighting. Williamson called Taplett on the radio and recommended that How Company be allowed to stop for the night; no one had been over the ground in daylight, but everyone knew it to be some pretty fierce terrain. Tap told him to hold in place until Regiment had approved or denied the request.

When Taplett got Ray Murray on the line, he first asked for some artillery support, something he had been promised but had yet to receive. Murray replied that he would try to muster some guns, but Taplett would not be put off: "Goddamnit, if you guys want to get out of Yudam-ni, we're the guys who can get you out. But you better give us the artillery support we need." Far from being put off by Taplett's peremptory tone — Tap was really wired — Murray insisted that he would try. In the meantime, he wanted the 3rd Battalion, 5th, to keep taking ground if it could.

There was a lot of groaning and moaning when Murray's request was passed forward to the line companies. Hal Williamson left an outpost detachment on the key height, and got How Company moving forward in the dark against numerous Chinese positions that could be smelled long before they could be seen. How/5's immediate objective fell without great difficulty.

Not so Item Company's objective, Hill 1520.

★

As the Item Company point moved into a draw, it was cut apart by a cross fire from high ground on either side. The position was completely untenable, and Captain Schrier urgently requested permission to return to his initial position, which he could at least defend against counterattack.

The Chinese closed on Item/5 almost before George Schrier had sufficient opportunity to deploy his troops. After an initial attack, which rattled the Marines before they could settle in, the Chinese withdrew while their mortars prepped their objective. Then the PLA infantry returned in great numbers, following which they withdrew under a heavy mortar bombardment.

Staff Sergeant William Windrich led a squad of his 1st Platoon to plug a gap, and met a Chinese assault force head on. Seven of the twelve Marines were wounded before reaching their objective. Windrich, who had received a severe head injury, declined evacuation and returned to the company CP to dig up volunteers who would move forward with him to evacuate the wounded. He was hit again, in the legs, as he led the remainder of his rifle platoon forward, but he again declined to be evacuated. The sergeant platoon leader continued moving from position to position, keeping his small unit viable for over an hour despite his injuries. In the end, however, cold and shock got to him, and William Windrich collapsed, dying.

Technical Sergeant Dale Stropes took charge on the flank opposite Windrich, directing his troops under intense fire with telling effect. He was painfully shot in the back while passing out ammunition, but got to immediate work evacuating casualties from his sector. He was then shot in the chest and killed.

Rushing forward to help Item Company hold, 1st Lieutenant Dorsie Booker's provisional platoon of artillerymen from the 1st Battalion, 11th, moved into the line just in time to absorb the shock of a particularly fierce clash. Booker looked up to see that the left flank was caving in. He told off the men nearest his position and led them forward to meet the attackers, who were stopped.

George Schrier — veteran of combat at Guadalcanal and New Georgia, a former Marine Raider who had been commissioned from the ranks on the field of battle, the Marine who had raised the first flag atop Iwo Jima's Mount Suribachi — was lightly wounded early in the fighting, an event he pretty much ignored. Later, however, he was shot through the neck and, unable to speak, had to relinquish command of Item Company and drop down to the roadway for medical treatment. His relief was the last and most junior of Item/5's officers, 2nd Lieutenant Willard Peterson.

Though Bob Taplett could hear the firing and even see some of the exchange, he had no means of communicating with Item Company, which had lost all its radios. The wounded who trickled, then poured, down from the heights got some of the story across, but Taplett could not call in supporting arms without being in direct contact with a qualified observer on the heights.

A portion of the battalion aid station had managed to push through the snarled traffic to the rear by 2300, and it was set up in a frozen rice paddy beside the MSR. About twenty vehicles in all were laagered in the field, and a native hut in the center of the circle served as the sick bay. The lightly wounded were treated and held for eventual return to their units, but the serious cases were driven back to the regimental aid station, which was better able to cope with the inflow. When Taplett saw George Schrier come in, he knew that Item Company was in serious straits.

But the company held, taking fearsome losses in the process. First Lieutenant Dorsie Booker's gunners put up a superb display of the versatility of combat Marines. Booker ventured forward time and again over a five-hour period to ambush the waves of attackers on their own ground, but he was eventually shot and killed.

Another artilleryman, Private First Class Amon Harvey, organized a counterattack that cleared a vital stretch of line the Chinese had held for some time. Harvey was wounded early in that encounter, but he remained on hand to shout encouragement to his fellow gunners for as long as it took them to stem the Chinese counterassault.

★

As the attacks on Item Company ground slowly to a standstill, Hal Williamson's How/5 ventured forward against sporadic and inaccurate long-range fire until the entire company was assembled in a thick stand of pine trees below a position manned by numerous unsuspecting Chinese. Williamson requested and received permission to halt and deploy; he wanted the full benefit of air support when he mounted his surprise attack, and he needed full daylight for that.

The 3rd Battalion, 5th, was well on its way to Hagaru-ri, and to being fought out.

There was very heavy fighting to the rear that night.

★

Lieutenant Colonel Hal Roise's 2nd Battalion, 5th, had watched all the other battalions at Yudam-ni move rearward and take to the road through December 1, and it had backpedaled as well, giving ground and creating rubble in the path of the Chinese who so badly wanted Yudam-ni. At the onset of the evening, the battalion was centered on Hill 1276, from which it could see up the length of the narrow central valley. Pyres of discarded equipment and supplies marked the sites of old bivouacs and dumps. As the sun set, the troops could see hundreds of Chinese soldiers rooting through the debris, determined to win some needed article of clothing or ruined can of food from the fire and ice.

To the rear, amidst the booming of mortars and artillery and the roar of turbo-charged aircraft engines, the main body of the Yudam-ni garrison was climbing the steep grade between Hill 1542 and Turkey Hill.

There were fleeting moments throughout the evening when many of Roise's men felt that they were being abandoned, a sacrificial offering to the gods of war, who might thus allow the greater part of the flock to survive.

The Chinese struck shortly after midnight, pitching a few hard left-right jabs against Fox/5, holding the summit of Hill 1276. Easy and Dog Companies, on the flanks, were hit by lighter probes, as was the provisional company from the 4th Battalion, 11th. But the flank attacks were feints, meant to draw off the battalion reserve. The real danger lay in the center, where the veterans of Captain Uel Peters's Fox Company braced themselves for the final showdown. If they held through the night, they knew they could leave Yudam-ni. If they broke, no one would be back to help.

Fox Company's 2nd Platoon took the brunt of the assault and, hit from three sides, moved to the rear of the knob on which it had dug in. Coming up the rear slope was Easy Company's 2nd Platoon, the battalion reserve. As the Fox platoon broke amidst cries of "Second Platoon, fall back," the reinforcing platoon, similarly designated, also took off in great haste. One of those things.

The Chinese, who installed themselves firmly in Marine fighting holes on the knob, were denied reinforcement because of some very fancy night-fighter work laid on by the battalion's forward air controller, who employed 60mm white-phosphorous marker rounds to guide his allotted division of Marine F7F two-place fighter-bombers.

That was at 0200. At 0230, Hal Roise ordered Captain Peters to retake the lost knob. Regimental 4.2-inch heavy mortars pounded the summit while Fox Company moved nimbly up the frozen slopes. Two attempts came close, but failed. Roise put a stop to the killing until there was light enough to see what was going on. Owning the hill was not of critical importance to Roise as long as the Chinese were denied access to the rear of the vehicle column.

Private First Class Bob Kennedy, a Dog/5 BAR-man, was set up with this company on a flat area beside Hill 1276. Kennedy, a Regular who had joined the battalion outside Inchon after a year's service guarding Japanese generals incarcerated on Guam, was impressed with the intricate strength of the line his company had developed beside the hill in little more than a day. Numerous heavy machine guns were sited to deliver effective, maximum cross fires and, though he had been unable to dig into the frozen earth, Kennedy was well protected by a wall of sandbags containing hard, frozen earth spoils. It was, in Bob Kennedy's estimation, the best defensive line he had seen Marines assemble during his Korean experience.

Sunrise found Kennedy sharing a can of frozen sweet cherries with his assistant gunner, Private First Class Tony Lima. The two, and hundreds of other Marines, were shaken by the sudden appearance of several divisions of early arriving Marine Corsairs, which machine-gunned and rocketed the Chinese-held knob while Fox/5 moved into position to deliver its third counterassault.

The early morning light also revealed hundreds of Chinese spread across the narrow central valley, some moving forward toward Hill 1276, and many moving northward to avoid the Marine aircraft.

As Bob Kennedy sucked furiously on the frozen cherries he had popped into his mouth moments earlier, he twisted in his place to assume a comfortable firing position behind his sandbag wall. Feeling as though he was on a practice range, the veteran BAR-man squeezed off short bursts at the more prominent knots of Chinese in his field of fire. As fast as the receiver clicked empty at the end of each magazine, Kennedy popped in another, barely missing a beat. The whole line had opened at pretty much the same instant, butchering Chinese by the scores, forcing them into a stupefied, lethargic general withdrawal.

Fox Company's attack, commencing at 0730, was swift and deliberate, and the Chinese were pitched off the summit of the hill. But the company was hurt by machine guns that had been expertly emplaced on the reverse slope. The fighting ground to a standstill until more air support could be called at 1000. The Marine Corsairs pummeled the Chinese with napalm and bombs, forcing them to join the general retreat.

★

George, Item and "Jig" Companies, 7th, all well below the summit of Hill 1542, west of the MSR, were hit by the four companies of the 79th PLA Division that had been holding the hill when the Marine attack began on the morning of December 1.

As luck would have it, the first Chinese assault, at 0430, ran into the unit least capable of withstanding it. "Jig" Company, the one-hundred-man hybrid composed mainly of scared artillerymen, simply collapsed after brief resistance. One of the artillerymen, Sergeant James Johnson, held his little platoon together through the first onslaught, but was ordered to displace to a more tenable position. Sergeant Johnson stepped forward and engaged the oncoming Chinese hand to hand while his platoon disengaged and withdrew. He was never seen again, and his platoon kept right on going to the bottom of the hill, where it dissolved itself.

On George/7's line, Sergeant Ray Aguirre looked up in time to see a mass of human forms stampede across the skyline above his fighting hole. Immediately, the platoon command post took a mortar round, which killed the radio operator and ruined the radio. Ray Aguirre got up to run for better cover, but another mortar round felled him, and he broke his ankle. Lying dazed upon the frozen ground, Aguirre sensed more than felt dark figures pass him by. A quick jerk brought him around as an unseen man — friend or foe? — tried to remove his field pack. Foreign voices muttered at the edge of his hearing for a few moments, then Ray Aguirre lost consciousness.

First Lieutenant Tom Sullivan, of Item/7, was lightly injured by a mortar round moments after the assault opened. He could see quite a bit of the action to his rear, where "Jig" Company had been, until, after a brief interval, Item Company was ordered to withdraw to the base of the ridge on which it had established its night defenses. Sullivan's platoon reached the designated draw and deployed. At least one platoon of George Company seemed to be in the same draw, and a large number of men Sullivan could not identify in the dark were moving through. The fighting higher up seemed to slacken a bit, but it did not really end.

Lieutenant Colonel Bill Harris and his staff, tied to the battalion CP over one thousand yards to the rear, received little information, and most of that was badly garbled. There was nothing they could do in any case but wait for the sun and hope for the best.

A squad leader serving with Sergeant William Vick's section of 75mm recoilless rifles arrived at Battalion well before dawn to say that his gun and its ammunition, which had been sent up Hill 1542 late the previous afternoon, had been captured intact. Captain Bill Earney, the battalion operations officer, was livid, but there was nothing he could do except sweat out the prospect of being bombarded by the highly accurate weapon at first light. No one seemed to know where Sergeant Vick was, and that was a blow, for he was one of the 7th Regiment's most aggressive troop leaders.

As the first signs of dawn were making themselves felt, the battalion staff was really beginning to sweat over the lost 75mm recoilless rifle. But someone spotted Sergeant Vick strolling down the road from the hill, a Chinese burp gun slung over his shoulder, and the breechblock from the lost recoilless rifle dangling from one hand. He tossed off a grin, and got plenty in return.

But dawn also revealed that "Jig" Company was gone, and that George and Item had been thrown off the hill. The battalion staff got right down to work, coordinating the available air and artillery. As much as could be spared of the battalion headquarters company was thrown into the fray, and a counterattack was mounted at 0700.

The fighting was perilous, but the Chinese, never committed in very great numbers, allowed themselves to be pushed back up the hill, though they made certain they retained several commanding positions.

Sergeant Ray Aguirre, who had been unconscious since about 0500, was shaken awake at about 0730 and dragged and carried to the roadway. He received rudimentary treatment along with thirty or forty others who had been injured in the night fighting and counterattack, and was placed in the care of the people operating Bob Taplett's battalion aid station in the lee of Turkey Hill.

By midmorning, the large company that was Bill Harris's 3rd Battalion, 7th, was in possession of a line screening the MSR from direct assault by the Chinese on the heights. There were some heated exchanges between Colonel Litzenberg's CP and Harris's, but, since Regiment would release no reinforcements, Bill Harris's demurrer that he had not the manpower to take more ground was grudgingly accepted.

★

Screened by Taplett's battalion, in the south, and Harris's and Roise's, in the west and north, several thousand Marine riflemen, gunners, specialists, clerks, and casualties were loaded aboard or walking beside several hundred vehicles of every size and function. It was upon those vehicles and upon the shoulders and feet of those men that the breakout from Yudam-ni would be borne.

The master plan had gone off with numerous unforeseen hitches. But it had gone off.

CHAPTER
32

There was the soft crunch of rubber-soled feet on the hard-packed snow. The soft jingle of metallic equipment. The soothing shirring sound of cloth-encased thighs rubbing together in mindless rhythm. The muted oaths and sighs of tired, struggling men. The labored, whistling rasp of breath drawn painfully between clenched teeth. The freezing saliva upon the roof of the mouth. The burning of cold-numbed ears. The painful clenching of fists and toes. The boring, mindless pace. The heightened sensation of imminent danger and the progressive grip of underlying terror. The throbbing discomfort of overtired eyes darting swiftly upward to check progress. The bobbing gait of seven hundred frozen men struggling against the worst nature could hurl into their faces.

The 1st Battalion, 7th Marines, was struggling overland in the general direction of Toktong Pass and Fox Hill. And each new step brought it closer to a weary, wavering collapse upon the uncharted wilderness it had to traverse.

★

Following its commitment in the early afternoon of December 1 to the battle to wrest Turkey Hill from the PLA, Able Company, 7th, mounted a direct assault in column of platoons to relieve much of the pressure that had built up around How/7, which had tried and failed to secure the height overlooking the MSR. The leading Able/7 platoon, commanded by 1st Lieutenant Leslie Williams, made good, steady progress until its right flank was pinned securely by Chinese machine-gun fire from higher up. The platoon had gotten as far as an abutment some five hundred yards below How/7's objective, but heavy casualties caused it to falter and seek cover wherever the jumbled ground allowed.

Lieutenant Williams paused just long enough to assess the situation, then pounded his platoon back to order and led the men who could still follow him directly into the teeth of the snarling Chinese guns higher up. The quick move took the platoon within grappling range, embroiling the Marines in rugged, unremitting hand-to-hand gouging and pounding with the defenders.

The action by Williams's platoon alleviated much of the pressure on hard-pressed How/7, which sprang forward several lengths to overwhelm Chinese emplacements scattered across its front.

Lieutenant Colonel Ray Davis's 1st Battalion, 7th, had seized the ground from which it would begin its overland march to rescue Captain Bill Barber's Fox/7 and secure the bottleneck at Toktong Pass. The wounded from Able and How Companies were passed quickly down to the MSR while the rear of the battalion column snaked uphill. As the injured were being given over to the care of Bob Taplett's medical detachment, Davis's battalion was severing its ties with the main body of the moving Yudam-ni garrison. When Charlie/7 moved uphill from the road to the rear of the battalion column, the 1st Battalion, 7th, became a thoroughly foot-mobile striking force, totally reliant upon itself for the leap into the unknown it was about to endure.

★

Preparations had been going on for fully twenty-four hours, from the moment Homer Litzenberg and Ray Davis agreed upon the plan that would hurl the crack 1st Battalion, 7th, across the Chinese rear to rescue Fox/7.

With his executive and operations officers, Majors Ray Fridrich and Tom Tighe, Davis devised a finely honed plan. The battalion divested itself of all but the most essential heavy gear, including all but two 81mm mortars and six .30-caliber heavy water-cooled machine guns. Crews for these and lighter crew-served weapons were doubled, and all hands were given at least double the normal ammunition allotment. Individuals were left to decide about what food to carry, but all the men were admonished to carry at least one full canteen of water. Most of the troops chose to subsist upon fruit cocktail and syrupy peaches and the like. By carrying such sugary canned foods close to the skin, they could rely upon having a quick energizer in reasonable condition for bolting down during brief breaks or on the move. Every man had to carry one 81mm round and his sleeping bag; all personal gear could be left with the battalion trucks, which, of course, would move with the main column on the MSR.

The battalion carried extra heavy pack radios to bolster its quirky SCR-300 wirelesses, and the artillery forward observer team had spent most of the day checking and rechecking the heavy radio by which it would be tied to the fire-direction center of the 3rd Battalion, 11th.

After culling sick and enfeebled Marines from the main body of the battalion, Davis and his officers and senior noncoms checked every man. By the time it was committed to taking Turkey Hill, Davis's battalion was in just exactly the shape the battalion commander desired.

★

Dusk, December 1. The 1st Battalion, 7th, and How/7 were settling down behind hastily contrived defenses on the summit of Turkey Hill. Baker/7 was patrolling along the proposed track of the battalion to the southeast. Ray Davis placed a hurried call to Regiment to tell Colonel Litzenberg of his success in gaining the summit of the hill, and expressed a desire to move out immediately lest his tired troops, sweaty and uncomfortable from the exhausting climb, freeze up in the −24-degree air. Litz told Davis to proceed, adding that he should take the small remnant of How/7 to make good some of the losses sustained in the seizure of the line of departure.

Davis pressed his officers and senior noncoms to reorganize in the shortest possible time and replaced Able Company at the head of the column with 1st Lieutenant Joe Kurcaba's Baker/7, which was to be followed by the cut-down battalion command group, then by Able Company, and then by Charlie Company. Major Ray Fridrich, the battalion exec, was to have brought up the rear with some weapons people and the battalion headquarters company, but tiny How/7 was given the rear guard.

It was just coming up 2100 hours when Ray Davis pointed to a particularly bright star and rattled off an azimuth to the lead Baker/7 platoon leader. After Baker/7 had moved out in its entirety, Davis placed a pair of guides at the cut atop the hill through which the entire column would have to pass; these men admonished each passing Marine to guide on the bright star.

All the troops had been up since dawn, and had taken part in the daylong effort of preparation, fighting, and climbing. Before them lay miles of trackless wastes and uncounted Chinese. But for a few rounds of white-phosphorous marker fired by road-bound artillery, Davis and his troops were strictly on their own.

The first leg was across the rear slopes of Hill 1520, a gargantuan hill mass overlooking the MSR about halfway to Toktong Pass, a terrain feature so large that Davis's battalion could hear nothing of the life-and-death struggle involving George Schrier's Item/5 on the other side of the hill.

The moment the troops set foot on the first downhill slope they lost sight of the guide star, and the column veered slightly as the point sought the path of least resistance. Compasses were broken out, but the abundance of metal the column was packing and the peculiar influence of the cold caused erratic readings, plunging the column into still deeper confusion. The artillery was called to place several marker rounds on the correct azimuth, but the shells were either off target or intervening ground blocked the splashes of white phosphorous from view.

The point, which had never really stopped moving, was hampered increasingly by deep snowbanks, which had to be breasted by brute force. Rear ranks were slowed by the need to negotiate a path worn smooth and slick by all the feet that had already tamped down the snow. It was quite typical to find Marines crawling up finger ridges on their hands and knees, grunting from the exertion, fuming with impatience, grumbling in general. In time, even these muted human sounds ceased as exhaustion wore in upon them. A cough sounded like a mortar round exploding in the calm, silent, starlit wilderness, and everyone was put on edge.

A crucial radio failure kept Joe Kurcaba, at or near the point, from hearing Ray Davis's increasingly worried warnings about a drift to the right, toward the MSR, which was to be the object of planned harassment and interdiction fires from Marine artillery miles to the rear. The battalion commander started a verbal message forward in relays, but ears muffled against the cold lost that message, and the steady drift to the right continued as Baker/7 trudged mindlessly forward.

Ray Davis stepped out beside the column, dragging his radioman and runner in his wake, and began inching past the men in front of him. Grunting and fuming, the battalion commander overtook trudging Marine after trudging Marine. When he sensed a distinct lack of alertness on the part of the troops he was passing, Davis broke his own edict for silence by berating the men in a loud voice. Never dreaming that the nondescript parka-clad figure passing down the column might be the battalion commander, the riflemen and gunners admonished him with curses to "pipe down."

As Davis was closing on the point, the point platoon leader's uneasy feeling that he was off the track erupted in a whispered order to the Baker/7 mortar officer, 2nd Lieutenant Joe Owen, to hurry back to the company commander, Joe Kurcaba, for some reassurance. The immensely tall lieutenant had taken only a few steps when he collided with a shorter man. As both men recovered, Owen recognized the battalion commander, who ordered an immediate halt while he and several Baker Company officers took a fresh compass reading, checked it, and reoriented the point.

Chinese fire, which had been sporadic and inexact through the hours it took to cover the ground between Turkey Hill and Hill 1520, picked up considerably as the point crossed the next sharp ridgeline and passed into a meadow studded with numerous rock outcroppings. It was clear that the PLA infantry holding the eastern and western slopes overlooking the meadow were willing to fight.

As the volume of fire steadily increased, Davis called in his company commanders and rattled off a quick plan for deployment and attack. The two 81mm mortars and six heavy machine guns were deployed in an infantry-supported base of fire while riflemen formed into two attack columns. Each man who passed the guns dropped off his spare 81mm round, which was pumped out with precision as Baker and Charlie Companies closed on a Chinese platoon. Oddly, many of the Chinese were caught asleep in their blankets. Taking advantage of the momentum of their attack, the Marines swept into the Chinese lines, resorting to liberal use of hand grenades and, in the case of two of Joe Owen's mortar gunners, entrenching tools to rout the Chinese. The light resistance was quickly overcome at the cost of several wounded Marines.

Despite the eradication of the opposition in the immediate vicinity of the meadow, Chinese guns farther out managed to injure several Marines. Moving his troops onto protected ground, the thoroughly exhausted battalion commander, not yet recovered from the exertion of his sprint to the head of the column, called a halt so that the wounded could be treated.

The troops — nearly all of them — found the limits of their endurance then and there. The reinforced battalion collapsed as a man into a great heap, triggering an immediate response by officers and noncoms, who wearily raced through the mounds of recumbent bodies, kicking and cursing their charges to a more acceptable state of semi-alertness. The men were utterly oblivious to the eerie Chinese tracer that was ricocheting through the unofficial battalion bivouac.

As his officers and noncoms kicked the battalion into shape, Davis dropped down into a Chinese rifle pit and had his runner place a poncho over the hole to seal the light of a small flashlight while he checked his compass. Davis had become so exhausted that, by the time he stood up, he had quite forgotten which way he intended to point the battalion. Shrugging, he repeated the process, taking the precaution of pointing his finger in the right direction. His attention span was so short, however, that the murmuring of his company commanders caused him to forget why he was pointing off into the unknown. He had to repeat the process yet again in order to get the sense of his actions through to his benumbed brain.

So intent was Davis upon forming cogent thoughts that he actually asked his senior officers if his instructions sounded logical. The fact was that they were as exhausted as Davis, and really had no idea. It was a revelation every bit as chilling as the sub-zero air.

Moving slowly on the corrected heading, the battalion ground wearily forward until nearly 0300. It had been on the move for nearly six consecutive hours, and had been awake and extremely active for over twenty straight hours. It was clear that everyone needed some rest. Ordering every fourth man to guard the slowly forming perimeter, around which ranged several light patrols, Ray Davis finally allowed the men to sack out in the open. The heaviest radio was broken out and used to establish contact with Regiment.

No sooner done than an urgent report arrived at the battalion CP from How Company, which was struggling up with the wounded. The company had come under direct attack by a determined Chinese force, which had apparently blundered into the Marines. A platoon each from Baker and Charlie Companies was dispatched to bail out the embattled rear guard. The reaction force swiftly took some intervening high ground, inflicted some casualties upon the Chinese, and closed on How Company to escort it into the still-forming perimeter.

The Chinese fire, which had been dogging the battalion for hours, all but petered out before dawn, December 2.

Fourteen hundred yards to the southwest — less than a mile away — Captain Bill Barber's Fox/7 remained alert for the final Chinese attack, the one that might yet bring the bleeding, battered company to ruin. Unlike any previous night on Fox Hill, however, the company received only long-range sniper fire, and not much of it. The eighty-five effectives remaining on Fox Hill were actually a bit disappointed at the lack of Chinese gumption that night.

★

Ray Davis delivered verbal orders at first light to Baker/7's commander, 1st Lieutenant Joe Kurcaba, who was to lead the approach on Fox Hill. Bill Barber knew that the relief force was nearby, but no direct contact had yet been achieved, and Davis wanted to minimize the chance of a brush between the two Marine forces. Unable to contact Marine Corsairs arriving on station overhead because all the battalion's radio batteries had failed, Davis ordered a swift attack aimed at achieving maximum surprise on the ground. Charlie Company was sent to seize a spur dominating the route of Able and Baker Companies.

Moving into the assault at daybreak, Baker/7 rapidly crossed one thousand yards of hilly ground without so much as a shot fired in protest. Then, approaching a jumble of small hills known as Rocky Ridge, Baker Company got hit, and hard.

As the attack elements ground forward to Hill 1653, Davis's radioman shouted to the battalion commander, "Fox-Six [Captain Barber] on the radio, Sir!"

Barber was in high spirits. Voicing a mixture of bravado and concern over the approach of Davis's reinforced battalion, he offered to send a combat patrol forward to guide Able and Baker Companies the rest of the way to Fox Hill. Davis politely declined, but asked that Barber coordinate the runs of the Marine Corsairs, which his communicators still could not reach.

Assisted by Marine Air and his own mortars, Davis urged his leading companies forward. Charlie/7 took its objective on the flank and settled in to guard the battalion's route into the Fox/7 lines.

The first Baker/7 riflemen reached Fox Company at 1125 hours, December 2. Charlie Company proceeded into the expanding perimeter next, while Able Company held the back door open for the remainder of the column. A reedy cheer went up from among the formerly beleaguered defenders of Toktong Pass. Backs were pounded and hands were gripped. Each group noted the signs of extreme weariness upon the faces and frames of the other.

The moment was not without its high comedy — and tragedy.

As Major Ray Fridrich snarled encouragement at the rear of the group laboriously humping litters and sleeping bags bearing the wounded, he was amazed to see a Marine who had claimed injury and who had been carried by his buddies across miles of frozen wasteland bolt from the bag in which he was being carried. As the "injured" man loped through the snowdrifts toward Fox Hill, the men who had been carrying him went berserk with anger and, as one, shook their weapons from their shoulders and opened fire. No hits were scored, but the man might well have wished he had been shot when his former buddies next contacted him.

The moment was an emotional homecoming for 1st Lieutenant

Ralph Abell, the young St. Louis Reserve officer who had accompanied General Almond from Hagaru-ri to Yudam-ni on the afternoon of November 27. Abell had commanded Fox Company's 1st Platoon until early November, when he had been transferred to the battalion staff and, from there, to become the regimental public information officer. After briefly whetting his taste for combat as commander of a provisional rifle platoon, Abell had been tabbed to accompany Davis's battalion and assume command of Fox Company, which was down to one able-bodied officer out of seven.

Abell made directly for the Fox Company sick-bay tent, where he looked up many old friends who had been wounded. As he was leaving, he passed Dr. Peter Arioli, the 7th Regiment's senior surgeon, who had accompanied the relief force as a volunteer. Moments later, as Arioli was standing in the entryway to the tent speaking with one of Davis's staffers, a single bullet pierced the thin canvas and snapped Peter Arioli's spinal column. The doctor was dead before he fell into the arms of the stunned staff officer.

Miraculously, not one other member of the relief force was killed during the entire march. Two of Davis's Marines, however, went completely berserk and had to be forcibly restrained. Both died before they could be evacuated.

As soon as Ralph Abell had recovered from the shock of seeing so many men he knew lying dead and wounded, he sought out Bill Barber and officially relieved him of command of Fox Company. Despite numerous wounds, including a particularly painful gunshot wound in the hip, Barber was as game as ever as he was led to the sick bay for some needed rest.

As soon as the troops had bolted a hot meal, Joe Kurcaba's Baker/ 7 was sent to seize some ground dominating the loop in the MSR below Fox Hill. Able/7 was sent later to bolster Kurcaba's position, and the remnant of Fox Company was left to hold its original, shrunken position. Charlie and How Companies outposted several low hills in the neighborhood, all without much action.

★

The main body of the Yudam-ni garrison was grinding forward. Slowly. Painfully.

CHAPTER
33

Lieutenant Colonel Bob Taplett's 3rd Battalion, 5th Marines, was in seven kinds of shock by dawn of December 2, but it was as game as it had ever been.

Lieutenant Colonel Ray Murray, commander of the 5th Marines, drove forward to Taplett's CP in the lee of Turkey Hill at about dawn to inspect the aid station Taplett's people had been running through the night. On finding Taplett, the regimental commander asked why the battalion's attack had not yet resumed. Over-weary and distraught, the battalion commander motioned with his hand: "Look around. We've been cleaned out."

Murray replied immediately, "We're going to attach the composite company from the 7th Marines," meaning the remnants of Dog and Easy Companies, 7th. "How do you want to employ them?"

"There's only one way," Taplett affirmed, "and that's straight down the MSR."

★

A little way off, 1st Lieutenant Herc Kelly, Taplett's communicator, was trying to get some food into Captain George Schrier, the wounded Item/5 commander. While keeping up a solicitous banter, Kelly peeled the metal from a tin of frozen fruit and pierced the lump with a heated bayonet. Schrier mumbled his gratitude, but was clearly in pain from his serious neck wound as he tried to handle the frozen mess. Sensing the captain's deep frustration, Kelly next peeled the can from around a frozen lump of salmon he had liberated from a burning truck, and pierced it with his heated bayonet. That was much better; the salmon was easier to eat, and the starving Schrier chewed through it as quickly as he was able.

Similar displays of friendship and mercy were going on throughout the sick-bay area, which Taplett's Marines had long since dubbed "Dante's Inferno."

And lest anyone think the battle had passed that bloody spot by, a regimental radio jeep was blown to pieces by a land mine as it moved to the verge of the narrow roadway to get around a traffic jam.

★

In the hills, Captain Chester Hermanson's George/5 moved through the bits and remnants of Item Company to begin its cautious sweep from the killing ground on which George Schrier had made his bloody stand in the night. The George/5 Marines counted three hundred forty-two Chinese corpses.

To the right of the road, Captain Hal Williamson's How/5 took some fire early as it hunkered down in a copse just below the summit of its next hilltop objective. Marine Air swooped to the rescue, placing pinpoint fires within thirty yards of Williamson's forwardmost elements. As the last Corsair pulled up, waggling its wings to signal the end of the strike, How/5 moved out of the trees and charged up the hill, securing it by main force.

By midafternoon, as How and George Companies continued to grind forward along parallel tracks on either side of the MSR, each had been reduced to a pair of operating platoons, and both were just about fought out.

On the roadway, Staff Sergeant Russell Munsell's D23, the only tank the Yudam-ni Marines owned, continued to lurch forward ahead of Dog-Easy/7, which was being chewed to bits.

D23 went into the attack at 0730, overwhelming the Chinese roadblock that had stopped Taplett's riflemen cold the previous evening. The flat *crack* of the heavy tank's 90mm main armament blocked out all other sounds of infantry battles in the hills. One, two, three rounds. . . . The block was reduced to bloody, smoking rubble, and D23 ground forward fully one thousand yards, drawing the tiny composite company in its wake.

Light resistance at a second roadblock was quickly overcome, but the tank's engine died at 1000 hours. Under direct fire from the hills and a third roadblock, dead ahead three hundred yards, the tank's crewmen jumped to the roadway and exchanged the depleted batteries for a fresh set. D23 moved out again at 1030.

The battles in the hills on either flank raged hot and hotter. First Lieutenant Bud Fredericks, a How/5 platoon leader, was on his company's left flank, overlooking the MSR, for most of December 2. The entire day was spent peeking and squeaking over the numerous little finger ridges that run down from the heights on the right to the road on the left. Amply protected by heavy woods and underbrush, the platoon employed simple fire-and-move tactics to maintain a steady momentum.

Clearing one of the numerous spurs, Frederick's platoon sergeant approached a litter of rice mats he found spread upon a hump overlooking the road. The noncom kicked the mats aside and faced a volley of fire from Chinese burp gunners who had been lying in wait. Leaping back in utter astonishment, the platoon sergeant turned to the man nearest him and said, "Why, those funny little guys were trying to *kill* me," as if that was news to anyone. The position was cleared, and more of the same ensued.

A bridge spanning a frozen stream crossing the roadway below How/5 had been blown, causing the advance by D23 and the composite company to grind down. A roadblock ahead and Chinese soldiers firing from the heights prevented the engineer platoon attached to the 3rd Battalion, 5th, from getting forward to scrape dirt and debris into the gap.

George/5, on the left, overlooking the blown bridge, was ordered to deliver an assault down the long axis of a spur above the Chinese who had the bridge site under direct observation, and Dog-Easy/7 was started on its way in defilade to outflank still other Chinese emplacements. Under the precise direction of Taplett's two forward air controllers, Marine Corsairs raged in on the deck, blasting Chinese wherever they dared peek over the parapets of their fighting holes. The air-infantry team blistered the opposition and sent the survivors packing for safety while the engineers clanked forward on their bulldozers to begin the painfully slow process of sealing the gap in the roadway.

To the right of the MSR, How/5 was stopped by cross fires on the north side of the same frozen stream that the engineers were spanning below. No air support was immediately available, so Captain Williamson asked for some artillery support.

Second Lieutenant Hank Ammer, the forward observer attached to Taplett's battalion, was placed in direct communication with Williamson and the firing batteries of his own 1st Battalion, 11th, several miles to the rear. After mouthing the coordinates of the Chinese position into his mike, Ammer instructed the guns to fire two white-phosphorous marker rounds. The first splash observed by How/5 was a bit over, but the second was right on the money. Ammer ordered the guns to "fire for effect," and thirty-six precious 105mm rounds were said to be "on the way."

Long after the guns had barked and the shells should have fallen, Hal Williamson got back on the horn to ask Hank Ammer where the artillery support was. Ammer told him to "wait one" and queried his fire-direction center, which averred that the mission had been fired. It turned out that the marker rounds observed by How Company had been fired by 81mm mortars. No one had any idea where the artillery had fired its two marker rounds, nor the thirty-six rounds of High Explosives that followed.

Captain Williamson cleared the opposition on his front with the aid of the company and battalion mortars which, incidentally, demolished the ice covering the stream, thus providing How Company with its first replenishment of water since it had climbed into the hills the previous afternoon.

As the engineers endeavored to fill the gap across the stream, D23 and elements of Dog-Easy/7 slipped forward to engage the next roadblock, the third encountered that day.

Following a lengthy delay, in which it was found that the composite company was hanging back, Bob Taplett moved forward to take control of the advance. He found the remnants of the sadly depleted composite unit an uncontrolled mob just back from the line of fire. The incredulous battalion commander asked after the captain who had been placed in command of the unit and was told that he was inside D23. Livid, Taplett went forward, first in a crouch, then at a crawl. The fire from the heights was so intense that his helmet was struck by a glancing round which, fortunately, did not penetrate. As soon as he reached the motionless tank, Taplett grabbed the intercom phone on the rear fender and loosed a verbal blast. The company commander refused to budge. The Chinese were blasting the top of the tank with small arms fire so, though he would sorely have liked to, Taplett was not about to climb up and try to pry open the turret hatch just to get his hands around the throat of the by-then-former company commander. He left in a huff to try to get his stalled attack going once again.

★

D23's 90mm gun slowly traversed the high-walled defile, pounding to dust every flimsy building in range. The coaxial machine gun remained in constant action, sweeping the roadway and approaches clear of the many PLA soldiers who were trying to get at the tank.

It took until nearly 1800 hours to reduce the third block to rubble and disperse the troops who had manned it with such splendid determination.

D23 was critically low on fuel and ammunition, so Staff Sergeant Munsell ordered two of his crewmen to drop down through their escape hatches and crawl to the rear to collect whatever they could beg, borrow, or steal. Only about fifteen gallons could be reclaimed from the fuel tanks of abandoned vehicles to the rear, and small quantities of .30-caliber machine-gun ammunition had to be donated by infantrymen, who were running dangerously low themselves.

It took until nearly 2200 hours to get D23 moving again, and that lasted only until the point infantry officer ordered her to back up. The heavy tank skidded out of control and slid into the ditch paraleling the roadway, impossible to recover under its own power.

The advance down the MSR stopped right there.

★

On the heights to the right of the MSR, How/5 continued a slow advance through the beginnings of a late-afternoon snow shower. The next objective was a high hill overlooking the spot where the road curved into its last uphill grade to the top of Toktong Pass.

First Lieutenant Bud Fredericks's platoon of How/5 darted across a large open field, one man at a time, while company weapons were deployed in a base of fire to hit a Chinese strongpoint farther up the hill. Three of Fredericks's men, including his corpsman, were hit on the run.

Fredericks and his men moved only a few feet up the slope before finding themselves pinned securely by heavy fire from above. When the platoon leader looked back through the waning light and wind-whipped snow, he saw that the company mortar officer had come to the particular attention of the Chinese. Peering out from behind a haystack in the stubbly field, the mortar officer tried vainly to spot for his 60s. Far from being of any use, however, though he jerked his head from one side of the stack to the other, he barely had time to show his helmet before he drew heavy fire, all of which was fortunately a beat or two late.

The troops were utterly exhausted. Bud Fredericks had less than twenty men left in his platoon, and he had to pace up and down behind them — punching, kicking, jabbing, and cursing — to get them to wake up. Each time he completed a circuit, he had to go right back to wake everyone up again. And again. And again. And again.

The attack resumed in the dark, an hour after being stalled at the base of the hill. The Chinese could see little, if anything, through the swirling snow and darkness, and three hundred additional yards fell to How Company without interference. How/5 was in possession of what it thought was the summit of its objective by 2300 hours, December 2. All it really held, though, was a shelf three hundred yards short of its goal. The same dark snowstorm that had baffled the defenders had stymied the attackers.

All hands fell where they had been standing the instant Captain

Williamson told them they could stand down. Within five minutes hardly more than a handful remained awake and vigilant.

★

To the left of the roadway, George/5 had secured Hill 1520 by noon, then had gone on to participate in clearing the ground overlooking the blown bridge. The company commander, Captain Chester Hermanson, was wounded later in the afternoon.

On hearing of Hermanson's evacuation, Bob Taplett called in his assistant operations officer, 1st Lieutenant Charlie Mize, and asked if he would like to resume command of the company he had led through Pusan and Inchon-Seoul. Taplett did not have to ask Mize twice, for the wiry, cocky Georgian fairly leaped up the hill.

What Charlie Mize found was a platoon in the guise of a company, and a mighty sad-looking platoon at that.

There were thirty-four of the original one hundred eighty left, plus eleven artillerymen who had been drafted into the infantry. No one seemed capable of giving a damn about anything. They had been on their feet, fighting, for four days in a row. No one had had more than a few spoonfuls of gooey, semi-solid food, nor very much water. No one seemed to relate to the concepts of physical warmth or well-being. Simply stated, George/5 was dead on its feet.

Charlie Mize reorganized all the riflemen and artillerymen into one platoon, led by 2nd Lieutenant Blackie Cahill, one of the spirited young officers who had retaken Hill 1384 with such élan on November 28. The machine-gun platoon was reorganized into a single section, and the mortars were retained by a lightly manned section. Mize's best hope was that the men whom he had known and with whom he had fought for all of fifteen months, counting prewar duty, would respond adequately when called upon to do so. They did not look it, Mize realized, but they were combat Marines, first and foremost, and that was all that counted.

★

As Taplett's attack wavered and ground to a halt in the hours around midnight, December 2, the nose of the long column out of Yudam-ni stood well within fighting range of Toktong Pass and Ray Davis's waiting 1st Battalion, 7th. Bob Taplett and his superiors were content to let the weary troops rest through the remainder of the night.

The attack would resume at dawn.

★

Straining, cursing Marines had been at work for hours freeing D23 from the roadside ditch it had slid into in the dark. Taplett's logistics officer had managed to come up with a stout towing chain, and the engineers had eased a heavy diesel tractor into place on the road beside the tank. The first attempt to pull D23 onto the roadway resulted in a broken chain and a torrent of cursing, but the second try was the charm, and Taplett's battalion regained its armored support.

The composite company had nothing left to offer, so Bob Taplett agreed to relieve it in favor of bringing the reinforced platoon that was George Company down from the heights to support D23's advance.

★

First Lieutenant Bud Fredericks awoke on December 3 with six inches of newly fallen snow on him. Rubbing his eyes, the young How/5 platoon leader sat up and saw that the entire company had been reduced to a patternless profusion of body-sized lumps on the level ground. A second look revealed that How/5 was still well short of the ridgeline it had thought it was on when it dozed off in the night.

Captain Hal Williamson ordered the sorry remnant that was How/ 5 back on its feet. The hilltop above had to be taken.

It was snowing heavily, a mixed blessing: the approach to the Chinese was well concealed, but air and artillery support was severely hampered. Chinese machine-gun fire was sweeping the approaches to the summit, and the Marines could no longer make any headway.

Hal Williamson got through to one of the battalion's forward air controllers, who told him that there were two Navy ADs overhead, but no reliable way to control them as he could not see the objective through the swirling snowstorm. Williamson allowed that he had no choice but to relay instructions through the air controller as he could not speak directly with the two Navy carrier pilots. At the last moment, however, the snow cleared just long enough for the pilots to roar in. Even after they had expended the enormous payloads they had hauled up from the sea, the two Navy men continued to make dummy runs on the Chinese strongpoint.

Bud Fredericks's platoon was having trouble resuming the advance despite the superb, if limited, air support. Then one of the automatic riflemen crawled forward under heavy machine-gun fire and sprayed the Chinese emplacements with his BAR; he continued to walk forward on his knees, firing all the while, until the Chinese cut and ran.

The Chinese flushed by the ADs and How/5 ran right into the

arms of an even larger Chinese force, which was itself retreating in the face of another Marine assault.

★

Lieutenant Colonel Ray Davis's 1st Battalion, 7th, had spent most of December 2 resting, and securing and patrolling the important ground around Fox Hill and Toktong Pass.

On hearing that Taplett had advanced to within several hundred yards of the vital pass, Davis and his operations officer. Major Tom Tighe, got to work fashioning a plan to link up with the road-bound force from Yudam-ni. So, while How/5 was clambering to its feet in the snow that had blanketed it in the night, Davis personally led Charlie/7 and How/7 against Chinese forces barring the road in the direction of Hagaru-ri. Linking the Toktong Pass garrison with the Yudam-ni column was left to Tom Tighe and Able and Baker Companies, 7th, which moved against the Chinese holding the high ground on the opposite side of the same hill that was Hal Williamson's objective.

The first phase of Tighe's attack was undertaken by 1st Lieutenant Hank Kiser's twenty-one-man 2nd Platoon of Baker/7, which advanced into heavy fire and cleared its objective. When the remainder of Baker/7 attempted to bypass the position, however, it was pinned by the heavy fire. Kiser hurriedly reorganized his small unit and led a spirited attack upon nearly fifty Chinese holding the ridgeline on Baker/7's flank. The Chinese broke, and forty of them died before the platoon's guns; five others were taken alive.

Once the opposition had been cleared, Tom Tighe led Able and Baker Companies against the rear of the Chinese facing How/5.

Those Chinese were routed, first by the Navy ADs attacking in support of How/5, then by the fire that Major Tighe's force pumped into their rear.

Things happened rather quickly from that point.

Bob Taplett was on the roadway, berating a lagging officer, when he was beckoned by a 5th Regiment staffer, who said, "Colonel Murray wants you to continue the attack because he's got a message from Colonel Litzenberg to tell you that Davis has reported he's running them right into your arms."

Taplett was as susceptible as anyone to the infantryman's normal paranoia concerning the motivations of anyone with whom he is not intimately associated. Thoroughly angered at the colonel of the 7th for what he saw as a deliberate lack of cooperation in beating the MSR clear all the way from Turkey Hill, the bone-weary battalion commander exploded at the young staffer: "You can tell Litzenberg that he's full of shit. If he wants me to believe it, he can come up here and look for himself. There's nobody running into our arms, and we're having one helluva time getting this attack going."

Tom Tighe *was* running the Chinese on his front into How/5, which was running the Chinese on its front into Tighe. Observers on the roadway forward of Taplett's vantage point could see it too.

First Lieutenant Art House, Taplett's 81mm-mortar-platoon leader, snapped out a few quick orders, and his guns were turned on the Chinese milling between Tighe and Williamson. Second Lieutenant Hank Ammer, Taplett's artillery forward observer, pleaded with batteries to the rear to relay their guns, and was heard yelling, "I got them! I got them!" when he was told to begin passing coordinates to the fire-direction centers. To top it off, a break in the overcast brought Marine Corsairs into the fray.

The Chinese between Tighe and Williamson were obliterated.

The turkey shoot, as the Marines on hand described it, was just winding down when a Marine two-place helicopter piloted by 1st Lieutenant Robert Longstaff whirred in to take out a wounded Marine. Hundreds of men watched in helpless terror as the fragile aircraft did an ungainly outside loop and plunged in flames against the hillside above the roadway. Bob Taplett instantly dispatched a patrol to rescue the pilot, but Lieutenant Longstaff had been killed on impact, and incinerated.

D23 lumbered through two Chinese roadblocks during the morning, trailing the remnant of George/5 and a provisional platoon scraped from Taplett's headquarters. Staff Sergeant Munsell and his crew were in dreadful shape, having been awake all night wrestling their tank from the roadside ditch. Fumes and internal heat caused the loader to pass out for some time, and the other four crewmen were sickened. But at just about noon, December 3, D23 passed to the control of Ray Davis's 1st Battalion, 7th, ending the first, and crucial, phase of the breakout from Yudam-ni.

It was downhill the rest of the way to Hagaru-ri — literally — but it was not smooth sailing. Not by any means.

CHAPTER
34

Though Lieutenant Colonel Bob Taplett felt that his heroic 3rd Battalion, 5th, deserved the honor of leading the Yudam-ni garrison all the way into Hagaru-ri, he was ordered to relinquish the lead to Lieutenant Colonel Ray Davis's 1st Battalion, 7th, which was already in motion toward the division base by the time Taplett reached Fox Hill.

To the rear, ten thousand other Marines were experiencing seventy-nine bitterly cold hours of footslogging, the likes of which even the saltiest of them would place as the most memorable of their careers.

★

The last unit to leave Yudam-ni was Lieutenant Colonel Hal Roise's 2nd Battalion, 5th, which had been left to stand across Hill 1276 while the remainder of the garrison bolted through the door held open at Hill 1542 by the remnant of the 3rd Battalion, 7th.

December 3 passed quietly, and slowly, for Roise's battalion. Too quietly, and too slowly.

Captain Stretch Mayer, the battalion headquarters commandant, was approached late in the day by one of the artillery forward observers, who told him that the last battery covering Hill 1276 had been ordered to limber up and withdraw down the MSR. A short time later, one of the battalion's forward air controllers mentioned that a pilot had reported spotting the head of the vehicle column some ten miles down the road, and that a gap was rapidly developing between Roise's battalion and the nearest friendly troops, on and near Hill 1542.

Alarmed, Mayer went over to Hal Roise, who was running the battalion out of his jeep. Roise was puffing away at his ubiquitous cigarette as Stretch Mayer reported the gist of his conversations with the forward observer and the air controller. The battalion commander's eyes sort of glazed over, but he never flinched. It was clear that he, too, was thinking that the battalion was baiting a trap while the remainder of the Yudam-ni garrison slipped away. Roise silently lifted himself from his jeep and strode over to his radio jeep. . . .

Before long, the rifle companies began filtering through the CP area; Roise had taken the step no one else seemed inclined to take in his behalf.

As the battalion was re-forming to leave the valley of Yudam-ni, a lone Marine Corsair roared in over the column, swung tightly around on its wing over the distant town, then roared away to the south. Stretch Mayer was certain that the pilot had been sent up to report on the final battle of the 2nd Battalion, 5th Marines, in Korea.

Then things began looking up. As the weary troops trudged southward through the gloomy late afternoon, a Marine fighter made a run on a hill west of the MSR, and the men on the road could see the six .50-caliber machine guns winking in the grayish light.

Passing Turkey Hill, Captain Mayer was surprised at the number of wrecked vehicles he saw. Chinese on the heights were firing down at the battalion. Mayer stepped to the verge and stumbled over a dead Chinese soldier, who released a great *"Yawhh!"* as the gases that had built up in his decomposing system were forced past his vocal chords. Then a round passed so close to Mayer's face that he felt the air rustle and his skin crawl back out of the way. An expert marksman, Mayer unslung his puny carbine and drew a bead on the sniper, who continued to fling bullets at the passing Marines. Taking up the slack on his trigger, Mayer held his breath and steadied himself against the pounding of his heart. As his breath eased out in practiced perfection, Mayer felt the recoil against his shoulder. Though he could not in honesty claim a kill, Mayer heard nothing more from the sniper.

Farther on, the headquarters commandant happened upon two Marines who were kneeling in the roadway beside a wounded buddy. Mayer hunkered down to see if he might be of assistance, but he immediately noted that the wounded boy's eyes were already glazing over. He left the dying man in the care of his buddies, and strode down the road until he found his own jeep, which was brimming over with riders. The thirty-two-year-old Reserve captain dozed off as soon as he found a warm place on the vehicle's hood.

★

Unbeknown to Stretch Mayer, Roise's battalion passed the 3rd Battalion, 7th, at Turkey Hill. The two remaining rifle companies of Lieutenant Colonel Bill Harris's small command were on the slopes of Hill 1542, holding the door open, and Harris and his headquarters people were in or near a small mud hut in the lee of Turkey Hill, right where Stretch Mayer had seen the wrecked vehicles. Supported by the last of the leapfrogging artillery batteries, Harris's battalion was to hold until Roise's train and infantry column were well clear.

It had been an anxious wait. During the day, Captain Bill Earney, Harris's operations officer, was sharing the warmth of a gasoline-drum fire beside the CP, chewing the fat with a noncom and two other officers, watching Chinese skirmishers on Turkey Hill venture closer and closer to the MSR. After a while Earney reached instinctively for a pack of cigarettes that was being passed around, then dipped his head to get a light from a match proffered by one of the men. Before he could straighten up, the young captain heard 2nd Lieutenant Vic Salvo, who had just returned to the battalion after being wounded at Sudong, exclaim, "Look! That bullet went right through my hand!" Earney and the others saw a neat hole in the hand that Salvo was waving in their faces. If he could make it to Hagaru-ri, Vic Salvo was entitled to a ticket home for his second wound.

★

As soon as Roise's battalion started passing Hill 1542, Bill Harris ordered the rifle companies halfway up the hill to get ready to drop down to the roadway. The battalion vehicles were moved a bit farther down the MSR to make room for the infantry, then the last available 105mm howitzers were leapfrogged down the road. A battery of the 3rd Battalion, 11th, was on hand to provide cover at the extremity of its range in a pinch, but that was somewhat speculative in light of depleted radio batteries.

Even before the order was passed, 2nd Lieutenant Pat Roe, the battalion intelligence officer, could see that riflemen on the heights were easing themselves toward the road. Higher up, little dark spots coalescing on the skyline showed Roe that the Chinese were preparing to mount a strike if the opportunity arose.

One Chinese group, more brazen than the others, set up a light mortar and began plunking rounds at the battalion command post. Roe, like most of the others, was too tired and cold to take cover. Instead, he stood with the other staffers and clerks, hunkering down in his filthy parka, stomping his feet in place to keep the blood circulating. The indifference of the troops to the mortar fire was palpable. In any event, no one was hit.

There was ample air support on call overhead, but the 3rd Battalion, 7th, had been reduced to an effective infantry strength of under three hundred men. The positions on Hill 1542 were utterly untenable; the battalion had been able to hold since December 1 only because the Chinese had been too tired or cold or passive or unseeing to press their considerable advantage. The battalion 81mm mortars had only two rounds of High Explosives, period. Fortunately, a large supply of small-arms ammunition was available.

All this was passing through Pat Roe's mind as he stood beside the radio jeep of one of the battalion's forward air controllers late in the afternoon of December 3, shortly after Roise's battalion had passed through. The airman was scanning the hills through his binoculars when he paused in mid-traverse and muttered, "Shit, here comes a million of them."

Pat Roe felt as though someone had yanked his spine out by the roots. He grabbed the airman's glasses and looked for himself. Breasting the crest of a low hill only two miles to the north was a column of twos in open order. The head of the column was obscured by an intervening hill, and the tail had yet to appear. But Roe could see six hundred yards of Chinese — something less than a million, but certainly more than a thousand.

The air controller cranked up his jeep radio and fired off a flash to Bill Harris. Pat Roe set up a spotting scope on the hood of the jeep and watched in blank amazement as the Chinese snaked through the gap between the hills.

Suddenly, four Marine Corsairs swept over the Chinese column on a dummy run while the air controller rattled off directions into his radio mike. The Chinese scattered, disappearing from view. The Corsairs followed up with several hot runs, spraying the hills with machine-gun fire, dusting them with rockets and napalm.

Roe looked up at Hill 1542 and he could see that the friendly riflemen were inching still closer to the road, ready to make their getaway. Bill Harris arrived and watched for some time before saying that some fire ought to be placed on the distant ridge to keep the Chinese off balance and dispersed. The artillery was no longer available, and the air controller could not immediately raise a fresh division of Corsairs, so Harris called over 2nd Lieutenant George Caridakis, the 81mm platoon leader: "George, I want you to lay down a mortar concentration along the top of that hill," and he pointed at the distant hill.

"What?" Caridakis replied. "*Both* rounds?"

When fighter-bombers were finally called in, Harris directed that they work over the ridgelines. The pilots reported, however, that there were an awful lot more Chinese on the reverse slopes than could be seen from the road. While the planes went to work, killing and maiming PLA infantrymen, a shiver ran through the men gathered around the radio jeep: What were all those Chinese up to, anyway?

The battalion's vehicles were well up the slope, past Turkey Hill. The rifle companies were called in and the rear guard strode away from the valley of Yudam-ni as quickly as its many legs could carry it. No one would miss the place.

★

Second Lieutenant Nick Trapnell, of Able/5, had been out on the flanks for most of December 2 and 3, humping his body across the ridges, keeping the Chinese well away from the soft vehicles on the road below.

There had been weird moments. Once, as the small company paused among the howitzers of an artillery battery deployed to cover units to the rear, Trapnell had to wonder about the artillery sergeant who made his way through the site, tapping every second man on the shoulder and telling him off for a provisional rifle platoon. Trapnell, who wanted to be an airman, had spent the entire year before the war training with a reconnaissance company, but he had not known a thing about infantry combat until he joined Able/5 in battle outside Seoul. On this night, he saw artillerymen with little infantry training, and probably no experience, being chosen at random to take on the most difficult job any soldier has to face. He wished them well with all his heart, then trudged forward when his company got moving again.

Once, when his platoon was on the roadway, Trapnell turned to see the source of a *clack-clack*ing sound that had finally penetrated the fog of his exhaustion. Making his way down the Marine column was a barefoot Chinese captive. The *clack-clack*ing was the man's frozen feet resounding against the frozen earth.

Nick Trapnell's taste for the absurd was fed yet again as he rested on the verge of the road amidst a stalled artillery battery. Some men preferred sitting, while others remained in nerve-driven motion. One of the latter was 2nd Lieutenant Dutch Blank, Able/5's mortar officer. Blank was so exhausted that he walked right into the muzzle of a 105mm howitzer time and time again as he paced back and forth, back and forth. And each time he butted the howitzer, he uttered the prescribed, "Pardon me, Mac."

★

Lieutenant Colonel Ray Murray sat through fifteen minutes of a halt on the road before stalking impatiently forward to see what the trouble was. After passing numerous vehicles, he found a gap in the column so large that he could not see the tail of the next vehicle ahead. Tearing open the driver's door of the first truck in line, he peered into the cab, amazed to see the driver and his assistant fast asleep, though the driver's foot was lightly pumping the accelerator. The colonel's penetrating voice and proven ability to get to the heart of a matter soon had the truck tearing down the road in search of the remainder of the column.

★

Private First Class Walker Merell, formerly of Charlie/7, was one of the uncounted casualties who had been crammed into jeeps and trucks for the ride out. Lashed onto the upper tier of a two-litter ambulance jeep, fully exposed to the cold but for a sleeping bag that had been pulled up around his ears, Merell dozed fitfully for what seemed an eternity of road-bound terror and discomfort. Except for a few crackers, Merell ate nothing whatsoever during his three days on the road. When there was firing, the driver left the jeep, but Merell and the unseen, unknown man in the litter beneath his had no way to do what they would have liked to do most: get off and run with the herd.

Crammed into a truck amidst tiers of other wounded and frostbitten Marines, Sergeant Bob Oldani, formerly of George/7, had to wait out the terror of being near a man who went slowly crazy because he was too fastidious to wet himself, though there was nothing else anyone aboard the truck could do. After more than a day of sobbing and pleading, the man, who had not been hurt badly to start with, drifted off into a coma, and died.

★

A typical Marine walking out of Yudam-ni might be wearing as much as, or even more than 2nd Lieutenant Tom Gibson, a 4.2-inch heavy-mortar officer who had served as an Army infantry officer with the 101st Airborne Division at the Battle of the Bulge (making him one of the very few Marines who had cold-weather-combat experience pre-dating Korea). Gibson had on regular cotton underwear; woolen long underwear; a pair of wool trousers; a wool shirt; a pair of waterproof outer trousers; a fleece-lined jacket; a parka with hood; mittens; two pairs of woolen socks; shoepacs; a steel helmet with liner and camouflage cover. On top of that, Gibson, and most other Marines, carried a normal load of web gear and pack, with all sorts of pouches and pockets crammed full of oddments and ammunition.

The result was a lot of well-rounded Marines. Very few men cared to undress very much in the freezing chill of the Taebeck Plateau, so an act as simple as urination became a hit-or-miss proposition.

More than one Marine who could not see past his belt pulled out a shirt tail and urinated into a pants leg. Following an instant of wet warmth there was an immediate sensation of liquid freezing from thigh to foot. There was little discomfort, but there was a perfect chance for winding up frostbitten. No one knows how many men went unfit for combat as a result of this rather singular hazard.

★

Captain Bill Earney, operations officer of the 3rd Battalion, 7th, was typically bundled up and encumbered with gear. So, when a stray round from the heights plowed into the buckle of his pistol belt, sending a shock wave through his torso, Earney had to think seriously about checking for a wound. He could not feel any blood, so decided to forego the opportunity to undress on the roadway.

★

In the middle of the last miserable night of the Yudam-ni withdrawal, 2nd Lieutenant Nick Trapnell, of Able/5, came down from the ridges and allowed himself to be guided forward by a wavering light in a hollow by the side of the road. Assuming it to be a command post of some sort, he went forward to investigate, hoping to get The Word and share in some warmth. It was not a tent, as he anticipated, but a tiny native hut crammed to the walls with an uncountable mass of huddling Marines. Looking at the blank faces inside, Trapnell saw an old friend and Basic School classmate, 2nd Lieutenant Pat Roe, of the 3rd Battalion, 7th. The interior of the building was in flames. In order to keep warm, the nearly insensate men inside were burning the hut down around themselves. Later, Pat Roe could never recall having been involved in so mad an act.

★

Major Fox Parry's two-battery 3rd Battalion, 11th, was the first artillery unit out to Yudam-ni. Because of limited ready-ammunition stocks, and an assumption that there might be little or no ammunition available at Hagaru-ri, there was a good deal of conservatism involved in decisions to support or not support the infantry. Still, in the event of emergency, the cold-hampered guns were generally kept within range of most or all infantry units on the road or in the hills.

One George Battery howitzer bailed out a line of trucks loaded with wounded that had become the target for a particularly accurate Chinese machine gun. Mindful of the low ammunition stocks, the gun chief sniped at the machine gun with careful precision, blowing it off the hillside with the fourth round.

Later that day, December 2, an Item Battery howitzer placed a round near a distant knot of moving figures, but was stilled when a sulphurous blast of profanity was blurted over the tactical radio net by a 5th Regiment platoon leader whose patrol had nearly been hit.

It took Item Battery until 1530, December 3, to negotiate the six thousand yards from the southern end of Yudam-ni to an ice-coated field near the town of Sinhung-ni, at Toktong Pass. The crews slid and rolled their six howitzers into positions they had dug into on the way to Yudam-ni two weeks earlier. The field was a mass of ice, but it was the best spot around for reaching forward and back along the MSR. Unable to dig in to avoid light harassing fires, the gunners drove their trucks in beside the guns, the best protection they could manage.

It was at Sinhung-ni that Fox Parry witnessed a brief emotional setback for Homer Litzenberg. The tall, square-faced colonel, who had taken a fatherly interest in Parry during their months together in combat, arrived with elements of his staff to inspect the battery site and deliver some new directives. As the two men talked, Litz became increasingly overwrought, saying that he thought he might have to break up the entire 1st Battalion, 11th, in order to provide yet more fillers for the depleted infantry units on the road. The tears nearly came, but the colonel shook off his feelings and found anew the brusque air he had been affecting since first he joined combat in Korea. He left Fox Parry a bit shaken.

★

Despite the frustration and downright weirdness of the journey, spirits remained generally high — and climbed higher — as the great column snaked over Toktong Pass and descended toward Hagaru-ri.

But there was fighting, and there were losses.

CHAPTER

35

Leading the long column was Ray Davis's 1st Battalion, 7th, which began the final leg of the march to Hagaru-ri about noon, December 3, almost as soon as it had linked up with Taplett's battalion.

Thanks to the aggressiveness of Marine and Navy airmen and the continuing efforts of the crew of D23, the lead battalion made rapid progress against diminishing opposition as it descended from Toktong Pass.

Certain of success in linking up with the Yudam-ni garrison, Major General O. P. Smith authorized the formation of a relief force comprised of tank-mounted Marines drawn from units within the perimeter and a large contingent of Royal Marine Commandos. This force left the Hagaru-ri perimeter at 1630.

Second Lieutenant Joe Owen, of Baker/7, was standing on the roadway beside Ray Davis's CP at about 1900 hours when the neat files of Royal Marines passed through the outguards the leading element of the 1st Battalion, 7th, had thrown out. A British officer, impeccably turned out, strode directly up to the tall, cruddy lieutenant, drawn by the binoculars which marked him as an officer, and reported in a calm, urbane voice. Joe Owen had not seen a salute in weeks of combat, and was particularly impressed by the wagging of the stiff British salute. The Royal Marine lieutenant asked where he could set up his machine guns, but before Owen could respond one of the more garrulous mortarmen, who had been wounded in the arm a short time earlier, chimed in, "We don't give a fuck where you set up your goddamn gun. Just do it so we can go in and get warm."

Davis's battalion moved off toward Hagaru-ri as soon as the relief column had set up.

Stopping six hundred yards short of the town's defenses, Davis's troops dressed ranks. They were a haggard, disheveled lot, but their pride was something to behold. Without anyone counting cadence, all of them stepped out in formation, their feet pounding the frozen roadway in unison. Passing the first knots of gawkers, the men of the 1st Battalion, 7th, threw back their shoulders and marched through the friendly lines, as if on review.

Dr. Bob Harvey, a sensitive aspiring pediatrician who had served as Bob Taplett's battalion surgeon at Pusan and Inchon-Seoul before being transferred to one of the medical companies, was as moved as he had ever been. Normally soft-spoken and eloquent, the young physician turned to a stranger beside him and exclaimed, "Look at those bastards! Those *magnificant bastards!*"

There were tearful, stirring reunions, and bear hugs from strangers, and hands pumped in admiration and thanksgiving. And a few inevitable misunderstandings.

As Major Tom Tighe, Davis's operations officer, staggered through the Hagaru-ri outpost line, he was greeted loudly by Lieutenant

Colonel Olin Beall, the curmudgeonly commander of the 1st Motor Transport Battalion. Asked if he needed some water, Tighe nodded eagerly, but was struck a blow when Beall laughingly suggested that he eat some snow. Since snow was precisely what Tighe had been eating for the past three days, he communicated his extreme displeasure over the unthinking gaffe. Beall moaned back that Tighe was an ungrateful so-and-so, the only arrival Beall had heard complain about anything.

The motor officer stalked off, but he returned a few minutes later with a sheepish look in his eyes, and shoved a canteen into Tighe's hands. Relenting, Tom Tighe tipped back the canteen and felt the warm, smooth flow of bonded bourbon trickle down the back of his throat. He was completely restored within minutes.

It was dark by the time Colonel Homer Litzenberg's command group passed through the thin screen of tanks, Marines, and Royal Marines sent forward earlier from Hagaru-ri. The departure of Marine and Navy aircraft brought out the Chinese, who harassed the column from the heights, but did not venture close enough to the road to cause a violent reaction on the part of Litzenberg's troops.

Major Hank Woessner, Litz's operations officer, was trudging down the road beside the much taller regimental commander when there was a rumbling explosion followed by a huge fireball only a few yards back along the darkened roadway. Without breaking stride or even looking to see the source of the blaze, Litz turned to Woessner and ordered him to put out the blaze before the Chinese used the light to help them cut the traffic on the MSR.

Woessner unslung his Garand rifle and turned on his heel, lurching quickly back toward the flames. He had gone only a few paces when he saw the outlines of a heavy tank which was being consumed by the flames. Young Woessner thought he ought to at least make a stab at obeying the colonel's order, but he took only two or three steps more before he gave the job up as hopeless. All he had on hand for fighting the flames was — what? — snowballs?

★

Preparations for the influx of thousands of weary Marines at Hagaru-ri had been made as well as could be expected. Guides were on hand to lead various units to predesignated bivouacs within the perimeter. Wherever possible, the weary men were placed in tents and given time to sleep. Hot stews, coffee, and pancakes were churned out in vast quantities, and replacement clothing and equipment was made available by supply officers who turned blind eyes to the wholesale pilfering of dumps, which began as soon as the first Yudam-ni Marine stepped through the forwardmost outpost.

All went well for what remained of December 3. Following Davis's battalion, the two regimental trains and most of the wounded succeeded in getting into the perimeter. The injured were lifted gingerly from their transport and given as much care as the overburdened medical system could muster.

Private First Class Walker Merell, who had been three days aboard an open ambulance jeep, was lifted from his perch and placed in a tent, where he was examined by a corpsman and prodded by a doctor (the first he had seen since being shot six days earlier). It turned out, as it did in too many cases, that Merell's initial shoulder wound was the least of his problems. After misplacing his gloves in the November 28 fighting on Turkey Hill, Merell had lost sensation in the fingers of his right hand, which had been bandaged upon his arrival at the battalion aid station at Yudam-ni. When corpsmen unwrapped the putrid dressing on December 3, they found that the fingers of Merell's right hand were black, the distinctive coloration of advanced frostbite. All they could do was sprinkle on some sulfa powder and tag the twenty-year-old Ohio Reservist for early evacuation. (Merell would, in time, lose the end joints of those fingers. And, years later, he had his ruined and useless right hand amputated at the forearm in order to gain the use of a metal hook.)

★

Lieutenant Colonel Carl Youngdale, who had succeeded to the command of the 11th Marines on November 30, when the previous commander was ordered out due to illness, was on hand at the first outpost to greet Major Bill McReynolds, commander of the 4th Battalion, 11th, who had given himself a voluntary bust and walked out of Yudam-ni as commander of a jackleg infantry company assigned to guard the medical column. Youngdale was appalled at the younger man's condition, and led him by the arm right across the perimeter to his own tent. He showed McReynolds to a cot and told him to get some rest so he would be in shape to re-form his battalion.

McReynolds mumbled, "Oh, fine. That's great," and took off his shoepacs.

Youngdale turned away for a moment, then turned back to see the young major dressing again.

"Mac, what the hell are you doing?"

"I have to see how the troops are."

"They're all right," Youngdale soothed. "We've arranged for everything. We've got guys to take care of them. We're picking them up as fast as they come in. The thing to do now is get some rest and sleep, because we're going to be shooting pretty soon."

McReynolds mumbled, "Oh, fine," and started shucking off his footwear once again. However, when Carl Youngdale next looked across the tent at the weary battalion commander, he caught the major pulling on his shoepacs. The regimental commander grabbed the footgear and hurled it across the tent, ending the matter there.

Neither Youngdale nor McReynolds had any idea that the 4th Battalion, 11th, was in the process of losing the greater portion of its guns in an unprecedented fiasco on the MSR.

★

The 155mm howitzers had been ordered to join the flow of vehicles from Yudam-ni at 1830 hours, December 2. Progress had been agonizingly slow, what with the damaged roadway, blown bridges, destroyed and abandoned vehicles that had to be removed from the right of way, constant small-arms fires, and probing attacks from the heights.

The result was a rapidly dwindling supply of diesel fuel for the 4th Battalion's tracked prime movers. When the guns reached Sinhung-ni, at the top of the pass, at 1400, December 3, the fuel supply was critically low.

Relaying a message through the 7th Regiment's tactical command net, the officers in charge of the guns requested an immediate resupply of at least one hundred fifty gallons of diesel fuel. The message was acknowledged and the guns were ordered forward; the fuel would be sent as soon as it could be mustered, and the resupply would take place wherever the guns met the fuel trucks.

As the column of 155s moved out to breast the pass, one of the guns jackknifed off the icy roadway and turned over, killing a man who had been riding on the trails. The gun had to be uncoupled and abandoned. The recoil mechanism was disabled in such a way as to render the big weapon useless until, hopefully, it could be recovered and refurbished.

It was a hazardous descent indeed. As soon as one mover was refueled from the dwinding fuel tanks of the others, another would run dry. Ambulances and trucks were also running out of fuel, and these were towed up to five or six at a time by the tracked movers. But the added weight meant added fuel consumption.

The guns had been hauled to within two miles of Hagaru-ri when they were stymied by a blown bridge. Marine engineers were hard at work widening a bypass, but the column was motionless for a full hour while fuel dripped away through idling engines.

Just as the first artillery vehicles crossed the bypass, PLA machine gunners on the heights fired in support of an infantry foray. Major Angus Cronin, the 4th Battalion's operations officer, formed a platoon from his gunners and counterattacked. Ten attackers were killed against the loss of twenty wounded Marines.

It all started coming apart there.

Elements of Lieutenant Colonel Harvey Feehan's 1st Battalion, 11th, were backed up behind the 155s, and all three battalions of the 5th Marines were clambering to get by. (Harris's 3rd Battalion, 7th, and Fox Parry's two 105mm batteries were well to the rear, guarding Toktong Pass.)

As bazookas were fired at Chinese emplacements on the hills all around, the lead tractor ran completely out of fuel. Gunners sent to scrounge for fuel reported that they were coming up dry in attempts to siphon more fuel from the other tractors. Major Cronin ordered the lead howitzer and the vehicles being towed by its prime mover to be bulldozed from the road. The dead and wounded who had been lashed to the trails of the howitzer were carefully removed and placed aboard trucks. Then the gun, the prime mover, and the vehicles that had been in tow were shoved over the edge and down the mountain.

Within a quarter-mile, the 4th Battalion, 11th, gave up eight more tractors and guns and three jeeps, all of which had run out of fuel or been crippled by gunfire from Hill 1226, which dominated that stretch of the MSR.

Miraculously, a driver found and uncovered a diesel fuel dump that had been cached beside the road during the advance to Yudam-ni weeks earlier. The vehicles were refueled, and an effort was made to recover one of the jettisoned 155s, but that came to nothing.

The earlier request for one hundred fifty gallons of fuel was met by 11th Regiment, which dispatched Major Tom Cave, a staffer, in the company of 1st Lieutenant Bill Meeker's platoon of Baker/Engineers. Cave and Meeker made a valiant effort to breast the inflowing tide of men and vehicles, but had to give it up. A message to Major Cronin pinpointed the spot where the fuel was left, but it did not get through, and the dogged effort was wasted. In all the 155mm battalion lost ten of its eighteen guns.

New trouble developed for the infantry battalions following the artillery.

★

The Chinese on Hill 1226 had managed to build up an impressive base of fire.

Bob Taplett, whose rifle companies had drifted on ahead of the battalion vehicle train and headquarters, had arrived sometime before, and had been able to offer some little help to Major Cronin's gunners. He was joined after a while by Lieutenant Colonels Hal Roise, of the 2nd Battalion, 5th, and Jack Stevens, of the 1st Battalion, 5th.

The three rifle-battalion commanders, who had little present in the way of infantry, fumed and fussed for a time as the fire from the heights intensified; all had particularly barbed comments reserved for the regimental command group, which had long since gone under canvas at the division base.

While elements of Taplett's headquarters company built up a base of fire on the verge of the roadway, a platoon from Captain Sam Jaskilka's Easy/5 moved toward the Chinese strongpoint by way of a ridgeline to the north.

Then, while the Easy/5 platoon in the hills was trudging across the skyline in the gathering light, Chinese sappers blew the repaired bridge once again. Drivers, who had been calm up to that point, started to panic, pressing on their accelerators, hoping to run the gantlet of fire by crossing the ice-covered stream.

Bob Taplett was trying to halt the column when he heard the heaviest streak of profanity he had heard in his decade in uniform. Commissioned Warrant Office Allen Carlson, of the 1st Battalion, 11th, had had enough insubordination, and he was thundering his emotions at the fleeing drivers. Clomping down the road after the nearest truck, Carlson disappeared from Taplett's view around a bend. But he returned a few moments later leading a truck that had a 105mm howitzer in tow.

As the Easy/5 platoon moved against the Chinese flank on the snow-covered skyline, Gunner Carlson dragooned the nearest warm bodies and formed a scratch gun crew. Nearby, Bob Taplett helped haul a 75mm recoilless rifle into place. Carlson aimed his 105 over open sights and blasted the Chinese strongpoint. Another 105 under the control of Major Bud Schlesinger, exec of the 1st Battalion, 11th, was wheeled into place beside Carlson's gun, and a .30-caliber heavy machine gun donated by Lieutenant Colonel Jack Stevens was soon spraying Hill 1226.

High up on the road, well out of the action, 2nd Lieutenant Pat Roe, who was with the 3rd Battalion, 7th's trucks, watched through

his binoculars as Hal Roise shook out several of his rifle platoons
and put them into motion.

Private First Class Bob Kennedy, a Dog/5 BAR-man, found himself wheeling off the road into a long field in the company of bayonet-wielding riflemen. The thin skirmish line of parka-clad Dog/5
Marines moved rapidly up the slope, prying PLA infantrymen from
their fighting holes, sending others fleeing into the guns on the road.

The first break in the overcast sky was filled with Navy ADs,
which spread rockets and napalm across the face of Hill 1226. Each
attack bomber waggled its wings in salute as it pulled back up into
the mists.

Marine heavy tanks coming up from the south turned their 90mm
guns on the Chinese atop a small hill across the road from the main
event, neutralizing a troublesome machine gun.

As Pat Roe's portion of the convoy began inching forward again,
1st Lieutenant Ace Parker, exec of Bill Harris's weapons company,
told off a provisional infantry platoon and led it across the ridges
against Chinese emplacements on Hill 1226 that had not yet been
touched by fire from the road or the Dog/5 attack.

As Parker moved forward, Dog/5 wheeled to face him, squeezing
the Chinese between them. A lone AD hurtled out of the overcast
and screamed along parallel to the roadway to prevent the Chinese
from escaping.

There was a well-hidden Chinese machine gun that had the roadway under direct high-angle fire from the heights. The vehicles and
walking men of the 3rd Battalion, 7th, formed up on the far side of
the gantlet, then took off in a group. As Captain Bill Earney, the
battalion operations officer, neared the beaten zone, he spotted a
pair of communicators plodding along with a radio-filled machine-
gun cart in tow. The two enlisted Marines seemed out of it, a surmise
that was more than confirmed when they shuffled apace through a
storm of machine-gun fire that shredded the rubber tires of the cart
and holed the radio equipment. As Pat Roe passed the beaten
ground, he saw riflemen from his battalion crouching and running
through the fire by way of a roadside ditch. On the opposite side of
the road was a squad and a platoon from Jack Stevens's battalion,
which were unleashing a vicious fire at the spot where they thought
the hidden machine gun might be. Roe dismounted from his jeep to
walk across the field over which Dog/5 had delivered its initial attack. The nearby platoon leader was 2nd Lieutenant Nick Trapnell,
the Basic School classmate who had seen Roe in the burning hut

during the night. Roe waved in recognition, but Trapnell was too intent upon his work to even see his friend. Caught by the intense high-angle machine-gun fire, Major Lefty Morris, who had faced the worst the Japanese had been able to dish out at Guadalcanal, Tarawa, and Saipan, was sure that he would lose his life traversing that last hot spot before Hagaru-ri.

Pat Roe crossed the roadside field on his hands and knees, then stumbled into the carnage that had been half the fighting power of the 4th Battalion, 11th. Dead Marines and overturned vehicles littered the verges of the road. Drifting among the wreckage were feathers from bullet-riddled down bags, which had been used as shrouds for men killed on the MSR who had been lashed to the gun trails.

The Chinese positions overlooking the MSR were completely overrun by 0830, December 4, and the elements of the five battalions involved trudged the short distance to Hagaru-ri.

★

The very last unit to reach the division base was Fox Parry's 3rd Battalion, 11th. Parry had been ordered by Colonel Litzenberg to fall in between the 4th and 1st Battalions, 11th, but he had been loath to leave several rifle battalions without some sort of artillery protection, so he had delayed his departure from Sinhung-ni. While Parry never intended to be tail-end Charlie, the delay saved his headquarters and two firing batteries from becoming entangled in the ambush below Hill 1226.

The battery sites at Sinhung-ni, which was just within range of How Battery, near East Hill, were abandoned in short order after dawn, December 4. Moving quickly down the MSR in the traces of the last infantry units clearing the ambush at Hill 1226, Parry's howitzers passed the first perimeter outpost at about 1400.

One of the most amazing sights of a combat career that had begun at Guadalcanal greeted Fox Parry as he trudged up the last rise into the Hagaru-ri perimeter. At the base of the hill was a 105mm howitzer belonging to the 1st Battalion, 11th. It had apparently been jogged loose from its prime mover and had rolled out of control down the long incline. When Parry saw it, the heavy weapon was sticking straight up out of the ground on its barrel.

When he was met by Lieutenant Colonel Carl Youngdale on entering the perimeter, Fox Parry was ordered to relinquish several of his howitzers to make good the 1st Battalion's loss of two guns prior to its arrival at Yudam-ni and four guns lost on the road back to Hagaru-ri. Stunned, Parry told the regimental commander that his

3rd Battalion had yet to lose a gun in Korea; if the 1st Battalion needed guns, let it send its gunners back up the road to retrieve what they had lost, starting with the grotesquely displayed piece at the foot of the hill. Youngdale chuckled over the heated response and let the matter rest. He led Parry to his tent and fed him a cheese sandwich, the very best cheese sandwich the major had ever eaten.

C H A P T E R
36

The Hagaru-ri garrison had been preparing for days for the arrival of the Yudam-ni garrison. The entire affair was totally beyond the experience of the Division senior staff, so no one knew quite what to expect, or do.

Several points were obvious, and all were to some degree within the capabilities of the organization.

With the completion of the airstrip on November 30, and the assignment of numerous Navy, Marine, and Air Force transports to the mission, nearly all the wounded and sick soldiers and Marines who had accumulated at the division base were started toward the rear hospitals at Hungnam, Hamhung, and throughout Japan.

★

Captain Joe McAllister, of the Air Force's 21st Troop Carrier Squadron, a crack C-47 unit known as the Kyushu Gypsies because of its numerous transfers during the five-month-old war, spent most of the last week of November, 1950, evacuating 8th Army casualties from dirt runways in northwestern Korea. In fact, on one mission, while the Chinese were fighting successfully to win one end of the runway he was using, he had lifted out over forty GIs in an aircraft built for a maximum of twenty-seven.

After completing several interim missions around Pyongyang, the North Korean capital, McAllister and his crew had flown to Yonpo to rejoin the bulk of the squadron, which had been involved in the rescue flights from Hagaru-ri from the very start.

It was well before dawn when McAllister's C-47 Dakota transport made its first hop to the embattled Marine base, alone and unescorted. The pilot had been involved in flying fuel tankers over The Hump into Burma and China during World War II, so he was not overly impressed with the Taebek Plateau when first he saw it, but he was impressed with how small Hagaru-ri looked from the air, though he had certainly flown into far smaller bastions.

Arriving over the field at about 0900, McAllister was ordered to orbit to the left until cleared for landing. He was two thousand feet above the plateau, about ten thousand feet above sea level. It was a bright, sunshiny day with unlimited visibility. A light mantle of snow on the ground reflected the sunlight, yielding an altogether picturesque view.

Higher up, Marine Corsairs orbited at minimum power to conserve fuel. As calls for air support came from the ground controllers, one or two of the fighters would break formation and plummet earthward. McAllister noticed right off that the Marine pilots almost never went around the orbiting cargo aircraft, but simply tipped over and roared on by, often at hairsbreadth distances. That kept the transport pilots and copilots pretty busy, and alert.

Clearance for landing was given in due course, and McAllister circled lower, homing on the single runway. Experience and a cool hand usually brought McAllister's C-47 to a stop on most fields within five hundred feet. At Hagaru-ri, on his very first landing, the veteran pilot had two immediate jolts. First, his tail wheel blew on touchdown, which resulted in a bout of some very heavy wrestling with his control yoke. Second, no one had warned the pilot that the second half of the strip ran uphill at a five-percent grade.

Though he had been ordered to turn at the end of the runway and taxi back to the dispersal area, Captain McAllister was severely hampered by the ruined tail wheel and had to pull off as far as he could to the side. Placing a call to Cyanide Control, the ground-control radio jeep, McAllister passed along word of his plight. Then, securing the aircraft, he and his crew jumped to the ground to check for damage and await a repair crew. They became some of the very few airmen to set foot on the strip.

Gawking at the surroundings, McAllister heard a low *woof-woof-woof* sound. Looking up, he saw large puffs of snow and dirt being lifted from the ground, each one closer than the last. Someone was trying to zero in a mortar, and McAllister's cargo area was filled with ammunition and gasoline. Understandably distraught, McAllister leaped aboard the stranded bird and told Cyanide Control of the danger. Within thirty seconds, a Marine heavy tank clanked up beside the Dakota transport and topped a small rise beside the runway.

McAllister and his co-pilot could not contain their curiosity, so they ambled up behind the tank, which had stopped. Peeking around the steel monster for a better look, Joe McAllister heard a thin, piercing whistling sound, oft repeated; a Chinese machine-gun crew had seen him. The turret above whirred back and forth on its servo-motors as the gunner sought a target. Then the turret stopped. *"Carumph! Carumph! Carumph!"* Three rounds left the 90mm gun in quick succession, and the backblast nearly grounded the curious airmen.

Getting into the spirit of things, McAllister loped down the hill to take a place beside a gasoline-drum fire as the tank rattled and clanked back out of sight. As he was roasting his hands before the open flames, the pilot was conscious of the stares his personal weapon was receiving. He had lifted a Chinese burp gun and several pancake ammunition drums during his last evacuation flight in the 8th Army area, and he had unconsciously slung the weapon over his shoulder when he left his aircraft. One Marine, bolder than his fellows, said, "Oh, man, I'd love to have that. I could really tear 'em up with that!" Without so much as a qualm, Joe McAllister shrugged the weapon from his shoulder and handed it over to the young Marine. "You can sure put it to better use than I can," he said as he gave the grinning boy an extra drum of ammunition.

As soon as the Dakota's tail wheel had been fixed, McAllister called his crew aboard and taxied over to the dispersal area. The transport was stripped within minutes by expert Marine cargo handlers, then a Navy corpsman took charge. Blanket-covered litters already on the flat beside the double cargo doors were loaded by men who had learned to make use of every square inch of deck space. Then the walking wounded shuffled aboard until the corpsman in charge cut off the flow and told Captain McAllister to get rolling.

As the Dakota taxied, roared into the air, and circled south for the quick flight to Yonpo, a touched Joe McAllister was gratified to hear the hitherto pensive passengers begin to joke and trade insults.

★

Not every flight ended as well, but only two transport aircraft were lost of the hundreds involved in carrying supplies to and the wounded from Hagaru-ri. The first Dakota was lost when its undercarriage collapsed on landing. It was Private First Class Jay Ransone's luck to be aboard the second.

Following the evaporation of Task Force Faith, Ransone had been picked up unconscious from the ice by a Marine truck crew and driven back to Hagaru-ri, where he was fed and treated by Navy corpsmen. Then, with thrity-one other ambulatory and three litter patients, he had been routinely loaded aboard Captain Robert Smith's C-47 for the quick run to Yonpo.

The takeoff was routine, and Jay Ransone's spirits soared with the aircraft. But as the Dakota flew through five hundred feet, Captain Smith pulled back on the control yoke and found that he was nosing *down*. The aircraft was skidding across an icy field almost before the pilot could react.

Jay Ransone and the other wounded were lifted from their bucket seats and hurled into the forward bulkhead. Panic developed quickly amidst warnings of an impending explosion. The cargo doors were kicked open and the walking wounded tumbled out onto the snow. A few had to go back inside for the badly injured and the three litter cases.

Captain Smith emerged from the cockpit, a large cut over one eye, and started organizing the disorganized mass of barefoot men. Those in the best condition carried the litter cases piggyback while the straggling column set off toward Hagaru-ri, two miles the other side of a lot of PLA infantry.

Marine Corsairs, arriving within minutes of the crash, began running opposition as soon as the column moved out. One, in fact, set fire to the downed Dakota with a .50-caliber tracer.

The jog back to Hagaru-ri was noisy and tense, but surprisingly uneventful. Jay Ransone had his new injuries treated and was hustled aboard the first available flight to the rear. He was safely tucked in bed at the MASH unit at Hamhung by dinnertime.

★

In the six days of its operational life, the Hagaru-ri airstrip (now a modern provincial airport) was directly responsible for the safe evacuation of 4,312 Army, Navy and Marine, Air Force and ROK casualties, relatively few of whom had been wounded or injured at Hagaru-ri.

During the same period, several hundred tons of ammunition and fuel, and other critically needed goods, were flown in or air-dropped by Air Force C-119 Flying Boxcars and Air Force, Army, and Navy Dakotas. Even more noteworthy, in its way, was the fact that five hundred thirty-seven Marine officers and enlisted men, scraped up from the Division rear and as far away as Japan, were flown in to help make good some of the losses in the embattled combat units.

Most of the men and matériel that arrived at Hagaru-ri got there largely through the efforts of the 1st Marine Division Logistics Officer, Colonel Francis McAlister. The senior officer at Division Rear, McAlister yearned to be in on the action, but was convinced by O. P. Smith and Al Bowser that he was the only man who could adequately represent the interests of the division at X Corps.

There was quite a bit of confusion attending the evacuation process. For the first two days of the operation, there was no adequate screening of the evacuees, and there is no doubt but that, to escape from Hagaru-ri, a fair number of laggards took the places of wounded men. Then the enormous influx of wounded from Yudam-ni added immeasurably to the confusion, for many of the injured were frostbite cases with no readily discernible symptoms.

In the end, after much soul-searching, the brass decided to relax their standards. The evacuation process was running smoothly, and no authentically injured man was in danger of being excluded. In a pinch, the garrison could hold the perimeter and airstrip a day or two longer than planned. In fact, the staff quickly came to realize that men who really wanted out would find ways to get out. (Sergeant Jim Friedl, of the 2nd Battalion, 5th, came within an ace of getting his hands on a sergeant who, it was said, intentionally froze his feet in order to buy a ticket out.)

The Word quickly spread: Any man who had any degree of frostbite could leave if he wanted to. A number of men took the option. What is commendable is that men who, perhaps, should have turned themselves in stayed with their units. And that made the troops who *had* to stay all the more comfortable with the reality of the situation: the undependable element, which would be a liability in the days and weeks ahead, had been cut free at one fell swoop. (Unfortunately, deep-seated reactions placed in the low regard of their peers a number of men who were authentically but not noticeably ill, and several promising career officers were eventually forced out of the Marine Corps because they elected to be flown out.)

★

The Hagaru-ri interlude was crucial to the well-being of the division and attached units. Just the opportunity to get some sleep went a long way toward restoring the Yudam-ni Marines to something like their former selves.

Discipline was loose, and that was good for everyone and, interestingly, for the organization. A lot of liquor was consumed by a lot of people, and not without its restorative effect or several notable excesses.

One of the more dramatic recoveries was made by Lieutenant Colonel Bill Harris. From a low point on the morning of November

28, when he seemed bound for a prisoner-of-war stockade once again, Harris's recuperative powers were constantly at work. At the low point, he had given away many of the fine personal items he had brought to the war in mid-November: his hunting rifle, his leather toilet kit, his binoculars. When the stability of the Yudam-ni garrison had been restored, Bill Harris's stability had likewise been restored, but his mental set seemed very much in tune with the ups and downs experienced by his battalion and his regiment. A good night's sleep under canvas at Hagaru-ri might have fully restored Bill Harris to the formerly positive, active, ebullient individual who had joined the 3rd Battalion, 7th, on the way up the mountain to Koto-ri.

But it was not to be.

After participating in an evening planning session, Harris had walked to his tent and turned in. At 2110 in the evening of December 5, the cold silence of the Korean night was pierced by the high-pitched roar of twin turbo-charged aircraft engines. A stick of 500-pound bombs was released between the bivouacs of the 1st and 3rd Battalions, 7th, and the bomber — an Air Force B-26 way out of its zone of operations — surged off into the night.

There was a mass of confusion, and bits of several kinds of hysteria. For example, Major Tom Tighe was thrown from his cot when one blast clashed with his keyed-up nerves. He found himself on the deck beside Lieutenant Colonel Ray Davis, who was trapped in his sleeping bag by a jammed quick-release zipper. It was one of the very few times that Tighe saw Davis in an agitated state, for the colonel was writhing about, totally helpless. Reaching over to help, Tighe could not resist asking, "What'll you give me if I let you out of this one?" A crazed look passed over the battalion commander's face, but it was immediately replaced by a smile and a hearty laugh.

Not so Bill Harris, who had last been bombed on Corregidor the day before the island in the entrance to Manila Bay was taken. The fragile sense of well-being that the young battalion commander had enjoyed during the previous few days was cut short. Bill Harris shielded himself behind a sullen, uncommunicative barrier that impacted upon his staff, which had to reshape a fighting battalion from bits and parts for a renewed offensive effort that was to begin within twenty-four hours of the bombing incident. Never a particularly communicative leader, Harris became all the more distant, inaccessible to all but a few of his most-trusted staff officers.

★

On the morning of December 5, Air Force Major General William Tunner, commander of the Far East Air Force Combat Cargo Command, flew into Hagaru-ri to lay a proposal before O. P. Smith. Tunner, whose stock with Smith was high for having overseen the resupply of the Marine base, was first given the profuse thanks of the normally reserved Marine division commander. But he next drew an icy stare, for he proposed evacuating the entire garrison by air. General Smith simply informed General Tunner that Marine cargo aircraft had flown in over five hundred replacements, and he could see no good reason to fly them back out.

★

X Corps had no role in the planning for the evacuation of Hagaru-ri over and above its unequivocal directive that the base be evacuated and obliterated. The task of planning the breakout fell upon the shoulders of Colonel Al Bowser.

Working for O. P. Smith had its benefits, but many of them sometimes seemed like mixed blessings. Al Bowser, at forty, was at the pinnacle of his profession. He was the chief planner for the only combat division the Marine Corps had in the field, a rare privilege with enduring honor. But, where most commanding generals participated actively in the planning process, O. P. Smith's style was to allow his subordinates to draw up plans that he would either approve or disapprove.

That style of command placed a heavy burden upon Al Bowser and Lieutenant Colonel Buzz Winecoff, and the lean operations staff upon which they relied at the Division Forward CP. Fortunately, Bowser had been operations officer of 3rd Marine Division during the Bougainville operation in early 1944. At that time he had had thirteen years active duty experience and no prior operations staff experience. In the winter of 1950 Bowser had served nineteen years in the Corps, and had as much staff and command experience as any of his peers.

Bowser envisioned the drive by the bulk of the reinforced division on Koto-ri as something like a moving laager. Infantry would lead the train out, and infantry would guard the flanks and the rear. The entire collection of men, vehicles, and equipment would move as a unit, everything in its place. But for needed air cover, the division would move as a self-contained entity and be self-supporting.

O. P. Smith looked at the plan and agreed to run with it, though he asked a few questions to hint at provisions *he* might have made. In the end, he left the matter entirely in Al Bowser's hands.

A meeting of senior staffers and troop commanders was called for the late morning of December 5 at the large tent Al Bowser shared with the Division Chief of Staff, Colonel Gregon Williams. Colonel

Bowser made the initial presentation, which was fleshed out with reports by staff section heads and their assistants. Specific assignments were handed out, and command relationships for the move were established.

While Al Bowser and other staffers were being questioned on specific points, the tent was rustled by the high-powered rotors of a helicopter. Within moments, an orderly announced that the X Corps commander was waiting outside for General Smith.

It soon became evident that Ned Almond had arrived with another pocketful of medals. The most senior officers were lined up and given their goodies: an Army Distinguished Service Cross for Ray Murray, and another for Litz; Lieutenant Colonel Olin Beall received a Silver Star for his part in rescuing the Task Force Faith survivors from the ice; and an embarrassing assortment of medals went to other men, too.

As Almond went about his chores, he turned to O. P. Smith, of the icy countenance, and chirped, "General, you have no worries. I have arranged for the Air Force to bomb a path clear for you all the way to the sea."

O. P. Smith just stared down at the corps commander, working a tart-enough response around in his mind: "I think, General, that there will be sufficient fighting for us all."

Later in the day, while explaining the breakout plan to several news reporters, Smith agreed to field some questions.

"General," one of the newsmen soon ventured, "all this adds up to a retreat."

O.P. gave that a moment's thought, for it was a fair surmise. The general, a man entirely bereft of any sense of personal aggrandizement, was about to utter what would become a legendary response, but he had no sense of that either. Ever the patient teacher, Smith said gently to the reporter, "No, not a retreat. It will be an attack in another direction."

Within twenty-four hours, newpapers throughout the United States were emblazoned with this headline: "Retreat Hell! We're attacking in another direction."

PART SEVEN

Retreat, Hell!

CHAPTER

37

Fox Company, 7th Marines — the *new* Fox/7 — had been placed under the command of 1st Lieutenant Ralph Abell at Toktong Pass within an hour of the relief of Fox Hill. And in the four days since the company had slowly made its way back to become as strong a fighting unit as there was in the 5th or 7th Marine Regiments. By stripping many technicians and clerks from the regimental and battalion headquarters companies, by cannibalizing the remnant of Dog/7 and dropping the unit from the battalion organization, by adding a sprinkling of excess artillerymen, by issuing new weapons and gear to the tough little cadre that had survived the ordeal of Fox Hill, higher headquarters turned Fox/7 into a worthy opponent for the Chinese holding the roadblocks south of the division base.

Of the four officers running the new Fox/7, only two — 1st Lieutenant Ralph Abell, the commander, and 1st Lieutenant John Dunne, the 1st Platoon leader — were trained combat infantry officers. The third officer was an artilleryman who at least knew about combat. But the fourth was 1st Marine Division's assistant historian, a likable young man fresh from the States, who was as bewildered to be with a combat infantry unit as the unit was to have him. After questioning the new man at length — after offering him the mortar section, or the machine guns, or either of the two vacant rifle-platoon commands — Ralph Abell took the new lieutenant's word for it that he was not a fighter. But the young man was game, and Abell kept him on as, of all things, his runner. Or, put another way, Ralph Abell might have been America's only first lieutenant with his own aide-de-camp.

Good, bad, or indifferent, Abell's Fox/7 was going to lead the division to Koto-ri, starting at 0400, December 6, 1950.

★

The very first moves from Hagaru-ri were made by Ray Davis's 1st Battalion, 7th, which moved immediately to the skyline east of the MSR, and by an Army company, which moved to the high ground to the left of the roadway to screen Ralph Abell's drive.

It was generally acknowledged that the key to the successful

march from Yudam-ni had been the ability of the Marines to control
the high ground dominating the MSR. The job facing the Hagaru-ri
force was in every way similar: the force on the road would have to
punch through the bulk of the opposition while units on the skyline
sought to control the Chinese response.

Mounting out at 0400, December 6, the Army company made initial rapid progress toward the heights, then stopped to await the
beginning of the drive by Lieutenant Colonel Randolph Lockwood's
2nd Battalion, 7th. Davis's battalion, which jumped off at the same
time, ran into some trouble effecting a passage of friendly lines, but
moved quickly once that maneuver had been completed. Progress
on the flanks was initially rapid. On the right, as Charlie/7 was passing Baker Company opposite the village of Tonsae-ri, it stumbled
into a Chinese platoon bivouac and butchered seventeen of twenty-
four Chinese before the startled defenders could roll from their blankets.

★

The Fox/7 men gathered in the shadow of East Hill were a grim
lot. Sergeant Brad Westerdahl, who had been seconded to Fox Company from the battalion intelligence section, had been told that all
opposition was to be swept aside no matter what, for Fox/7 was
stopping for nothing.

Ralph Abell spoke briefly with 1st Lieutenant Richard Primrose,
the tank officer who had conned D23 to Yudam-ni on November 27.
Primrose was raring to move in support of Fox/7, and he told Abell
that he could be on the line of departure in plenty of time, as soon
as his crews had warmed the engines of their heavy tanks.

It was impossible to surprise the Chinese with the initial thrust.
Demolition of the division base had been going on for more than a
day, and the many smoke plumes that marked burning dumps and
piles of debris were dead giveaways as to the intentions of the garrison. Fox/7, augmented to a strength of one hundred fifty effectives,
was in for a fight, no doubt about it.

The weather was bad. A great misty fog hung over the valley, so
aircraft overhead could not be accurately directed.

There was zero resistance. Fox Company advanced cautiously,
but quickly. The tanks, initially too cold to start, but cursed to life
by the embarrassed crews, roared up and began overtaking the company point.

Looking to the left as the heavy tanks were going by, Ralph Abell
spotted a knot of Chinese standing by the railroad embankment that
rose several feet above the roadway on that side. Rushing to the

nearest tank, the rifle company commander grabbed the intercom phone from the rear fender and attempted to reach the tank commander. The line was dead. Almost beside himself, Abell slung his rifle over his shoulder and clambered aboard, making his way to the turret through sporadic gunfire. After banging on the turret hatch for a moment, the infantry officer was relieved to see it raised an inch or two. A voice from within asked, "Who's there?" Feeling himself to be the butt of a grotesquely dangerous knock-knock joke, Abell shouted, "You idiot! Open up!"

The hatch popped open and the commander blinked in Abell's face. "What's going on?"

"Do you think you can turn this goddamn tank around and hit those people over by the embankment?"

"Oh, sure," the tanker replied. "Nothing to it." The turret motors whirred electrically as Abell dropped to the ground and scrabbled over to the far side of the roadway. The 90mm gun was lowered a few degrees. There was a brief pause, then a solid *"Carumph!"* The Chinese in the middle distance, who had not moved in long moments, were transformed to a shower of bone and gristle and blood.

★

To the rear, 1st Lieutenant Bob Bey's reconstituted Easy/7 was running into trouble just south of East Hill. The Chinese had let Abell's company pass without incident, but they had lowered the boom on Bey's.

A Marine fell dead under the sudden onset of Chinese fire. Everyone else flopped behind any available cover. Machine guns were set up beside the road, and the company 60mm mortars went into action as soon as the gunners had targets.

One of the machine gunners was hurled, dead, from behind his gun. The assistant gunner leaped forward to the trigger. Three Marine Sherman medium tanks equipped with bulldozer blades wheeled to the right side of the roadway and surged across a small field, throwing out 75mm rounds as quickly as the gunners could reload. The battalion 81mm mortars were humped forward by their crews and set up.

The Chinese bolted. First Lieutenant Neal Heffernan, the 2nd Battalion, 7th's forward air controller, called for air support, and walls of napalm were soon searing the Chinese line of retreat.

Moving forward to assist a wounded radioman, 1st Lieutenant James Chandler, the battalion intelligence officer, asked if he could be of help. "Hell no, Lieutenant," the cheery reply started, "I got my airplane ticket out of here. I'll crawl to the airfield if necessary!"

Farther on, Chandler picked up a platoon leader who had been shot in the legs and piggybacked him to the road for a quick ride to the airstrip.

The Chinese resistance was broken, but not before Bob Bey, who had survived the rigors of Hill 1282 and the attack down the MSR to Hagaru-ri unscathed, was lightly wounded. The last of the original Easy/7 officers, he opted to remain with his command.

★

High up on the flank, Able/7 took the lead from Charlie/7 and continued to struggle along the military crest above Fox Company, painstakingly crossing the many side valleys and draws that cut through the ridges at odd but frequent intervals, endeavoring to keep pace with Fox Company below — a losing proposition, but gamely tried. The flanking unit to the right of the MSR was less sure of itself.

The three hundred fifty members of the 31st Infantry who had reached Hagaru-ri and could still serve had been formed into a provisional battalion, known as 31/7, under the command of Major Carl Witte, the 31st's intelligence officer. King Company, 31st, one of the small companies of 31/7, had been sent to the ridge west of the road to protect that flank.

Emerging from the fight at the first roadblock, 1st Lieutenant Ralph Abell watched incredulously as a small Army unit filed off the heights and entered Fox/7's column. Searching out the bitterly cold Army captain who had led those troops to the road, Abell asked why the unit had abandoned its position on the heights. The Armyman mumbled something about the weather. And Ralph Abell blew up at him. The altercation that resulted was nearing an impasse when Litz stormed up and stalked from his jeep; he ordered the thin Army unit back onto the flanking ridge.

★

Marines evidenced a growing hostility to the Armymen in their midst. It was unfair for them to do so, but there was not a member of 1st Marine Division who did not feel that his plight in some way reflected a lack of concern on the part of the Armymen who ran X Corps. Since the Corps staff was not available to bear the Marines' rage — and since most Marines viewed the Chinese as being too pathetic to be the objects of smoldering derision — the full burden fell upon the survivors of Task Force Faith and several smaller elements of the 31st Infantry which had been north of Hagaru-ri. Those were the last soldiers who should have drawn such hostility, for they were men who had survived up to eight days of combat with the

Chinese. Moreover, theirs were small companies with no organic supporting arms taking on a job that would have troubled larger, rested, better-equipped units. It was an unfortunate turn of emotions, and it lingers yet.

★

After stopping briefly to wait for Easy Company to close up (it was still embroiled in its initial fight just south of East Hill), Ralph Abell was approached by the battalion executive officer, Major Buzz Sawyer, who ordered Fox Company to punch forward without waiting for the rest of the battalion; if Abell ran into serious opposition, he could call all available air and artillery to help bail him out.

Abell's company quickly gobbled up a total of four thousand yards from its line of departure. At that point, coming around a jog in the road, the lead squad drew fire from Chinese positions centered on a tiny cluster of straw huts known as Sangpyong-ni, which was situated on a hill-backed flat to the left of the MSR.

Sergeant Brad Westerdahl had recoiled to an icy stream bed to the right of the road — as did everyone else — the moment the shooting started. When the order "Fix bayonets!" was passed, Westerdahl prepared himself for a bloody fight.

Ralph Abell called his forward observer, 2nd Lieutenant Don Campbell, and asked if the Chinese positions could be reached by his 105s. "Sure can," Campbell replied.

"Okay. When you're on target, give me three star clusters. Then we'll go."

The artillery fired, the star clusters burst, and Sergeant Brad Westerdahl found himself in motion across the roadway.

Ralph Abell, who had never before called an air strike, gained contact with an orbiting Corsair division leader. After fumbling for the correct jargon for several precious seconds, Abell simply asked the airman if he could see Sangpyong-ni and the defended hillock right behind it.

After running one orbit, the Marine pilot said he had the defenders spotted. Then, while Abell rattled off a stream of quick grunts at his command group, the aircraft were cleared for the first run.

Sergeant Brad Westerdahl was not even conscious of the roaring aircraft engines as he legged across the open field toward the hillock. He was completely intent upon getting behind some cover at the expense of the slowly breaking defenders. Pockets filled with white-phosphorous grenades, Westerdahl evolved a neat gimmick for destroying one defended fighting hole after another. Leading another intelligence sergeant by a few feet, he dropped one of the grenades into each hole. As the Chinese, usually two to four to a hole, popped up to escape the burning chemical, the sergeant who was trailing simply blew them away with his Garand rifle.

After a few moments of trying to hold off the Marines, the Chinese broke and ran across the open fields to the rear of their positions.

Brad Westerdahl, on his way to becoming one of the Marine Corps' best rifle shots, had already won two of the three competitions required to earn his Distinguished Marksman badge, and he was armed appropriately with an old Springfield '03 bolt-action rifle. As the Chinese receded across the fields, Westerdahl found a comfortable spot, carefully wrapped his left forearm in the leather rifle sling, calmed himself down a mite, and flung round after round into the backs of the retreating enemy. One after another, the Chinese were bowled over onto their faces to lie motionless on the frozen fields beneath Brad Westerdahl's firing position.

After firing steadily for a few minutes, Westerdahl noticed that the fleeing Chinese were channeling into a narrow pathway across a deep ravine. Realigning his heavy Springfield rifle, he placed his sights on a particular spot and fired into the back of every mustard-yellow quilted uniform that appeared before his eye.

The turkey shoot went on for some time before a Chinese grenade pounded off the expert marksman's helmet and exploded, driving small metallic slivers into his head and shoulder. At the urging of his buddies, Westerdahl loped back down the hillock, crossed the road and settled onto the bank of a frozen stream bed to have his wounds treated. He was just getting ready to rejoin his platoon when someone he knew came by to say that a fellow member of the intelligence section had been killed.

Directed to a tree farther down the stream, Westerdahl came upon the seated body of Private First Class Jerry Kearns, an Indiana Regular who had served with the 2nd Battalion, 7th, since its formation. A bullet had entered Kearns's temple just below the helmet rim, and had killed him instantly. Knowing that Kearns was recently married, Sergeant Westerdahl removed the dead man's wedding band and took some personal papers from his field pack. If he survived, Westerdahl vowed, he would return the ring and the papers to his friend's widow.

Then, shouldering his rifle, he strode back across the roadway and mounted the slope behind Sangpyong-ni to rejoin his platoon. On the way up, he looked into Chinese fighting holes and saw the litter of hundreds of Christmas packages, which, though Westerdahl did not yet know it, had been rifled from the wreckage of the so-called Drysdale convoy that had been stopped and destroyed on the MSR on November 29.

Ralph Abell was approached by a rifleman from 1st Lieutenant John Dunne's 1st Platoon. "Sir, Mr. Dunne has been killed. He's up ahead."

Ralph Abell went into mild shock, for he and John Dunne were the last of the seven officers who had formed Fox Company at Camp Pendleton in July. Abell forced himself to take control as he stalked forward to stand over the small-seeming corpse of one of the men with whom he had been baptised in blood. He looked for only a moment, said a silent good-bye, and returned to the road to call his victorious platoons together. The roadblock had been opened, and Fox/7 had to get back to its advance.

When Fox/7 moved out of Sangpyong-ni, it left its 3rd Platoon leader behind, wounded and bleeding in the roadside ditch. Staff Sergeant John Audas, who had led his platoon with incredible drive after the first night on Fox Hill, had fought his first battle in November, 1942, as a young aerial gunner flying the rear seat of a Marine dive bomber sent to join in the sinking of a mortally damaged Japanese battleship that wallowed in the swells north of Guadalcanal. That had been quite a baptism, and three years of aerial combat in the Solomons and the Philippines had ensued. As with many former aircrewmen, John Audas had gone into the infantry when the dive bombers were phased out at the end of the Pacific War. He had led his troops brilliantly on Fox Hill and coming out of Hagaru-ri. But John Audas was not thinking about his career as he lay in that roadside ditch opposite Sangpyong-ni. He was thinking of his shattered, ruined foot; of the blood he was losing; of freezing to death; of the possibility of never being found, dead or alive, by fellow Marines.

To the rear, Easy/7 had completed the rout of the Chinese at the first roadblock and had closed up behind Fox Company, leading the first serials of the 7th Regiment's vehicle train. The Army company, King/31, could be seen trudging uphill to the left, and Baker/7 could be seen as it moved downslope to the right, under orders to support the roadbound companies in any future actions.

★

Fox Company, 7th, advanced a total of five thousand yards down the MSR by nightfall. The last thousand yards were taken without any form of opposition. When Lieutenant Abell requested instructions, he was told to continue his advance until he drew some fire.

The company moved cautiously into the defile near Pusong-ni, where the main body of Dog/Tanks and 41 Commando had been bushwacked on the night of November 29.

Even in the rank, cold darkness, the men of Fox and Easy Companies could discern wrecked, twisted vehicles on and beside the roadway. Increasingly, as they passed through the large laager that had been the haven of Major John McLaughlin and Captain Charlie Peckham, the men had to tiptoe around mounds of frozen corpses.

During one break, while troops on the flanks sought out a hidden machine gun which had engaged the company, Ralph Abell was called forward by one of his riflemen, who had heard a low voice from within one of the canted trucks beside the road. The voice was speaking in English, but the riflemen around it had convinced themselves that they could discern a trace of an accent.

"Who's in there?" Abell called out.

"I'm a wounded American. I'm trapped."

Mulling that over for a moment, Abell hurled back, "Who's Stan Musial?"

"Um, . . . I think he plays baseball for the Cards."

Somewhat reassured, Abell helped free the injured man, who turned out to be a very lucky GI from Ohio. "I don't know much about baseball, Sir," the boy apologized, "but I sure know about Stan Musial, huh?"

But for that one bright spot, the task of walking through Hellfire Valley, as it came to be called, was a somber affair.

★

Fox Company was held up by a Chinese machine gun again at 2200 and sideslipped by Easy Company while the gun was hunted down and destroyed. The point next moved about twelve hundred yards to a blown bridge and set up a perimeter defense while 1st Lieutenant Ozzie Vom Orde's platoon of Dog Company, 1st Engineer Battalion, clanked forward to construct a bypass. Movement recommenced at 0200, December 7, to a second blown bridge, then picked up again at 0300 when Easy/7 moved off for the last leg into Koto-ri. But for the wrecked bridges, Lockwood's battalion encountered zero opposition while covering the last several miles into the southernmost American bastion on the Taebek Plateau.

Another vital link had been forged. A chain of men and vehicles extended along the full length of the MSR between the diminished base at Hagaru-ri and the suddenly burgeoning base at Koto-ri. While Lockwood's two-company battalion had been moving doggedly down the road to link up with Puller, serious fighting on the road and on East Hill was threatening to destroy the carefully conceived plan by which the breakout was being directed.

***

CHAPTER

38

At 1000 hours on the morning of December 5, 1950, after Lieutenant Colonel Hal Roise's battalion had had a night's rest within the protection of the Hagaru-ri perimeter, the officer received a call from his boss, Lieutenant Colonel Ray Murray. The 2nd Battalion, 5th, was to relieve Captain Carl Sitter's George/1 and attached units on East Hill in order to protect the column of twelve hundred vehicles and seven rifle and three artillery battalions that would be passing beneath the hill on the way to Koto-ri.

Private First Class Bob Kennedy, a Dog/5 BAR-man, was sitting on the straw-covered floor of a native house, contemplating the two blackened toes he had found upon pulling off his shoepacs in order to replace his worn socks with a fresh pair liberated from one of the many open supply dumps within the perimeter. Officers filtering through the mass of recumbent bodies in the straw-filled room passed The Word: Roise's battalion was rear guard again. It would have to hold East Hill until the 7th Marines, the 11th Marines, the remnants of 7th Infantry Division units, the Marine division headquarters and service units, splinters of X Corps service units, the other two battalions and headquarters of the 5th Marines — everyone else — left the base.

The face of East Hill was so steep, and the snow upon it was worn so slick, that the troops had to pull themselves uphill hand over hand on ropes that previous occupiers had rigged. The Chinese farther up did not hamper the relief, and the move was carried out fully by 1600 hours, December 5, when Roise's troops were tied in with Lieutenant Colonel Jack Stevens's 1st Battalion, 5th, on the left, and Lieutenant Colonel Tom Ridge's battered 3rd Battalion, 1st, on the right.

At a meeting held on the afternoon of December 5, Ray Murray outlined the evacuation plan for his senior commanders and their staffs: "We'll hold our present positions until the 7th Marines clear the road to Koto, after which we'll move out. When we do move out, we will come out as Marines, and not as stragglers. We're going to take our dead, wounded, and equipment when we leave. We're coming out, I tell you, as Marines, or not at all. Any officer who doesn't think that we can get out of here will kindly get frostbite and go lame, and I'll see that he's evacuated."

Later that day, at 2200 hours, Murray informed Hal Roise that the 2nd Battalion, 5th, was to seize the high ground on East Hill northeast of the present Marine line on the slope. Someone had belatedly realized that the Chinese atop the hill could lay their weapons upon the roadbound column that would be passing beneath the hill beginning at 0400 the next morning. Division had requested that the attack be mounted to minimize the danger to the soft vehicles. Captain Sam Smith's Dog Company, 5th, augmented by a platoon from Easy/5, was to mount the sweep from its positions high on the slope. The attack would commence after a bombardment by the regimental 4.2-inch heavy mortars and an air strike at 0700.

★

The four-deuces opened fire on schedule. As the tense riflemen waited for their officers to signal the attack, the heavy mortar rounds plowed up rubble at the summit for fifteen minutes, ceasing in time to allow the scheduled air strike to begin.

It was quiet for a full minute. No aircraft were yet on station. A quick call from Battalion got the heavy mortars back into action until 0725, when the leading Corsair pilots reported to Roise's forward air controller, Captain Manning Jeter. The pilots told Jeter not to expect any napalm because of a shortage of tanks that day.

A total of seventy-six Marine and Navy land- and carrier-based aircraft participated in the East Hill strikes, the largest single air operation against a single objective during the campaign. They blew and blasted and strafed and stung the Chinese for fully ninety minutes while the Dog/5 riflemen, sitting on a hump across a saddle from the main body of the hill, blasted away ceaselessly with their small arms.

Captain Jeter, the forward air controller, was seriously wounded as he stood in full view of the Chinese, the better to see what was going on. He was immediately and smoothly replaced by Captain Dave Johnson, whose familiar Boston-accented voice cheerily broadcast calls for precision strikes against known Chinese strongpoints.

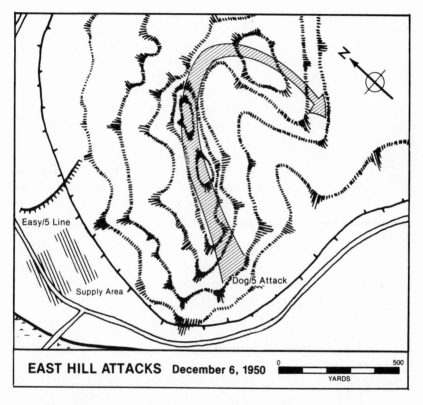

EASY/5 Line

Supply Area

Dog/5 Attack

EAST HILL ATTACKS December 6, 1950

0   500
YARDS

(See endpapers for GUIDE TO MAP SYMBOLS AND ABBREVIATIONS.)

Assisting the precision air strikes was Dog/5's 3.5-inch rocket expert, Private First Class Oakie Douglas, who had won acclaim outside of Seoul in September when he knocked out five North Korean T-34 tanks within twenty minutes; General Douglas MacArthur, who had arrived at the front minutes after the destruction had been completed, had smilingly accused Douglas and the Marine Corps of staging the event to bring the then-underrated 2.36-inch bazooka some needed publicity. On the morning of December 6, Oakie Douglas put on another display of pinpoint fire, pitting his bazooka against Chinese entrenchments. Judging from the crazed smile that remained fixed on his bearded countenance, he enjoyed the work immensely.

At 0900, precisely, Captain Sam Smith passed The Word to 1st Lieutenant Swede Sorenson, whose 3rd Platoon rose to lead the way up the steep, slippery slope, pulling 1st and 2nd Platoons behind it. However, before Sorenson progressed fifty yards across the saddle, his unit was pinned by a withering cross fire. As the veteran platoon leader attempted to rally his men, he was wounded severely in the left shoulder and evacuated. His replacement, 1st Lieutenant John Hinds, the company mortar officer, reorganized 3rd Platoon while sister units a short distance to the rear maneuvered to place flanking fire on the Chinese guns.

Private First Class Bob Kennedy, of the 2nd Platoon, loped forward, firing his heavy BAR from the offhand position as his platoon prepared to attack in Hinds's support. Captain Smith ordered 1st Lieutenant Richard Johnson's 1st Platoon to deliver a flank attack upon the Chinese strongpoint.

At a word from the company commander, the three rifle platoons rose as one and pressed in upon the Chinese line, which simply evaporated.

As soon as Hinds's 3rd Platoon seized the first knob, Sam Smith ordered 1st Lieutenant George McNaughton to lead his 2nd Platoon against the second knob, which was higher up. At the same time, Hal Roise ordered Fox/5 to dispatch a platoon to relieve the Dog/5 units on the first knob so that they could support McNaughton's platoon.

The ground that Dog/5 would have to seize lay in a rough U, with the base pointing north. Thus, the initial moves were northward, and would be followed by moves to the south. The saddles connecting the staggered heights were too narrow to support more than one rifle platoon at a time, so Dog/5 was faced with the problem of delivering very limited assaults against Chinese positions which could, in the beginning at any rate, be supported by flanking fire from still other Chinese positions on the opposite arm of the U.

While his 3rd Squad engaged the Chinese on the next knob with long-range fire, Lieutenant McNaughton ventured into the open with the remainder of the platoon. As soon as he got moving, the officer sent a sergeant back to bring 3rd Squad forward. When it did not get forward, McNaughton just continued without it. The lost squad had, in the meantime, taken brutal flanking fire, which injured all but two men and the sergeant who had been sent to fetch it.

McNaughton delivered his assault with twenty men. Stepping into the open, each man had to pass the company machine-gun officer, 1st Lieutenant Karle Seydel, the last of the officers who had brought Dog/5 to Korea. Seydel, a Seattle Reservist, was standing tall, firing his .45-caliber automatic pistol at the Chinese across the way.

Bob Kennedy and his assistant gunner, Private First Class Tony Lima, clomped across the open ground, mounted the next slope and chased a knot of Chinese down the reverse slope of the platoon objective. Nearby, a Marine went down, hit by gunfire from the next knob forward. The platoon's Navy corpsman passed Kennedy and Lima and let himself down the steep slope to help the wounded Marine. Unable to hold his stance on the steep, slippery ground, however, the Navy man held up his left hand, which Kennedy and Lima grasped while he worked on the wounded Marine. A minute later, the corpsman was hit, and the two BAR-men had to pull him and the earlier victim back onto the saddle. Before they could do more, the BAR-men were ordered forward to take part in an assault on the next knob.

There was heavy fire from Chinese emplacements across the way, to the right. Bob Kennedy was trailing Tony Lima when a round penetrated his right thigh, leaving a clean through-and-through wound, knocking Kennedy on his butt. While feeling around with his grimy fingers to assess the damage, Kennedy noted how gooey the hole was. Within moments, a rifleman from another platoon came by and asked what the matter was. On hearing that the BAR-man had been hit, the rifleman demanded that he hand over the automatic rifle. Kennedy was glad to oblige, but insisted that he be given the other man's Garand rifle in exchange. The trade was hastily consummated, and the other man charged forward. Bob Kennedy's first reaction was to see if the Garand had any bullets in it, for he had also handed over his beltful of BAR magazines. Cranking the chamber open, he found that he had four rounds. He also realized that he had fought his last fight of the day.

Using the Garand rifle as a crutch, Bob Kennedy hobbled after Dog Company until he found a corpsman, who slit through several layers of trousers and poured liberal doses of sulfa powder onto the wound before bandaging it. Kennedy next joined a larger group of casualties, and stayed with it when everyone slid down to an aid station at the base of the hill.

While Dog/5 continued to take ground on East Hill, Bob Kennedy boarded a jeep and was driven to the door of a C-47, which was filled with colorful parachutes recovered from air-dropped supply containers. Kennedy jumped aboard and curled up in the soft, warm silk as the aircraft surged into the air. He was at Yonpo before Dog/5 finished its day's fighting.

★

By the time George McNaughton's platoon crossed the saddle on which Bob Kennedy had been hit, only fifteen of the twenty riflemen who started the attack remained, and four of them had been lightly injured. Coming into position, the platoon leader spotted about two hundred fifty PLA infantrymen between him and the road to Koto-ri, which was to the south. The two men from the destroyed 3rd Squad arrived at that point, and word from Captain Smith indicated that the bulk of Fox Company was moving forward to relieve the other Dog/5 platoons, which were outposting knobs to the rear. Meantime, McNaughton was to mount a patrol into the Chinese-held draw and eliminate the Chinese force there. That put eighteen Marines up against two hundred fifty Chinese.

Leaving his wounded on the hill under the protection of the bulk of the demi-platoon, George McNaughton led only four riflemen into the draw. To the rear, 1st Lieutenant Richard Johnson's 1st Platoon built up a base of fire which could reach out and support McNaughton and his four men. One of the four was hit in the foot, and McNaughton placed him in a position from which he could support the others.

Unbelievably, the Chinese opposition evaporated under the lightest touch. Over one hundred fifty PLA soldiers *surrendered* to the astonished Marine platoon leader and his three cohorts.

While Fox Company and elements of the 5th Antitank Company, bolstered by thirty-two members of the Army's 4th Signal Battalion, moved into positions to the rear, Captain Sam Smith ordered his understrength Dog Company to dig in. The Chinese seemed to be preparing a massive counterattack as the day gave way to the night.

★

The Chinese who were planning to drive through the newly won Marine positions on East Hill were embarked upon a high-stakes game that neither side could really afford to lose. The entire 7th Marine Regiment and the first divisional motor convoy, with a significant portion of the 11th Marines, had already left Hagaru-ri and were strung along ten miles of the MSR. At the same time, several PLA divisions, at the least, were moving along parallel valleys to try to mount blows they hoped would segment the long vehicle columns.

The entire 5th Marine Regiment, with Tom Ridge's 3rd Battalion, 1st, and Harvey Feehan's 1st Battalion, 11th, had remained at the former division base, as had a number of Marine and Army service and special units, which were to complete the job of destroying the defenses and the dumps.

The Hagaru-ri garrison was, as always, most vulnerable in the East Hill sector, partly because of the ability of the Chinese to build up assault forces in the broken terrain behind the hill, and particularly because of the critical vulnerability of the MSR, which passed right alongside the hill. If the MSR could be severed, the Americans remaining at Hagaru-ri might escape, but they would have to forfeit all of their soft vehicles and all of the supplies those vehicles carried.

The last of the division fuel and ammunition dumps, which had neither been emptied nor readied for demolition by crews that expected to work through the night, lay across the road from and directly beneath East Hill. Those dumps had to be kept safe above all else, for the vast stocks of explosives and ammunition within them could have been used to destroy 1st Marine Division several times over were they to fall into the hands of Chinese soldiers long used to putting American matériel to use against Americans.

Preparations for the defense of Hagaru-ri began in earnest well before nightfall, which was at 1730.

It began snowing at 1930.

The Chinese mounted what appeared at the outset to be a spirited, last-ditch effort against Dog/5, which was spread thin, covering all the knobs along the U-shaped summit of East Hill. Tanks on the flanks and the battalion's own 60mm and 81mm mortars, coupled with well-situated machine guns, lashed out at the Chinese who swarmed up the slopes toward Dog Company and its supports. The attack was driven back, but erupted anew within moments, as the Chinese regrouped to deliver their customary one-two left-and-right jabs.

The brunt of the attack fell upon 1st Lieutenant John Hinds's 3rd Platoon of Dog/5. The Chinese eventually closed to within grenade-throwing range, and inflicted numerous casualties upon the desperate Marines. First Lieutenant James Honeycutt, the Dog/5 exec, was wounded as he moved to plug a gap in the 3rd Platoon line.

First Lieutenant Karle Seydel, the Dog/5 machine-gun platoon leader, was right on top of his light machine guns, pumping out automatic pistol rounds as fast as he could, accounting for at least seven of the attackers.

Corporal Fred Walz, one of Karle Seydel's machine gunners, sent his assistant, Private First Class Warren Howard, to fetch hand grenades while he strove to hold off the Chinese. When Howard returned, the two gunners alternated between firing their little air-cooled .30-caliber machine gun and bowling grenades downhill at the swarming Chinese. Many of the attackers were killed within ten feet of Walz's gun.

The pressure undulated for nearly three hours. First Lieutenant George McNaughton was badly wounded, as was the 1st Platoon leader, 1st Lieutenant Richard Johnson. Neither would accept relief.

By 0300, Smith's company could not hold any longer, and the company commander reluctantly ordered his troops to sideslip to the left, toward the lines of Captain Uel Peters's Fox/5. Despite their wounds, Lieutenants George McNaughton and Richard Johnson sparked a tough delaying action as the bulk of the company moved to the left. Lieutenant Karle Seydel was shot to death as he moved to rally his withdrawing gunners.

When Dog Company reassembled within Fox Company's lines, Captain Smith and his last uninjured officer could muster only eighty men.

★

On the far side of Fox Company, Captain Sam Jaskilka's Easy/5, strung out along an embankment supporting narrow-gauge railroad tracks, received blistering mortar fire before the Chinese launched a massed assault against Staff Sergeant Russ Borgomainero's 1st Platoon. The initial thrust was so swift, in fact, that the Chinese nearly carried Borgomainero's position, a near repeat of the initial fighting the night of November 27–28. The attackers actually captured a Marine light machine gun, which they were in the process of turning upon Americans, when Corporal Jack Williams swung around the heavy machine gun he was manning thirty yards to the left. However, Williams's gun could not reach, so he took off alone across the open ground, killing several Chinese and recapturing the light machine gun, which he turned back to its Marine crew. Corporal Williams was shot to death as he returned to his own gun.

As pressure upon Borgomainero's position mounted steadily, Sergeant Andrew Dunay, a section leader with the regimental antitank platoon that had been sent to flesh out the Easy/5 line, dashed forward to take a bazooka from the hands of a gunner who had been knocked unconscious by a Chinese concussion grenade. Dunay fired white phosphorous at the Chinese until the launcher failed, then hurled charged rockets by hand, thus saving a machine-gun position that was severely threatened.

The attacks against Easy/5 continued until 0630, December 7, but the Chinese never really penetrated the company line.

★

To the rear, confusion was complete among Roise's headquarters troops, who had been deployed around one of the huge dumps at the foot of East Hill.

Initially, Captain Stretch Mayer, the battalion headquarters commandant, had had a dreadful time getting his clerks and technicians out of their snug tents and onto a perimeter line around the huge dump. While the fighting raged atop East Hill and over by Easy Company's line along the railroad embankment, the headquarters people had to battle only the cold.

Then the dump began taking mortar fire from the far side of East Hill. Captain Mayer actually heard a round boring closer and closer, and was not surprised when it landed six or eight feet in front of his CP, followed immediately by a second round. Both were duds. (When Mayer dug them up in the morning, he found two rusted 82mm rounds, which must have been carried by hand from Manchuria.)

As the mortar barrage continued, the headquarters people looked through flashes of gunfire on the perimeter and saw Chinese soldiers scrabbling up the stacks of crates that filled the dump.

The headquarters company line was thin. There was a lot of ground to cover, and limited numbers for covering it. Moreover, Mayer was certain that a number of his men — including his two senior sergeants — had walked back to their warm tents.

Opening with his own carbine, Mayer soon had the entire line banging away at the briefly lighted targets among the crates. Suddenly a huge fire fight erupted on the right, where Easy Company was holding forth. The dump began burning in several places, and

hordes of Chinese swarmed over the crates, clearly intent upon finding food and warm clothing. They were a disorganized rabble, incapable of fighting.

The headquarters Marines became confused by the mounting action. It was clear that Easy/5 was in desperate straits, so the headquarters people began plugging away in the general direction of the
greatest hubbub. Immediately, Stretch Mayer ventured along the
line, booting Marines in their butts to get their attention, to get them
to stop firing into the rear of Sam Jaskilka's company. A furious,
scathing call from Captain Jaskilka got a hurried acknowledgement
from Captain Mayer, who strove even harder to control his troops. It
was an honest error by inexperienced troops, and no one was hurt.
But there were a lot of angry, rattled Easy/5 riflemen come morning.

The Chinese never were driven from the dump.

★

To the left of Easy/5, holding positions astride the road from
Yudam-ni, Captain Jack Jones's Charlie/5 withstood an extremely
heavy attack at just about the time Easy Company was hit. The
troops were in well-developed positions, and the Chinese had to
mount their assault across open ground, right into the teeth of pre-
registered mortar fire, which was directed with brutal accuracy.
Pressing closer despite grievous losses, the Chinese nearly penetrated the Marine line. Captain Jones called forward an Army Sherman tank, one of three from the 31st Medium Tank Company which
were backing the line. The tank and the ground troops chewed the
attackers to bits, forcing the living Chinese to withdraw before midnight.

★

To the left of Charlie/5, Captain James Heater's Able/5 had settled
in early. The company had drawn several small Chinese probes
shortly after the snowfall began, between 1930 and 2000 hours, and
Chinese artillery dropped a few rounds into the company sector.

Second Lieutenant Nick Trapnell, as rested as anyone after a day
of sleeping and eating and lying around, fell into a bunker filled
with headquarters people to share the warmth. One of the senior
noncoms was proudly sharing his family snapshots with anyone who
cared to look, then left to check on his heavy machine guns, which
had to be fired at regular intervals lest they freeze in the brutal cold.
Minutes after he left the bunker, the proud family man was killed
by one of the intermittent Chinese registration rounds, the battalion's first casualty of the night.

At about 2100, while the Chinese were mounting serious assaults against Dog/5 on East Hill and light probes against Charlie/5, adjacent to the right, Nick Trapnell heard from the troops holding the right sector of the Able/5 line; they were growing restless, their senses abuzz with the instinctive taste for combat that veterans work themselves up to on such nights.

Although no one in the company could actually see or hear anything extraordinary on their front, Trapnell allowed the troops to toss out a few illumination grenades, of which only one in four worked. All that could be seen was a panorama lifted from a Christmas card; it was that peaceful.

The anxiety passed by osmosis from the right to the middle sector of the company line, and then on to the left. Everyone became increasingly jumpy; perhaps there was a Chinese patrol somewhere "out there."

Nick Trapnell settled in behind one of the heavy machine guns with Gunnery Sergeant Orville McMullen and the Able Company gunney, an old salt named Hodge. Hodge was tearing adhesive tape from the tops of grenade canisters, getting ready for some heavy fighting; the others were trying to decide whether or not they should fire a burst of tracer to see what happened. Trapnell was reluctant to reveal the gun's position, but eventually agreed to a quick burst when the sergeants suggested that the gun could be moved farther along the line to a new position.

The three men — Trapnell, McMullen, and Hodge — hunched over the shoulder of the gunner like three baseball umpires, straining their eyes to see what the snowy blackness might reveal in the wispy light of several tracers. The tension was electric.

Nick Trapnell, the youngest but most senior in rank, whispered a choked, terse command: "Fire!"

The gunner expertly squeezed off a five-round burst.

Gunnery Sergeant Hodge murmured a choked, *"G-a-w-d-damn!"*

The tracers and brief muzzle flash illuminated a small portion of a solid wall of tightly packed PLA infantrymen extending completely across the front. The PLA soldiers had crept noisely through the new snow and had crossed the barbed wire in front of the gun emplacement.

There was one beat of still, dead silence. Then pandemonium.

Every round, aimed or not, struck human flesh amidst the tightly packed phalanx of mustard-yellow infantry.

Chinese artillery and mortars opened with full salvos.

Trapnell's ammunition supply drained before anyone noticed. None of the officers or noncoms could exert much fire control over the keyed-up Marines, whose fire simply chewed the Chinese ranks to ribbons. But there were more Chinese than any of them had ever dreamed there might be.

★

In his own opinion, Lieutenant Colonel Jack Stevens won his spurs as a battalion commander that night.

Originally an airman, Stevens had been kept from the Pacific to train many of the men who did see battle. A wrangle with a superior over training procedures had kept him from receiving a key promotion to major late in the war and, though he was a Basic School classmate of both Hal Roise and Bill Harris, Stevens was junior to both. In fact, he had joined Roise's battalion as executive officer some months earlier, and had not been moved up until the former commander of the 1st Battalion, 5th, had been rotated home after the fall of Seoul. Until the night of December 6, Stevens had been spared the hard decisions that are the inevitable lot of rifle-battalion commanders, and he had not been willing, until that night, to really assert himself in his important role.

The battalion CP, set up hastily in a large empty structure about one hundred fifty yards behind the line manned by Able and Charlie Companies, was used by many Marines that early evening as a place to warm up. Some of the visitors were pretty senior people, including Ray Murray and his exec, Lieutenant Colonel Joe Stewart.

When the main Chinese attacks hit Charlie and Easy Companies, both Murray and Stewart had urged Jack Stevens to commit his reserve company, 1st Lieutenant John Hancock's Baker/5, to the fight. But something on the back edge of the battalion commander's instinct caused him to dig in his heels and wait. As the pressure on the line, and from the senior officers, mounted, Stevens determined to stick it out. He had an open line to the Baker Company CP, and he knew that the company could be fully committed with a few hasty syllables.

Then word of the hornet's nest in front of Able Company flashed aloud on the command net. Reports of fierce action and several penetrations galvanized Stevens and his staff, and Baker Company was ordered to battle.

★

When 2nd Lieutenant Bull Collins, the smallest of the Able/5 platoon leaders, spotted many Chinese stretcher bearers knifing through his platoon's position, it dawned on him that the enemy was being more thorough than usual about policing the battleground.

Though usually highly sensitive to the plight of injured men, Collins resorted to a simple trick to drive away the stretcher bearers. When a stretcher team passed close enough, the wiry lieutenant dropped a live grenade onto the stretcher. To his amazement, the grenade set off a case of ammunition. After that, every time a stretcher passed close enough to Collins or any of his men, a grenade was deposited on it with no thoughts about maiming wounded Chinese.

Five times that night, Nick Trapnell's platoon ran so low on ammunition that the survivors had to resort to cold steel to hold the line while new supplies were carried forward under intense fire. The minefield constructed by engineers on the wooded nose leading to the Able/5 line was the company's salvation, for Chinese using the spur to cover their approach eventually activated every one of the hundreds of mines, booby traps, and trip flares that studded the frozen field.

It got quiet at about 0400, just long enough to give an over-optimistic squad leader time to say, "Hot dawg! They're goin' home!" Whistles and horns were sounded before the last word had evaporated in the wind. By that time, Able/5 was down to seventy-five of the one hundred men it had fielded at sunset. Baker Company was just about used up, and there were no more reserves. Everyone prayed out loud for the sun, which would bring Marine Air into the fight.

The spirit of the Chinese attacks waned appreciably as the survivors were called upon to negotiate the growing mounds of their dead and wounded countrymen. The tide slowly turned, but the killing continued.

As the wispy sun appeared over East Hill, trained marksmen took to their gunslings and went to prone positions in the clear, each with his own coach to spot targets and hits. The Able Company line soon resembled a Stateside target range. Nick Trapnell had fallen heir to a Garand rifle with a sniperscope the day before, when one of his crack squad leaders had been evacuated. Even using the scope, he needed two or three rounds for each target. On the other hand, Gunnery Sergeant Orville McMullen peered over iron sights at sunrise and squeezed off but eight rounds, killing eight Chinese.

At dawn, every Marine in Able Company found that he was covered from head to toe with picric acid dust from the cheap explosive the Chinese used for their concussion grenades. Brass cartridge cases were knee-deep in some places, and, here and there, bodies were piled up to six feet deep. The shock of the cold no doubt took the lives of many lightly wounded Chinese and several Marines who might otherwise have survived.

★

In the middle of the morning, after the shooting had stopped, but before his Marines moved forward to police up the incredible mixed array of weapons the Chinese carried into battle, Ray Murray crossed the small stone bridge on the road leading north from the 1st Battalion's sector. Murray had been a battalion commander at Guadalcanal, Tarawa, and Saipan (where he had been badly wounded on the beach), and he had commanded the 5th Marines at Pusan, Inchon, Seoul, and through the advance to Yudam-ni. As he ambled forward four or five hundred yards in the dead silent sunlight, he saw more enemy dead than he had ever seen in one place before. In fact, spread in an arc from Able/5's left front to the slopes on the back side of East Hill, and on into the dumps at the base of the hill, at least eight hundred Chinese lay in grotesque attitudes of the violent ends they had met in the night. Here and there, even hours after the shooting had stopped, Murray saw that their quilted tunics were still smoldering from smudges of white phosphorous. It had been a ghastly execution.

When he returned to his CP, Murray learned that the 7th Regiment was well along on its walk to Koto-ri, and he authorized the troops and vehicles under his command to begin moving out of the former division base.

Between the head of the column, which had begun straggling into Koto-ri at about 0500, December 7, and the tail of the column, which would not leave Hagaru-ri until after noon, battles large and small raged among Marines and soldiers on the ridges and the Chinese divisions that had been sent quickly to stop them.

There were triumphs. And tragedies.

C H A P T E R

39

As Dog/5 struggled and bled upon the slopes and across the saddles and knobs of East Hill, as the bulk of the 5th Marines and its supports waited to see what the Chinese around Hagaru-ri might do, the 7th Marines, two battalions of the 11th Marines, one of two divisional motor columns, and the demi-battalion of Army combat infantrymen called 31/7 passed beneath the hill and turned south toward Koto-ri — and salvation.

While the two companies of Lieutenant Colonel Randolph Lockwood's 2nd Battalion, 7th, led the column forward, PLA regiments moved across the jumbled hills and ridges on the flanks in a mad effort to place their superior and maneuverable numbers on positions from which they might block the MSR, segment the Marine column, and destroy, piecemeal, the entire American force.

Following Lockwood's battalion was Lieutenant Colonel Bill Harris's 3rd Battalion, 7th, which was providing a security screen on the heights to the left of the roadway. Harris's troops were following the 3rd Provisional Battalion, 31st Infantry (known to Marines as 31/7) and were directly above the divisional and regimental vehicle column that was in the care of the 7th Marines.

For most of the daylight hours of December 6, the bulk of the column on the roadway experienced only long-range fires by clusters of Chinese machine guns, a favorite Chinese tactic aimed more at slowing the column than at doing much killing.

While the leading companies of the 2nd Battalion, 7th, made steady progress through most of the day, the vehicle column, of necessity, moved much more slowly. In fact, except for the leading companies, the roadbound troops barely passed Tonsae-ri, at the head of Hellfire Valley, by nightfall.

★

The small Army rifle companies had a miserable day of it.

Nearly all of the able-bodied American and South Korean survivors of Task Force Faith and the 31st Infantry's forward headquarters group had been organized into four small provisional rifle companies. Three of the companies — Item, King, and Love — were designated the 3rd Provisional Battalion, 31st Infantry, and placed under the 31st's Intelligence Officer, Major Carl Witte. The fourth company was actually a "battalion unit" which retained its identity as the 1st Battalion, 32nd Infantry, though, like each of the other companies, it mustered only about one hundred effectives. The entire Army combat unit, known to Marines as 31/7, was placed under the command of Lieutenant Colonel Barry Anderson, the 31st Infantry's haughty operations officer.

Nearly all of the men in those small companies were survivors and, though the desire to bring the war to the Chinese burned fiercely in their hearts, many of those men had been fought out days earlier. At most, 31/7, which lacked organic supporting arms, mustered four hundred officers and men, including troops from the disbanded 57th Field Artillery Battalion.

Captain George Rasula, the 31st Infantry's assistant operations officer, had been given about one hundred American artillerymen and South Korean infantrymen designated Item/31. He was happy to be commanding a combat unit, but he was depressed over the condition of that company, only too well aware that he had had not nearly enough time to get it organized. An accomplished tactician, Rasula sensed that his boss, Lieutenant Colonel Barry Anderson, had sold the Marine planners on sending the ill-equipped Armymen to the left flank without giving much attention to the incredibly jumbled terrain, or the possibility that the Chinese would use that easily defended ground to base their main resistance to the breakout. He did not particularly blame Anderson for arranging an important role for the disenfranchised little command, but he had to wonder at the enormity of the task Anderson had wangled.

Though Rasula was gratified by the spirit exhibited by his platoon leaders, a mixed bag of artillerymen with little if any infantry combat experience, he found himself reacting to a dose of depression and previous combat-command experience at Peleliu in a bizarre sort of way; fearing that the Chinese might be as avid collectors of trinkets as he knew some Americans were, the captain camouflaged his wedding ring with a Band-Aid in the hope that the ring finger would not be severed from the corpse he might become once the shooting started.

After watching an impressive show put on by Marine and Navy fighters and attack bombers, George Rasula prepared to lead an assault against a ridge about two hundred yards out and somewhat lower than his vantage point. As the air show wound down, Rasula waved his troops on, thankful to be moving.

The one hundred Armymen surged forward to encounter the surprise of their lives. Keyed up to deliver a desperate assault against fearsome resistance, the GIs and South Koreans walked across the proposed battleground, collecting all of one hundred-fifteen cowed Chinese who stood up, hands in the air, the moment Item/31 jumped off. Not one shot was fired by either side, partly because the one machine gun that had been assigned to Rasula's company went out of commission before pumping out even one round.

Though it was Rasula's desire to continue to lead the advance along the left flank hills, he was certain that doing so would spell the demise of the fearful Chinese prisoners, so he decided to turn the point over to the next company in column and see the Chinese safely to the roadway. Torn between relief and disappointment, Rasula had his troops usher the prisoners down the hill and see them safely into the care of Marine MPs.

Unable to communicate with higher authority because his one radio had quit working, Captain Rasula decided to keep the meager company on the road.

At nearly dusk, December 6, Major Carl Witte, commander of the 3rd Provisional Battalion, 31st, came upon a house bordered by a low stone fence that crossed the road and ran up the slope to the right. Witte knew that the fence might serve as a useful checkpoint for units on the flank, so he stood by it in the gloom until he saw a sputtering Chinese concussion grenade land on the road. That grenade did no damage, but before Witte could react other grenades went off around him. Although one exploded on his left shoulder and sent him reeling, he got right back up and joined a group of fellow GIs in an attack upon the walled house compound. The garden-wall door was kicked down, and a room behind it was liberally sprayed. Four or five Chinese were killed, as was Witte's radioman and an Army officer.

When the excitement died down and the effect of the adrenalin in his system tapered off, Carl Witte felt considerable pain in his injured shoulder. A Marine tank officer appeared at that moment and helped Witte up to the rear deck of his tank, where the major could warm up.

A tanker by trade, Carl Witte was helped into the Marine heavy tank and briefly got a seat when the gunner dropped to the roadway to pace the circulation back into his cold, cold feet. Later, after climbing woozily back to the roadway, Witte tottered the remaining several miles to Koto-ri.

Captain George Rasula was next senior to Major Witte, but he was lost among the masses of men on the darkened road and did not receive a message from Witte appointing him to command the 3rd Provisional Battalion, which had no leadership for what remained of its journey into Koto-ri.

For his part, George Rasula got a dose of the bile that was rising in the throats of many Marines when it came to dealing with the Army men in their midst. Rasula paused to assist a young Marine to his feet after the boy had simply collapsed from fatigue. The Marine was about to take the captain's proffered hand, but pulled back when he saw the Army insignia on Rasula's cap: "No thanks, I'm a Marine." Rasula had helped relieve shattered Marine units on Peleliu, and he bore no grudge.

★

An astute observer of Chinese tactics would have seen, from dusk onward, that a particular pattern to the fighting was developing.

Such an observer was Captain Bill Earney, operations officer of the 3rd Battalion, 7th. Coming up on Pusong-ni at about 2100 hours, December 6, Earney heard and saw the first really heavy concentrations of machine-gun fire from the heights. As he and his troops moved through the village, the Chinese opened fire. The pattern was quite clear as green tracer squirted out from between the wrecks of the houses and from deep draws behind them. Red American tracer probed the darkness, going after the sources of the green death. For the time being, the American motor column continued to grind forward.

Bill Earney looked to the right to see what was going on and spotted several flashes on the low ridgeline. He walked out a ways with his radioman; thought for a while that friendly mortars might be out there, firing over the MSR at the Chinese on the left; considered for a while that it might be gunfire from Ray Davis's 1st Battalion as it mopped up on a distant ridgeline; then gave up and trudged forward to report to the battalion commander, Bill Harris.

A short time later, after leaning against the warm hood of a truck which was stopped in the middle of the road, Earney joined the tail end of his battalion's column. Cognizant of classic Chinese divide-and-conquer tactics, Earney was determined that a senior officer be present at the front, center, and rear of the battalion serial in case separate attacks had to be mounted or received.

There was no end to the delays. At one point, a heavy tank crew was overcome by carbon-monoxide fumes, and their vehicle blocked the MSR for long minutes, until someone on the outside broke in and roused the suffocating men.

★

Minutes before sunset, Lieutenant Colonel Randolph Lockwood, commander of the 2nd Battalion, 7th, was directing a mop-up operation beside the MSR when a jeep pulled up beside him and stopped. Colonel Homer Litzenberg strode briskly forward, shouting at the troops, "Move out! Move out!"

Miffed by the regimental commander's behavior, Lockwood tried to explain that he thought he should re-form the troops on the roadway before sending them farther. Litz began yelling again: "Re-form on the road!" Then, pounding Lockwood's back in impatience, Litz bellowed, "Move out!"

The troops quickly re-formed and began moving south again. Darkness had almost enveloped the hills, but it was just light enough for Litz to spot three or four huts by the side of the road. "Burn them down," he ordered in confirmation of his long-standing policy that the Chinese be left without shelter. Randolph Lockwood moved to protest the order because of the darkness, but the huts already flickered and flared, lighting a considerable stretch of the roadway.

★

The command group of the 7th Marines had been on the road for well over twenty hours as it rounded a nondescript curve in the roadway at about 0200 hours, December 7. Colonel Litzenberg was somewhere out ahead, alone with his driver, no doubt grumbling at his troop leaders, making impatient noises at the engineers who were struggling in the cold and dark to bypass several blown bridges.

Lieutenant Colonel Fred Dowsett, Litz's exec, was huddling against the cold that infiltrated the canvas top of his jeep when his driver braked to avoid the rear of a Marine medium blade tank that loomed suddenly out of the darkness.

As the column straggled to a halt behind Dowsett's jeep, several buildings to the left of the roadway flared up, and the entire area was bathed in brilliant firelight.

After jumping down from his own jeep just behind Dowsett's, Major Hal Roach, the regimental logistics officer, led his radioman forward and joined the regimental exec on the right side of Dowsett's vehicle.

Machine-gun and rifle fire opened from the left from atop or just beyond the railroad embankment behind the burning huts. One round immediately hit Fred Dowsett in the ankle, and he was let down into the roadside ditch.

Instantly sizing up the situation, Hal Roach rushed forward to the nearest tank. The former commander of the 3rd Battalion, 7th, and Damnation Battalion grabbed a crowbar from among the tools and gear strapped to the armored vehicle, and climbed to the turret. He banged with the crowbar on the hatch, which lifted an inch a moment later. While he pointed at the burning buildings, Roach rattled off a stream of orders, then clambered back to the roadway to see what was going on farther back.

Fred Dowsett, calmly nursing his wounded ankle, was on the radio, speaking with Colonel Litzenberg, who was well forward. While the colonel got to work organizing a relief force, Dowsett and Roach indulged in a few moments' vitriol directed at Litz's habit of being too far forward, though for once being forward was keeping him out of danger.

The first infantry unit to reach the stalled command column was the shadow that had been How Company, 7th, under the command of 2nd Lieutenant Minard Newton. These troops were placed between the stalled vehicles and the railroad embankment and ordered to establish a base of fire. By that time, also, the two Marine medium blade tanks that had stopped the column had moved far enough to the verge of the road to provide a passage for the vehicles to the immediate rear.

The staffers and clerks in the column reboarded their vehicles and prepared to move out, steeling themselves for the ordeal of making the fire-swept passage.

Major Hank Woessner clambered aboard his jeep beside his driver, who let out the clutch and gunned the jeep forward. They had not gone more than a few yards before the young driver slumped over the wheel, a killing round through the head. The jeep slowed and stopped.

Woessner climbed to the roadway, ran around the jeep and, with the help of several other men, pulled the profusely bleeding man to the ground. Then, noting that his vehicle was blocking the column, the regimental operations officer climbed into the driver's seat. Just as he was about to start the jeep forward, Woessner was stopped by one of his technicians, who volunteered to take the wheel. The major climbed over the gearshift into the passenger's seat and the enlisted Marine climbed into the driver's seat and roared off.

The few moments in which Woessner's jeep had been stopped spelled doom for several men just to the rear. A line of machine-gun bullets passing through the jeeps behind Woessner's killed Captain Don France, the regimental intelligence officer, and his assistant, 1st Lieutenant Clarence McGuinness.

Other Chinese guns, which were moved into position behind the regimental command element during the initial halt, tore at the portion of the divisional train that was being escorted by the 7th Marines. Major Frederick Simpson, the divisional headquarters commandant, hastily called his clerks and cooks and technicians out of their trucks and booted them in the direction of the fire, which was spreading along the railroad embankment and the hills beyond.

Master Sergeant William McClung, who had been captured by the Japanese at Bataan and had spent four years as their prisoner, took immediate charge in one sector of the forming line. By directing fire and pulling men in from isolated positions, McClung slowly built up a viable defense. When two trucks flared up and illuminated a stretch of the crowded roadway, Master Sergeant McClung directed his men to concealed positions, then ran back into the firelight to pull wounded Marines to safety. He dragged two men to the side of the road, but was shot to death as he carried a third man through the firelight.

The chain reaction Marine vehicle stoppages along the roadway, and the dawning awareness on the part of the disorganized Chinese that they were facing a golden opportunity to inflict serious harm upon the Americans combined to spread a growing swath of death and destruction.

★

While the tiny companies of the 3rd Battalion, 7th, fought to control the Chinese buildup beside the road, the convoy remained rooted to its position. Ranging the long column to help with the wounded, Father Connie Griffin, the 7th Regiment's Catholic chaplain, and his clerk, Sergeant Matt Caruso, climbed into the 3rd Battalion's cracker-box ambulance to administer the Last Rites of the Church to a young Mexican-American Marine who felt that his time had come. Griffin grasped the hand of the severely wounded youngster, stared into his dark eyes and spoke gently to him in his native Spanish, assuring him that all was well on the outside despite the sounds of gunfire.

Among the wounded Marines looking on was Staff Sergeant John Audas, of Fox/7. He had spent most of the day lying wounded in a ditch across the road from Sangpyong-ni. He had nearly frozen to death before being discovered by fellow Marines at dusk and placed aboard the cracker-box ambulance and treated.

Connie Griffin began to thaw out as he exchanged words with the dying Marine. The firing seemed to be subsiding, so he turned to his clerk, Sergeant Caruso, and suggested that they really get warm before stepping back out onto the road. The priest was attempting to will the tension from his mind and body, paying no heed, when he was engulfed by a spray of bluish flashes. Caruso screamed, "Look out, Father! Look out!" And throwing himself between the bullets and Father Griffin, he died in a sheet of blood. One of the many bullets passing through the driver's window at an oblique angle struck Connie Griffin in the jaw and passed into his right shoulder and out his back. As the priest collapsed across Matt Caruso's bloody corpse, Dr. Robert Wedemeyer, who had been sitting in the front passenger's seat, sprang to action, yelling at Chief Pharmacist's Mate Pete Ciani, "My God! Watch him! Don't let him *exsanguinate!*" The last word, meaning "run out of blood" in Latin, was spoken to keep the still-conscious priest from worrying. Despite his shattered jaw and the onset of shock, Griffin muttered, "You son of a bitch, I've forgotten more Latin than you'll ever know!"

Chief Ciani, who was taking desperate action to staunch the great gouts of blood from the priest's face and shoulder, interrupted, "Shut your damned mouth, Padre, and let me work on you!"

Dr. Wedemeyer reluctantly ordered Sergeant Caruso's body removed from the ambulance. Moaning a protest, the priest drew a sharp rebuke from the surgeon: "Padre, this ambulance is for the living, and not the dead." When he realized the effect Caruso's stiffening corpse was having upon the spirits of the other wounded men, Griffin nodded his assent and finally allowed the doctor and Chief Ciani to do their work.

★

Major Ray Fridrich, exec of the 1st Battalion, 7th, had spent the entire day on the road with his battalion's vehicle train while the rifle companies worked the ridgeline to the west of the MSR. As the fighting progressed, Fridrich's serial made it nearly to the point where the 7th Regiment's command group had first been ambushed. The Chinese, who had built up a considerable force in a very short time, stopped the column cold and forced Fridrich and his men into the ditch on the right side of the roadway.

Several Marine heavy tanks were on the roadway, firing lines of tracer from their coaxial machine guns in order to mark targets for the knots of riflemen all around. Casting about for troops with whom he could build up a line, Fridrich found that he was surrounded by weaponless Armymen who had dived into the ditch with the senior Army officer in the column, Lieutenant Colonel Barry Anderson, operations officer of the 31st Infantry.

Bullets from the heights were ripping through the vehicles on the roadway, and the tanks and infantry were firing back, but without much effect. At length, the tank crews reported that they were running out of .30-caliber machine-gun ammunition. They could not fire their 90mm turret guns for fear of the treacherous backblast causing casualties among the many troops huddled nearby.

On hearing that the tanks needed ammunition, Ray Fridrich yelled for his battalion armorer, who had last been seen only yards away aboard a truck loaded with bullets. The calls were answered after several minutes when the sergeant appeared out of the gloom, crawling along the ditch on all fours. There was a large bandage where a bullet from the heights had clipped off the end of his nose. "Those tanks out there need ammunition," Fridrich called above the din of the firing. "We've got to move that truck out there regardless."

"Yes, Sir!" The sergeant pulled himself to his feet and hurtled out onto the roadway, climbing through the passenger's door to the driver's seat of the ammunition truck. No one ever turned ignitions off on the road, even under fire, so the armorer only had to throw her into gear and pull up on the lee side of the rearmost of the four heavy tanks. The sergeant grabbed two cases of .30-caliber machinegun ammunition, climbed up behind the turret and banged on the hatch until the tank commander cracked it open. Then, standing fully exposed in the heavy fire, the armorer passed the ammunition cases through the hatch. He resupplied all four tanks in much the same manner, though Ray Fridrich never saw the tank crewmen expose more than a hand.

Moments after the ammunition sergeant leaped back into the ditch, Fridrich saw a young Marine carrying a ten-foot length of telephone pole that was burning furiously from end to end — a portable warming fire, for there could be no other purpose.

★

First Lieutenant Paul Sanders, commander of a Dog/Tanks platoon, was driven onto a section of the road bordered by several buildings just as they flared up and the Chinese on the heights opened with several machine guns. The commander's turret hatch was open and locked, so Sanders was unable to pull it down as he slid into the turret beneath a torrent of bullets.

Sanders ordered his gunner to lay on the Chinese, then noted immediately that the turret was stuck fast. A voice came over the phone attached to the tank's rear fender, informing Sanders that a corpse was wedged between the turret and the engine compartment upon which several riflemen had been riding. Sanders asked the disembodied voice if the corpse could be pulled free, and the man agreed to give it a try. The turret suddenly traversed and the coaxial machine gun was immediately laid against the source of the streams of green Chinese tracer.

Sanders vaulted through the hatch and landed in a ditch filled with South Korean soldiers, to whom he pantomimed orders to fire at the heights. The Koreans were scared. One got to his knees, aimed his Garand rifle straight up, and fired all eight rounds. Then he threw down the rifle and crawled off. Disgusted, Paul Sanders climbed back into his tank, and promptly came unglued.

A trained infantry officer new to tanks, Sanders felt a great gout of primal fear rise through him as he realized what a sitting target he was in that tank. He got on the radio and excitedly called his other commanders to get them into action. The calm voice of his veteran platoon sergeant talked Sanders out of his panic and produced some calm, cogent action until the column resumed its progress.

★

The last Major Lefty Morris and Captain Bill Earney saw of Lieutenant Colonel Bill Harris was when they crawled into the battalion commander's Weasel to thaw out and discuss conditions on the road, well before the fighting turned serious. Both men noticed that Harris was in a rather sullen mood, but neither pressed him.

Though he was routinely admonished by his subordinates, Harris had taken to wandering about without an escort, without even a radioman. He was off in another world, and Lefty Morris had been slowly taking firmer control of the battalion. Still, until Bill Harris was relieved by higher authority, Morris and Earney knew he would have to be treated as though things were normal.

The last anyone saw of Bill Harris was at 0530, December 7, 1950. He was standing alone a few hundred feet up a draw to the left of the road. Then he simply vanished.

Lefty Morris, one of the calmest combat officers in the Marine Corps, took control of the 3rd Battalion, 7th, as soon as Harris's disappearance had been noted. By that time, the Chinese in the immediate vicinity of the battalion — which was just south of the initial point of contact — were about used up. A flurry of action continued, but Morris's battalion was able to grind forward, pulling a substantial portion of the regimental and battalion columns along with it.

★

Farther south, 1st Lieutenant Ozzie Vom Orde's platoon of Dog/ Engineers had completed the bypass around the site of the last blown bridge before Koto-ri.

Within an hour of sunrise, Major Hal Roach, who had remained in the thick of the fighting for most of the early morning hours, discovered Major Hank Woessner's jeep and trailer at the end of the unblown northern half of the wrecked span. Woessner was nowhere to be found, nor were any of the men who were known to have been with him. The last Roach had seen of the regimental operations officer had been when Woessner was climbing into the driver's seat of the jeep after pulling out his dead driver — just before he had moved to the passenger's seat to make room for another driver. On closer inspection of the jeep, Roach found a deep pool of frozen blood on the floor on the driver's side. Fighting down a huge lump in his throat, Roach asked the engineers if they had seen anything, but they had not been there long, and had nothing to report.

Hal Roach drove on into Koto-ri passing the word that Hank Woessner was missing and possibly killed. However, he found the exhausted regimental operations officer running a control point just inside the town's defensive perimeter. Flabbergasted, Roach asked Woessner what had happened.

Just as it was becoming light enough to see, Woessner's replacement driver missed the unmarked engineer's cutoff onto the bypass and drove out onto the blown bridge, braking just before he would have driven into the gully. The jeep's reverse gear had given out near Yudam-ni, and the trailer it was hauling prevented Woessner and the driver from pushing it back to the cutoff. Gunfire from the east forced the two Marines to drop about four feet to the ground to the right of the bridge abutment, where there was good cover and where they found eight or ten fellow Americans. As the Marines exchanged fire with the Chinese, a grenade landed right at Hank Woessner's feet, a dud. After about five minutes Woessner and his driver managed to retrieve a "salvaged" machine gun from the rear seat of the jeep and put it into action until, a short time later, with no other traffic or help visible, the major decided to abandon the jeep and move the entire group to Koto-ri. They arrived safely without further incident.

★

Major Fox Parry, the commander of the 3rd Battalion, 11th, drew little fire that long night as he followed the 4th Battalion, 11th, down the road in fits and starts. Though all his battalion's guns were to the rear, Parry and his executive officer, Major Red Miller, were forced along with the flow.

As Parry's jeep was approaching a barrier composed of green tracer thrown out by a machine gun on the heights, the battalion commander ordered his driver to bull through. A few rounds penetrated the canvas top, so Parry remarked, as the jeep roared to safety, "Boy, that was close!" Red Miller, who was sitting beside Parry, responded, "It sure was," and showed the battalion commander where a round had passed through the fleshy web between his left thumb and forefinger.

As Parry and Miller passed safely to Koto-ri, one of their batteries was beset at dawn and forced to fight a battle right out of the textbooks that governed artillery during the Civil War.

★

To support the drive of the reinforced 7th Marines down the MSR from Hagaru-ri to Koto-ri, the 3rd Battalion, 11th, had been resupplied with ample ammunition of all types and split into three self-contained firing units — basic six-gun batteries with beefed-up fire-direction centers which could operate without aid from the larger battalion FDC. Captain Ben Read's How Battery, which had been in position on a spur of East Hill throughout the siege of Hagaru-ri remained where it was for most of December 6 to support the beginning part of the breakout. George and Item Batteries rolled out with the 7th Regiment's vehicle column.

By nightfall, December 6, the advance of the main body of the 7th Marines had ground over only three thousand yards of the MSR, less than two miles. How Battery, which had been feeling increasing pressure during the day, closed station at 1730 and moved into the vehicle column, covering only one thousand yards in over two hours. While How Battery closed up on East Hill, George Battery pulled out of the column and went into position by the side of the road, where it was to remain at least until Item Battery reached Koto-ri and was set up to cover the MSR from there. It was a neat, mathematical plan, well within the experience of the veteran gunners. And it went well until the point of the 7th Regiment's motor column was stopped about fifteen hundred yards south of the George Battery positions.

After struggling forward only two thousand yards in four hours, How Battery's Captain Ben Read decided to move forward toward the sound of the firing, which seemed to be several thousand yards ahead; if his guns were needed, he could set up in a relatively short time. Read motioned for his exec, 1st Lieutenant Red Herndon, to join him and walked rapidly forward along the darkened roadway.

Well forward of where they left the guns, Read and Herndon found Lieutenant Colonel Olin Beall in among the trucks of his portion of the column. Beall explained that at least three Chinese machine guns had been placed in a strongpoint overlooking the roadway, and that no one had been able to silence them, though several bazooka teams were trying. Read suggested that he and Herndon go back along the column to get a Marine heavy tank they had passed on the way down. Beall warmed to the notion, and the two gunners turned back to the north.

The tank commander was a skeptic. After Read and Herndon put their suggestion before him, he got onto his radio and spoke with his superior elsewhere in the column: "Two characters here think they can break the roadblock if they have a tank."

The two battery officers fumed over the description and the wait, but an affirmative response came over the radio. Read returned to the battery, which was just behind the stalled tank, while Herndon and one of the battery sergeants guided the tank forward.

In the end, the tank's 90mm gun did little to crack the Chinese strongpoint. Nor did some fire from one of George Battery's 105s, which was set up on the road and aimed in the general direction of the offending machine guns. A George Battery bulldozer, however, pushed several burning vehicles from the roadway, allowing the stalled column to resume its journey. At the same time, a George Battery forward-observer team picked its way across the darkened landscape to a knob from which the Chinese strongpoint could be observed. When it became light enough to see, the observer team would direct fires from George Battery guns.

While George Battery worked on the strongpoint, How Battery continued to move forward in fits and starts. Reaching a point where the railroad embankment paralleled the roadway seventy-five yards to the left, Ben Read shook out a precautionary machine-gun platoon composed of his own gunners and settled in to await the next jump forward.

Dawn was just breaking when Sergeant Russell Rune, the machine-gun platoon leader, called down from the embankment, "Here they come!"

Hundreds of Chinese were on the flanks, ready to attack across the railroad embankment, right where the six How Battery howitzers were waiting for the column to start forward again. Rune and his machine gunners swung the muzzles of their weapons down to try to catch the leading ranks of PLA infantry, but the two sides were too close to each other for that. Two of the Marines picked up the rear tripod legs so their guns could be depressed sufficiently to rake the Chinese.

Ben Read and Red Herndon yelled at Sergeant Rune to withdraw his vastly outnumbered security platoon, then kicked the battery to order. There were all sorts of immobile trucks in the way. Almost without thinking, the officers and gun chiefs directed the crews to point the stubby muzzles of the six howitzers through the gaps between the trucks. There was no time to dig in the trails, so Read ordered all the available men in the vicinity to brace their bodies behind the gun shields to take up the brutal recoils. Dozens of other men were throwing ammunition canisters out of the stalled trucks onto the roadway.

White phosphorous, High Explosives, antitank, star clusters — whatever the type of ammunition — was set at Charge-One, the lowest power available, and fired as quickly as it could be thrown into the next available breech. Each recoil pushed the guns back another three feet against the straining shoulders of the men braced below the gun shields. After every fifth or sixth round, the assembled crews pushed each gun back to its starting point between the trucks.

Number-6 Gun inadvertently fired a round set at Charge-Seven, the heaviest powder load, and the heavy chassis and tube shot back a full twenty feet, running right over the beefed-up crew. Ben Read bellowed for the attention of the startled mass of fallen Marines and ordered them to regain control of the weapon.

The Chinese died in windrows atop the railroad embankment as air bursts kissed off in their faces. But they got off a torrent of gunfire as they went down.

A five-gallon gasoline can strapped to the side of one of the trucks erupted in flames. Red Herndon and one of the forward observers grabbed several sleeping bags and smothered the flames before the ammunition in the vehicle could begin cooking off.

One of the crews turned their piece to lay it on a machine gun deployed in a nearby culvert. The Chinese weapon and its crew were pulverized by the first 105mm round.

The road was strewn with wounded Marines and intense, nimble corpsmen, who braved the fire to repair damaged tissue and staunch blood from severed arteries and veins.

The gruesome destruction continued. The gunners got better at it as they settled in. The Marines fired into the trees just beyond the embankment to spread lethal shrapnel into the hordes of Chinese who were hiding behind the railroad embankment. Houses nearly a mile beyond the embankment were leveled around the mortars the Chinese had concealed in and behind them. Four rounds fired from a single howitzer vaporized a group of Chinese officers watching the slaughter from a knob three thousand yards out from the road.

Ben Read took a painful wound in the knee when a concussion grenade landed at his feet; the sergeant beside him went down with steel slivers in the groin.

Passing among the wounded as the firing subsided within an hour of sunrise, Ben Read felt hot tears brim over from his eyes. The wounded put up a cheerful front for the limping battery commander, and he for them. As Read spoke with the fallen Marines, he was accosted by Sergeant Rune, who slapped him on the back; the Chinese were on the run.

Eight hundred Chinese died on and behind the railroad embankment. Within ninety minutes of the onset of the Chinese attack, How Battery was limbered up and on the move.

★

As the 7th Marines and the first divisional train lumbered forward, the 5th Marines, its supports, and the second divisional train prepared to abandon Hagaru-ri to the People's Liberation Army.

CHAPTER

40

Captain Hal Williamson, commander of How Company, 5th, stalked up to a clump of dark figures gathered in the lee of a tank and berated them for standing around, idle, while Chinese firing from the heights had their way with the stalled column. A dark form detached itself from the group by the tank and stepped forward a few paces before addressing the rifle company commander. "You're talking to Lieutenant Colonel Milne," the form said. Williamson, who would have recognized the commander of the 1st Tank Battalion in daylight, backed off a mite, but insisted that his mission of leading the 5th Marines and the second divisional train from Hagaru-ri was being jeopardized because the line of tanks under Milne's direct control was blocking the roadway. Milne agreed to get rolling, and returned to the group of men he had left a moment before. Within a minute, the group had dispersed down the line of tanks and, as Chinese fire from the heights magically subsided, the great tank engines roared to full power. After Williamson motioned to his fellow company commander, 1st Lieutenant Charlie Mize, of George/5, he returned to his waiting troops and stepped off down the road.

A little farther along, Mize and Williamson approached a checkpoint and began looking for Lieutenant Colonel Joe Stewart, exec of the 5th, who was to modify their orders if necessary. They found

Stewart huddled up inside his covered jeep, but before he could speak Lieutenant Colonel Bob Taplett's jeep skidded to a halt on the verge of the roadway and the aggressive commander of the 3rd Battalion, 5th, stepped down and issued a stream of orders in his usual forthright manner. Taplett was all business this early morning; there was no stopping him or his troops.

Taplett's battalion soon came upon another large clump of stalled vehicles and indecisive men. Several hundred Chinese were on the heights, banging away at a short stretch of the roadway ahead, and no one dared run the gantlet. Deploying his two rifle companies (Item/5 had been temporarily disbanded), Taplett moved among the milling Marines around the trucks and jeeps, pushing them to the side of the road, establishing a long firing line.

Six Chinese armed with bolt-action rifles were murdering the men on the roadway. Several howitzers from the 1st Battalion, 11th, were in the stalled serial, but no one had made a move to unlimber them and fire at the bushwackers.

Lieutenant Colonel Olin Beall emerged from the knot of men behind a clump of trucks and sidled up to Taplett, his matched pearl-handled revolvers rising and falling jauntily with the action of his hips. "I'm gonna get down the road," Beall blustered.

Taplett was nearly staggered by the words. "Don't go! I've got two companies, and I'll get them out in front. Don't go until they get those guys up there."

Beall shrugged and walked away. Before Taplett could act, Beall had his drivers cranking up their idling engines and rolling out. Less than a mile ahead, where the railroad embankment impinged on the roadway, Chinese soldiers dropped hand grenades right down onto the vehicles, killing and maiming numerous passengers.

Acting quickly, Taplett ordered Charlie Mize's George Company to sweep the embankment while Hal Williamson's How Company supported. It took an hour for the smoothly functioning rifle companies to clear that section of the roadway and proceed toward Koto-ri.

★

Fox/7 had enjoyed a meal and a few hours' rest when Major Jim Lawrence, the operations officer of the 2nd Battalion, 7th, found 1st Lieutenant Ralph Abell, the Fox/7 commander, and requested — not ordered — the company to undertake the rescue of a group of Task Force Drysdale survivors that had been spotted in the hills several miles off the MSR. Abell was beat, and he knew his men were beat, but he nodded grimly and shook the company out of its warm billets and back onto the road.

The hike north on the MSR and into the hills was exhausting, punctuated by the sarcasm of Marines heading south, but it was largely uneventful. Nearly a dozen shaken Armymen were herded and carried to ambulances which had been driven as far into the hills as possible.

One of the scary little details that gave Ralph Abell some bad moments was the fact that an elderly Army warrant officer, who appeared to be in good physical condition, clutched four letters he had taken from the litter of a wrecked mail truck on November 29, more than a week earlier. Nothing anyone said to the man could induce him to turn those letters over to anyone but a military postal representative.

★

The wreck of Task Force Drysdale figured prominently in the impressions of many of the Marines who passed it in daylight on December 7, though it made no impression whatsoever on others.

Lieutenant Colonel Ray Murray, who barely had time to pause, had but one impression register: the corpse of a very young Chinese boy dressed in the uniform of a Marine first sergeant.

First Lieutenant Herc Kelly, Bob Taplett's battalion communicator, helped retrieve an officer's footlocker from the debris. Inside was a Marine major's blue and white dress uniforms and four bottles of Canadian Club. Holding two bottles in reserve, Kelly passed the other two around. It was like pouring syrup, the liquor was that smooth.

Farther on, Kelly and his men found the remnants of the divisional administrative section. Dead Marines were sprawled in attitudes of agony all up and down the column. The most grisly bodies were frozen in firing positions, resting rifles on snow embankments or the hoods of their stalled vehicles. The really sick part was that just about every vehicle kicked right over the instant anyone tried to start it up.

Startling though it was, Herc Kelly actually came upon a Christmas parcel addressed to him. There were plenty of chocolate-chip cookie crumbs, a note from his wife, and a pedometer, which he strapped to one of his ankles then and there.

Corporal Alan Herrington, a machine gunner attached to Item Company, 1st, had been off and on the roadway all day, working his way into the hills when there was opposition, angling toward the moving vehicles with his company when there was not. As Herrington was approaching the debris of Task Force Drysdale, he started when he saw two frozen corpses beneath one of the many damaged trucks. Between the pair of dead Americans lay the body of a puppy, its head on its paws in the attitude of sleep.

Farther on, Herrington peered into the cab of yet another damaged truck. The driver and his assistant were crowded into the far corner of the cab, half raised up, their rigid arms held before their faces to ward off unseen bullets, their eyes frozen wide in the face of the terror they had felt in the last instant of their lives.

★

Lieutenant Colonel Carl Youngdale, commander of the 11th Marines, was stalled on the road for nearly an hour at the spot where How Battery had made its stand at dawn. Hundreds of Chinese were in plain sight in the hills, moving away from the area in which so many of their countrymen had been butchered by Marine howitzers. Several howitzers from the 1st Battalion, 11th, were unlimbered, and shells were soon screaming toward the slowly moving, defeated mustard-yellow mass as it trudged through deep snow toward the skyline. Observers of this new carnage cheered the gunners on.

Incongruously, one of the Chinese stopped in plain sight within several hundred yards of the Marines and dropped his pants. As he squatted over the snow, many Americans drew out their rifles and popped away at him. There were no telltale puffs in the distant snowfield to give a clue as to the accuracy of the rifle fire, and there were too many men participating in any case, but that incredibly detached PLA soldier finished without paying any heed to the men on the road, hitched up his trousers, and trudged over the ridgeline to safety.

When at last the second divisional train of which Carl Youngdale was a part began moving again, he idly broke off pieces of a giant Mr. Goodbar candy bar he had been given by Dr. Bud Hering, the division surgeon, before leaving Hagaru-ri. As Youngdale nibbled at the candy, he noticed that his regimental operations officer, Lieutenant Colonel Jim Appleyard, was sidling closer. At last, nose atwitch, Appleyard asked the regimental commander why he smelled of peanuts and chocolate. Reluctantly, Youngdale reached into his pocket, broke off a piece of the Mr. Goodbar and handed it to Appleyard. From then on, whenever Youngdale reached into his pocket for any reason, he could be certain that Appleyard would be right at his elbow. It was as good a way as any for the two seasoned artillery officers to pass that long day on the MSR.

★

Thoroughly exhausted by a night of fighting, and days on short rations and long exercise, 2nd Lieutenant Nick Trapnell, of Able/5, passed December 7 in a fog. The only thing he could ever recall of the tramp to Koto-ri was the particular kindness of 2nd Lieutenant Dutch Blank, who shared his very last Lifesaver with him.

★

As at Yudam-ni, the final unit to leave Hagaru-ri was Hal Roise's 2nd Battalion, 5th, which was to guard the engineers who would be blowing the town and its remaining dumps all to pieces.

In their preparations to blow the stone bridge over the Changjin River the engineers were severely hampered by masses of North Korean civilians who were fleeing the Chinese, hoping to be evacuated to South Korea along with the American invaders. And Chinese in the hills added to the confusion by dropping heavy mortar rounds randomly upon the emptying town and its environs.

Adding immeasurably to the confusion was the last-minute decision by Marine MPs to release one hundred sixty Chinese prisoners from the town brig. These men were given food and clothing and fuel for fire building, then left to their own devices. A number did not want to be all that free, and they followed and badgered the engineers and riflemen who were preparing the town for demolition. The prisoners were made to understand that they would have to march to their own lines. They were formed up on the road and were just beginning to move when a PLA company mounted an attack. The former prisoners were caught in the cross fire, and one hundred thirty-seven of them were shot to pieces, killed, before Marines beat off the attackers.

Private First Class Rick Seward walked into a hut and came face to face with four injured PLA soldiers just as a nearby dump filled with mortar ammunition was blown by the engineers. It rained unexploded shells, canisters, and debris for a full minute, but Seward, who never took an eye from the four Chinese, saw that none of them so much as twitched a hair in all that time.

Sergeant Jim Friedl, Easy/5's 81mm forward observer, was passing through the center of town when a great *pop* from a nearby bonfire made him turn. A Marine a few feet away was nursing a bloody face, caused by a C-ration can that had exploded in the fire.

Captain Stretch Mayer, the battalion headquarters commandant, joined the staff and company commanders for a final briefing from Hal Roise. Speaking quickly, his ubiquitous cigarette bobbing up and down in one corner of his mouth, Roise gave out with the withdrawal plan. Then he looked around at the great hilly bowl and said, almost wistfully, "You know, if I had air and plenty of artillery, I think I could hold this place all winter."

Mayer looked across the crowd of officers at his close friend, Captain Sam Smith, of Dog/5, and felt his eyes fog over. Smith just raised his eyebrows and shrugged his shoulders. No one said a word; none dared encourage Roise, who was perfectly capable of doing what he said he might.

It was late in the afternoon of December 7 when the rear guard of Roise's battalion took to the hills and the road and looked back down on the former base. The engineers were methodically blowing the place to pieces. A carpet of Chinese was descending from the hills, making for the burning food dumps. Thousands of North Korean civilians, intent upon reaching the sea, streamed through the center of town, across the icy Changjin, between the exploding dumps. Hundreds, perhaps thousands, of Chinese and North Koreans died upon the pyre of Hagaru-ri.

★

Major Lefty Morris and Captain Bill Earney, of the 3rd Battalion, 7th, were setting up shop in Koto-ri late in the morning when a message from Regiment ordered the battalion back north to keep the MSR open for the vanguard of the 5th Marines, which was still some hours away.

Bill Earney led out the thin battalion column with his radioman and a mixed bag of headquarters troops and riflemen; Lefty Morris was a little farther back with the three rifle companies.

Rounding a bend in the road, Earney's point was fired on by Chinese visible on a hill to the right. The captain ordered up his only machine gun, which was emplaced to return the fire. A 60mm mortar put out five or six rounds while Earney got through to several orbiting Corsairs, which pounced on the Chinese position, silencing it.

It was during the latter stages of this minor confrontation that Lefty Morris had the opportunity to utter as grim a commentary as could be uttered on the plight of the fought-out rifle battalions.

As his minuscule battalion was maneuvering to cover the Chinese positions, high-ranking officers to the rear urged Morris to commit his reserve and mount a serious assault. To which Lefty replied ominously, "George Company has forty men left. How Company has thirty men. And Item Company has fifty men. I have nothing left to commit."

Morris's battalion moved cautiously up the road through the noon hour and rounded a curve from which its leading element could see a long, long way to the north. At about 1330, Bill Earney spotted troops on the road a mile distant. He ordered his men to take cover among a small cluster of abandoned vehicles to meet a massed assault or link up with the 5th Marines, whichever.

Earney and his men remained concealed until they were absolutely certain that the approaching troops were Marines, at which time the tall, thin battalion operations officer signaled and approached them. He saw that one of the leaders of the column was Bob Taplett, with whom he had served in 1945. Morris's tiny battalion fell in right behind Taplett's.

★

Private First Class Rick Seward, of Easy/5, rode into Koto-ri aboard the last tank in the column. Warrant Officer Bill Downs, of Able/Engineers, walked in eating a can of ham and lima beans he and another engineer had heated on a truck manifold during the last break just outside of town.

Walking or riding, eating or hungry, the last Marines closed on Koto-ri at 2130, December 7, 1950.

★

Corporal Alan Herrington, of Item/1, was visiting with a wounded buddy who was awaiting a flight out of Koto-ri's tiny airstrip that night when they were approached by a special-seeming civilian war correspondent, Marguerite Higgins.

Maggie Higgins had a great reputation among the senior officers, with whom she had been spending a great deal of time since Pusan. She was fairly well known by enlisted Marines. When she got to Alan Herrington and his doped-up, hurting buddy, she affected a brusque, almost superior, air. She had a story to write, and the pain the wounded Marine was experiencing touched her not at all. Her questions were perfunctory, as were the first few answers. At length, she asked the wounded Marine what, for him, had been the hardest part of the action.

The boy thought for a moment, then beamed through the haze of his pain and a pretty heavy dose of morphine. The answer he gave the haughty lady reporter summed it up for all the men who had participated: "The hardest part of all this was getting four inches of dick out of six inches of clothes to take a leak."

PART EIGHT

The Bridge

CHAPTER
41

There were twenty-five thousand men crammed into the confines of the tiny Koto-ri base by nightfall, December 7, 1950.

Koto-ri had not been an especially tranquil setting since it had been taken by the 7th Marines weeks earlier during the drive on the Reservoir, but the base had had a life of its own, and the hordes of Americans and South Koreans that descended upon it that first week of December changed immutably the town's primary characteristic, its isolation.

The ten days since November 27 had been, by far, less frenetic at Koto-ri than at the bases farther up the MSR, but they had been no less memorable for the men who got no farther forward.

★

With the demise of Task Force Drysdale on November 29, Koto-ri ceased to be a transit point and became a terminus.

Garrisoned initially by Lieutenant Colonel Allan Sutter's 2nd Battalion, 1st Marines; Easy Battery, 2nd Battalion, 11th; the headquarters of the 1st Marine Regiment; and assorted Marine and X Corps headquarters and service elements, the base had grown steadily since November 29, and wound up containing a bewildering assortment of units and splinters of units. By the morning of November 30, the 1st Marine Division Reconnaissance Company and the whole of Baker Company, 1st Tank Battalion, had been added to the garrison. And word was that day that the fresh 2nd Battalion, 31st Infantry, would be passing through from Hamhung to bolster the 7th Infantry Division units east of the Reservoir.

★

Major Joe Gurfein, an assistant X Corps operations officer based at Hamhung, was just knocking off work at 1600, November 30, when a call came through from the Corps Operations Officer, Lieutenant Colonel Jack Chiles. General Almond had just learned that the commander of the 2nd Battalion, 31st, which had started north from Majon-dong in the morning, was in some confusion as to his mission, and that a corps staffer was needed to go forward to deliver definitive orders. The officer who had been specifically requested begged off and asked Joe Gurfein if he would take the duty. The thirty-two-year-old New Yorker, a 1941 West Point graduate and veteran of mountain warfare in Italy, said sure, he would take the duty. He reported to Lieutenant Colonel Chiles at 1630, and was soon heading north on the MSR, alone but for his driver. By 1800, Gurfein had passed through the blocking position held by the 1st Battalion, 1st Marines, at Chinhung-ni, the railroad terminus at the foot of the Taebek Plateau. From there, he continued north several miles and reported to Lieutenant Colonel William Reidy, commander of the 2nd Battalion, 31st, at about 1830.

The confusion that had dragged Joe Gurfein up the MSR that evening had been caused by two separate orders issued by senior Corps officers during the day. Early that morning, General Almond had personally ordered Reidy to attack up the MSR to Koto-ri to clear it of roving bands of Chinese bushwackers and North Korean guerrillas. By early afternoon, the battalion (less Easy Company, which had been left as 7th Division reserve near the Fusen Reservoir) had been stopped by PLA units between Chinhung-ni and Koto-ri. A message sent by officer courier to X Corps headquarters characterized the confrontation as "threatening." The Corps Operations Officer, Lieutenant Colonel Chiles, ordered Lieutenant Colonel Reidy to keep the road open, which was interpreted as quite a different order than that issued early in the day by the Corps Commander. Faced with conflicting orders, Reidy decided to honor the last issued, and to sweep back south. Joe Gurfein had been sent to get Reidy going north again. It was that simple. Almost.

Bill Reidy seemed a cooperative enough sort to Joe Gurfein, who, though junior in rank, spoke with authority as the corps commander's personal representative. The truncated battalion, which had been placed on the slopes around the vehicle column in what Gurfein considered an excellent hedgehog defense, was reassembled and under way, northward, by 2300. Fires at the former campsite were left burning to mislead the inevitable Chinese observers.

The lead company, Fox/31, got off to a good start, but was hit moments after midnight, before the rear guard actually began moving.

Private First Class Rex Cramer, a Fox/31 rifleman, was sprawled on the bed of his truck with the rest of his squad when slugs from the heights began hitting the vehicle, which shimmied to a halt. Everybody bailed out except Cramer, whose legs had been cramped and had fallen asleep. As he was cussing his buddies for taking off, hands and an arm appeared over the tailgate of the truck, and Private

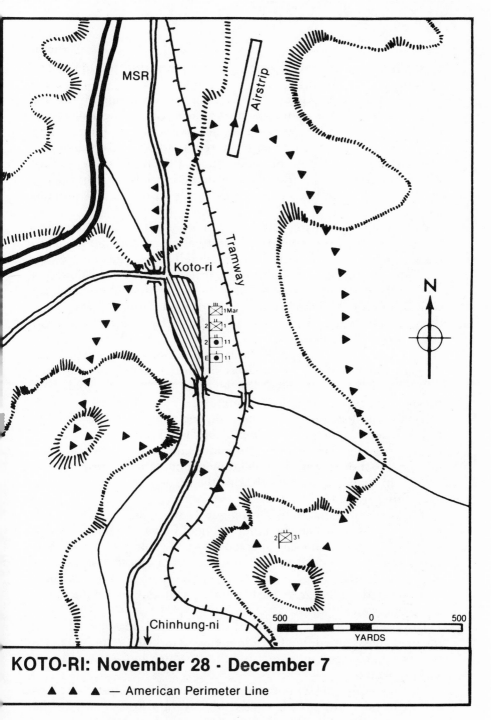

MSR

Airstrip

Tramway

Koto-ri

N

|III|
|X| 1Mar
2 |X| 1
2 |●| 11
E |●| 11

2 |X| 31

Chinhung-ni

500   0   500

YARDS

KOTO-RI: November 28 - December 7

▲ ▲ ▲ — American Perimeter Line

(See endpapers for GUIDE TO MAP SYMBOLS AND ABBREVIATIONS.)

First Class Joe Lapacola dragged Cramer out and tossed him down a nearby embankment.

Fox Company quickly deployed and began advancing up the hill alongside the road to eliminate the ambush. After going a short distance, the counterattackers saw that there was only one burp gunner on the heights. They got to within three hundred yards of him and began tearing off plenty of ammunition. But the Chinese soldier would not give an inch. Rex Cramer found himself secretly rooting for the bushwacker, but another squad circled around and killed the man.

By then it was snowing, and plenty of other interested Chinese on neighboring hills were pouring a great volume of fire into the leading elements of Reidy's battalion, which fell back in great haste.

Major Gurfein had thought about driving back to Hamhung as soon as the battalion started moving, but something told him to stay with Bill Reidy until the battalion had reached Koto-ri. It was a good thing, for Reidy, an untested infantry officer, fell apart at the seams at the sound of the first shot.

Joe Gurfein took charge of the battalion and got it moving right through the roadblock. There was no further opposition for two miles, until the point entered a deep cut which prevented flank patrols from getting up onto the heights.

It was a perfect spot for an ambush, and it was snowing heavily. Dead ahead was the heavy humming of Chingjin Power Plant Number-1, a rectangular concrete structure surmounting a sheer two-thousand-foot drop, and dominated by a mountain that rose beyond sight. The power plant was brilliantly lighted by arc lamps, but everything around it was dark and still.

It was coming up 0100, December 1, when heavy fire hit the convoy. The troops panicked and plunged forward, which was fine with Joe Gurfein, who saw speed as the only solution. A machine-gun squad at the tail of the column was dropped off, a sacrifice to slow pursuit, and the column wore on up the steep incline. All hands were startled by the great heat thrown off by the power plant, but the comfort was fleeting.

The pace continued rapid until the lead truck reached a fork in the road and stopped. Joe Gurfein bounded forward, relied upon his intuition to choose the correct right fork, which looked more worn, and plunged on.

The battalion, shaken but sound, continued on another two miles and descended from a high pass directly into Koto-ri, where the troops were warmly received. By that time, the battalion commander had regained his composure and immediately requested that a tank-supported infantry force be sent back to rescue the machine gunners who had blocked pursuit near the power plant. It was something of a miracle that the gunners were returned alive.

When Joe Gurfein broached the subject of his return to Hamhung, he was told that that was impossible.

At a stroke, the infantry strength of the Koto-ri garrison had been nearly doubled. Colonel Puller placed the newly arrived battalion on the southern and eastern hills overlooking the tiny base.

★

Actually, from the moment the road to the north of Koto-ri had been closed by the destruction of Task Force Drysdale, Colonel Puller's garrison had been amply endowed by a sizable manpower reserve in the form of bits and parts of a large number of X Corps and 7th Division units, which had either been assigned directly to the base establishment or caught there when they arrived too late to join the ill-fated convoy. Though the potential of this mixed group was great, the key to its effectiveness lay in organization.

Fortunately, the key to organization of that force had also arrived — in the unlikely personage of a bespectacled, slightly built lieutenant colonel of artillery who had arrived in Korea only two days before.

John Upshur Dennis Page had been born to a soldier's life. His father, a career officer, had been married in the Philippines in 1900, and had had his marriage witnessed by General Arthur MacArthur, a future Army chief of staff, the father of General Douglas MacArthur.

Born in early 1904, John Page longed to be a soldier, and had learned all he could about soldiering throughout his youth. But weak eyes had kept him from his appointment to West Point, and he had gone to Princeton instead, to become an engineer. On graduation in 1926, Page was commissioned a second lieutenant in the Field Artillery Reserve and, while building a fine career in engineering, he had pursued a soldierly career of a sort, taking one military course after another. He became a crack shot. He learned to fly. He went to summer camp every year through the '20s and '30s.

His opportunity came on the eve of World War II, when he was called to active service and sent to Fort Sill, Oklahoma, to become an instructor. He gained such a fine reputation as a teacher that he had to fight the brass to be assigned overseas, and he fulfilled his lifelong ambition in Europe, where he commanded an artillery battalion in combat.

Following the war, when he might have returned to his lucrative business, he became one of the few Reserve officers to be accepted into the Regular Army at his former rank, major.

In 1950, Lieutenant Colonel John Page was stationed, with his family, in New Orleans. Orders had already been cut for a transfer to the Command and General Staff School, at Fort Benning, a step to higher command. On the eve of his departure for the prestigious school, however, the orders were changed. John Page was to go to the war in Korea.

He arrived at Hamhung on November 27 and was told that he would be filling the first available command vacancy with an X Corps artillery battalion. On November 29, he was assigned a driver, Corporal David Klepsig, and sent north along the MSR to establish checkpoints between the port and Koto-ri. It was a temporary assignment, to give him a useful chore while he was marking time.

Within the next twelve days, John Page was to become an immortal.

Corporal David Klepsig, a young Georgian midway through what he planned to make his only tour in the Army, was on temporary duty with a topographical-meteorological unit assigned to X Corps when, at 1630, November 28, he was told by his first sergeant to draw a jeep and meet a Colonel Page at 1700 in front of the X Corps Artillery headquarters.

Klepsig pulled up right on time and walked with John Page to pick up the colonel's gear. While they were loading the jeep, Page suddenly said, "Here, Corporal, here's something for you." Klepsig held out his hand, almost without thinking, and received three chocolate bars. He immediately fell under the spell of the bespectacled, mustachioed officer, who treated him, a stranger, better than any officer ever had.

Corporal Klepsig was directed to drive over to the headquarters of the 52nd Transportation Truck Battalion, a Corps unit responsible for running convoys up the MSR. John Page was to meet with the battalion commander, Lieutenant Colonel Waldon Winston, for a briefing. It turned into an all-night stay. Winston told Page that the traffic-regulating points that needed to be contacted each day were strung out along sixty miles of the MSR; Page and Klepsig would have to log one-hundred-twenty-mile round trips starting the next day, November 29. The party that would be manning the control points was introduced to John Page, and he to it, and all hands were told to be ready to move at 0500.

The party, in seven jeeps, got off at 0530, November 29, and made good progress up the mountain, falling in behind Baker Company, 1st Marine Tank Battalion, as it crunched slowly up the incline into the Taebeks from Chinhung-ni to Koto-ri. Within a quarter-mile of Koto-ri, Page and Klepsig saw their first Marine Corsairs making runs on the Chinese who had stopped Task Force Drysdale on the far side of town. They also saw their first dead enemies, a pair of otherwise unidentifiable gunners who had been seared by napalm near their small mountain gun when the Marines first came to Koto-ri, weeks earlier.

On the final lap into the Marine base, Klepsig shrugged off the first intimation that he might not survive first combat, and confided in the forty-six-year-old officer in the seat beside him, "You know, Colonel, I'm a fatalist. If I'm going to get it, I'm going to get it."

"By golly, Corporal," Page said in a jovial voice, "I like you. So am I. We'll get along!"

Koto-ri was in a state of siege. Searching through the town for a regulating point manned by several artillerymen who were to be under his control, John Page issued his first order: The MSR was closed; no vehicles were to proceed north from Koto-ri until the Marines had reopened the road.

Page decided to return to Hamhung at 1500. He and Klepsig had neither a sleeping bag between them, nor a can of C-rations. They got only a few hundred yards out of town, however, before they were stopped by a pair of MPs, who were interrogating a North Korean man and his wife. Asking what was wrong, Page was told that, as far as the MPs could make out, the Chinese were in possession of the valley to the south, that the road was closed.

Asked how many Chinese there were in the valley, the MP said he thought there were only six.

Page simply had to see for himself. The two MPs were asked to go along, and they agreed, climbing aboard the jeep, which Klepsig had driven less than a mile when Page ordered him to park in the middle of a field just short of the house the Korean couple said they had been run out of.

The four Americans spread out in a thin, ragged little line and advanced across the field toward the house. About three hundred yards from the objective, David Klepsig glanced up at a clearing on a nearby hill and spotted a formation of Chinese walking into view, two abreast. He hollered to John Page, who checked the clearing with his binoculars, then ordered everyone to commence firing. There were four Americans and dozens of Chinese, and the Americans were forced to run for their jeep. Instead of going back to Koto-ri, however, Page ordered Klepsig to drive to the top of the pass, south, to a regulating station manned by several Army artillerymen. Klepsig thought of driving all the way to Hamhung, but Page had him pull over so he could speak with the officer in charge of the station. The artilleryman thanked the colonel for the latest news and said he needed ammunition if he was to hold against a Chinese attack.

That was a fateful request, for it obliged John Page to leave the MPs at the regulating point and return to Koto-ri. The jeep was fired on as it bypassed a damaged bridge, which a Chinese machine gun on the heights had zeroed in. Page and Klepsig bolted from the jeep and hid behind an embankment.

As the sky grayed over in the late afternoon, Page said that he thought they ought to move. "Corporal, go get the jeep, and I'll cover you and meet you where you turn back into the road." Thinking that Page meant he would fire from behind the embankment, Klepsig steeled himself and lit out. When he first looked back, the driver was astounded to see John Page standing in the middle of the road, firing his carbine on full automatic. Klepsig leaped into the jeep and roared off, barely missing John Page, who jumped in on the run.

The colonel, who had been absolutely nerveless to that point, suddenly noticed how fast Klepsig was going on the icy road. "Slow down, Corporal! Do you want to get us killed?"

They were back in Koto-ri within ten minutes, and had proof that the MSR had been severed to the south.

Later that evening, while Page and Klepsig and other Armymen were loading ammunition for the regulating detachment down the road, the Chinese launched a heavy attack. About fifty of them got into the perimeter, and roving Marine patrols nearly shot Page and Klepsig as they ran toward the sound of the firing. The attack, however, was beaten back, and the infiltrators were rooted out of their hiding places by sunrise.

Also at sunrise, John Page organized a party of volunteers to rescue the regulating detachment. Equipped with several jeeps and machine guns they were just about to go when Colonel Page decided to make one last radio check. Stopping off at the 1st Marines CP, he learned that the regulating party had made off into the night and had gotten to the lines of the 1st Battalion, 1st, at Chinhung-ni.

Sometime later that morning, John Page spoke with Chesty Puller, and the two decided that Page would amalgamate into a reserve force all the Armymen who were not attached to combat units. The job of equipping and organizing the troops went on through the day, November 30.

★

There is no accurate information concerning the start of the idea that evolved into the small runway at Koto-ri. Perhaps, and logically, the plan came down from X Corps, or 1st Marine Division. Many men who were at Koto-ri think it was John Page's idea. Whatever the case, elements of the 185th Engineer Combat Battalion selected a site half in and half out of the northern defensive line. It was an awkward sort of place which could not be defended or worked on at night, but it was the only suitable piece of ground accessible to the tiny perimeter. Colonel Page selected 1st Lieutenant Claude Roberts, a staff member of the 2nd Engineer Special Brigade, an X Corps unit, to oversee the construction. The strip was to provide a means for evacuating the many wounded who were piling up in the sick bays within the perimeter.

Lieutenant Roberts and officers of Charlie Company, 185th Engineers, staked out a runway two thousand feet long and one hundred feet wide. When they assembled their equipment, no one doubted but that the task would be impossible. The provisional company that Page had organized from service elements was to provide daytime security for the engineers.

There was little heavy action during the first week of December. Night attacks were the norm, but they were desultory, meant more to harass than to break through the perimeter line. Days were filled with random shooting and maiming and killing. Everyone soon became inured to the incessant popping of small arms and the possibility of instant death in the open, or in tents, or in the latrines.

Miraculously, enough runway was leveled in the first twenty hours of work to allow small, then larger, aircraft to land and take off with the wounded. A motley assortment of aircraft was assigned the job. In addition to several helicopters, which could land just about anywhere, light planes from Marine Observation Squadron 6 (VMO-6) and several Army artillery spotting units could carry out two men apiece on each flight. Old Martin TBM Avenger torpedo bombers, converted to staff planes for 1st Marine Aircraft Wing, were hurriedly refitted to allow a total of seven men to be lifted out in each of their fuselages and bomb bays. Later, C-47s began hauling out twenty-five to forty wounded at a time.

The engineers under Claude Roberts never stopped lengthening and widening and improving the strip. And as they did, they drew more and more attention from the Chinese, who saw the direction in which things were heading.

At one point a TBM tried to make an approach in a snowstorm. Lieutenant Roberts relayed a message for the pilot to circle until the snow on the runway could be plowed, but the driver of the road grader sent to do the job was shot in the back on his first pass. John Page materialized in the center of the action, organizing a response to the sniper fire, which was picking up. After getting the engineers onto a firing line of sorts, Page ran to the nearest Marine heavy tank, B22, and ordered it into the fray.

The tank's driver, Private First Class Nick Antonis, an aggressive nineteen-year-old San Francisco Reservist, cranked up the idling engine and, as John Page latched onto the exposed turret .50-caliber machine gun, burst forward from his hull-down position on a rise overlooking the runway. While Page banged away, Antonis headed for a little wooden shanty beside the runway, a place he thought might be harboring one of the snipers. Antonis lost control of the forty-six-ton behemoth barreling down the icy slope and, though he had both sets of brakes locked tight, slid right over the flimsy structure, crushing it, and flattening the Chinese rifleman inside.

The very next day, John Page was in the air with 1st Lieutenant Charles Kieffer, an Army artillery spotter pilot, in a light, unarmed aircraft — an *almost* unarmed aircraft.

All John Page had intended doing that morning was making a quick check of Koto-ri's defenses from the air. Though loosely attached to the 1st Marines, Page had long since seized the opportunity to run his own show. (Chesty Puller, normally disdainful of the Army, saw in John Page a kindred spirit, and allowed the Armyman to have his way.) Just to be on the safe side, Page trundled aboard the light plane loaded for bear: an automatic carbine, plenty of ammunition in his parka pockets, grenades in other pockets and dangling from his web gear, probably a combat knife in his boot top.

Once in the air, Page directed Lieutenant Kieffer to buzz a tent that the Chinese had erected near the top of the pass south of town. After studying the trails running through the area, Page motioned for another pass. Pilot Kieffer was astounded when the artillery colonel uncorked three of his hand grenades and dropped them on the tent from several dozen feet. When Kieffer had pulled up and leveled off, he saw that the tent was in tatters.

His blood up, Page pointed to a long ridge west of Koto-ri. Kieffer headed for it and saw that the ridgeline was covered with fighting holes overlooking the encampment and the airstrip. He heard John Page yelling in his ear, and obeyed the order to descend. John Page "bombed" the fighting holes as quickly as he could pull grenade pins and lean into the slipstream. At the end of the ridge, Kieffer, who by this time was a willing participant, was ordered to circle back, lower still. John Page raked the fighting holes with his carbine. A Chinese soldier who stood up and leveled his rifle at the light plane was cut down where he stood. The last grenade accounted for three PLA infantrymen in a single foxhole.

Minutes later, pilot and passenger were on the ground, hoping to scrounge more ammunition for a second sortie. But a seriously wounded man had to be evacuated immediately, and John Page, bombardier, had to relinquish Lieutenant Kieffer and his "bomber."

Thanks in part to John Page's extraordinary efforts, the Koto-ri airstrip was fully operational by December 6, and seven hundred men were flown out that day to make room for the many wounded who were expected from the fighting on the MSR to the north.

That ended John Page's contribution at Koto-ri, but it certainly did not end the continuing contribution — the ultimate contribution — he was to make within the week.

★

X Corps had given Major Joe Gurfein up for lost. For some reason, a radio message he sent upon arriving at Koto-ri to explain that he would be — well — detained did not get through. In fact, he was somehow listed as having been killed in action, and his obituary was printed in the United States before the issue was resolved. Attaching himself to the staff of the 2nd Battalion, 31st, whose Lieutenant Colonel Reidy had fully recovered from his lapse by the power plant, Gurfein had assembled a report he felt he had to get to Corps Headquarters in order to let the operations staff know how critical the situation at Koto-ri had become. So, on the night of December 3, Joe Gurfein bundled up and trudged out to the airstrip to hand a hastily scrawled "flash" to the pilot of a light plane that had arrived late to evacuate a pair of wounded men.

The report to Corps covered the period from noon, December 2, until 1800 hours, December 3, and read, in part:

All quiet until [1330, December 3]. F Company, 31st Inf attacked Hill 1328 about 1330. By 1700, F Co had secured the hill and could control the remainder of the ridge to the south. Air hit the valley leading to the west with excellent results. Our 4.2s hit approx. 30 enemy infantry coming up on west side of Hill 1328 and dispersed them.

Estimate [PLA] battalion minus on hills to west and south. Lots of machine guns well dug in. No mortars or artillery. Enemy losses 2 POWs, 100 KIA, not counting air, who apparently killed about 300 (?). Our losses 5 KIA, 10 WIA.

We now hold all hills within 1,000 yards of *edge* of camp except that to east, which is concave, and we have a reverse slope defense on it.

Supply drops are 80% efficient. About one out of 6 or 7 drops land outside our perimeter. We have recovered one of these, and may be able to get the other two. About 10% of all loads break loose from chutes. The chutes open, but the belting is not on properly.

Please send us information through these liaison pilots. What is happening at Hagaru-ri? How far south has the enemy cut the MSR? Where are the nearest friendly troops to the south? How is 8th Army doing?

I recommend most highly that [Funchilin Pass] be seized [as soon as possible].

★

The airdrops were certainly sustaining Koto-ri, after a fashion. But what Joe Gurfein wrote about loads breaking loose in the air was all too true. First Lieutenant Ernie Hargett, a Marine reconnaissance-platoon leader, saw his personal jeep cut in half by such a free-falling cargo load. And a Marine who hid under another jeep to avoid being hit in the open was crushed to death when that jeep was hit from the air.

Luckier than most, Joe Gurfein was ordered out of Koto-ri by Corps Headquarters, and he arrived safely back at Hamhung on December 5 to show people that he really was still alive.

★

Although the sense of danger — and the reality of being overrun — were keen throughout the period of Koto-ri's isolation, the several thousand men crammed into the tiny perimeter did not once despair of the outcome. News from the north and south was slim, as indicated by Joe Gurfein's flash, but no one doubted that the outcome for the greatest number of men would be positive.

Hours before the arrival of the lead companies of the 7th Marines, the Koto-ri garrison began preparing to feed and care for over twenty thousand newcomers.

As at Hagaru-ri earlier in the week, the rush of emotion attending the arrival of the bulk of 1st Marine Division was palpable.

Private First Class Norm Deptula, attached to an Army signal relay station atop the highest knob at the south end of the perimeter, dropped down to the valley floor to look for a section of his unit which had been caught at Hagaru-ri on November 27. While waiting for his own buddies to arrive, Deptula noticed another man who was waiting for a buddy in the milling crowd. The Marine's face beamed after a time, and he ran to embrace and shake the hand of an incoming buddy. A moment later, Deptula saw a dead Marine who had been strapped to the bumper of an incoming truck. And, as another truck passed, a buddy told him to look into the back, where he saw dead Marines stacked like cordwood. Moments later, a jeep nosed through the crowd, and Norm Deptula saw four of the living upon stretchers tied across its trailer. Farther on, within the perimeter, Deptula counted thirty-five bodies lying in a row.

Sergeant Brad Westerdahl, who had picked up a minor wound while serving with Fox/7, emerged from a sick-bay tent to see engineers blasting and bulldozing a great hole within the perimeter. This was to be the common grave of well over one hundred Marines, soldiers, sailors, and Royal Marines. As at Yudam-ni and Hagaru-ri, the mass grave was plotted in by Marine engineer surveyors following a brief service.

While the dead and wounded were cared for, the tired living refugees moved off, with friends if they could find them, to the tents and shelters of the Koto-ri garrison. Every available stove was fired up, and continuous stews and pancakes were served to anyone who cared to eat.

As the division and its supports sorted themselves out, the senior staff and unit commanders got right to work planning a withdrawal.

Colonel Al Bowser thought, and Major General O. P. Smith agreed, that a successful move to Chinhung-ni, where the Army's fresh 3rd Infantry Division had established a forward defense line, would bring 1st Marine Division to ultimate safety. Chinhung-ni was a dozen miles across Funchilin Pass, the hairiest dozen miles anyone had yet to face.

CHAPTER

42

Colonel Al Bowser, who had flown from Koto-ri to Hagaru-ri with O. P. Smith on December 6, had learned a thing or two about planning withdrawals in the past few weeks, and he was about to plan his best withdrawal of the campaign as he settled down to work in a cramped tent in the center of the Koto-ri perimeter.

The withdrawal from Yudam-ni had been pretty much out of Bowser's hands, but he had taken from it the crucial lesson of the need to hold the high ground. Admitting to himself that the words "withdrawal" and "retreat" meant pretty much the same thing, at least as far as outcomes were concerned, Bowser attempted to apply O. P. Smith's perception of "an attack in another direction" to his plans for the Hagaru-ri breakout. The results were not especially to Bowser's liking. When he took a close look at the plan and the reality of its execution, he saw, first of all, that he had been far too sanguine as to time and space requirements; the move had taken twice as long as he had visualized, and it had been something of a shambles because of the violence of the Chinese response.

As he sat in the tent in Koto-ri, musing over his errors and the firm lessons he had learned in nearly twenty years in the Marine Corps, Al Bowser saw the ultimate sanity of O. P. Smith's attack-to-the-rear analysis. Forget the "rear" part, Boswer told himself; the objective lies across Funchilin Pass, at Chinhung-ni.

Attacks were something Al Bowser knew how to handle. Had he not already planned Inchon, the attack on Chinhung-ni would have been Al Bowser's technical magnum opus.

★

As far as the vastly inflated Koto-ri garrison was concerned, every platoon of every company of each small combat battalion had an objective to seize or a contingency plan to follow as they formed up to deliver the attack on Chinhung-ni. Bowser's greatest advantage — one he shared with many of the division's senior combat unit commanders — was that the 7th Marines had attacked northward over the same ground only a few weeks earlier. Junior officers and

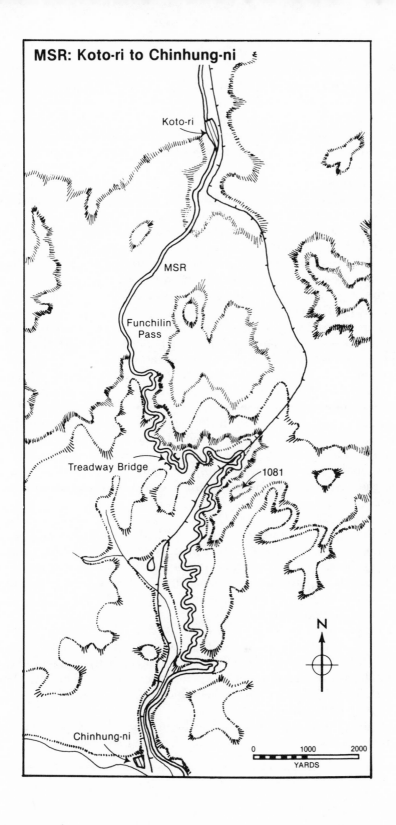

MSR: Koto-ri to Chinhung-ni

Koto-ri

MSR

Funchilin
Pass

Treadway Bridge

1081

Chinhung-ni

N

0   1000   2000
YARDS

the troops themselves all knew where things were and what to expect.

The division was on the slim side; there was no fat. While most units had to make do with less men than they should have, the men who were left were the heartiest, or the luckiest. And that counted for a great deal in those mountains.

In successive, closely timed moves, Marine and Army combat units would seize and hold firm the hills overlooking Koto-ri and the first stretch of road in the direction of Funchilin Pass. Other combat battalions would pass through the portals seized and held open in the initial moves, and still other units would pass through them in successive waves. Few combat troops would be among the thousands of men and vehicles on the narrow roadway, for the skyline all the way down to Chinhung-ni would be held, and firmly, by elements of Bowser's force.

As an added bonus, Bowser had full control over a fresh battalion of Marines — Lieutenant Colonel Buck Schmuck's 1st Battalion, 1st, which had been only lightly probed at Chinhung-ni — and he planned to use the fresh troops and their supports to seize Hill 1081, the tactical key to the passage through the choke point below Changjin Power Plant Number-1.

There was one major "if" in Bowser's plan, and it was crucial. *If* the assembled force at Koto-ri, which had over fifteen hundred wheeled and tracked vehicles to ride out on, was to reach the foot of the Taebek Plateau as a fully equipped fighting force, it was a given that the road and its bridges would have to be intact all the way down.

A battery of 3rd Infantry Division's 50th Anti-Aircraft Artillery Battalion, mounted in gun carriers and halftracks, had been forced by an estimated battalion of PLA infantry to turn around only three miles from Koto-ri. The action had been stiff, but several gunners had had an opportunity to see that the bridge spanning the two-thousand-feet-deep chasm adjacent to Changjin Power Plant Number-1 had been demolished.

That heart-stopping possibility was confirmed on December 6 by aerial reconnaissance. And on that same day Lieutenant Colonel Jack Partridge, commander of the 1st Engineer Battalion, had flown from Hagaru-ri aboard a Marine spotter plane to see for himself. His report: The bridge had indeed been blown.

There was a solution.

An Army bridging company had been trapped at Koto-ri on November 29, but it lacked the crucial bridging sections. With much attendant hassle, eight Treadway Bridge sections were loaded aboard Air Force C-119s and dropped over Koto-ri. Six of the sections were safely delivered; one fell into Chinese hands, and the last was damaged. The six were placed in the care of 1st Lieutenant Charles Ward, of the Army's 58th Treadway Bridge Company, whose unit was attached to Dog Company, 1st Engineer Battalion.

All anyone at Division could do about preserving the bridges was pray.

C H A P T E R

43

The 1st and 3rd Battalions, 7th, jumped off at 0800 on the morning of December 8, 1950.

Major Lefty Morris, who had been confirmed as commander of the 3rd Battalion, 7th, had had discussions with the commander of Fox Company, 31st Infantry, whose positions he would be attacking through on his way to Hill 1328, the first hill south of Koto-ri on the west side of the MSR. The Army captain had assured Morris and his staff that the area in front of Fox/31's lines had been adequately and aggressively patrolled during the previous week, and that the approach to the summit of the hill was relatively clear of PLA infantry.

The tiny battalion — hardly more than a reinforced company — jumped off from a good covered approach below the Army company's lines and made good initial progress while a fearsome snowstorm kicked up in the faces of the leading Marines. However, almost as soon as the first files of George/7 passed through Fox/31, they were hit by heavy fire thrown out by dozens of well-entrenched Chinese emplaced almost on top of the Army company's line. Suspicious, many of the veterans in the assault noted the quantity of litter in and around the Chinese fighting holes and concluded that, far from undertaking active patrolling, Fox/31 had clung to its line and allowed the Chinese to build up their defenses for at least several days.

As the troops ground forward, finding dozens of miserable Chinese soldiers frozen to death in their holes, their officers remained mindful that the last report from air observers before the snowstorm began had indicated that large formations of PLA infantry, supported by heavy mortars and light artillery, were moving on Hill 1328 from across the broad valley to the west of Koto-ri. It was too snowy, however, for Morris's troops to make out these formations.

All three of the 3rd Battalion, 7th's platoon-sized companies plugged away at the Chinese for the whole of the next three hours, until well past noon. Progress was minimal. Great manpower losses accrued from taking casualties, evacuating the casualties, and humping loads of fresh ammunition to the front.

At 1300, 7th Regiment ordered its reserve battalion, Lockwood's two-company 2nd Battalion, into action to support Morris's. Leaving 1st Lieutenant Bob Bey's Easy/7 on the road to contain the results of the fresh attack, Lockwood's executive officer, Major Jim Lawrence, ordered 1st Lieutenant Ralph Abell, the only officer left in Fox/7, to hook around to the southern end of Hill 1328 and launch an attack upon the rear of the Chinese contesting Morris's advance.

Moving quickly, Abell and his handful of Marines found that the only way to get into position to launch their attack was to climb a sheer, icy slope. It was a punishing effort, but the company slipped through the snowstorm unnoticed, re-formed quickly and quietly, and went into the assault.

After overpowering several Chinese emplacements, the attack ground to a halt when Abell ordered his men to throw up a hasty defensive line. Just in time, for the Chinese flipped a quick counterattack into the faces of the Fox/7 Marines. Ralph Abell sustained a severe wound in the arm, but stood firm when he remembered that he had no officers to whom he might relinquish command.

While Abell was struggling to maintain his foothold on the southern end of Hill 1328, Morris's left-flank unit ran a few patrols down to the roadway and tied in with Easy/7, thus containing the Chinese on three sides, leaving them a convenient bolt-hole to the west.

The slugfest continued on into the night as the division's vehicle train passed safely down the MSR.

★

Upon its arrival at Koto-ri, the 1st Battalion, 7th, had lost its incomparable commander, Lieutenant Colonel Ray Davis, who went up to Regiment to replace the wounded Fred Dowsett as Litz's executive officer. Replacing Davis was Major Buzz Sawyer, who had been the 2nd Battalion's commander until mid-November, and its exec thereafter.

Sawyer's battalion, the longest-suffering, hardest-fighting of all the rifle battalions, was to mount its assault on down the high, long ridge to the east of the MSR in conjunction with Lefty Morris's attack to the west. But something had gone out of the battalion after it had reached Koto-ri. The troops and their officers were on the ragged edge of being fought out. Every man was resigned to death.

When Sawyer's exec, Major Ray Fridrich, found the last four Baker/7 officers huddled around a tiny cook fire at sunrise, he had to use some pretty harsh language to get the company commander, 1st Lieutenant Joe Kurcaba, to shake off his fatigue and get the company saddled up. Kurcaba, one of the best troop leaders in the division, was just that far gone.

Sawyer's battalion managed to jump off on time. First Lieutenant Gene Hovatter's Able/7 had the vanguard, with Baker and Charlie Companies close behind.

Able/7 moved quickly down the ridgeline, covering a thousand yards as fast as the point platoon leader, 1st Lieutenant Bobbie Bradley, considered prudent.

The Chinese struck suddenly, holding Bradley's platoon where it stood, forcing Buzz Sawyer to establish a strong base of fire with elements of the battalion weapons company.

The weather quickly closed in, obviating air and artillery support. The fight grew in intensity. First Lieutenant Leslie Williams moved to Bradley's right and tried to pull his men forward, but both platoons were quickly pinned from three sides. Williams's runner, Private First Class Frederick Stouffer, loped off across several hundred yards of open ground and let himself down to the road, where he quickly convinced the commander of a Marine heavy tank to support the Able/7 attack. Though wounded, Stouffer stood exposed by the turret and directed fire. Able/7 moved forward a bit. Lieutenant Williams was shot to death.

First Lieutenant Joe Kurcaba, long since over his dawn attack of the blahs, spoke briefly with Major Tom Tighe, the 1st Battalion operations officer, then walked fifteen or twenty feet to where his officers had come in from the company line to assemble for a quick confab; Baker/7 was to take the Chinese strongpoint by the flank.

The Baker/7 officers were unable to see the enemy positions they would shortly be attacking, but gunfire spilling over from the Able/7 area was whistling all around them. First Lieutenant Woody Taylor took his orders wordlessly and strode off to find his 1st Platoon. Second Lieutenant Joe Owen, the company mortar officer, and 1st Lieutenant Chou Ein Lee, the 3rd Platoon leader, hit the deck, but

Joe Kurcaba remained on his feet. Owen and Lee pleaded with the company commander to get off his feet, but Kurcaba just looked at them through puffy eyelids and muttered his stock response: "You know, if I get down, I don't think I'll ever be able to get up again."

At length, Lieutenant Lee got up and returned to 3rd Platoon, leaving Joe Owen to urge Kurcaba to get down. The gunfire was growing more intense, but Kurcaba stood his ground, peering intently through the falling snow in the hope of spotting the Chinese.

Feeling challenged by the company commander's disdain for the enemy fire, Joe Owen lifted himself wearily to his feet. As Major Tom Tighe glanced over from his position nearby, Joe Kurcaba pitched back into Owen's arms, dead with a round square between the eyes.

The same flurry of fire killed Tom Tighe's operations chief and lodged a ricochet in the sleeve of the major's parka as he was speaking by radio with Colonel Litzenberg.

Owen pulled his dead friend to the ground, grabbed Kurcaba's map case and sent a runner to find Chou Ein Lee, who was next senior.

Meantime, Joe Owen took off for the left front, toward the sound of the heaviest firing. He heard on the way up that Lee had been wounded, and no one seemed to know where Woody Taylor was. Owen, a second lieutenant, took command of Baker/7.

Circling higher, hoping to come in behind the Chinese, Owen received an urgent call to come back down the hill to deliver a report. He found a single heavy tank at the base of the hill and immediately realized that he could lay its 90mm turret gun on the strongpoint that had reduced Baker/7 to a shadow. Owen grabbed the infantry phone and rattled off a stream of coordinates and landmarks to the tank commander.

Once the tank was squared away, Owen charged back up the hill and took control of every Baker/7 Marine he could find, a total of twenty-seven. The thin line moved forward. Then Owen's contact with the tank was lost, and what looked to him like the entire People's Liberation Army surged into sight on the ridgeline. Hoping to bluff them, Owen trudged forward. On his left, a BAR-man, one of the first men mustered into the company, went down. In the instant he had to mourn the loss of that fine combat Marine, Joe Owen caught a round in his left chest. Spun by the impact, he caught the next round in his right elbow. All sense of invulnerability, built up painstakingly over months of intense combat, dissipated in a spray of blood and bone. Then Joe Owen went down, screaming for the thin line of Marines to keep on moving forward.

While the tiny remnant of Baker/7 re-formed and held the Chinese by their noses, Charlie/7 laid down a heavy flanking fire and Able/7 delivered a spirited attack that broke the Chinese resistance.

The battalion, such as it was, continued moving forward for what remained of the day, digging in with Baker/7 about seven hundred yards ahead of the other companies about an hour before sunset. When Woody Taylor counted noses, he found that his command mustered twenty-nine men including himself and an artillery forward observer. It seemed to Taylor that nearly everyone was manning an automatic weapon of some sort.

★

A corpsman, on his first day with the company, ran afoul of Joe Owen when he could not produce a morphine ampule to ease the intense pain. But, despite his anger and frustration, Owen gave in to the Navyman's ministrations and allowed himself to be eased back down to the roadway. There he lay for some time, drifting in and out of sleep, trying gamely to offset the potential for frostbite by wiggling his toes whenever he was conscious, coughing blood from his nicked left lung. Three of the Baker/7 mortarmen Owen had led since first combat in September found him on the road and commandeered a corpsman's jeep virtually at gunpoint. The enormously tall officer was stuffed into the vehicle and driven back to the Koto-ri airstrip, where he was given some aid and a ride out of the war.

★

Progress on the MSR that day was negligible because of the unexpectedly heavy fighting on the skylines.

It was nearly noon before Lieutenant Colonel Jack Stevens's 1st Battalion, 5th, was ordered out of Koto-ri to attack its objective, Hill 1457, several miles south of town and about two thousand yards east of the MSR, which it dominated.

Baker/5 moved first, seizing some intermediate high ground and establishing a base of fire from which it would support Charlie/5's assault on the hilltop objective. Falling in with a patrol from the Army provisional battalion, 31/7, Charlie/5 moved rapidly and managed to drive the Chinese from the high ground by 1550, then beat back a weak Chinese counterthrust. Baker and Charlie Companies were in full possession of Hill 1457 by nightfall, backed by 41 Commando and covered from a separate enclave established by Able/5 overlooking the MSR.

★

Despite serious setbacks at the outset of the drive, and some un-completed occupations by nightfall, three of the first day's key objectives had been secured or nearly secured. In real numbers, casualties had been relatively light. But, in terms of proportions, the badly depleted assault units had suffered grievous losses. All, however, were game for more fighting.

The Chinese mounted several desultory attacks against the dwindling Koto-ri perimeter, but were easily repulsed by the 2nd and 3rd Battalions, 1st, which were rear guard.

One of the most difficult and distressing dilemmas facing the shrunken garrison that night was the refugee question.

Thousands upon thousands of North Korean civilians had been pouring out of the hills, hopeful that the departing Americans would take them south, to freedom. Despite very basic human feelings about the suffering masses, most Marines preferred to keep the civilians at arm's length.

As Corporal Alan Herrington, of Item/1, lay sleeping well within the northern arc of the Koto-ri perimeter, he was awakened by a buddy whose animal instincts had been aroused by very faint rustlings at the rear of the crowded tent. A knife rent a long gash in the canvas. Herrington and the other Marine leveled their carbines on the gash and blasted away, killing eight Chinese who had apparently infiltrated the perimeter with the unmanageable hordes of civilians.

Elsewhere in Koto-ri that night, Navy corpsmen assisted two Korean women giving birth.

CHAPTER

44

First Lieutenant Dave Peppin had been a Marine since early 1942, an officer since early 1945, an engineer since 1948, and a combat veteran since July, 1950, when he went into action near Pusan as the 1st Marine Brigade's engineer liaison officer. At twenty-six, despite his years in the Corps, he had been a troop leader for exactly nine days, since he had wangled a place aboard a C-47 bound from

Yonpo to Hagaru-ri on December 1 to fill a vacancy in the command of the 2nd Platoon, Dog Company, Engineers.

Thus far in the campaign Peppin had seen little action: some small-arms exchanges with the Chinese at Hagaru-ri, and some patrolling on the skyline overlooking the MSR on the way to Koto-ri. On December 8, as his platoon chugged forward in column with the 7th Marines, Peppin had rounded a blind curve and spotted three figures standing stock-still on the roadway several hundred feet ahead. The engineer platoon leader paused and strained his eyes to make out details. The men, who did not move, each wore a scarlet-lined cape. Concluding that he was facing Chinese officers of high rank, Peppin called out for them to surrender. The three men continued to stand stock-still, silent, staring back at Dave Peppin, who called again. Nothing. A third try brought no response. Peppin calmly leveled his carbine, as did several of his engineers, and blasted the three men from the roadway. None of those men ever uttered a sound.

Following that bizarre incident, Peppin's platoon was ordered into the hills to the left of the roadway. The platoon's vehicles were left in the care of the drivers, and thirty-odd engineers mounted the slope and huffed and puffed up the distant ridgeline. Hours of almost mindless walking ensued. The ridge on which Peppin's platoon had been placed angled slowly back to the MSR, so the engineers were out of the hills and back in the road-bound column by nightfall, December 8. The column was by then firmly stalled by fighting to the south, so the engineers bedded down as best they could.

On the morning of December 9, Dave Peppin's platoon was ordered to the head of the regimental column along with 1st Lieutenant Ozzie Vom Orde's 1st Platoon of Dog/Engineers and 1st Lieutenant Charles Ward's four Army bridging trucks. If all went well before the day was out, the two engineer platoons and the bridging unit would have the opportunity to improvise a span across the gap in the MSR beside Changjin Power Plant Number-1.

★

Captain George Rasula's tiny provisional company of the 31st Infantry was higher up and farther out than any other American unit south of Koto-ri on December 8 and 9. Getting up there had involved a very long and arduous climb followed by a tough tramp through dry, cold, crotch-deep snow along a razorback ridge meandering for four or five miles from Koto-ri.

It happened that George Rasula, a Finn from the wilds of northern

Minnesota, was peculiarly endowed for such rugged duty. By dumb luck, and his linguistic abilities, Rasula had spent several months before the war conducting cold-weather exercises with former Finnish Army officers in Alaska. He had learned much; probably, he knew more about cold weather combat and survival techniques than any man in X Corps. His experience and knowledge, and a slight bent toward motherhood, had kept many of his poorly equipped troops from succumbing to the cold. While men farther down were experiencing a rise in temperature, George Rasula and his tiny company climbed steadily into colder weather.

Visibility was severely limited. Landmarks could not be spotted. The climb and advance went off by dead reckoning, by instinct.

There had been one scary incident in the swirling mists on December 8. As Captain Rasula dropped back in the column to prod the slowpokes, all hell broke loose at the point. Men all around were dropping to cover, though there was precious little of that. Rushing forward, the captain kicked the lead platoon into an enveloping maneuver. But before Rasula could really get going, the firing stopped. Suddenly and completely.

The men were cold and hungry, but there was no way to heat their rations. When Rasula checked through their gear, he was stunned to find that several men had chucked their sleeping bags, the most essential of survival tools.

Reluctantly, Rasula decided to leave his men in position while he and a platoon leader descended to the roadway for orders and a briefing. Visibility had improved by the early afternoon, and the hearty Finn felt he could make it down and return by nightfall. It was a grueling descent, but Rasula found his commander, Lieutenant Colonel Barry Anderson, and asked about relief. Anderson just shook his head without uttering a sound and went on about his business, leaving George Rasula and the platoon leader, two pretty frozen specimens, out in the cold, literally and otherwise.

Getting back up to the ridgeline to rejoin his company involved a very tiring climb for Captain Rasula, no doubt the result of poor diet and lack of sleep over the past few weeks. To compound his discomfort that cold, cold night Rasula, who did not think it wise to sleep in his down bag because of earlier enemy activity, sat in his foxhole with the bag pulled tightly about his shoulders.

There was no action that night, but Rasula found himself beneath several inches of new snow when he awoke at sunrise. The new day was glorious, clear and bright beneath a gorgeous blue sky. As the men stood up, pounding their feet and hands to get the blood circulating, three PLA infantrymen were spotted standing motionless about four hundred yards farther along the ridgeline. One soldier asked to be allowed to fire, and Rasula let him get off a single round, which resounded across the dead silent snowscape and sent the Chinese shuffling from sight.

Way below, the point of the column on the MSR was beginning to grind forward.

★

Easy/7, which had spent the night on the roadway by Hill 1328, tied in with the 3rd Battalion, 7th, and Fox/7, moved up to the southern end of the hill to join its sister company. First Lieutenant Ralph Abell, who had been shot in the arm the previous afternoon, asked his colleague, 1st Lieutenant Bob Bey, to take charge of both tiny companies while he turned himself in to have the wound treated.

An hour later, as air and artillery worked over Hill 1328 under the unblemished sky, Abell hiked back up the hill to rejoin his command. His arm had not been badly injured, as he had first thought, and he did not care to stay with the wounded; though his arm was immobilized in a sling, he opted to return to his company.

The afternoon wore on as the 2nd Battalion, 7th, cleared the slopes of Hill 1328 nearest the MSR. Morris's battalion pulled out just before noon, and Tom Ridge's 3rd Batalion, 1st, arrived shortly after that to free Lockwood's troops for their move to the road.

After moving less than a mile, Fox/7 was sent to cover by sporadic fire from the heights across the road. Most of the men, including Ralph Abell, went to ground in a ditch beside the road. One man, however, stood his ground.

Sergeant Clyde Pitts, a slow-drawling, deliberate Southerner with an authentic cornball sense of humor, clomped up and down the roadway beside the ditch. Like most of the men at his feet, Pitts had earlier filled his pockets to bulging with assorted candy; in Pitts's case, the candy was Charms.

Above the roar of the gunfire and the throaty rumble of hundreds of idling engines, Clyde Pitts pitched the troops in a whining, nasal carnie barker's voice each time he saw a Marine squeeze off a particularly well-prepared round. "And here's a pack of Charms for this lucky Marine," or any of a dozen variations. Some of the haggard boys were so broken up with laughter that they could not shoulder their weapons. It helped pass the time.

★

First Lieutenant Woody Taylor, the last of the Baker/7 officers, awoke to find that all of the thirty South Korean soldiers assigned the night before to eke out his tiny company had made off in the night.

Taylor pressed outward from his tiny perimeter as soon as he could organize patrols. Dozens of frozen, dying Chinese were found on all sides, within one hundred fifty yards of the company perimeter. With some reluctance, but with the sense that he was performing an act of mercy, Taylor ordered his troops to dispatch every Chinese soldier they could find.

Homer Litzenberg arrived at the Baker/7 position at 0930 with Major Buzz Sawyer, the new battalion commander, and ordered Taylor to dispatch a platoon to contact Marine units farther down the ridgeline.

Woody Taylor had about had his fill of patrolling. He had only twenty-eight men in a company that could have mustered nearly two hundred two weeks earlier. "Hell, Colonel," he thundered, "I haven't got a platoon left in the whole damned company."

Buzz Sawyer jumped in and told Taylor to sit tight and send whatever he could spare to secure a knob overlooking the power plant.

After Litz and Sawyer left, Taylor told off half his company and sent it down the hill toward the road: thirteen men and a sergeant.

★

Engineers were needed at the point of the column. The Chinese had blown great holes in the roadway, and these had to be filled in if the long column was to pass.

First Lieutenant Dave Peppin got The Word from his company commander, Captain Craig Turner, to move forward with his bulldozers.

The first crater was huge. Unbelievably huge. And the ground was frozen solid. Short of blasting for fill, Peppin could not imagine a way to restore the roadway. Looking for an out, the twenty-six-year-old platoon leader thought of snow, something he had plenty of. The bulldozer was put to work scraping snow into the hole and running over it to pack it down. It took forty-five minutes of hard work, but the ten-foot deep crater was filled, the roadway was restored, and the column clanked forward — with Dave Peppin and his bulldozer in first position. (Very few of the thousands of men who crossed that snow-filled crater, or many others, realized what Peppin had done. Not so the North Korean government, which was in for quite a shock come the first thaw.)

Watching infantry units advance along the ridges and slopes adjacent to the road, Peppin adjusted his pace to their pace. There was no gunfire for a long time, but as Peppin and the lead bulldozer rounded a sharp turn dominated by a sight-impeding swale, the air was suddenly filled with machine-gun bullets. Changjin Power Plant Number-1 and the blasted bridge were just around the curve, and so were several dozen Chinese.

Peppin looked up the adjacent slope for some help, but saw that the infantry had fallen behind. He walked along the road-bound column a short distance and found an officer and a small knot of riflemen. The officer was willing to lead the advance and, hopefully, take the power plant.

While the infantry moved on the power plant, Dave Peppin and Ozzie Vom Orde, whose platoon had come up to join Peppin's, got to work preparing the bridging trucks for the ticklish job that lay ahead.

The road was too narrow for a truck to turn around on, and the bridging trucks, which had to be backed into position, were longer than most. But there was a turnout that had been leveled weeks earlier, and the first bridging truck was backed up and turned around.

While the infantry moved on the power plant and Peppin and Vom Orde sweated out the reversal of the bridging truck, Colonel Litzenberg stalked into view to yell about the delay. The colonel ordered Peppin and Vom Orde to send their engineers out to attack the power plant. Dave Peppin was not particularly awed by Homer Litzenberg's exalted rank, so he dug in his heels, suggesting that the colonel send his riflemen to do that job while the engineers prepared to do theirs. Litz backed off.

By that time, Charlie/7 and the squad that was half of Baker/7 had captured the power plant after a brief fight that netted a dozen prisoners and their weapons. Farther on, as the Baker/7 element fanned out to defend the bridge site, it found fifty more Chinese frozen and dying in their fighting holes. Charlie/7 moved forward to outpost those same holes, and the battalion weapons company set up its mortars and machine guns.

On questioning one of the chilled prisoners, Buzz Sawyer learned that a thousand-man infantry force had raced on foot across the mountains the night before to get into position to defend the power plant and the heights. A sudden drop in temperature had caused nearly every one of those PLA soldiers to freeze in his own sweat. Only a few dozen survived to be captured.

★

No one was going anywhere until the former bridge spanning the two-thousand-foot chasm had been replaced by the two engineer platoons and the Army bridging detachment.

It was 1230 hours, December 9, 1950.

C H A P T E R
45

Lieutenant Colonel Buck Schmuck's 1st Battalion, 1st Marines, was spoiling for a fight. Composed almost entirely of Regulars, the battalion had been kept back from any really serious fighting by the need to hold the railhead at Chinhung-ni secure against Chinese investment.

Turning back a light PLA probe during the night of November 28, and mounting a two-company foray to destroy a Chinese base camp west of Chinhung-ni on November 30 had done little to sate the battalion's appetite for action.

It was clear by December 1 that the road through Chinhung-ni had been cut to the north and south, but a continuing flow of troops from Hamhung to and through the base had shown the Chinese to be in rather light strength in the area. Nevertheless, the bulk of a Marine engineer company on duty by Changjin Power Plant Number-2, some miles south of Chinhung-ni, had been driven into Schmuck's perimeter.

Buck Schmuck personally led a tiny patrol about eight miles north along the MSR to see what he could see of the vaunted roadblocks near Changjin Power Plant Number-1. The small force got to within a few miles of Koto-ri, penetrating a major Chinese troop concentration. In a brief but thrilling action, Schmuck's patrol had called artillery fire from Koto-ri onto the main Chinese force, then had effected a hairsbreadth escape down the steep incline near the power plant. The most important result of that patrol was Schmuck's gaining firsthand knowledge about the terrain to the north of Chinhung-ni. One of the battalion commander's deepest impressions was the obvious importance of a jumbled mass of ridges known as Hill

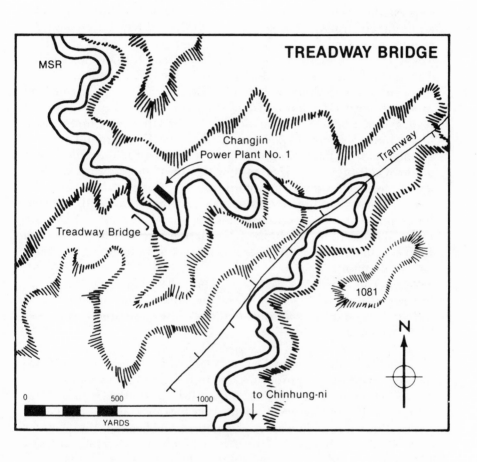

TREADWAY BRIDGE

MSR

Changjin
Power Plant No. 1

Tramway

Treadway Bridge

1081

N

to Chinhung-ni

0   500   1000

YARDS

1081; whoever held the topmost heights, he realized, controlled the MSR for miles in either direction.

★

Nothing much happened at or with regard to Chinhung-ni until the evening of December 6. At that time, as O. P. Smith was preparing to fly from Hagaru-ri to Koto-ri, he contacted Ned Almond and requested that the 1st Battalion, 1st, be replaced at Chinhung-ni by a reinforced Army battalion. For once, Almond had anticipated the requirement, and he had already gained permission from GHQ-Tokyo to utilize elements of the fresh 3rd Infantry Division (which Tokyo had for a time considered transferring to 8th Army, in northwestern Korea). Almond called in Brigadier General Armistead Mead, the 3rd Division assistant commander, and ordered him to lead a task force to relieve Schmuck's battalion at Chinhung-ni. Mead built his force, known as Task Force Dog, around the 3rd Battalion, 7th Infantry Regiment, and the 92nd Field Artillery Battalion, a self-propelled 155mm howitzer unit whose guns would be able to reach all the way to Koto-ri.

Task Force Dog brushed aside meager opposition south of Chinhung-ni and arrived to relieve Schmuck on the afternoon of December 7. By that time, the bulk of 1st Marine Division had closed on Koto-ri, and Colonel Al Bowser was hard at work planning the drive on Chinhung-ni.

When The Word was passed to Schmuck's troops that they were to seize Hill 1081, the last barrier the bulk of the division would have to face on its long journey to the sea, they prepared themselves with a vengeance.

★

In the early morning of December 8, with hours of darkness remaining to cover its approach, Captain Robert Wray's Charlie Company, 1st, moved quickly up the MSR from the Chinhung-ni perimeter. Following was Captain Bob Barrow's Able/1, the battalion headquarters and weapons companies, and Captain Wes Noren's Baker/1. Baker Battery of the Army's 50th Anti-Aircraft Artillery Battalion clanked along in the column, an important addition of self-propelled twin-40mm gun carriers and halftracks mounting quad-.50-caliber machine guns.

For 1st Lieutenant Brandon Carlon, a twenty-six-year-old 1947 Annapolis graduate who had seen first action at Inchon, the move from Chinhung-ni had the particular air of a raiding foray. Carlon's platoon of Charlie/1, near the head of the column, padded silently through the fierce snowstorm that had begun almost as soon as the battalion point had cleared the defenses manned by Task Force Dog.

A cough rang like a gunshot through the dark silence, and the embarrassed culprit was roundly *shushed* by everyone nearby.

Captain Bob Barrow, a brilliant young officer who had served as an advisor to Communist guerrillas in Central China during World War II, had begun the evening in a depressed state. At the verbal briefing preceding the move from Chinhung-ni, Barrow had been told that his crack Able/1 would be the battalion reserve. The tall, slim Louisiana native had been within a breath of demanding a more important role, but the spectre of losing even one man in the name of unit pride stilled his tongue. In the end, however, Buck Schmuck had juggled the missions of his rifle companies, and Captain Barrow was given the job of leading the main attack upon Hill 1081.

The six-mile approach on the objective was made in almost total silence, a condition appreciably enhanced by the sound-deadening qualities of the billowing snowstorm. It took fully five hours for the troops to trudge up the steep incline, and for Charlie Company to position itself for the opening move of a most delicate operation. To the rear, five halftracks and gun carriers were ready to spring forward to lay direct fire on the heights; for the moment, however, the approach had to be made by unsupported, silent infantry.

★

Charlie/1 arrived at the foot of Hill 1081 and Captain Wray ordered Brandon Carlon to lead his platoon up the slope to secure the ridgeline overlooking a hairpin turn in the MSR.

It was hardly an attack. There was no way for Carlon to deploy his troops without slowing to a crawl, so he simply started up the nose as quickly as he could climb. The platoon strung itself out in a long, loose single file and followed. No one could see the remainder of Charlie Company, nor, after a few minutes, the road.

While praying that he would be able to overcome opposition by surprise alone, Lieutenant Carlon met no Chinese, though he passed a number of seemingly abandoned bunkers that smelled of recent occupation. Carlon continued to struggle up the steep, slippery slope until he arrived atop the commanding knoll. Sounds from nearby indicated that the Chinese were digging in higher up and to the left. Gaps in the snowstorm revealed the bodies of several Chinese sprawled in the snow nearby, probably victims of an earlier air strike.

Carlon's platoon stopped on the knob to wait for units from the rear to close up.

★

Captain Wes Noren's Baker/1 moved through the remainder of the reinforced battalion, trudged a few score yards up the steep, wooded slope to the right of the roadway and swept forward to find and hold blocking positions north of Able Company's line of attack. Looking through the billowing storm, Captain Noren saw hundreds of footprints in the fresh snow on the roadway below his route of advance.

Machine-gun fire revealed the presence of a manned Chinese bunker directly in front of the company. A platoon was ordered to reduce the opposition, and mortar fire was called in, though there was no way to gauge its effectiveness. The snow that obscured the results of the mortar fire also covered the approach of the assault platoon, which defeated the Chinese gunners in a short, sharp fight.

Next up was a large, well-built command bunker that Noren's point took without opposition. The Chinese had left so precipitously, in fact, that the Marines found rice cooking on the fire and fresh clothing so recently laundered that it was still warm.

The advance paralleling the roadway resumed, cautiously, through the remainder of the day. Groups of Chinese put out harassing fires, which forced Baker Company to deploy and mount numerous profitless attacks. The advantages and disadvantages of the incessant snowfall just about canceled each other out. While there was no serious opposition, Baker Company did lose several men killed and wounded. Unable to get an exact fix on his company's location in the midst of the continuing snowstorm, Captain Noren halted the advance late in the afternoon and ordered his men to dig in as best they could.

★

Shortly after 1st Lieutenant Brandon Carlon stopped his platoon on the knob overlooking the curve in the MSR, he was joined by Captain Bob Barrow, the Able Company commander. Barrow, however, paused for only a moment to get his bearings, then moved on through, followed by his company gunnery sergeant, King Thatenhurst, and the column of platoons. As soon as Able Company had passed through, an increase in the snowfall reduced Carlon's vista to a mere twenty-five yards.

The going for Bob Barrow and Able Company was treacherous in the extreme. Having started the mission at eleven hundred feet above sea level at Chinhung-ni, the battalion had climbed twelve hundred feet on the MSR. The summit of Hill 1081 was about one thousand feet above the roadway, about thirty-three hundred feet above sea level. The thin mountain air and chilling cold took a toll upon the energy reserves of the climbers, slowing the column considerably, as did the precipitous, rocky route that Barrow was forced to blaze for his bulkily clad, heavily laden riflemen and gunners. The care that had to be exerted to avoid traps set out by the Chinese only added to the general misery.

Captain Barrow and Technical Sergeant Thatenhurst reached the top first, on their hands and knees. Remaining at the end of a narrow ridge running south from Hill 1081, Barrow sent Thatenhurst down to bring the rest of the company forward as quickly — and as quietly — as possible.

Leaving the troops in defilade just below the summit, Thatenhurst led the platoon leaders and forward observers to speak with the captain, who in the meantime had surveyed the ridge ahead.

The ground was treacherous. The attack would have to be mounted along a very narrow razorback ridge; Barrow doubted that as much as a platoon could be deployed in line on that ridge. A few men with a machine gun could stop Able/1 in its tracks. Just before the platoon leaders and forward observers reached him, Barrow had had a fleeting glimpse of the waiting Chinese through a wind-whipped gap in the storm. The ridge ahead sloped upward and widened considerably nearer the top, where Chinese were deployed seventy-five to one hundred yards dead ahead.

The platoon leaders and forward observers were led by the company commander to covered positions from which they could observe the terrain and the enemy deployment. It was clear to all that the Chinese were waiting for trouble; rifle fire heard faintly from below told both sides that Noren's Baker Company was still advancing on the roadway.

Barrow asked his 4.2-inch forward observer if his guns were deployed. When he heard that they were, the company commander asked that a mission be fired against the Chinese emplacements. The forward observer, however, looked askance at the captain; he could not be certain of observing the effects of the fire, and there was every reason to anticipate that it would alert the Chinese to the imminent attack.

Barrow was prepared to tough it out. Even if the mortar fire tipped his hand, he reasoned, he could be certain that the Chinese would experience a few crucial moments of confusion, during which he could drive home his initial moves. Responding to the possibility of bringing the first salvo down on his own head, Barrow allowed as the first rounds should be fired to the right and then corrected by sound alone onto a line parallel to the company's axis of advance.

It was midafternoon when 2nd Lieutenant Don Jones led his 2nd Platoon and a machine-gun squad quietly forward. One infantry squad was perched precariously upon each of the steep slopes on either flank and the third infantry squad and machine guns were deployed in line across the razorback ridge. Barrow and his executive officer, with the 60mm mortar section, were right behind Jones's platoon. To the immediate right was Staff Sergeant William Roach's 3rd Platoon and, in the reserve position, 1st Lieutenant Bill McClelland's 1st Platoon, which would have no room to deploy until the Chinese positions dead ahead had been overrun.

The 4.2-inch rounds landed in bone-jarring proximity, and the forward observer mouthed a few terse corrections into the mouthpiece of his mike.

Jones's platoon moved quickly and quietly through the snow. The leading fire team had crept and crawled about one hundred yards when an eddy in the snowstorm placed it squarely in the sights of a Chinese machine gun, which opened fire. It was obvious, as the lead squad went to ground, that the Chinese were firing blindly, in panic. The Marines continued to inch forward, but only a very few could return the heavy fire.

Bob Barrow, realizing that he had committed too few men to grapple effectively with the fully alerted defenders, ordered Lieutenant Jones to halt in place and build up a firing line with one of his squads and the light machine gunners; the two remaining rifle squads were to find a way around the Chinese flank and mount an attack from that quarter.

Jones moved to the left with the two squads, covered by the snowstorm. He would swing right once he was in a good position, and once Barrow had built up a strong base of fire with Staff Sergeant Roach's 3rd Platoon.

Corporal Joseph Leeds, one of Jones's fire-team leaders, slithered forward on the extreme left, taking nearly an hour to move one hundred fifty yards. The remainder of Jones's two assault squads followed just as slowly.

Bob Barrow painstakingly built up his base of fire. The 60mm mortars were carried forward under wild, heavy fire and set up in such a way as to be fired directly at the Chinese emplacements. While waiting for Jones to gain adequate positions on the left, the company commander contented himself by dueling with the Chinese on his front.

Though the 60mm gunners were unable to see their targets, they opened as soon as word was passed from Lieutenant Jones that he was ready to attack. Satisfied that he had done all he could, Barrow ordered Jones to move out on the left while Roach's platoon moved from the right.

Blinded by snow, hampered by their own heavy equipment, slipping and sliding on the steep, rocky slopes, Barrow's Marines closed on the Chinese, screaming and taunting to steady themselves and rattle the enemy.

On the extreme left, Corporal Joseph Leeds spotted the strongpoint throwing out most of the Chinese fire just as the Chinese turned several machine guns to meet Jones's flank attack. Pulling his fire team behind him, Leeds lit out over the impossible terrain, through heavy machine-gun fire, and killed nine Chinese before he was felled with a mortal wound.

The way was open. With Marines pitching through the gap opened by Corporal Leeds, the Chinese abandoned their bunkers and took off blindly through the snowstorm. Many escaped down the reverse slope, but others ran headlong into Roach's platoon, which was driving in from the right front. All of the bunkers were cleared with hand grenades, and the Marines immediately moved in, seeking a respite from the howling wind and deepening chill.

Nine Able Company Marines had been killed, and eleven had been wounded.

It was dark within minutes. Bob Barrow called all his men to the newly won ground and ordered them into a tight hedgehog defense.

The wounded bore the brunt of the suffering. By organizing litter teams immediately upon the close of the action, Captain Barrow moved to get his injured safely to the road before they succumbed in the cold to even very minor wounds. Each litter team, working in relays, took fully five hours just to reach the intermediate position held by Brandon Carlon's Charlie/1 platoon. Carlon's corpsman did what he could for the freezing wounded, then accompanied them the rest of the way to the battalion sick bay on the road. The litter teams, which turned the wounded over to Carlon's men, began humping reserve ammunition and supplies back to Able Company, a most grueling task for men who had already found the limits of their endurance.

The Marines atop Hill 1081 spent the night huddled up against the unremitting wind. They found that everything was frozen solid when they broke out their rations. This was the company's first experience with frozen rations, and it took some time before the troops mastered the art of warming what could be warmed and chipping away at the rest.

Before the nine dead Marines could be decently laid out in the Able Company perimeter, the atmosphere had frozen them in grotesque attitudes, which helped the morale of the living not one jot.

Though Bob Barrow did not then know it, the advance of the 7th Marines from Koto-ri had been delayed; it would be at least another day before the head of the divisional column could get as far south as Hill 1081.

The Chinese tried once to win back their former positions, but their attack was weak and brief, and Able/1 held with ease.

★

December 9 dawned clear and cold.

Before even considering a move against the integrated system of bunkers that still lay before his position, Bob Barrow ordered all hands to test-fire their weapons. It was a prudent move, for many rifles and machine guns had frozen in the night and had to be cleared before the action could resume.

The battalion's senior air controller climbed to Barrow's command post to call air support for the coming assault, and mortar and artillery observers who had spent the previous day and night with Able Company checked in with their fire-direction centers. Below, the battalion 81mm mortar platoon was tearing open canisters of ammunition and stacking the shells neatly beside the guns.

After forming a base of fire with his blooded 2nd and 3rd Platoons and the company weapons, Bob Barrow huddled with his 1st Platoon leader, 1st Lieutenant Bill McClelland, to work up a plan for the final assault on the Chinese bunkers ahead.

Bill McClelland had dropped out of the University of Pennsylvania in the middle of his junior year, in late 1940, to enlist in the Marine Corps. He had seen action in the Solomons and Marianas before being ordered to Basic School in 1945, and he had been commissioned a Regular second lieutenant in 1946. He had joined the 6th Marines at Camp Lejeune in June, 1950, just in time to be shipped with his unit to California to become part of the 1st Marines. He had been through Inchon and Seoul and had participated in actions against North Korean guerrillas in northeastern Korea, around Wonsan. Bill McClelland was a career professional, as were nearly all his men, and he was faced with one of the most important tasks of his career.

First Platoon would mount the final assault on the topmost knob of Hill 1081. Though he would have ample fire support, McClelland could not count upon infantry support in pressing his assault across the severely restricted approach to the objective.

While 1st Platoon moved carefully forward, the company machine gunners squeezed off aimed volleys, hoping to drive the Chinese deep into their fighting holes. The tactic, which drew little blood, seemed to be working, for the return fire slackened.

The key to the Chinese position was a rocky shelf to the left front of the objective, a position from which McClelland hoped to mount a two-squad assault. The platoon's third squad was placed in the care of Staff Sergeant Ernest Umbaugh and sent to the right, along the military crest.

The attack opened with heavy fire from the supporting arms and Roach's 3rd Platoon. McClelland's split 1st Platoon jumped off on time, but the two left squads were almost immediately driven to ground by heavy machine-gun fire. Staff Sergeant Umbaugh, with the right squad, launched himself directly across the topographical crest and, with Bill McClelland, ranged behind the two stalled squads to get the men up and moving once again.

The first Chinese emplacements were quickly overrun, but the assault squads moved onto ground covered by machine guns on a bare knob some two hundred fifty yards to the north. While McClelland steadied the left squads, Ernie Umbaugh crossed back over the topographical crest to halt the right squad and build up a base of fire, which he directed against the strongpoint to the north. Once the left squad had been adequately directed, Umbaugh again crossed the open ground to rejoin Lieutenant McClelland and the bulk of the platoon.

First Platoon was by then down to twenty effectives.

As McClelland's platoon halted in place to reorganize, Captain Barrow ordered William Roach's 3rd Platoon forward to the newly won line, and Donald Jones's 2nd Platoon moved up to establish a new base of fire.

McClelland's new line of departure provided a screened approach upon the enemy base of fire. As McClelland and Umbaugh rose to the attack, Sergeant Henry Noonkester, a squad leader, passed both of them and delivered a splendid one-man grenade assault upon the two nearest Chinese emplacements.

Unable to fire because the assault platoons were in the way, the company machine gunners left their weapons and joined the attack, firing their pistols into the faces of Chinese who had been bypassed by 1st Platoon's screaming charge.

In rolling up the Chinese defenses from end to end, the attacking

Marines stampeded the defenders through the complex of trenches and bunkers, dropping grenades from above onto the fleeing, panicked PLA soldiers.

When Bill McClelland stopped to let the riflemen pass in the final assault upon two stubbornly held bunkers at the center of the collapsing Chinese complex, he saw that Ernie Umbaugh was legging it toward him from the opposite flank. Before the platoon sergeant could speak, however, both men were blanketed by a flurry of small-arms fire. The lieutenant had many holes shot through his parka and equipment, but he suffered no injury. Ernie Umbaugh, who was only five feet away, was shot full of holes and fell bleeding to the ground. His wounds would be mortal.

At the center of the diminishing action, Corporal Earl Flowers stalked resolutely through the beaten zone, depositing American and captured Chinese grenades in each emplacement he passed. When the grenade supply was nearly exhausted, a 2nd Platoon rifleman ran across the open, fire-swept ground to deliver two sackfuls to McClelland's riflemen.

Coming up behind the assault units, Bob Barrow had his attention wrenched from the action by a 1st Platoon rifleman. "Look! Look," the man shouted, pointing down toward the road. Barrow's heart stood in his throat as he watched the leading elements of the 7th Marines breast the top of Funchilin Pass far below.

Hill 1081 cost Able Company, 1st Marines, one hundred twelve dead, wounded, and frostbitten out of an original complement of two hundred twenty-three.

The road was clear. But there was trouble at the power plant.

C H A P T E R

46

The bridge sections were too short.

Seven feet too short.

The gap in the roadway was twenty-nine feet across, and the steel Treadway Bridge was twenty-two feet from end to end.

First Lieutenant Dave Peppin rose from his haunches and threw aside the length of communications wire he was holding across the chasm. The man on the far side of the gap in the roadway had told off a full twenty-nine feet, and there was no getting around it. Peppin picked his way past the squat, rectangular form of the silent concrete power-plant building to rejoin the two engineer platoons arrayed on the northern side of the gap and bent his ear close to hear if anyone had a reasonable solution. For his own part, Peppin felt that the power plant itself could be razed to the ground to provide a precarious but flat bypass around the gap. But that would take most of the day.

As Dave Peppin and 1st Lieutenant Ozzie Vom Orde bemoaned their egregious luck, an enlisted engineer came forward and told the two officers that he had uncovered a large stock of precut bridging timbers — stout wooden beams that could be built up to support either end of the short bridging sections.

Elated, Vom Orde and Peppin carefully surveyed the gap. There was no purchase at the northern end, but there was a ledge on the far side, about eight feet below the surface of the road and about ten feet in length.

The solution was a textbook approach: the timbers would be stacked in alternating layers to form an open crib on the ledge; the crib would be filled in to form a solid base; the steel treadways would be placed across from the solid roadway to the crib; the bridge would be solid and stable for the fifteen hundred vehicles that would have to cross.

Every available man pitched in to help. While the engineers brought up the bridging timbers, Chinese prisoners captured in the fight to take the power plant were ordered up to collect the grotesque corpses of their countrymen who had frozen to death in their fighting holes during the night; the bodies would be used to fill in the open latticework of the wooden crib as the earth nearby was too hard for so extensive a digging operation.

As the timbers were being put in place, a harried Dave Peppin was accosted once again by Homer Litzenberg, who huffed and fumed and looked repeatedly at his wristwatch. "How long will it take to put the bridge in?"

"Two hours, Sir," Dave Peppin responded.

"I'll hold you to that." The tall, square regimental commander stalked back up the road and around the swale several hundred feet to the north. And Dave Peppin went right back to work.

Word arrived that, a mile or so to the south, the Chinese had dropped the steel trestle carrying the mountain tramway onto the road. Lieutenant Peppin sent seven men to survey the damage; it seemed to be every bit as big a job as placing the Treadway Bridge. The seven returned in less than ten minutes to report that the Chinese had the road covered and they could not proceed to the damaged trestle without ample infantry support. There were thousands of riflemen to the rear, but only a few dozen that Peppin could see around the power plant. He was too busy to take the time to argue with an infantry officer about mounting a combat patrol.

★

When Captain Wes Noren, commander of Baker/1, awoke on the morning of December 9, he was thankful to see that the heavy snowfall that had hampered his advance northward past Hill 1081 the previous day had ceased altogether.

When Noren checked his surroundings, he noted that he had stopped his company a little short of the ridgeline that had been his objective, an easy enough error to commit in the late afternoon light and blinding snowstorm. The company moved forward a few hundred feet to the correct position and deployed to defend the ground. A large number of Noren's men had developed severe frostbite, so the captain organized litter teams and had the casualties evacuated to the battalion command post, which had been set up in a large, warm bunker that Baker Company had taken the day before. A damaged American helicopter abandoned by the side of the road provided some recreation for gawkers, but the immediate task for Baker/1 was to dig in and establish viable communications with Battalion and supporting arms. The extreme cold, however, had frozen Noren's radio batteries, and these had to be replaced. Also, Noren learned the hard way of the effect of the cold upon the flight of artillery shells; 155mm registration rounds, fired by the Army's 92nd Field Artillery Battalion at Chinhung-ni, could not be accurately placed on a Chinese unit passing across the skyline, but they did send that unit running from the scene in disorganized haste.

From his vantage point on the high ground, Wes Noren could see Dave Peppin and Ozzie Vom Orde putting in the Treadway Bridge.

As the afternoon wore on, a tiny combat patrol from Major Buzz Sawyer's 1st Battalion, 7th, dropped down from the heights and stalked forward to join Noren's company. The linkup had been made. All that remained, it seemed, was the successful placement of the bridge.

★

The Army bridging truck was backed into place the moment the crib had been completed and filled. First Lieutenant Charles Ward, the Army bridgemaster, oversaw the placement of the two massive I beams which, with the help of the Marine engineers, were spaced correctly and made absolutely parallel to each other. A huge four-inch-thick plywood sheet was run out onto the spacing bars, and the lead bulldozer clanked gingerly forward to level a short earthen ramp across the crib.

The Treadway Bridge was ready. The 1st Battalion, 7th, had linked up with the 1st Battalion, 1st. Able/1 was winning its fight atop the commanding height. Everything was set; the column could proceed.

Lieutenant Colonel Jack Partridge, commander of the 1st Engineer Battalion, climbed aboard his waiting jeep and drove back to the top of Funchilin Pass to have a word with Lieutenant Colonel Gus Banks, commander of the 1st Service Battalion and the officer in charge of Division Train Number-1. Partridge, a reticent man, simply told his colleague that the engineers were beginning to cross the bridge and that the divisional column could proceed slowly down the steep grade to cross right behind them and several combat units. Then Partridge had his driver reverse the jeep, and he flew down the hill to oversee the crossing.

★

Ozzie Vom Orde's platoon stayed to keep an eye on the bridge, while Dave Peppin assembled his platoon at the southern end of the Treadway Bridge and resumed his position at the head of the column to have a look at the tramway trestle. There was, he had been told, plenty of infantry out ahead.

After he had covered most of the one thousand yards between the Treadway Bridge and the destroyed tramway trestle, Lieutenant Peppin called a halt so that he could study what he was up against.

The huge latticework trestle, complete with narrow-gauge railroad tracks, had crossed the road on fifteen-foot-high abutments. Chinese sappers had simply blown the trestle at both ends and it had dropped neatly, and intact, upon the MSR, blocking it.

There appeared to be several solutions available. Peppin could place ample explosives and reduce the trestle's mass by blowing it to its components, or, because there was a wide, sloping meadow just to the left of the roadway, he could construct a bypass.

He needed a closer look.

Noting that infantry on the heights to the left had advanced apace with his mechanized platoon, Peppin mounted the lead bulldozer and ordered the driver forward.

The bulldozer moved noisily until it came even with a draw winding down from the heights to the left. A tiny mountain streamlet debouched from the draw and cut across the road in a tiny gully. The bulldozer was driven gingerly across the narrow cut, right up to the trestle.

Dave Peppin dropped to the road and placed his hand on the steel framework. It was a heavy one. The engineer lieutenant thought to return to the platoon trucks to pick up explosives, but he had a second thought. Peppin motioned the bulldozer operator to place the blade against the trestle, then directed him to push, just once.

The bulldozer roared and strained, and the entire steel structure slid aside as easily as a well-oiled gate. The MSR was open.

★

The first vehicles across the Treadway Bridge belonged to the engineers, who would have to rebuild any damaged bridges farther down or fill holes the Chinese had blown in the roadway. The infantry had filed across and taken positions on the heights to hold back any last-ditch attacks the Chinese thought to launch against the vulnerable bridgesite.

Only a dozen vehicles had crossed when a bulldozer, hauling a huge earth-moving pan, came up and edged out slowly onto the massive I beams.

It was about 1800 hours, and dark.

The dozer operator, tense and tired, misjudged and went off the steel beams onto the heavy plywood centerboard. The weight of the bulky earth pan broke through the board and the work vehicle sank clumsily into the crack. It seemed that any attempt to move the bulldozer would further destroy the centerboard and, possibly, push the beams far enough out of line to send the bridge plunging into the chasm.

Technical Sergeant Winfred Prosser, one of the best bulldozer operators in the world, departed from the crowd of onlookers at the end of the bridge and stepped forthrightly onto the span to climb into the operator's seat of the canted vehicle. Gingerly, Prosser inched the bulldozer back to an upright position, then backed ever so gently onto the solid roadway.

Jack Partridge, the engineer battalion commander, stepped in and began running mental calculations through his engineer's brain. If the ruined centerboard — which could support the weight of most of the narrower vehicles — was removed altogether, as it had to be, then the I beams would have to be readjusted to a width of one hundred thirty-six inches. At that interval, the wide Pershing heavy tanks would have about two inches' purchase on either beam, and jeeps would have the use of a mere half inch of the metal lips in the inboard edges of the beams.

It was going to be a cliff-hanger.

★

As soon as 1st Lieutenant Dave Peppin had moved the tramway trestlework, he was bedeviled by several 81mm mortar concentrations, which landed on either side of the road. Sporadic small-arms fire also started up, but it seemed to have no direct relationship with the mortar fire. As soon as the mortar fire began, Peppin ordered the bulldozer back to the main body of the platoon, but it became momentarily ensnared in the gully carrying the tiny stream across the road. The fourth or fifth salvo threw a steel shard into the bulldozer operator's wrist, forcing Peppin to take the controls and beat a hasty retreat to the unmolested main body of the platoon. The fire stopped entirely as soon as Peppin moved from the trestle.

Regaining the platoon vehicles, Peppin placed a call for instructions, but was unable to reach another radio. He waited patiently for fifteen minutes before stalking back up the road in the hope of finding someone who could give him a definitive order; anything was better than waiting in the open. He had gone only a few hundred yards when he found an enlisted Marine, alone in a radio jeep. Peppin ordered the man to get in touch with a senior officer, and the man said he could put the lieutenant through to engineer battalion headquarters. A request for instructions was sent, and answered after some minutes: Peppin was to proceed with his platoon right down the MSR; the column would follow at length. Satisfied, Dave Peppin turned on his heel and trotted back to his waiting vehicles.

To the rear, Major Buzz Sawyer was standing in the southern end of the Treadway Bridge, sweating out the resumption of radio contact with the 7th Regiment command group, which was out of sight and up the road. Sawyer, who had been wounded in the leg coming out of Hagaru-ri, had limped a short distance up the road in the hope of finding Colonel Litzenberg, but he decided to return to his battalion before he got too far away from the point. When he returned, Sawyer found that his excited radioman had received a cryptic unsigned message (which turned out to be from Ray Davis, now the regimental exec): "As Moses was taken through the bullrushes, so lead him to the bottom of the pass."

It took a moment for Sawyer to realize what the message meant. The officer who would be in charge of the engineer units accompanying the lead battalion was Major Emile Moses. Thus, Sawyer was to provide an escort for Moses and the engineers, who were to lead the road-bound column to the bottom of the mountain, to Chin-hung-ni.

It was coming up midnight. All the engineer vehicles were across the modified treadways, and the first vehicles of the first divisional train were just inching toward the beams. Buzz Sawyer called his forward command group together for a hurried confabulation. The low, muttered exchange went on for a few moments before Sawyer's operations officer, Major Tom Tighe, sensed the presence of a new-comer at his elbow. He turned idly to see who that might be, and exclaimed, "Why, the sonovabitch is a Chinaman!" The freezing enemy soldier, who was taken alive, had joined the knot of American officers simply to share some body heat.

Sawyer's command group moved off down the MSR to get the tiny 1st Battalion, 7th, moving once again. They passed the trestle that Dave Peppin had swung aside, padded quietly through Baker/1's blocking position, and joined Lieutenant Colonel Buck Schmuck at his bunker command post in the shadow of Hill 1081.

The road to Chinhung-ni was open.

CHAPTER

47

The night of December 10, 1950, was one of the coldest on record. Thousands of Marines and soldiers — and Chinese — arrayed on the heights and along the narrow mountain pass were overtired and malnourished, unable to fight the deep bone chill of the frigid win-ter night. The Chinese continued to succumb in legions to the cold and the sweat of their exertions, and American Marine and Army units continued to decline as more and more men were felled by the effects of frostbite and upper-respiratory infections.

The column ground forward through that impossibly chill night, but at an agonizingly slow pace, for of the fifteen hundred vehicles only one at a time could cross the fragile Treadway Bridge.

As 2nd Lieutenant Pat Roe, the intelligence officer of the 3rd Battalion, 7th, waited impatiently in the gathering gloom for the show to get back on the road, he suddenly realized that he was just below the spot where he had discovered a large artillery bunker during the advance northward weeks earlier. With the thought of a relatively warm bunker fixed in his mind's eye, Roe had no trouble rationalizing a little climbing expedition.

It was well after dark by the time Roe and his section chief, a Sergeant Mitchell, stumbled upon the entrance to the bunker. Mitchell ducked down, shined his flashlight into the maw of the emplacement and found it was occupied by two Chinese. One of the enemy soldiers had already frozen to death. The other was not quite that far gone; his entire body was frozen, including his head, which resembled a block of ice, but the two intelligence men could see a thin puff of vapor coming out of his nose, and his eyes seemed to follow the beam of their flashlights.

Uncertain as to what he should do about the frozen man, Roe went off with Sergeant Mitchell to find some men to help carry him to the road. When he returned, however, Roe found that other men had also entered the bunker and that both of its former occupants lay dead where they had been dumped in a nearby snowbank. By that time, the column seemed to be moving, so Roe called in everyone that he could find and headed back to the road.

★

Captain Craig Turner, commander of Dog Company, 1st Engineer Battalion, was walking beside one of his sergeants on the road south of the bridge when they passed a low ridge. Chinese on the ridge-line were rolling concussion grenades down the shallow slope, and one of them burst between Captain Turner and the sergeant.Both men were thrown clear into a snowbank on the verge of the road. When they stood up to take inventory, the sergeant found that his leg had been riddled in many places. Craig Turner, however, was not harmed in the slightest.

★

First Lieutenant Ralph Abell, his wounded arm swatched in ban-dages and suspended by a sling, was leading the remnant of Fox/7 down the road when he and his men came upon a year-old child sitting alone by a burned-out hut beside the road. A quick search failed to turn up either of the infant's parents, so a burly, filthy Marine who earned his keep by killing, picked him up and carried him. All hands became involved, trying to feed the child, and keep him warm, until a chaplain could be found and the child placed in gentler hands.

★

Sergeant H. D. Bales, a wireman with the 4th Battalion, 11th, was beset by numerous civilians that night. He and a fellow communicator spent hours keeping the miserable natives from bypassing their truck serial, but finally relented and took one toddler apiece to keep warm in their heavy parkas.

On the other hand, Private First Class Rex Cramer's element of Fox/31 passed a miserable Korean schoolboy who was standing barefoot in the snow, crying. Only minutes after he passed the boy, Cramer was chilled to hear a single shot from back up the road.

★

During one stop, Private First Class Bob Young, a member of the 4th Battalion, 11th's headquarters security section, jumped down from his truck to check on the Chinese corpses beside the road, just to make sure none was a sniper awaiting an opportunity. As he had done many times on the road from Yudam-ni, Young jabbed his bayonet into the nearest body. The man's eyes snapped open and registered a deep pain. The Marines got the PLA soldier into a truck and warmed him up as best they could. Later that night the prisoner willingly helped push stalled vehicles off the road.

★

Father Marty Hoehn, of the 31st Infantry, walked forward from his jeep during one delay and found that the column was stalled because a heavy tank had slid sideways toward the abyss to the right of the roadway. All the men who had been riding in and on the tank were standing helplessly on the icy verge beside the behemoth, so Chaplain Hoehn took charge. He directed several men to pour gasoline on the roadway at either end of the tank, and to light it. The flare of the gasoline lasted only a brief instant, but the ice quickly melted. When the tank driver gave it a try, he found that he could pull into the vehicle column and move forward.

★

Technical Sergeant Carl Hanson, the 2nd Battalion, 1st's atomic warfare specialist, was breasting the top of Funchilin Pass on foot, complaining with his buddies about a crowd of Korean civilians that had gotten mixed into the column, when he collided with a bony object that had stopped dead on the road in front of him. Startled, Hanson came to realize that the obstruction was the hind end of a cow.

★

Colonel Ed Snedeker, deputy chief of staff of 1st Marine Division, had attempted to fly from Hamhung to Chinhung-ni on the morning of December 9, but had been turned back by weather. An attempt later in the afternoon, however, had been successful, and the colonel went to work establishing a traffic-control point from which he could direct arriving units to holding areas in and around the tiny base.

Ed Snedeker's job was a crucial one if 1st Marine Division was to come out of its ordeal as a cohesive combat unit. Organizations that had been mixed on the road had to be sorted, and hundreds of footsore men had to be found rides to the rear. Besides, any semblance of order that Snedeker could instill would help the morale of the weary Marines and soldiers inching forward across the Treadway Bridge and down the mountain pass.

After conferring with Brigadier General Armistead Mead, commander of Task Force Dog, Colonel Snedeker and his few enlisted helpers set up a squad tent just to the north of the Army perimeter and ran a phone line to the task force CP. The control point was up and functioning by about 1800 hours, just as the first engineer vehicles were passing across the Treadway Bridge.

Having arrived alone without much of a briefing, Ed Snedeker had to rely upon the willingness of other men to get the help he needed. One of the most willing officers he found was Lieutenant Colonel Waldon Winston, commander of the Army's 52nd Transport Truck Battalion, which was in the process of displacing forward to Chinhung-ni from Hamhung. Winston revealed that he could get about one hundred fifty trucks into Snedeker's hands if X Corps bought the plan. Snedeker contacted General Mead, who contacted X Corps. However, because of communications problems, Mead never received a response to his request. Lieutenant Colonel Winston intimated, nevertheless, that he would provide the trucks on his own authority if clearance could not be obtained from Corps.

★

As elements of Major Buzz Sawyer's 1st Battalion, 7th, moved cautiously down either side of the road, 1st Lieutenant Dave Peppin clanked forward on his engineer platoon's lead bulldozer.

Shortly after passing the tramway trestle Peppin came upon a grisly scene. A small truck convoy had been stopped by the Chinese on the road, and about eighty dead American soldiers were strewn across a roadside field; some had been frozen in attitudes that suggested a sudden onslaught by a vastly superior force. The engineers pushed aside the wrecked vehicles obstructing the MSR and stacked the dead bodies in their equipment trucks, then moved on.

Farther down, Peppin received a message that he would be met by a mechanized Army unit which would escort him into Chinhung-ni. Rounding a bend a short time later, the engineer lieutenant peered through the crystal-clear darkness and perceived that several armored fighting vehicles were parked on the shoulder of the road. Closing on the buttoned-up vehicles, Peppin found the Army company commander and asked if he was there to escort the point of the Marine column into Chinhung-ni. The Army officer, who handed Peppin several loaves of fresh bread, said that he was indeed, and he ordered his vehicles to turn southward. Then, while Dave Peppin looked on in open-mouthed incredulity, the whole Army unit scooted down the road and out of sight.

Clanking and sliding, with Sawyer's loyal riflemen still guarding his flanks, Peppin and his platoon passed Ed Snedeker's tent and ground on into Chinhung-ni at about 0230, December 10.

Chinhung-ni was home plate.

★

The 7th Marine Regiment — what was left of the 7th Marine Regiment — flowed through Chinhung-ni for what remained of the dark hours, and well into the early morning. Ed Snedeker had managed to gather twenty-two Marine trucks from artillery and base units at Chinhung-ni, and these were used to carry the foot-borne infantry and about sixty Chinese prisoners the rest of the way to Hungnam. While no word had yet been received from X Corps regarding the use of Lieutenant Colonel Winston's trucks, no member of the reinforced 7th Marines had to walk a step beyond Chinhung-ni.

In the light of day, thousands of stupefied, thoroughly worn-out Marines passed Ed Snedeker's squad tent. There were moments of pity and sorrow, and others of undisguised happiness.

As the 3rd Battalion, 7th — down to under two hundred effectives — passed the control tent, a jeep detached itself from the column and pulled to the side of the road. There, 1st Lieutenant Tom McBee, the battalion supply officer, pulled a fine pair of barber scissors from his personal toilet kit and proceeded to cut the scraggly centerpieces from scores of snot-festooned, dripping moustaches. That simple, silly, loving act caused morale to soar.

★

There was a long wait between the tail of the 7th Marines and the head of the 5th Marines, which was escorting Division Train Number-2 off the Taebek Plateau. For Ed Snedeker, it was the most nerve-wracking wait of a long career.

By the time the 5th Regiment's column hove into view in the defile above Chinhung-ni, Colonel Snedeker had learned that O. P.

Smith and his staff were safely established in Hungnam, preparing to evacuate the entire division from North Korea.

As late as the previous afternoon, 1st Marine Division had been assigned a position in the great perimeter that was to have guarded Hamhung and Hungnam while service units pulled out. At the very last minute, just as General Smith was boarding his helicopter for a flight to Chinhung-ni, Corps sent word that the Marines would be evacuated first, and that Smith should return to his Division Rear Command Post in the port city. The change in order was so precipitous, in fact, that, as the helicopters bearing the general's party passed over Chinhung-ni, Smith's aide-de-camp had tried to get the pilot to land in compliance with the last orders he had heard about.

Troop leaders were told of the evacuation order as they passed Ed Snedeker's control point.

★

In the hills, on the last leg of the journey to Chinhung-ni, Private First Class Rick Seward, of Easy/5, felt that the journey to the sea would never end. Dawn had revealed the damaged carcasses of dozens of broken-down vehicles which had been abandoned by the side of the road. Seward's feet were sore, and the pace was agonizingly slow. Dead Chinese littered the landscape; those who had fallen on the roadway had been pancaked by the passing vehicles, and resembled flat pink and yellow cartoon caricatures.

Looking down across endless switchbacks, Rick Seward despaired of ever getting out of the mountains. Easy/5 was spread over hundreds of yards of twisting roadway, and was thoroughly intermingled with other units of its own and other battalions. As long as he knew anyone in close proximity, however, Rick Seward felt safe.

The only BAR-man left in Seward's squad lurched down the incline as though drunk, dragging his automatic rifle behind him by the sling, crying noiselessly.

Furious at his inability to keep his steel pot perched atop the hood of his parka, Seward tossed the helmet aside and watched it tumble into the gorge. A truck ahead, piled high with dead bodies, caught the rifleman's eye; arms and legs were pointing stiffly over the side in all directions. As hard as he tried to outdistance the charnel wagon, Seward invariably found himself looking at those dead Marines.

The rush of 155mm rounds boring through the air overhead from Chinhung-ni was a constant reminder that the danger was not yet passed, and that made Seward wish he had kept the helmet he had tossed aside in helpless rage.

Together with another Marine, Rick Seward collided woozily with an empty jeep trailer and tumbled aboard to ride the last hundred yards into Chinhung-ni, where a quick nose count revealed that Seward's platoon had fallen to the level of thirteen effectives.

★

The last shots Corporal Bill Wyda fired in North Korea made the whole trip worthwhile.

Ordered to break out their light machine gun, Wyda and his crew from How/1 found a spot on a hill at the head of Funchilin Pass, from which they would screen the passage of the rearmost element of the division, the bulk of the 1st Marines.

Looking down a side valley, Wyda spotted a lone Chinese soldier walking across a field in plain view several hundred yards out. Drawing a bead, the veteran gunner cut loose. The strong wind obscured the light of the tracer rounds so, unable to see the effect of his fire, Wyda used up an entire chest of .30-caliber ammunition, two hundred fifty rounds, without hitting the enemy soldier, who did not even lengthen his stride. A second chest was nearly used up without effect, and still the Chinese soldier walked slowly across the side valley.

The wind let up for just an instant. The last tracer in the second belt left the muzzle of the machine gun and slowly described a path right into the behind of the casual Chinese. The man staggered to his knees, rested for a moment, then hobbled from sight.

Dozens of American onlookers cheered.

There was one final, mutually profitless little exchange with a Chinese patrol, then Bill Wyda and his squad were ordered back to the road for the final leg out of North Korea.

★

As the rear elements of the 1st Marines were clearing the tiny valley of Koto-ri, Marine Corsair pilots spotted several thousand Chinese legging down a broad valley to the southwest of the village, heading right for the now-blown base.

Marine and Navy attack aircraft swarmed over those luckless PLA battalions, killing and maiming hundreds of men before the tightly packed ranks had an opportunity to scatter into the countryside.

★

The 5th Marines trudged through Chinhung-ni during the late afternoon and evening of December 10, largely without incident, though at about 1800 hours PLA blocking units south of the town stopped the column briefly with long-range machine-gun fire.

C H A P T E R

48

Lieutenant Colonel John Page left Koto-ri shortly after noon on December 10, one of hundreds of Armymen who had been casually attached to the 1st Marine Regiment for the final leg of the journey to Chinhung-ni and Hamhung.

Page's eleven days at the tiny mountain base had been profitable for him, for the 1st Marines, and for the hundreds of wounded and frostbitten servicemen that his efforts at overseeing the airfield construction had helped see to the safety of rear hospitals.

Now John Page could look forward to a fast, safe trip to the Corps base, where he would freshen up, change his clothing, and see if there was not an artillery battalion that he could take charge of, for that was the mission that had brought him to North Korea thirteen days earlier.

Page and his driver, Corporal David Klepsig, had not gone more than five hundred yards from the Koto-ri perimeter line before their serial was stopped by fire ahead. Typically, as soon as the column ground to a halt, dozens of men jumped from their vehicles to the roadway and began stomping their feet and pacing back and forth to keep warm. Curious about the delay, John Page left Corporal Klepsig with the jeep and hiked forward toward the sound of the firing.

When the convoy started up again, Sergeant Basil Peterson, an Army communicator, spotted a heavy tank out on a flat to the left of the roadway, up a broad side valley. The tank was stopped, but a lone figure standing behind the turret was banging away at the distant heights with the .50-caliber turret machine gun.

David Klepsig, who had his eyes peeled lest he miss John Page's return, let the clutch of his jeep out and ground slowly forward. After he passed the side valley, where he saw the tank, he inched up the incline to the top of the pass, worrying that he would miss his rider. Looking over his shoulder one last time before beginning his descent, Klepsig saw the bespectacled officer run up alongside the jeep, laughing. Just as Klepsig's foot went to the brake, John Page reached out to leap aboard, but missed, and was sent sprawling into the icy roadway. He got up and climbed into the passenger's seat, still laughing heartily, telling Klepsig how invigorating had been his little exchange with the Chinese gunners on the heights.

The colonel's jeep inched forward with the column. At another delay, Page jumped out and jogged forward, leaving Klepsig with the jeep once again. After passing a long line of Marine and Army tanks which had been placed by the side of the road in order to let lighter vehicles cross the Treadway Bridge first, Klepsig found John Page photographing the power plant and the bodies of dozens of Chinese who had frozen to death there the night before. Page jumped into the jeep for the harrowing ride across the chasm, then offered to relieve Klepsig at the wheel so that the young corporal could warm his limbs. Klepsig, however, declined the offer, so Page, who seemed eager for some action, went ahead on foot.

Corporal Klepsig remained in the column until he arrived at Chin-hung-ni late in the night of December 10. He had kept a lookout for John Page, but had been unable to find him. Not knowing what he should do, the corporal pulled over onto a flat beside the road.

While looking for John Page in the town, Corporal Klepsig ran into 1st Lieutenant Claude Roberts, the engineer who had overseen the construction of the Koto-ri airstrip. Roberts responded to Klepsig's inquiry after the colonel by calling attention to a delay the corporal had experienced at a giant mudhole several hundred yards back up the road. A truck had been hit by gunfire from the heights as it had tried to bypass the obstruction, and a dark figure, obscured by the shadows, had climbed aboard to man a machine gun on the truck cab roof. The corporal said that he had witnessed the incident, but was amazed to learn that the machine gunner was none other than John Page.

Certain that Page would soon be along, Klepsig joined an MP at a roadside checkpoint. After a long, fruitless wait, the MP offered to keep an eye out for the colonel while the exhausted driver went into a nearby squad tent to get some rest. Klepsig agreed reluctantly, and left the checkpoint. After a time, in which he could not sleep, Klepsig looked out and saw that the MP was letting each vehicle pass without asking after John Page. Following a terse exchange with the MP, Klepsig threw his bedroll into his jeep and pulled into the column.

It was nearly midnight before Klepsig approached tiny Sudong-ni, the place two miles south of Chunhung-ni where the 7th Marines had stood off the PLA's First Phase Offensive in early November. There was heavy firing ahead, and the column was halted.

★

True to his word, Lieutenant Colonel Waldon Winston, of the 52nd Transportation Truck Battalion, began making up shortages in Colonel Ed Snedeker's vehicle requirements after nightfall on December 10. Working closely with the 1st Marine Division Motor Transport Officer, Major Pop Seeley, the doughty survivor of the Task Force Drysdale tragedy, Winston saw to it that no Marine or GI coming down from Funchilin Pass had to walk a step beyond Chinhung-ni.

Though there had been some excitement on the road south of Chinhung-ni in the late afternoon, Winston had heard that two battalions of the 65th Infantry Regiment, a Puerto Rican National Guard component of 3rd Infantry Division, had been sent out to patrol the ridgeline overlooking the narrow Sudong Gorge.

Just as he got word that the harassing fires had been broken up, Winston looked up to see John Page enter his tent. The two had first met the night before Page had set out for Koto-ri, and they had taken an instant liking to each other then. There was a brief handshake and a quick mutual update. Winston had heard of Page's yeoman service at Koto-ri, and congratulated him on his fine achievements.

Page inquired after Corporal Klepsig, whom he had not seen since leaving him at the Treadway Bridge. Winston declared his ignorance of the driver's whereabouts and saw John Page off.

Because of overloaded telephone circuits, Colonel Ed Snedeker had been unable to get word to or from the next large town down the line, Majon-dong, and he needed to know about road conditions lest he put too many vehicles in motion. Lieutenant Colonel Winston volunteered to drive down to the town to find out what was going on. Because of reported enemy action on the road, Winston organized an escort composed of a weapons carrier and a jeep manned by several military policemen. He left Chinhung-ni at about 2300 hours, December 10, falling into the column with elements of the 1st Marine Regiment's Antitank Company.

The vehicles had gone less than a mile when word came from farther ahead that the Chinese had interdicted the road. It was obvious that Winston's patrol could not get through to Majon-dong, so the truck battalion commander turned back to Chinhung-ni to tell Colonel Snedeker that the road had been cut.

While Winston drove south again, toward the roadblock, Ed Snedeker and Pop Seeley began cramming incoming vehicles into every available inch of flat ground in and near the tiny village. It was impossible to stop the flow of trucks and jeeps from the pass, for the backup might telescope all the way to the precarious Treadway Bridge.

★

Private Marvin Wasson, a member of Captain George Petro's Antitank Company, 1st Marines, was driving a jeep he had found abandoned beside the road near the top of Funchilin Pass when he was stopped by a Marine warrant officer and informed that the Chinese had ambushed several of the antitank company's armored personnel carriers (cut-down Sherman tanks outfitted with .50-caliber machine guns). Wasson grabbed his rifle, got out of the jeep and loped forward until he found Captain Petro, who was building up a base of fire below the Chinese guns. John Page was standing beside the Marine captain, carbine in hand, looking to Wasson as if he was ready for some big-game hunting.

Petro moved off to organize other troops nearby, leaving Wasson alone with the bundled-up Army lieutenant colonel. Page suggested that they "go up and find out what's holding up the convoy." Wasson agreed to that.

An eerie, dark form materialized from beside one of the stalled trucks, a Chinese soldier laden with armfuls of food he had pilfered from the vehicle. Page ordered Wasson to shoot the infiltrator, but the quarry ran around the back of the truck before the Marine could raise his Garand rifle. The Army officer and the Marine private rounded the back of the truck and ran head on into a score of other Chinese, who cut and ran toward several houses up the nearby slope.

The two Americans pursued, firing as they ran. A grenade hurtled down from the houses and exploded near Private Wasson, cutting him in an ear and an arm. When Page saw that his young companion had been injured, he yelled, "I'll draw their attention while you run for it."

The words had just left the forty-six-year-old officer's mouth when a furious burst of gunfire from the hillside engulfed him, throwing him from his feet, killing him.

Private Wasson tumbled down to the roadway, landing beside a personnel carrier full of wounded Marines. He told the corporal in charge to move out before the Chinese charged down from the hillside. As the bulky vehicle crashed through several nearby houses, Wasson leaped aboard and rode into the clear, then jumped to the roadway to find Captain Petro and report the death of John Page. Petro ordered Wasson to turn himself in at an aid station to have his wounds treated.

When Lieutenant Colonel Waldon Winston's second attempt to get through to Majon-dong had been frustrated because of the action on the MSR, the truck-battalion commander walked toward the sound of the firing. He first encountered two Marines assisting an injured companion from a personnel carrier that had borne the brunt of some heavy firing from the hillside. Moving on to the carrier itself, Winston peered over the chassis to get a better look at the Chinese, and was splattered by fragments of bullets shattering on the armored vehicle.

A flare burst overhead, silhouetting several Chinese soldiers as they scrabbled across a boulder-strewn stream. Winston leveled his carbine, which had a full clip of tracer rounds, and stitched the bodies of three Chinese he had caught in the open.

Slowly, as Captain Petro ranged the line of stalled vehicles, small groups of Marines formed a viable base of fire. Winston found the Marine company commander seated in a jeep and asked who was in charge. Petro gave the name of the Marine truck-company commander, who was stuck well to the rear. Winston felt that he outranked everyone nearby, so he identified himself to Captain Petro and said that he was assuming command, that he wanted Petro to get the stalled vehicles moving.

After a hurried survey of the traffic jam, Colonel Winston ordered all jeeps off the road to make space for the heavier vehicles.

In the meantime, Private Marvin Wasson had had his ear and arm bandaged and had volunteered to help set up his company's 75mm recoilless rifles. Wasson fired three rounds and managed to demolish one of the houses on the hillside. He then left the gun in the care of other men and organized a scratch crew for a machine gun he found beside the road. The Chinese attacked at that point, killing one Marine and wounding a corpsman before being driven back. The houses that the recoilless rifle was setting aflame yielded adequate light for numerous machine gunners, who were having a field day.

As the fighting wound down because the Chinese all went to ground, Marvin Wasson trudged back to the roadway to see if he could help move stalled vehicles.

Waldon Winston was doing his best to find drivers when he was approached by a bandaged Marine who volunteered to do anything that might get the show on the road. Thus far, the frustrated Army officer had been able to find only two other Marines willing to help. He sent Wasson to the rearmost vehicle, a truck with a trailer in tow. The truck's battery was low, and Wasson could not get the motor to catch. He returned to Winston for instructions, and was told to get the next-to-last vehicle moving while the colonel and a Marine covered him. If Wasson was successful, Winston reasoned, the rearmost vehicle could be pushed out of the way. The effort failed, however, because of the trailer on the rearmost truck. However, the aborted effort caught the attention of Marines who had been standing around in helpless paralysis, and many of them moved to unhitch the trailer and roll it out of the way.

Winston and Wasson and two other Marines — the original group — took charge of the disorganized rabble and slowly, very slowly, turned the tide of apathy and confusion. One by one, Marines moved to the firing line or to the burgeoning work crews. Order eventually appeared from chaos. A volunteer driver took charge of the personnel carrier that had first been hit by the bushwackers, and that tracked vehicle was used repeatedly to tow stalled trucks from the roadway.

Leaving the work on the road to others, Colonel Winston organized five Marines into a combat patrol and moved up the hill to see how many Chinese were there. Passing beside a ransacked truck, Waldon Winston nearly tripped on a body. Peering more closely, he looked into John Page's face. Winston fanned his men out in a protective semicircle and searched for some sign of life. But John Page was gone. Winston sent for a corpsman and a litter team, and had John Page's body carried to a truck where an Army master sergeant with magnificent waxed moustaches lay dead on a litter. Both bodies were placed in an ambulance.

Dozens of Marines probed across the lower slopes of the ridges overlooking the MSR, while scores of others cleared the roadway. It took until 0630, December 11, before Lieutenant Colonel Winston led the reorganized convoy out of the Sudong Gorge.

The Chinese were by no means finished with their efforts to stop the evacuation columns, and a good deal more American and Chinese blood was spilled that day. But the road was open and the confusion and apathy that had bedeviled the night's fighting did not reappear in the daylight.

John Page and many other Americans who were killed on the road from Koto-ri to the sea were laid to rest in a military cemetery at Hamhung. The Marine Corps awarded the Army officer a posthumous Navy Cross. In 1956, three years after the statute of limitations had run out, the Congress of the United States enacted a special bill awarding Lieutenant Colonel John U. D. Page a posthumous Medal of Honor.

C H A P T E R
49

The last vehicles over Funchilin Pass were the tanks — forty-six armored vehicles from Baker and Dog Companies, 1st Tank Battalion; the medium blade platoon of the 1st Tank Battalion; the 31st Medium Tank Company; and the heavy-tank platoons of the 1st, 5th, and 7th Antitank Companies. They had all been held at the rear of the column or bypassed by wheeled vehicles because it was feared that their weight might knock over one or both of the treadway beams spanning the gap at Changjin Power Plant Number-1.

Dog/Tanks, which left Koto-ri during the early afternoon of December 10, had laagered in the broad valley just south of town, well before the incline to Funchilin Pass. When Captain Bruce Clarke left for what he expected to be a brief trip to the rear to check on fuel supplies, he turned command of his company over to his senior platoon leader, 1st Lieutenant Paul Sanders.

When Clarke did not return in a reasonable period, Sanders became nervous. The tanks had been using fuel throughout the wait because they had to keep their engines idling. Somehow, while Sanders was running back up the road in a jeep to look for Captain Clarke, a partially filled fueler truck passed through the company's laager, but no one thought to stop it. One of the heavy tanks soon ran dry, and Sanders reluctantly ordered it pushed over the edge of the road into the deep abyss. Later, when the battalion commander, Lieutenant Colonel Harry Milne, arrived from the rear to explain that Captain Clarke had been hit in the leg by a stray round and had been driven through the tank park in an ambulance, Lieutenant Sanders admitted to his lapse in letting the fuel truck get by. Milne commiserated and told Sanders to take command of Dog Company. It was getting dark by then, so, as soon as Milne drove forward, Sanders ordered the company back on the road; the battalion commander had informed him that there were no soft vehicles behind Dog Company. Rather than risk losing tanks and crews on the narrow roadway, Sanders allowed his drivers to use their head lamps. The trip over the pass and down the defile would be treacherous enough without having to do it blind.

To the rear, Captain Bruce Williams, of Baker Company, came to the same conclusion. All of the company's soft vehicles had been sent ahead with the battalion train. As soon as Sanders moved Dog Company over the pass, Williams put his platoons on the road. He had had a word with the commander of the division reconnaissance company, who told him that a reconn platoon under the command of 1st Lieutenant Ernie Hargett would provide security for the rear-most tanks. Williams asked the reconn-company commander to have Hargett check in with the rear tank-platoon leader, 1st Lieutenant Philip Ronzone, and he told Ronzone to look after the reconn men. This was a fairly typical exercise; no one anticipated any difficulties.

Getting to the top of Funchilin Pass was no piece of cake, what with the blind hairpin turns, the pitch-darkness, and the icy road-way. But there was no untoward incident on the way up.

The descent to the Treadway Bridge was another matter. Tanks in motion gain many, many tons of momentum, and their steel tread shoes are eminently unsuited for icy road conditions. Each and every driver literally stood on his left brake to keep his vehicle up against the nearly vertical rock wall on that side. There was a lot of skidding, and sparks flew as armor plate ground against rock. Incessant stopping and starting just made the proceedings more interesting.

Thousands of North Korean civilians pressing in from the rear added to the general confusion of the descent. After a time Captain Williams ordered Lieutenant Ronzone to fire short bursts over the heads of the close-packed civilians, but that had little or no effect in breaking them of their desire to stay close to the slowly moving tank column.

Things were going rather well for Captain Williams when, all of a sudden, the transmission went out on his command Weasel. There was no way to work on the little amphibious jeep without stalling most of the company column, so Williams moved to his command tank, B41, and had the next tank behind the Weasel push it over the edge.

There was no communication with units ahead or, in fact, his own platoons behind. The occasional bullet that whistled by from the heights was ignored, as were the 155mm rounds that the 92nd Field Artillery Battalion, at Chinhung-ni, fired blindly into Koto-ri. Some of the big rounds dropped a lot closer to the tanks than anyone would have desired, but the nature of the terrain blotted out radio communications, obviating the usual corrective procedures.

At about 2300 hours, December 10, Captain Williams heard that the lead tanks and reconnaissance platoons had reached the Tread-way Bridge. The only men on the ground by the bridge were engi-neer demolitions experts commanded by Captain Ray Gould of Able/Engineers, who was impatient for the tanks to pass, for he and his men were in an incredibly vulnerable position. A foul-up in communications had put Lieutenant Colonel Buck Schmuck's 1st Battalion, 1st, on the road south when it was to have remained at the tramway trestle and Hill 1081 until the last of the tanks, engineers, and reconnaissance men had passed through. That meant that there was nothing to guard the relatively helpless tanks but a small reconn platoon and a few engineers.

One by one, the Baker Company tanks inched across the wobbly span. By the time Bruce Williams reached the bridge and jumped down from B41 to speak with Ray Gould, the engineers were nearly peeing themselves with concern. There had been a report from the middle platoon leader that one of the heavy tanks had suffered a brake failure. Just before turning the last corner toward the bridge, which effectively brought an end to radio communications, Captain Williams told the platoon leader to push the balky tank into the abyss. Williams reassured Ray Gould that there were only two pla-toons left to cross, and that that should take no longer than ten or fifteen minutes.

It was not to be.

The tank that had failed was in the worst possible position for being pushed over the side. Its balance was to the left, while the abyss was to the right. The next tank to the rear could push it, but it would only go farther to the left. It could not be towed by the next tank forward because it might skid sideways and pull that tank over the edge if it went out of control on the icy road, a pretty sure bet.

Including the stalled tank, there were eight heavies stuck on the road: all of Lieutenant Ronzone's five 2nd Platoon tanks and three from 1st Platoon.

★

First Lieutenant Ernie Hargett, commander of the division recon-naissance company's 1st Platoon, had the rear guard. He had not expected to be there when he left Koto-ri late in the afternoon of December 10, but Schmuck's battalion had been put on the road too early, and someone had to be last. Hargett and his men, who had had an intermediate point to hold, were told off to screen the last of the heavy tanks of Captain Williams's company from the press of civilians following the column down from the pass. Hargett was to be the last man to cross the Treadway Bridge. When he reported to

Captain Ray Gould, the engineer company commander was to drop the treadways into the chasm below the power plant.

As soon as the tanks ahead stopped — Hargett had no idea why — he placed a squad under Sergeant Peter Bland in a blocking position about thirty-five yards behind B22, the last tank in the column. The civilians were getting restless, and Bland had orders to open fire if they got too close.

The lieutenant left Bland's squad, walked to B22 and asked the gunner, Corporal Andrew Aguirre, to blink his spotlight as a warning to the civilians. Aguirre complied. In the meantime, Hargett had some harsh words for Sergeant Willie Ayres, who had allowed his squad to climb up on the metal plates over B22's engine to steal some of the warmth. Ayres's men were ordered back onto the roadway.

Hargett had just finished reading off Sergeant Ayres when a runner from Sergeant Bland's squad arrived and asked for him. Pushing through the knot of Marines, Hargett took the runner's report: Bland needed help controlling the civilians.

Lieutenant Ronzone, leader of the rear tank platoon, had left his tank earlier to walk forward to the stalled tank. For all practical purposes, no one was in command of the rear platoon, though the platoon sergeant was the commander of the rear tank, B22; Ronzone, however, had told him nothing.

The five men in B22 had no cause for concern at that point. The driver, Private First Class Nick Antonis, was playing with a puppy that some reconn men had handed over when Sergeant Ayres's squad had been evicted from the warm spot over the engine. It was just another wait.

Ernie Hargett, who reached Sergeant Bland within moments of the summons, was approaching a civilian elder for a confab when there was a sudden flurry of shots. Hargett jerked his carbine up to fire on a knot of Chinese soldiers which had pushed through the crowd of civilians, but the weapon jammed. Without missing a beat, the former Quantico football star killed two of the enemy soldiers with the butt of his small rifle.

Private First Class George Ziegler, a light machine gunner who had been attached to Hargett's platoon as it was exiting Koto-ri, looked up the road and saw two PLA infantrymen sliding crablike toward him from the head of the civilian column. Both men were holding their rifles by the forestocks, as if in surrender. Cautious, Ziegler turned his machine gun on them and lifted the trigger. The gun, however, jammed on the first round. Ziegler stood up and shook off one of two rifles he was carrying on his shoulder, but the two Chinese darted forward before he could act, grabbed the light machine gun and made off into the throng of civilians. After jerking his rifle to his shoulder, Ziegler attempted to squeeze off a round, but the rifle jammed.

The very instant the shooting started, Staff Sergeant Robert Dolby, the commander of B22, bolted through his turret hatch and ran past three intervening tanks to B21 to speak with Lieutenant Ronzone, who had not left word that he would be well forward. The rest of B22's crew buttoned up and prepared to fire on the crowd at the rear, though the gunners were fearful of hitting fellow Marines. Informed by the gunner of B21 that Lieutenant Ronzone was forward, and out of touch, Dolby elected to continue on down the road to find him. The tank platoon was, thus, leaderless in addition to being in a communications blackout because of the terrain.

Back at Sergeant Bland's roadblock, Corporal Billy Paige leveled his BAR on the nearest squad of Chinese and felled it to a man. Ayres's BAR-man, Corporal George Amyotte, who had accompanied Lieutenant Hargett back from B22, likewise dropped an entire squad of PLA infantry. The fight developed into a real hand-to-hand brawl.

After a few moments of close infighting, Ernie Hargett detached himself from the melee and raced back to B22 to prepare Ayres's squad for its part in the defense. Bland's squad was outnumbered by incredible odds, and it would soon be pressed back.

Leaving Ayres's squad in the care of Gunnery Sergeant Stanley LaMonte, Hargett hurried back to the next-to-last tank, B25, to try to talk the driver into moving back a dozen yards so that his turret machine gun could be brought to bear on the Chinese. The driver refused.

In the time it took Ernie Hargett to return to B22, the entire rear-tank platoon fell apart. The crew of B22 locked itself in and refused to answer the reconn men, who were banging on the turret hatch. The crew of B25 panicked and left the vehicle, as did the crew of each successive tank down the line.

Arriving at B22 just as the crewmen of the other tanks took off amidst shouts of "Let's get out of here," Private First Class George Ziegler joined Ernie Hargett on the turret. Hargett, who was bleeding from a superficial facial wound, ordered Ziegler back to the roadway. The weaponless machine gunner dropped down amidst an impromptu aid station, where the platoon corpsman was working on a corporal who was leaning forward against the tank with his trousers around his ankles. Ziegler asked for and received a functioning Garand rifle from one of the several injured Marines sitting in the lee of the tank. He turned the weapon on a knot of Chinese soldiers who were climbing the slope to his right in order to get above the defenders. A grenade landed at his feet.

A million impressions passed through George Ziegler's mind in the instant he had to act. He had no helmet, so could not cover the projectile. And he could not press it into the solid, frozen earth with his rifle butt. He kicked it toward the abyss, but it went off in midair and sprayed the gunner with a liberal dose of shrapnel. He managed, however, to stay on his feet.

At that instant, after Ernie Hargett had ordered the wounded to the rear, he pulled the defenders back to B25, which was by then abandoned, though its motor was still ticking over. Just as the platoon got moving, a large satchel charge from the heights blew Private First Class Robert DeMott over into the abyss. He was knocked unconscious by the blast and landed on a ledge, but was otherwise uninjured. Everyone who saw the blast was sure he had been killed.

The reconn platoon was being pressed back a tank at a time when Corporal George Amyotte was saved by an operational experiment. Hargett's platoon was the first Marine Corps unit to test body armor in combat, and George Amyotte had become the platoon's foremost proponent of the article. A Chinese grenade that landed squarely on his back did not even rattle the BAR-man, who continued to pile the enemy up on the roadway.

The platoon was down to twenty-four effectives, many of whom had been injured by the time it passed all the way through the rear tank platoon and on toward the damaged tank, beyond which was a long gap all the way to the Treadway Bridge.

When Hargett arrived at the damaged tank, he found several Marines still standing around trying to work out a solution. Corporal C. P. Lett, the gunner of the tank immediately behind the stalled vehicle, refused to leave his tank to the Chinese. It was a good thing, for the frozen brake of the lead tank was freed just as Hargett arrived, and the tank was driven clear. Corporal Lett, who had never before driven a tank, hopped into the vacant driver's seat of his tank (the rest of the crew had bolted) and moved toward the Treadway Bridge, maneuvering around obstacles ahead more by guts than by knowledge.

★

Captains Ray Gould and Bruce Williams, standing in the open on the south side of the bridge, were becoming increasingly apprehensive as the sound of the gunfire flared up beyond their line of sight to the north. After a few minutes, the two rear-platoon leaders arrived on foot with about twenty-five tank crewmen, claiming that the tanks had been overrun and the missing crewmen killed. Captain Williams had no alternative but to accept these statements as fact, and he left the bridgesite with what remained of his company.

Ernie Hargett's platoon was joined as it neared the Treadway Bridge by a second reconn platoon, which had been sent back over the bridge to help. By then, however, the Marines had outdistanced the Chinese. In all, Hargett's twenty-eight-man platoon suffered two killed (including BAR-man Corporal Billy Paige), one missing and presumed dead (Private First Class Robert DeMott), and an even dozen wounded.

As soon as Hargett's platoon and the last two tanks crossed the bridge. Ray Gould gave the nod to his demolitions officer, and the Treadway Bridge was dropped neatly into the two-thousand-foot-deep chasm beside Changjin Power Plant Number-1.

★

Private First Class Robert DeMott, who had been blown over the edge of the road earlier, came to on his ledge just as the bridge was blown. He climbed back to the roadway, joined the hordes of civilians who were pressing forward, and was carried by the crush all the way down the defile to Chinhung-ni, where he reported in. Robert DeMott was the last American to pass through Colonel Ed Snedecker's control point.

C H A P T E R
50

With the arrival of Robert DeMott at Chinhung-ni and the closure of Colonel Snedeker's traffic-control point, 1st Marine Division's role in the Chosin Reservoir Campaign drew to a close.

In a period of three days, the entire division — with the exception of a shore-party company that was kept back to help run the port of Hungnam — was lifted by troop transport and LST to South Korea for a rest and refitting in a complex of bean fields near the city of

Masan, the same staging ground on which 1st Marine Brigade had prepared for its first fight in defense of the Pusan Perimeter in July.

Waves of illness and fatigue felled nearly every man who had survived the ordeal of the Frozen Chosin, though many remained on duty or were returned to their units after relatively brief hospital stays.

Though South Korea was in danger of being overrun by the Chinese field armies that had destroyed 8th Army in northwestern Korea, the Marine division was allowed to refit and get back up to strength before it went back into action.

The mutual dislike that was shared by Generals Almond and Smith boiled over when O.P. Smith categorically refused to rejoin X Corps so long as Ned Almond was its commander. The matter was smoothed over at higher levels, but 1st Marine Division was transferred to IX Army Corps in west central Korea until General Smith was routinely rotated home in April, 1951.

Epilogue

People are crawling all over the tank. They might be anyone. Chinese soldiers. Korean civilians. Even fellow Marines.

Sounds of gunfire flare and recede ahead, then disappear.

The sounds of people on the tank drives the gunner, Corporal Andrew Aguirre nearly to distraction. He is in command, and he exercises his authority by ordering the loader, Private First Class James Glasgow, to inventory the remaining stock of shells. After a moment, Glasgow reports that he has thirty-eight rounds left. Aguirre says that they will fire all of them; the backblast of the 90mm gun will pitch anyone on the tank over the edge of the precipice.

The thirty-eight rounds are fired in quick succession, blindly up the former MSR. After the ringing in their ears subsides the crewmen hear no more sounds of human movement atop the heavy tank.

Sounds of people walking on the road around the tank resume after only a brief pause. The puppy that the reconnaissance men passed to driver Nick Antonis earlier begins whimpering. Gunner Aguirre tries to quiet the mutt, but its screeching rises in pitch, panicking the crew. Aguirre strangles the pup with a twist of his wrist.

Later, as Nick Antonis is peering through the periscope in the locked hatch over his driving compartment, he stares right into the face of a Chinese soldier who is himself staring into the periscope. The driver flinches violently and ducks away, though the Chinese surely cannot see him.

The tank crewmen listen for what seems like hours to the gabble of passing crowds — civilians, soldiers, whomever.

After a long quiet spell, Nick Antonis drops the escape hatch between his feet and draws his .45-caliber automatic pistol. Within thirty seconds, the head and shoulders of a PLA soldier appear in the open hatchway. Antonis places the muzzle of his pistol right between the intruder's eyes and fires. He is more surprised by the spray of blood and bone and brain than appalled by the coldness of his act.

The four crewmen wait with baited breath for a reprisal, but none comes.

No one sleeps that bitter cold night in B22.

★

Early the next morning, at about 0400, Corporal Aguirre orders the crewmen out of their steel box onto the roadway so that they can assess their chances for an escape.

The bedding rolls and spare clothing that had been lashed to the tank are gone, pilfered by the passing crush of humanity. Each man has on his thin tank suit and whatever underwear he is used to wearing. The food supply consists of two packs of Charms candies that the assistant driver, Private Joe Saxon, happens to find in a pocket. Each man has an automatic pistol and a Thompson submachine gun, but there is only one magazine per weapon. Three hand grenades complete the arsenal.

Certain that the Chinese are outposting the road ahead, the four Marines struggle over the side of the chasm and manage to descend two thousand feet to the valley floor without injury. They have, however, gone a long way toward depleting their energy reserves.

As the tank crew plods southward, Navy and Marine carrier aircraft roar by overhead, on the way to blast to scrap the six abandoned heavy tanks on the road above.

★

They are taken as they root through a garbage heap at Chinhung-ni two days later. They are exhausted and weaponless after two days of battling Chinese patrols and the elements. Nick Antonis, the cockiest of the four, pulls the pin from the last hand grenade and obligingly hands the armed bomb to the nearest of the PLA soldiers. The man stares at it until it blows him away. The four captives are all wounded in the legs as the Chinese reflexively open fire. They would be killed but for the intercession of an English-speaking PLA officer, who harshly orders his troops to cease firing.

Their blood staunched by the freezing cold, the four miserable Americans are placed in a six-foot-by-six-foot trench, certain that they are to be executed. Andrew Aguirre, who served with the Marines in China during the late Forties, understands enough of the officer's stern orders to realize that he and his companions are to be spared. In fact, the Chinese officer orders his men to share their ration of dried peas with the captives.

★

They march aimlessly through the hills below the Taebek Plateau for the next ten nights, carefully avoiding American carrier aircraft. The Chinese are not gentle keepers; they prod the hungry, faltering captives with their bayonets at every opportunity.

On Christmas Day, before noon, the Marines and their captors top an enormous hill miles north of Hamhung and Hungnam. The outline of the twin cities and their broad boulevards can be discerned faintly in the distance. Nick Antonis stares intently and is able to make out a few warships sailing out of the harbor.

Suddenly a great billow of smoke and flame rises over the harbor and dock areas. As the silent pillar continues to rise and expand, a deep-throated rumble roars and echoes through the mountain fastness.

The pillar of smoke and debris collapses into itself and the roar subsides. Nothing of value has been left by the departing American invaders; Hungnam's post facilities have been blown to dust.

Merry Christmas, Nick Antonis thinks as he is prodded forward to begin the eleventh day of his three years in captivity.

A Word About Organization

First Marine Division mustered about 25,000 souls, mostly Marines, but also several hundred Navy doctors and corpsmen.

The main strength of the division was provided by its three infantry regiments, the 1st, 5th, and 7th Marine Regiments. Each of these regiments mustered three 1,000-man rifle battalions, a 4.2-inch heavy mortar company, an antitank company, and a headquarters-and-service (H&S) company. In all, the average regiment — and each differed slightly from the others — mustered about 3,500 officers and men.

The three rifle battalions of each infantry regiment (a total of nine in the division) deployed three rifle companies, one weapons company, and one headquarters-and-service company. The rifle companies were identified by alphabetical designations as follows: *1st Battalion* — A, B, C; *2nd Battalion* — D, E, F; *3rd Battalion* — G, H, I.*

Each rifle company consisted of three rifle platoons, one .30-caliber air-cooled light-machine-gun platoon, and one mortar section of three 60mm mortars. The rifle platoons each mustered about 45 men divided into three 13-man squads (further divided into three four-man fire teams plus squad leader) and a platoon headquarters team, including platoon leader, platoon sergeant, guide, runner, radioman,

*Unlike Marine battalions, Army battalions used letter designations for their weapons companies. Thus: *1st Battalion* — A, B, C and D (where D is weapons); *2nd Battalion* — E, F, G and H (where H is weapons); *3rd Battalion* — I, K, L and M (where M is weapons). Moreover, the organization of Army battalions and regiments differed significantly from those of somewhat smaller Marine battalions and regiments.

and corpsman. The battalion weapons company deployed three heavy-machine-gun platoons of six .30-caliber water-cooled heavy machine guns each, and an 81mm mortar platoon of three two-gun sections. The battalion H&S company incorporated the battalion staff officers and their enlisted clerks and technicians, a communications platoon, a motor pool, the Navy medical team attached to the battalion, and several supporting arms liaison teams, such as forward air controllers and artillery forward observers.

The division's fourth regiment, the 11th Marines, was the artillery regiment. It deployed three 18-gun 105mm howitzer battalions of three six-gun batteries each (designated identically to the rifle companies), and an 18-gun 155mm howitzer battalion (the 4th Battalion, comprising K, L, and M Batteries). Each of the three 105mm battalions was assigned to the operational control of an infantry regiment (1st Battalion to the 5th Marines; 2nd Battalion to the 1st Marines; 3rd Battalion to the 7th Marines), and the battalion commander of each artillery battalion doubled as the artillery adviser on the staff of the infantry regiment commander. The 155mm battalion was a divisional support unit, and was technically under the direct control of the division commander, though it was not uncommon for 155mm batteries, or even the entire battalion, to be placed under the operational control of subordinate headquarters. Technically, each of the 105mm batteries was assigned to support a particular rifle battalion, and at least two junior lieutenants from each battery were assigned to live with the rifle battalion to which their guns were assigned; these lieutenants and their communicators were so-called "forward observer" teams, which is an adequate enough description of their function in combat.

All of the dozen-odd support and service battalions that served as organic parts of the division were under the nominal command of the division commander, though he had a senior colonel on his staff to oversee their performance. Because the Marine division was built for an amphibious role, several specialized support battalions (the amphibious tractor and shore-party battalions) were not employed in the mountain fighting. Several others were committed piecemeal to the actual fighting because of the wide dispersement of the division (among these, the tank, motor transport, signal, service, headquarters, medical, and engineer battalions). In a campaign to which the division was better suited the various companies of most of the support and service battalions were generally assigned, one apiece, to the infantry regiments; and one platoon of each of those companies was assigned to each of the rifle battalions; this configuration yielded what were known as "regimental combat teams" comprised of "battalion landing teams."

The overriding characteristic of the organization, as amply demonstrated in the incessant and distressing actions of the two-week period herein described, was its flexibility. Whatever troops, weapons, and equipment the division or its components had on hand could be used in the most flexible configurations imaginable, depending upon the needs of the moment.

While such ideals hardly ever work out in real life, it was the aim of the training programs by which Marines were indoctrinated that every man be basically interchangeable with every other man of the same rank, irrespective of specialty. At the heart of the training program was the drive to make each and every Marine a rifleman. In that respect, given the exigencies of this campaign, the training paid dividends far beyond even the loftiest ideals and expectations.

APPENDIX A
Staff & Command Lists*

FIRST MARINE DIVISION
(November 27–December 11, 1950)

Division Forward Command Post
CG MGen Oliver P. Smith
CofS Col Gregon A. Williams
G-1 Col Harvey A. Walseth
  (WIA,30Nov)
Asst Maj Donald W. Sherman
G-2 (Asst)
  LCol John G. Babashanian
G-3 Col Alpha L. Bowser, Jr.
Plans LCol Floyd R. Moore
  (NBC,30Nov)
  LCol Joseph L. Winecoff
G-4 (Asst)
  LCol Arthur Chidester
  (MIA,29Nov)
  Maj Charles T. Hodges
Communications
  LCol Albert Creal
Surgeon
  Capt Eugene R. Hering,
  MC, USN
Motor Transport
  Maj Henry W. Seeley
Headquarters CO
  Maj Frederick Simpson

1st Military Police Company
CO Capt John H. Griffin

1st Reconnaissance Company
CO Maj Walter Gall
ExO 1stLt Ralph Crossman

CoO 1stLt Ernest C. Hargett
  (WIA,10Dec)
  1stLt Francis R. Kraince
  1stLt Donald W. Sharon
  2ndLt Phillip D. Shutler

41 ROYAL MARINE COMMANDO
OinC LCol Douglas B. Drysdale,
  RM (WIA,29Nov)
2inC Maj Dennis Aldridge, RM
Adjutant
  Lt Donald Goodchild, RM
  (WIA,29Nov)
Surgeon
  Lt Douglas Knock, RMC
  (WIA,29Nov)

1st MARINE REGIMENT
CO Col Lewis B. Puller
ExO LCol Robert W. Rickert
S-3 Maj Robert E. Lorigan
Communications
  Capt William R. Holt
Chaplain
  Lt Kevin J. Keaney, ChC,
  USN
  Lt James Lewis, ChC, USN

Antitank Company
CO Capt George E. Petro
ExO 1stLt John A. Dudrey

---

*As many records were lost or intentionally destroyed during the withdrawal from the Reservoir, the reconstructions that take their place in the archives are not completely reliable. That unreliability could well be reflected in this appendix; corrections have been made wherever possible.

CoO   1stLt Chester E. Tucker
        2ndLt Harold L. Coffman

4.2-Inch Mortar Company
CO   Capt Frank J. Faureck
ExO   1stLt Otis R. Waldrop
CoO   1stLt Edward E. Kaufer
        2ndLt Richard C. Eykyn
        2ndLt Francis R. Hittinger,
            Jr. (WIA,28Nov)

Headquarters-&-Service Company
CO   Capt Frank P. Tatum

1st Battalion, 1st Marines
CO   LCol Donald M. Schmuck
ExO   Maj Maurice H. Clarke
S-3   Maj David W. Bridges
Communications
        1stLt Paul Vnencek
Surgeon
        Lt Hubert C. Pirkle,
            MC, USN
        Lt Harry Whitaker, Jr.,
            MC, USN
Air Liaison
        Capt Robert B. Robinson
Headquarters CO
        Capt William B. Hopkins

Able Company, 1st
CO   Capt Robert H. Barrow
ExO   1stLt Richard P. Wilson
CoO   1stLt William A.
            McClelland
        2ndLt Jack A. Cohoon
        2ndLt Donald R. Jones
        2ndLt Bud F. Nelson
        P1Sgt William C. Roach

Baker Company, 1st
CO   Capt Wesley C. Noren
ExO   1stLt Chester V. Farmer
CoO   1stLt George G. Chambers
        1stLt Jack S. Cooper
        1stLt James H. Cowan
        1stLt John K. McLeod
        MSgt Matthew D. Monk

Charlie Company, 1st
CO   Capt Robert P. Wray
ExO   1stLt James M. McGhee
CoO   1stLt F. Brandon Carlon
        1stLt William A. Craven
        2ndLt Henry A. Commiskey
            (WIA,3Dec)

Weapons Company
CO   Maj William T. Bates, Jr.
ExO   Capt Richard L. Bland
CoO   Capt Thomas J. Bohannon
        1stLt William Koehnlein
        2ndLt Allen S. Harris
        2ndLt William J.
            Masterpool
        2ndLt Eugene J. Paradis

2nd Battalion, 1st Marines
CO   LCol Allan Sutter
ExO   Maj Clarence J. Mabry
S-3   Capt Gildo S. Codispoti
Communications
        1stLt Frank P. Stivers
Surgeon
        Lt(jg) James F. Fitch,
            MC, USN
        Lt(jg) Roger E. Fox,
            MC, USN
Air Liaison
        Capt Norman Vining
Headquarters CO
        Capt Raymond Dewees, Jr.

Dog Company, 1st
CO   Capt Welby W. Cronk
CoO   1stLt Theodore Culpepper
            (WIA,28Nov)
        1stLt Jay J. Thomas, Jr.
        1stLt Theodor Westervelt
        2ndLt Robert R. Dickey
        2ndLt Howard O. Foor
            (KIA,29Nov)
        2ndLt Carl C. Thompson,
            Jr.

Easy Company, 1st
CO   Capt Jack A. Smith
CoO   1stLt John T. Arcady
        1stLt Robert W. Blum

1stLt Owen E. Clapper
1stLt Edward Constantine
1stLt Harold B. Wilson

Fox Company, 1st
CO   Capt Goodwin C. Groff
CoO   1stLt Donald L. Evans, Jr.
     1stLt Thomas E. McQuay
     1stLt Alexander Michaux
     1stLt James B. O'Bannon
     1stLt Charles B.
       Stephenson, III
     2ndLt Bruce W. Cunliffe
     2ndLt Lewis H. Devine

Weapons Company
CO   Capt William A. Kerr
CoO   1stLt Adlin P. Daigle
     1stLt Russell A. Davidson
     1stLt Leland E. Ziegler
     2ndLt Raymond Glodowski
     2ndLt Littleton W. Waller

3rd Battalion, 1st Marines
CO   LCol Thomas L. Ridge
ExO   Maj Reginald R. Myers
S-3   Maj Joseph D. Trompeter
Communications
     1stLt Robert A. Foyle
Surgeon
     Lt Robert J. Fleishaker,
       MC, USN
     Lt(jg) George R. Farrell,
       MC, USN
Air Liaison
     1stLt Lawrence Simmons
Headquarters CO
     Capt Thomas E. McCarthy

George Company, 1st
CO   Capt Carl L. Sitter
     (WIA,1Dec)
ExO   1stLt Charles R. Merrill
     (WIA,29Nov)
CoO   1stLt Carl R. Dennis
     (WIA,3Dec)
     1stLt Frederick J. Goff
     2ndLt James D. Beeler
     2ndLt John J. Jaeger
     2ndLt Frederick W.
       Hopkins

How Company, 1st
CO   Capt Clarence E. Corley
     (WIA,28Nov)
ExO   1stLt Horace L. Johnson, Jr.
     (WIA,28Nov)
CoO   1stLt Harrison F. Betts
     2ndLt Roscoe L. Barrett, Jr.
     2ndLt Wendell C. Endsley
     (KIA,28Nov)
     2ndLt Harvey A. Goss
     (KIA,28Nov)
     2ndLt Ronald A. Mason
     2ndLt Edward W. Snelling

Item Company, 1st
CO   1stLt Joseph R. Fisher
ExO   2ndLt Charles H. Mattox
     (KIA,28Nov)
CoO   2ndLt James J. Boley
     2ndLt Mayhlon L.
       Degernes, Jr. (WIA,
       28Nov)
     2ndLt Wayne L. Hall
     (WIA,29Nov)
     2ndLt John H. Miller
     (WIA,29Nov)
     2ndLt Robert C. Needham
     (WIA,28Nov)

Weapons Company
CO   Maj Edwin H. Simmons
ExO   Capt John C. Shelnutt
     (KIA,28Nov)
CoO   1stLt John L. Burke, Jr.
     1stLt Donald C. Holmes
     (WIA,30Nov)
     1stLt Harold E. Savage
     2ndLt Nate L. Adams, II

5th MARINE REGIMENT
CO   LCol Raymond L. Murray
ExO   LCol Joseph L. Stewart
S-3   Maj Lawrence W. Smith, Jr.
Communications
     Maj Kenneth B. Boyd
     2ndLt Harold A. Thomas
     (WIA,11Dec)
Surgeon
     Cdr Chester Lessenden,
       MC, USN

Lt(jg) Alan A. Basinger,
   MC, USN
Lt(jg) Howard P. Creaves,
   MC, USN
Chaplain
   Lt Bernard L. Hickey, ChC,
   USN
   Lt Orlando Ingvolstadt,
   ChC, USN

Antitank Company
CO   Capt Rex O. Dillow
ExO   1stLt Almarion S. Bailey
CoO   1stLt Donald E. Estes
         2ndLt Paul R. Fields
         2ndLt Charles M. C. Jones

4.2-Inch Mortar Company
CO   1stLt Robert M. Lucy
ExO   2ndLt Tom L. Gibson
CoO   2ndLt Rollie D. Newsom
         2ndLt Wendell O. Beard

Headquarters-&-Service Company
CO   Capt Jack Hawthorn

1st Battalion, 5th Marines
CO   LCol John W. Stevens, II
ExO   Maj Merlin R. Olson
S-3   Maj Albert Hartman
Communications
         1stLt William L. Peter, Jr.
         (WIA,28Nov)
Surgeon
         Lt(jg) John P. Luhr, MC,
         USN
         Lt(jg) Daniel M. O'Toole,
         MC, USN
Air Liaison
         1stLt Forrest B. Holderidge
         1stLt James W. Smith
         (WIA,28Nov)
Headquarters CO
         Capt Walter E. G. Godenius

Able Company, 5th
CO   Capt James B. Heater
ExO   1stLt Orrin H. Shelton
CoO   1stLt James Lichtenberger
         (WIA,28Nov)

1stLt Robert E. Snyder
2ndLt Howard G. Blank
2ndLt Edward E. Collins
2ndLt Nicholas M.
   Trapnell, Jr.

Baker Company, 5th
CO   1stLt John R. Hancock
ExO   1stLt James T. Cronin
CoO   1stLt Louis B. Kohler
         1stLt Michael V. Palatas
         2ndLt Austin C. Jenson
         (KIA,29Nov)
         2ndLt Edward C. Morris
         WO Robert A. Clement

Charlie Company, 5th
CO   Capt Jack R. Jones (WIA,
         28Nov & 7Dec)
ExO   1stLt Loren R. Smith (WIA,
         28Nov & 7Dec)
CoO   1stLt William E. Kerrigan
         1stLt Robert J. Richter
         2ndLt Robert H. Corbet
         (WIA,7Dec)
         2ndLt Harold L. Dawe, Jr.
         2ndLt Byron L. Magness
         (WIA,7Dec)
         2ndLt Max A. Merritt
         (WIA,28Nov)

Weapons Company
CO   Maj John W. Russell
ExO   Capt Almond H. Sollom
         (WIA,4Dec)
CoO   1stLt Frank J. Meers
         2ndLt Harry L. Alderman
         2ndLt Dale L. Brown
         2ndLt Francis E. McDonald
         2ndLt Ralph J. Tuley
         (WIA,28Nov)

2nd Battalion, 5th Marines
CO   LCol Harold S. Roise
ExO   Maj John L. Hopkins
S-3   Maj Theodore F. Spiker
Communications
         2ndLt Peter Osterhoudt

Surgeon
Lt(jg) Henry Litvin,
MC, USN
Lt (jg) James E. Sparks,
MC, USN
Air Liaison
Capt David G. Johnson
1stLt Manning T. Jeter
(WIA,6Dec)
Headquarters CO
Capt Franklin B. Mayer

Dog Company, 5th
CO   Capt Samuel S. Smith, Jr.
ExO 1stLt James H. Honeycutt
(WIA,7Dec)
CoO 1stLt John R. Hinds
1stLt Stanley D. McElwee
(WIA,2Dec-
DOW,8Dec)
1stLt George C.
McNaughton
(WIA,7Dec)
1stLt Karle F. Seydel
(KIA,6Dec)
1stLt George A. Sorenson
(WIA,6Dec)
1stLt George H. Grimes
2ndLt Richard M. Johnson
(WIA,7Dec)

Easy Company, 5th
CO   Capt Samuel Jaskilka
ExO Capt Lawrence W. Henke,
Jr.
CoO 1stLt Raymond R. Jorz
(WIA,28Nov)
1stLt Robert L. Uskurait
2ndLt Edwin A. Deptula
(WIA,27Nov)
2ndLt Donald Marchette
(WIA,3Dec)
2ndLt Jack L. Nolan

Fox Company, 5th
CO   Capt Uel D. Peters
(WIA,6Dec)
1stLt Charles H. Dalton
ExO 1stLt Charles H. Dalton

CoO 1stLt Bernard W.
Christofferson
1stLt Gerald J. McLaughlin
1stLt S. E. Sansing
2ndLt Albert F. Belbusti
2ndLt Donald J. Krabbe

Weapons Company
CO   Maj Glen E. Martin
ExO Capt James W. Bateman
CoO 1stLt George Janiszewski
1stLt William E. McLain
(NBC, 7Dec)
1stLt David W. Walsh
1stLt John J. Walsh
2ndLt James E. Harrell
2ndLt Damon J. Larson

3rd Battalion, 5th Marines
CO   LCol Robert D. Taplett
ExO Maj John J. Canney
(KIA,28Nov)
Maj Harold J. Swain
S-3   Maj Thomas A. Durham
Communications
2ndLt Hercules R. Kelly, Jr.
Surgeon
Lt(jg) John H. Moon,
MC, USN
Lt(jg) John E. Murphy, MC,
USN
Air Liaison
1stLt Leo Corboy
1stLt Daniel Greene
Headquarters CO
Capt Roland A. Marburgh
(to 4Dec)
Capt Raymond H. Spuhler

George Company, 5th
CO   Capt Chester Hermanson
(WIA,2Dec)
1stLt Charles H. Mize
ExO 1stLt August L. Camarata
CoO 1stLt Robert L. Owen
1stLt Robert G. Price
(KIA,30Nov)
2ndLt John J. H. Cahill
2ndLt Dana B. Cashion
(WIA,28Nov)

2ndLt Lawrence O'Connell
2ndLt Andrew T. Watt

How Company, 5th
CO Capt Harold P. Williamson
ExO 1stLt Donald E. Watterson
CoO 1stLt Harold D. Fredericks
     1stLt Herbert Preston, Jr.
     1stLt Robert W. Schoning
     1stLt Denzil E. Walden
     2ndLt John O. Williams

Item Company, 5th
CO Capt Harold G. Schrier
       (WIA,4Dec)
     2ndLt Willard S. Peterson
ExO 1stLt Myrl E. Boys
CoO 1stLt Robert S. Hackney
     1stLt Thomas S. Rheman
     1stLt Mason H. Wiers
     1stLt Wallace Williamson
       (KIA,1Dec)
     1stLt George M. Zellick
     2ndLt Willard S. Peterson

Weapons Company
CO Maj Harold W. Swain
       (to 28Nov)
     1stLt Hubert J. Shovelin
ExO 1stLt Hubert J. Shovelin
CoO 1stLt Robert W. Bell
     1stLt George W. Bowman
     1stLt Arthur E. House, Jr.
     2ndLt Lucius V. DiLorenzo
     2ndLt Frank C. Peterson

7th MARINE REGIMENT
CO Col Homer L. Litzenberg,
       Jr.
ExO LCol Frederick R. Dowsett
       (WIA,7Dec)
     LCol Raymond G. Davis
S-3 Maj Henry J. Woessner, II
Communications
     Capt George E. Zawasky
       (WIA,6Dec)
     CWO Stanley A. Nowak
Surgeon
     Lt Peter E. Arioli, MC, USN
       (KIA,2Dec)

Lt(jg) George W. Bremner,
  MC, USN
Lt(jg) Edward C. Byrne,
  MC, USN
Chaplain
  LCdr John H. Craven,
    ChC, USN
  Lt(jg) Cornelius J. Griffin,
    ChC, USN (WIA,6Dec)

Antitank Company
CO Maj Walter T. Warren
       (WIA,8Dec)
     1stLt Earl R. Delong
ExO 1stLt Earl R. DeLong
CoO 1stLt Raymond J. Elledge
     2ndLt Francis W. Tief

4.2-Inch Mortar Company
CO Maj Rodney V. Rieghard
CoO 1stLt Albert A. Briscoe
       (KIA,6Dec)
     1stLt Nicholas Seminoff
       (WIA,28Nov)
     1stLt Gordon Vincent

1st Battalion, 7th Marines
CO LCol Raymond G. Davis
       (to 7Dec)
     Maj Webb D. Sawyer
ExO Maj Raymond V. Fridrich
S-3 Maj Thomas B. Tighe
Communications
     1stLt Kermit W. Worley
Surgeon
     Lt(jg) Robert G.
       Wedemeyer, MC, USN
Air Liaison
     1stLt Dan C. Holland
     1stLt John Theros
     1stLt Robert Wilson
Headquarters CO
     1stLt Wilbert R. Gaul

Able Company, 7th
CO 1stLt Eugenous M.
       Hovatter
ExO 1stLt Jack F. Boles
CoO 1stLt Bobbie B. Bradley
     1stLt William J. Davis

1stLt Frank N. Mitchell
(KIA,26Nov)
2ndLt James W. Stemple
(WIA)
2ndLt Leslie C. Williams
(KIA,8Dec)

Baker Company, 7th
CO   Capt Myron E. Wilcox
(WIA,27Nov)
1stLt Joseph R. Kurcaba
(27Nov-KIA,8Dec)
1stLt William W. Taylor
ExO   1stLt Joseph R. Kurcaba
CoO   1stLt Harrol Kiser
(NBC,8Dec)
1stLt Chou Ein Lee
(WIA,8Dec)
1stLt Harrison Saturday
(NBC,4Dec)
1stLt William W. Taylor
2ndLt Joseph R. Owen
(WIA,8Dec)

Charlie Company, 7th
CO   Capt John F. Morris
ExO   1stLt William E. Shea
CoO   1stLt Francis I. Donohoe
1stLt George C. Kliefoth
2ndLt Merrill L. Norton
2ndLt. Warren J. Skvaril
(WIA,28Nov)
P1Sgt Earle J. Payne

Weapons Company
CO   Maj William E. Vorhies
ExO   Capt Robert J. Polson
CoO   1stLt Richard Blandford
1stLt Edward B. Shepard
2ndLt Donald S. Floyd

2nd Battalion, 7th Marines
CO   LCol Randolph S. D.
Lockwood
ExO   Maj Webb D. Sawyer
(to 8Dec)
Maj James F. Lawrence, Jr.
S-3   Maj James F. Lawrence, Jr.
Communications
1stLt Leslie L. Davenport

Surgeon
Lt(jg) Laverne F. Pfeifer,
MC, USN
Lt(jg) Stanley I. Wolf, MC,
USN
Air Liaison
1stLt Neal E. Heffernan
Headquarters CO
Capt Walter R. Anderson

Dog Company, 7th
CO   Capt Milton A. Hull
(WIA,28Nov)
1stLt James D. Hammond,
Jr.
ExO   1stLt James D. Hammond,
Jr.
CoO   1stLt Paul V. Mullaney
(WIA,27Nov)
1stLt Edward M. Seeburger
(WIA,28Nov)
1stLt Anthony J. Sota
(WIA,28Nov)
1stLt Thomas Thomson
(KIA,27Nov)
1stLt Richard C. Weber
(WIA,28Nov)

Easy Company, 7th
CO   Capt Walter D. Phillips, Jr.
(KIA,28Nov)
1stLt Robert T. Bey
ExO   1stLt Raymond O. Ball
(KIA,28Nov)
CoO   1stLt Robert T. Bey
1stLt Leonard Clements
(WIA,28Nov)
1stLt William J. Schreier
(WIA,28Nov)
1stLt John Yancey
(WIA,28Nov)
2ndLt Richard A. Wells
(WIA,2Dec)

Fox Company, 7th
CO   Capt William E. Barber
(WIA,28Nov-to 3Dec)
1stLt Welton R. Abell
(WIA,8Dec)

ExO 1stLt Clarke B. Wright
       (WIA,2Dec)
CoO 1stLt Joseph Brady
       (WIA,28Nov)
       1stLt John M. Dunne
       (KIA,6Dec)
       1stLt Robert C. McCarthy
       (WIA,28Nov)
       1stLt Elmo G. Peterson
       (WIA,28Nov)
       1stLt Lawrence Schmitt
       (WIA,28Nov)

Weapons Company
CO   Capt Harry L. Givens
CoO 1stLt Joseph M. Dwyer
       1stLt Robert A. Henderson
       (WIA,29Nov)
       1stLt Robert T. Stroemple

3rd Battalion, 7th Marines
CO   LCol William F. Harris
       (MIA,6Dec)
       Maj Warren Morris
ExO Maj Warren Morris
       (to 6Dec)
       Maj Jefferson D. Smith
S-3 Capt William R. Earney
Communications
       1stLt Earnest H. Stone
Surgeon
       Lt(jg) Robert E. Dent, MC,
       USN
       Lt(jg) John J. Flynn, MC,
       USN
Air Liaison
       1stLt John Mortan
Headquarters CO
       Capt Eric R. Haars
       (to 29Nov)

George Company, 7th
CO   Capt Thomas E. Cooney
       (KIA,27Nov)
       Capt Eric R. Haars (29Nov-
       WIA,3Dec)
       1stLt George R. Earnest
ExO 1stLt William E. Buckley

CoO 1stLt Richard H. Clark
       1stLt Kenneth O. Cook
       (NBC,4Dec)
       1stLt George R. Earnest
       1stLt Howard J. Taylor
       (WIA,4Dec)
       2ndLt John M. Jackson
       2ndLt Arthur R. Mooney

How Company, 7th
CO   Capt Leroy M. Cooke
       (KIA,27Nov)
       1stLt Howard H. Harris
       (27Nov-WIA,1Dec)
       1stLt Harold J. Fitzgeorge
       (1Dec-WIA,5Dec)
       2ndLt Minard P. Newton,
       Jr.
ExO 1stLt Harold J. Fitzgeorge
CoO 1stLt William C. Foote
       1stLt Elmer A. Krieg
       (MIA,27Nov)
       2ndLt Paul E. Denny
       (WIA,27Nov)
       2ndLt Clarence W. Friesen
       (WIA,3Dec)
       2ndLt James M. Mitchell
       (WIA,27Nov)
       2ndLt Minard P. Newton,
       Jr.

Item Company, 7th
CO   1stLt William E. Johnson
       (NBC,3Dec)
       1stLt Alfred I. Thomas
ExO 1stLt Alfred I. Thomas
CoO 1stLt Joseph McPartland
       (NBC,8Dec)
       1stLt Jerome N. Pieti
       1stLt Thomas M. Sullivan
       (WIA,3Dec)
       2ndLt Joseph Mordente

Weapons Company
CO   Maj Jefferson D. Smith
       (WIA,5Dec; to 6Dec)
       1stLt Austin S. Parker
       (WIA,6Dec; to 10Dec)
       1stLt Robert E. Hill
ExO 1stLt Austin S. Parker

CoO   1stLt John J. Deppe
      1stLt Robert E. Hill
      1stLt Austin S. Parker
      1stLt John Siebenthaler
      2ndLt George Caridakis

11th MARINE REGIMENT
CO   Col James H. Brower
      (NBC,30Nov)
      LCol Carl A. Youngdale
ExO   LCol Carl A. Youngdale
S-3   LCol James O. Appleyard
Communications
      Maj Clarence T. Risher
      2ndLt Louis W.
        D'Allesandro
      WO James C. Price
Surgeon
      Cdr George M. Bell,
        MC, USN
      Lt James E. Keenan,
        MC, USN
      Lt(jg) Preston D. Parsons,
        MC, USN
Chaplain
      LCdr Otto E. Sporrer,
        ChC, USN
      Lt(jg) Barker C. Howland,
        ChC, USN

Headquarters Battery
CO   1stLt William C. Patton

Service Battery
CO   1stLt Joseph M. Brent

1st Battalion, 11th Marines
CO   LCol Harvey A. Feehan
ExO   Maj Francis R. Schlesinger
S-3   Capt Philip N. Pierce
Headquarters CO
      Capt James W. Brayshay
Service CO
      1stLt Kenneth W. Quelch

Able Battery, 11th
CO   Capt James D. Jordan
ExO   Capt William A. Lang
BtryO   1stLt Joseph C. Kellett
      1stLt Phillip H. King

      1stLt Howard W. Rogers
      1stLt Joris J. Snyder
      1stLt Calvin C. Waters
      2ndLt Robert R. Kiernan
      2ndLt Orlo C. Paciulli, Jr.
      2ndLt Evieo Ragsdale

Baker Battery, 11th
CO   Capt Gilbert N. Powell
ExO   Capt Haskell C. Baker
BtryO   1stLt Kenneth E. Davis
      1stLt Frank Mockli
      1stLt Mark A. Rainer
      1stLt Edward W. Smith
      2ndLt Robert D. Risinger
      2ndLt Henry Ammer
      CWO Allen Carlson

Charlie Battery, 11th
CO   Capt. William J. Nichols
BtryO   1stLt Joseph A. Goeke, Jr.
      1stLt Howard W. Rogers
      1stLt John T. Thompson
      CWO Marvin G. Myers

2nd Battalion, 11th Marines
CO   LCol Merritt Adelman
ExO   Maj Neal G. Newell
S-3   Maj Bruce E. Keith
Headquarters CO
      Capt George J. Batson
Service CO
      Capt Herbert R. Merrick, Jr.
Communications
      Capt John H. Maher

Dog Battery, 11th
CO   Capt Andrew J.
        Strohmenger (to 8Dec)
      Capt Richard E. Roach
BtryO   1stLt Robert A. Brobst
      1stLt Harold J. Jantz
      1stLt Joseph A. Piedmont
      2ndLt Dalton A. Hielscher
      2ndLt Alexander Ruggiero
      CWO Samuel G. Gilbert

Easy Battery, 11th
CO   Capt John C. McClelland,
        Jr.

BtryO 1stLt Foster W. Blough
1stLt Paul Mazzuca, Jr.
1stLt Richard J. Randolph
2ndLt Harvey W. Baron
2ndLt Edwin M. Rudzis
2ndLt Kenneth C. Williams
WO Raymon Cragg

Fox Battery, 11th
CO   1stLt Howard A. Blancheri
BtryO 1stLt Walter L. Blocker, Jr.
1stLt Clifford J. Peabody
1stLt Robert E. Young
2ndLt Richard M. Doezma
2ndLt Edwin W. Hakala
2ndLt Robert G. Tobin, Jr.
CWO Jesse Y. Walker

3rd Battalion, 11th Marines
CO   Maj Francis F. Parry
ExO   Maj Norman A. Miller
S-3   Maj James M. Callender
Communications
Capt Herbert Williamson
1stLt James K. Dent
Headquarters CO
1stLt John J. Brackett
Service CO
Capt Ernest R. Payne
(to 30Nov)
Capt Samuel A. Hannah

George Battery, 11th
CO   Capt Samuel A. Hannah
(to 30Nov)
Capt Ernest R. Payne
ExO   1stLt Willis L. Gore
BtryO 1stLt David D. Metcalfe, Jr.
1stLt William R. Phillips
1stLt Michael B. Weir
1stLt George E. Wilkerson

How Battery, 11th
CO   Capt Benjamin S. Read
(WIA,7Dec)
1stLt Wilber N. Herndon
ExO   1stLt Wilber N. Herndon
BtryO 1stLt Donald H. Campbell
1stLt Edward V. Easter
1stLt Lawrence T. Kane
1stLt Robert B. Metcalfe

Item Battery, 11th
CO   Capt John M. McLaurin, Jr.
(to 30Nov)
Capt Robert T. Patterson
BtryO 1stLt Robert C. Cameron
1stLt Marshall Campbell
1stLt Robert T. Jorvic
1stLt William A. Mather
2ndLt James R. Gallman, Jr.
CWO Alphonso E. Buck

4th Battalion, 11th Marines
CO   Maj William McReynolds
ExO   Maj Maurice J. Coffey
S-3   Maj Angus J. Cronin
Communications
1stLt Edmond V. Villani
Headquarters CO
Capt Paul L. Hirt
Service CO
Capt Armand G. Daddazio

King Battery, 11th
CO   1stLt Robert C. Messman
(POW,27Nov)
1stLt Robert E. Parrot
ExO   1stLt Robert E. Parrot
BtryO 1stLt Donald R. Thomas

Love Battery, 11th
CO   Capt Lawrence R. Cloern
BtryO 1stLt Paul R. Joyce
1stLt Kenneth E. Rice
CWO Robert H. Alderson

Mike Battery, 11th
CO   Capt Vernon W. Shapiro
ExO   1stLt William J. J. Vetter
BtryO 2ndLt Timothy Mulrennan
CWO Carl Fazio

**1st MOTOR TRANSPORT
  BATTALION**
CO   LCol Olin L. Beall
ExO   Maj John J. Barriero, Jr.
S-3   Capt Robert C. Ronald

Able Company
CO   Capt Arthur W. Ecklund
CoO   1stLt Ned W. Emmons
1stLt Lawrence I. Taylor

2ndLt Arnold F. Bynum
CWO Thomas E. Duggett

Baker Company
CO Capt James C. Camp, Jr.
ExO 1stLt Lorne Froats
CoO 2ndLt Robert G. Hunt, Jr.
CWO Frank L. Mason

Charlie Company
CO Capt Garfield M. Randall
ExO 1stLt Norman E. Stow
CoO 1stLt John E. Ferguson, Jr.
2ndLt Robert C. Tilton

Dog Company
CO Capt Bernard J. Whitelock
(to 9Nov)
1stLt Philip R. Hade
ExO 1stLt Philip R. Hade
CoO 1stLt Harold W. Johnson
1stLt William E. Nilson
1stLt Ira P. Norfolk

7th MOTOR TRANSPORT BATTALION*
CO LCol Carl J. Cagle

1st TANK BATTALION†
CO LCol Harry T. Milne
S-3 Capt Lester T. Chase
(KIA,29Nov)
Medium Platoon
Capt Robert M. Krippner

Baker Company
CO Capt Bruce F. Williams
ExO 1stLt William T. Unger
CoO 1stLt B. J. Cummings
1stLt Robert Gover
1stLt Jack Lerond
1stLt Philip Ronzone

Dog Company
CO Capt Bruce W. Clarke
(WIA,10Dec)

1stLt Paul E. Sanders
ExO 1stLt Herbert B. Turner
(POW,29Nov)
CoO 1stLt Robert L. Nelson
1stLt Richard A. Primrose
1stLt Paul E. Sanders

1st ENGINEER BATTALION†
CO LCol John H. Partridge
S-3 Maj William V. Schwebke

Able Company
CO Capt George W. King
(WIA,2Dec)
Capt William R. Gould
CoO 1stLt Nicholas A. Canzona
1stLt Wayne E. Richards
(WIA,2Dec)
1stLt Ernest P. Skelt, Jr.
WO Willard Downs

1st Platoon, Baker Company
CO 1stLt Ermine L. Meeker

Dog Company
CO Capt Byron C. Turner
CoO 1stLt Harold L. Javins
1stLt David D. Peppin
(from 30Nov)
1stLt Ewald W. Vom Orde,
Jr.
WO Otey H. Shelton

X ARMY CORPS
CG LGen Edward M. Almond
CofS MGen Clark L. Ruffner
Deputy
Col Edward F. Forney,
USMC
G-3 LCol John H. Chiles

92nd Field Artillery Battalion (Armored)
CO LCol Leon H. Lavoie

*A Fleet Marine Force Unit, 7th MT Bn was nominally under 1st MarDiv control, but was held back by X Corps. Undetermined elements of the battalion were forward of Chinhung-ni.

†Only staff and units actually committed are listed.

52nd Transportation Truck Battalion
CO   LCol Waldon C. Winston

7th INFANTRY DIVISION
CG   MGen David W. Barr
ADC   BGen Henry I. Hodes

31st INFANTRY REGIMENT
CO   Col Allen D. MacLean
        (MIA,29Nov)
        LCol Barry K. Anderson
        (Acting)
S-3   LCol Barry K. Anderson
31st Tank Company
        Capt Robert E. Drake

Baker Company, 31st Infantry
CO   Capt Charles L. Peckham
        (POW,30Nov)

2nd Battalion, 31st Infantry
CO   LCol William Reidy

3rd Battalion, 31st Infantry
CO   LCol William R. Reilly
        (WIA,28 and 30Nov)
        Maj Harvey Storms
        (KIA,1Dec)
        Maj Carl G. Witte
        (WIA,6Dec)—unit
        disbanded

1st Battalion, 32nd Infantry
CO   LCol Don C. Faith
        (KIA,1Dec)—unit
        disbanded

57th Field Artillery Battalion
CO   LCol Ray O. Embree
        (WIA,27Nov)
        LCol Robert J. Tolly
        (NBC,1Dec)—unit
        disbanded

1st MARINE AIRCRAFT WING
CG   MGen Field Harris
AWC   BGen Thomas J. Cushman

*Operationally attached to 1st MarDiv

MARINE AIR GROUP 12
CO   Col Boeker T. Batterton

MARINE AIR GROUP 33
CO   Col Frank C. Dailey

Marine Tactical Air Control Squadron-2*
CO   Maj Christian C. Lee

Marine Observation Squadron 6*
CO   Maj Vincent J. Gottschalk

Marine Transport Squadron 152
CO   LCol Deane C. Roberts

Marine Fighting Squadron 212
CO   LCol Richard W.
        Wyczawski

Marine Fighting Squadron 214
CO   Maj William M. Lundin

Marine Fighting Squadron 312
CO   LCol "J" Frank Cole

Marine Fighting Squadron 323
CO   Maj Arnold A. Lund

Marine Night Fighting Squadron 513
CO   LCol David C. Wolfe

Marine All-Weather Fighting Squadron 542
CO   LCol Max J. Volcansek

FAR EAST AIR FORCE COMBAT CARGO COMMAND
CG   MGen William H. Tunner

347th TROOP CARRIER WING
CG   BGen John P. Henebry

21st Troop Carrier Squadron
CO   LCol Phil B. Cage

61st Troop Carrier Squadron
CO   Col Frank P. Norwood

APPENDIX B
Medal of Honor Recipients

WILLIAM E. BARBER, Captain, USMC
> Commanding Officer, F Company, 7th Marines
> November 28–December 2, 1950

*WILLIAM B. BAUGH, Private First Class, USMC
> Attached, G Company, 1st Marines
> November 29, 1950

HECTOR A. CAFFERATA, JR., Private, USMCR
> F Company, 7th Marines
> November 28, 1950

RAYMOND G. DAVIS, Lieutenant Colonel, USMC
> Commanding Officer, 1st Battalion, 7th Marines
> December 1–4, 1950

*DON C. FAITH, Lieutenant Colonel, USA
> Commanding Officer, 1st Battalion, 32nd Infantry
> November 27–December 1, 1950

THOMAS J. HUDNER, JR., Lieutenant, Junior Grade, USN
> Fighter Squadron 32, U.S.S. Leyte
> December 4, 1950

*JAMES E. JOHNSON, Sergeant, USMC
> "J" Company, 7th Marines
> December 2, 1950

ROBERT S. KENNEMORE, Staff Sergeant, USMC
> E Company, 7th Marines
> November 27–28, 1950

*FRANK N. MITCHELL, First Lieutenant, USMC
> A Company, 7th Marines
> November 26, 1950

REGINALD R. MYERS, Major, USMC
> Executive Officer, 3rd Battalion, 1st Marines
> November 29, 1950

*JOHN U. D. PAGE, Lieutenant Colonel, USA
> Attached, 1st Marines
> November 29–December 11, 1950

CARL L. SITTER, Captain, USMC
> Commanding Officer, G Company, 1st Marines
> November 29–30, 1950

*WILLIAM G. WINDRICH, Staff Sergeant, USMC
> I Company, 5th Marines
> December 1, 1950

*Killed or Missing in Action.

APPENDIX C

Marine
Navy Cross Citations

ABELL, Welton R.
Fox/7 6–8Dec50
ALLEY, David W.
George/5 30Nov50
BANKS, Charles L.
1st Service Bn 29Nov–6Dec50
BARROW, Robert H.
Able/1 9–10Dec50
BEARD, James T.
Baker/7 3Dec50
BETTS, Harrison F.
How/1 28–29Nov50
BLICK, Joseph A.
——— 7–8Dec50
BOOKER, Dorsie H., Jr.
1st Bn, 11th 3Dec50
BRAATEN, Palmer S.
Item/5 2Dec50
BRADLEY, Bobbie B.
Able/7 8Dec50
CANNEY, John J.
3rd Bn, 5th 28Nov50
CHRISTOFFERSON, Bernard W.
Fox/5 28Nov50
DIRST, Lloyd V.
1st MP Company 29–30Nov50
DUNAY, Andrew F.
Antitank/5 6–7Dec50
EHRLICH, Leland E.
Item/7 7Dec50
FISHER, Joseph R.
Item/1 28–29Nov50
GALLAGHER, James P.
Easy/7 27–28Nov50
GEORGE, Walter W.
Fox/5 2Dec50
GZIK, Richard S.
——— 2Dec50
HAMBY, John H. C.
George/7 27Nov50

HARRIS, William F.
3rd Bn, 7th 7Dec50
HARVEY, Amon F., Jr.
1st Bn, 11th 2Dec50
HERNDON, Wilber N.
How/11 7Dec50
HOLLADAY, Morse "L"
1st Service Bn 29–30Dec50
HOLT, William P.
Antitank/1 10Dec50
HOWARD, Warren C.
Dog/5 7Dec50
HULL, Milton A.
Dog/7 27Nov50
JACKSON, "R" "A"
Easy/5 28Nov50
JENSON, Austin C.
Baker/5 29Nov50
JOHNSON, Horace L., Jr.
How/1 28–29Nov50
JONES, Donald R.
Able/1 8Dec50
JONES, Jack R.
Charlie/5 27Nov–7Dec50
KISER, Harrol
Baker/7 3Dec50
KNOX, Edwin L.
1st Engineer Bn 1–3Dec50
KURCABA, Joseph R.
Baker/7 21Oct–8Dec50
LAWRENCE, James F., Jr.
2nd Bn, 7th 6–7Dec50
LEEDS, Joseph R.
Able/1 8Dec50
LEVASSEUR, Ronald N.
Item/1 28–29Nov50
LITZENBERG, Homer L., Jr.
7th Marines 6–7Dec50
MATHEWSON, Bruce J.
——— 29Nov50

McCLUNG, William J., III
Division HQ *7Dec50*

MEADE, John F.
Fox/5 *27Nov50*

MITCHELL, Frank N.
Able/7 *26Nov50*

MONROE, Charles H., Jr.
How/1 *28–29Nov50*

MURPHY, Daniel M.
Easy/7 *27–28Nov50*

MURRAY, Raymond L.
5th Marines *6–7Dec50*

NOONKESTER, Henry E.
Able/1 *9Dec50*

OGDEN, James W.
Baker/Engineers *30Nov50*

ORSULAK, Edmond T.
George/5 *30Nov–1Dec50*

PETERS, Uel D.
Fox/5 *27Nov–6Dec50*

PETRO, George E.
Antitank/1 *10Dec50*

PHILLIPS, Walter D., Jr.
Easy/7 *27Nov50*

PULLER, Lewis B.
1st Marines *5–10Dec50*

READ, Benjamin S.
How/11 *7Dec50*

ROISE, Harold S.
2nd Bn, 5th *27Nov–11Dec50*

SCOTT, James E.
——— *30Nov50*

SELDAL, Russell J.
Baker/11 *4Dec50*

SMITH, Loren R.
Charlie/5 *28Nov50*

SMITH, Samuel S.
Dog/5 *6–7Dec50*

SNELLING, Edward W.
How/1 *28–29Nov50*

STEVENS, John W., II
1st Bn, 5th *27Nov–11Dec50*

STOUFFER, Frederick E.
Able/7 *3Dec50*

STROPES, Dale L.
Item/5 *2Dec50*

SUTTER, Allan
2nd Bn, 1st *25Nov–10Dec50*

TAPLETT, Robert D.
3rd Bn, 5th *28Nov–10Dec50*

UMBAUGH, Ernest J.
Able/1 *9Dec50*

WASSON, Marvin L.
Antitank/1 *10Dec50*

WILLIAMS, Jack V.
2nd Bn, 5th *6–7Dec50*

WILLIAMS, Leslie C.
Able/7 *1Dec50*

YANCEY, John
Easy/7 *27–28Nov50*

Guide to Abbreviations

AD	Navy Skyraider Attack Bomber	**FAC**	Forward Air Controller
ADC	Assistant Division Commander	**FDC**	Fire Direction Center
Asst	Assistant	**FO**	Forward Observer
AWC	Assistant Wing Commander	**F4U**	Marine Corsair Fighter-Bomber
		F-51	Air Force Mustang Fighter-Bomber
BAR	Browning Automatic Rifle		
BGen	Brigadier General	**G-**	Staff Section Head, division or corps
Bn	Battalion	**G-1**	Personnel Section Head
Btry	Battery	**G-2**	Intelligence Section Head
BtryO	Battery Officer	**G-3**	Plans & Operations Section Head
B-26	Air Force Medium Bomber	**G-4**	Logistics Section Head
		GHQ	General Headquarters
Capt	Captain	**GySgt**	Gunnery Sergeant
CCF	Communist Chinese Forces		
CG	Commanding General	**H&S**	Headquarters-&-Service
ChC	Chaplain Corps	**HQ**	Headquarters
CO	Commanding Officer		
CofS	Chief of Staff	**InfDiv**	Infantry Division
Col	Colonel		
Commo	Communications	**KIA**	Killed in Action
CoO	Company Officer		
CP	Command Post	**LCdr**	Lieutenant Commander
Cpl	Corporal	**LCol**	Lieutenant Colonel
CWO	Commissioned Warrant Officer	**LGen**	Lieutenant General
		LST	Landing Ship, Tank
C-47	Dakota Cargo Plane	**Lt**	Lieutenant
C-119	Flying Boxcar Cargo Plane	**1stLt**	First Lieutenant
		2ndLt	Second Lieutenant
		Lt(jg)	Lieutenant, Junior Grade
Dec	December		
Div	Division	**MAG**	Marine Air Group
DOW	Died of Wounds	**Maj**	Major
		MarDiv	Marine Division
ExO	Executive Officer	**MC**	Medical Corps
		MGen	Major General

MGySgt	Master Gunnery Sergeant	**-San**	Korean suffix for "mountain"
MIA	Missing In Action	**S-**	Staff Section Head, regiment or battalion
MLR	Main Line of Resistance		
MP	Military Police	**S-1**	Personnel Section Head
MSgt	Master Sergeant	**S-2**	Intelligence Section Head
MSR	Main Supply Route		
MT	Motor Transport	**S-3**	Operations Section Head
MTACS	Marine Tactical Air Control Squadron	**S-4**	Logistics Section Head
		SCR-	
MTSgt	Master Technical Sergeant	**300**	Signal Corps Radio Model 300
		SFC	Sergeant First Class
NBC	Non-Battle Casualty	**Sgt**	Sergeant
		SSgt	Staff Sergeant
-ni	Korean suffix for "town"	**SMaj**	Sergeant-Major
Nov	November		
NKPA	North Korean People's Army	**TBM**	Avenger Torpedo Bomber
		TSgt	Technical Sergeant
O	Officer		
OP	Observation Post	**UN**	United Nations
		US	United States
Pfc	Private First Class	**USA**	United States Army
PLA	People's Liberation Army	**USAF**	United States Air Force
		USMC	United States Marine Corps
POW	Prisoner of War		
Pvt	Private	**USN**	United States Navy
RAAF	Royal Australian Air Force	**VMF**	Marine Fighter Squadron
		VMO	Marine Observation Squadron
-ri	Korean suffix for "town"		
RM	Royal Marines		
RMC	Royal Medical Corps	**WIA**	Wounded In Action
ROK	Republic of Korea (Army)	**WO**	Warrant Officer

RESEARCH NOTE

The books and articles cited below formed the framework and provided much important detail for this study. However, the bulk of the work went into corresponding with and interviewing over one hundred Marine, Army and Navy participants. The resulting files, all based upon such firsthand data collected by the author, have been donated to the United States Marine Corps and are presently in the care of the Marine Corps Historical Division.

BIBLIOGRAPHY

Books:

Aguirre, Emilio, *We'll Be Home By Christmas: A True Story of the United States Marine Corps in the Korean War.* New York: Greenwich Book Publishers, 1959.

Blakeney, Jane F., *Heroes, U.S. Marine Corps 1861–1955.* Washington: Blakeney Publishers, 1957.

Geer, Andrew, *The New Breed: The Story of the U.S. Marines in Korea.* New York: Harper & Brothers, 1952.

Gugeler, Captain Russell A., USA, *Combat Actions in Korea: Infantry-Artillery-Armor.* Washington: Combat Forces Press, 1954.

Leckie, Robert, *The March To Glory.* Cleveland and New York: World, 1960.

Montross, Lynn, and Captain Nicholas A. Canzona, USMC, *U.S.* *Marine Operations in Korea, 1950–1953,* Volume III: *The Chosin Reservoir Campaign.* Washington: U.S. Marine Corps Historical Branch and Government Printing Office, 1957.

Whiting, Allen S., *China Crosses the Yalu: The Decision to Enter the Korean War.* New York: Macmillan, 1960.

Periodicals:

Canzona, Captain Nicholas A., USMC, and John C. Hubbel, "The Twelve Incredible Days of Colonel John Page," *Reader's Digest* (April, 1956).

Chandler, 1st Lieutenant James B., USMC, "Thank God, I'm A Marine," *Leatherneck* (June, 1951).

Davis, Captain W. J., USMC, "Fire for Effect," *Marine Corps Gazette,* (July, 1954).

Drysdale, Lieutenant Colonel D. B., RM, "41 Commando," *Marine Corps Gazette* (August, 1951).

Giusti, Ernest H., and Kenneth W. Condit, "Marine Air Covers the Breakout," *Marine Corps Gazette,* (August, 1952).

Herndon, Boonton, "Retreat to Victory," *Saga,* (September, 1960).

Jaskilka, Captain Samuel, USMC, "Easy Alley," *Marine Corps Gazette,* (May, 1951).

McCarthy, Captain R. C., USMC, "Fox Hill," *Marine Corps Gazette,* (March, 1953).

Marshall, S. L. A., "Last Barrier," *Marine Corps Gazette,* (February, 1953).

Montross, Lynn, "Breakout From The Reservoir: Marine Epic of Fire and Ice," *Marine Corps Gazette* (November, 1951).
"Hagaru: Perimeter of Necessity," *Marine Corps Gazette* (December, 1958).

"March of the Iron Cavalry: Marine Tanks in Korea," *Marine Corps Gazette,* (October, 1952).

"Ridgerunners of Toktong Pass," *Marine Corps Gazette,* (May, 1953).

"Trouble in Hell Fire Valley," *Marine Corps Gazette,* (March, 1957).

Owen, 1st Lieutenant Joseph R., USMC (Ret), "Chosin Reservoir Remembered," *Marine Corps Gazette,* (December, 1980).

Parry, Colonel F. F., USMC, "Fat Cats," *Marine Corps Gazette,* (December 1963).

Read, Captain Benjamin S., USMC, as told to Hugh Morrow, "Our Guns Never Got Cold," *Saturday Evening Post,* (April 7, 1951).

Shisler, Major Michael F., USMC, "Gen. Oliver P. Smith's Life Was a Commitment to Excellence," *Marine Corps Gazette,* (November, 1978).

Smyth, Major Frank, USMC, "Night Support: A New Weapon," *Marine Corps Gazette,* (November, 1951).

Stamford, Captain Edward P., USMC, as told to Captain Hubbard Kuokka, USMC, "What I Lived Through in Korea," *The Catholic Digest,* (November, 1951).

Taplett, Lieutenant Colonel R. D., USMC and Major R. E. Whipple, USMC, " 'Darkhorse' Sets the Pace," *Marine Corps Gazette,* (June, 1953, and July, 1953).

Acknowledgments

Eyewitness history of this sort cannot be completed without the selfless assistance of scores of participants willing to tell their stories and answer questions about oft-forgotten details. It is axiomatic that some men recall and describe life's events in far richer detail than others, but it is the telling that is crucial, and not the color, though it is useful to be the beneficiary of such vivid reports.

It was a surprise to the author that over five hundred participants could be located and contacted in just under nine months, and that nearly one hundred fifty of them would make contributions of time and effort — indeed, of friendship — and, I have no doubt, of sleepless nights. Contemporary concerns about privacy preclude a detailed listing of the names of the good souls who contributed to this effort, and concerns about fairness preclude that any one of them be singled out for special mention, though the impulse is certainly there.

I would, in a general sort of way, like to thank the editors of service and veterans' publications for placing timely pleas for help where their readers could find them. Some of the very best accounts came from men who, on reading such announcements, came forward of their own volition. I doubt that I would have been able to find as many as four or five of those men by other means — so stringent are today's privacy laws.

The professionals at the Marine Corps History and Museums Division, in Washington, D.C., were, as a group, the most influential in getting this study off the ground and aimed in the right direction. Of all of them, I owe the greatest debt of gratitude to Gabrielle Neufeld Santelli and Danny Crawford. Between them, hundreds of letters were forwarded to retired participants, and dozens of often-urgent requests for specific information were answered. A special thanks to both of them for putting up with a very ill and no doubt eccentric author/researcher during ten of the hottest spring days Washingtonians recall. In that vein, my thanks also to my very old friend, Jack Hilliard, curator of the Marine Corps Museum, and to Ben Frank and Tim Wood, of the History Division, and to the boss, Brigadier General Ed Simmons.

A special thanks for the maps to Carol Moody and the staff of Moody Graphics, of San Francisco. That was a job well beyond the range of their usual duties in my behalf.

And my profound thanks to my agent, Michael Larsen, for his good humor, advice, loyalty and friendship.

Thank you all.

— E.M.H.

Index

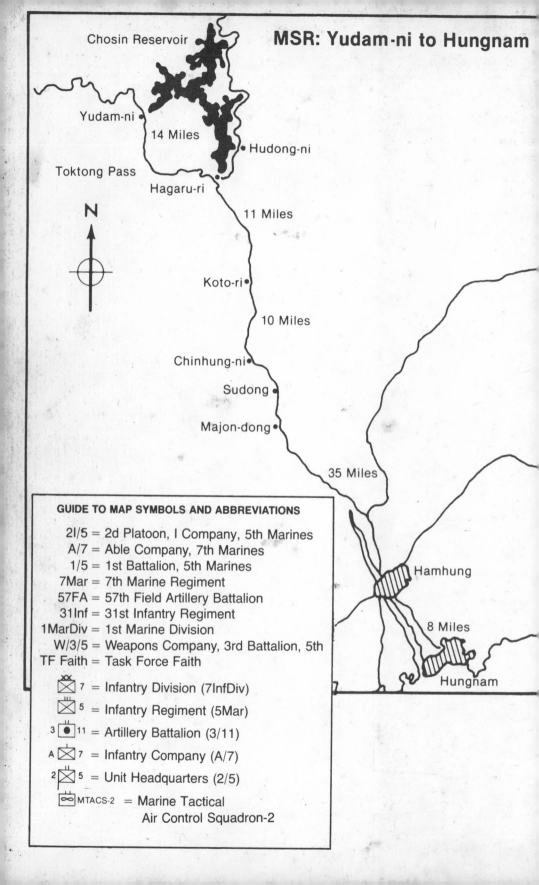

MSR: Yudam-ni to Hungnam

Chosin Reservoir

Yudam-ni
14 Miles
Hudong-ni
Toktong Pass
Hagaru-ri
11 Miles
Koto-ri
10 Miles
Chinhung-ni
Sudong
Majon-dong
35 Miles
N
Hamhung
8 Miles
Hungnam

GUIDE TO MAP SYMBOLS AND ABBREVIATIONS

2I/5 = 2d Platoon, I Company, 5th Marines
A/7 = Able Company, 7th Marines
1/5 = 1st Battalion, 5th Marines
7Mar = 7th Marine Regiment
57FA = 57th Field Artillery Battalion
31Inf = 31st Infantry Regiment
1MarDiv = 1st Marine Division
W/3/5 = Weapons Company, 3rd Battalion, 5th
TF Faith = Task Force Faith

⊠ 7 = Infantry Division (7InfDiv)

⊠ 5 = Infantry Regiment (5Mar)

3 ⊡ 11 = Artillery Battalion (3/11)

A ⊠ 7 = Infantry Company (A/7)

2 ⊠ 5 = Unit Headquarters (2/5)

⊶ MTACS-2 = Marine Tactical
Air Control Squadron-2